Joyce and Militarism

The Florida James Joyce Series

UNIVERSITY PRESS OF FLORIDA

Florida A&M University, Tallahassee
Florida Atlantic University, Boca Raton
Florida Gulf Coast University, Ft. Myers
Florida International University, Miami
Florida State University, Tallahassee
New College of Florida, Sarasota
University of Central Florida, Orlando
University of Florida, Gainesville
University of North Florida, Jacksonville
University of South Florida, Tampa
University of West Florida, Pensacola

Joyce and Militarism

GREG WINSTON

Foreword by Sebastian D. G. Knowles

University Press of Florida
Gainesville · Tallahassee · Tampa · Boca Raton
Pensacola · Orlando · Miami · Jacksonville · Ft. Myers · Sarasota

Copyright 2012 by Greg Winston
All rights reserved
Printed in the United States of America on acid-free paper

This book may be available in an electronic edition.

First cloth printing, 2012
First paperback printing, 2015

Library of Congress Cataloging-in-Publication Data
Winston, Greg.
Joyce and militarism / Greg Winston ; foreword by Sebastian D. G. Knowles.
p. cm.—(The Florida James Joyce series)
Includes bibliographical references and index.
ISBN 978-0-8130-4240-4 (cloth: alk. paper)
ISBN 978-0-8130-6134-4 (pbk.)
1. Joyce, James, 1882–1941—Criticism and interpretation. 2. Militarism
in literature. I. Knowles, Sebastian D. G. (Sebastian David Guy) II. Title.
III. Series: Florida James Joyce series.
PR6019.O9Z9535 2012
823'.912—dc23   2012018906

University Press of Florida
15 Northwest 15th Street
Gainesville, FL 32611-2079
http://www.upf.com

Endues paramilintary langdwage.

Finnegans Wake 338.20

Contents

Foreword ix
Acknowledgments xi
Abbreviations for Cited Works by James Joyce xiii
Introduction 1
1. Joyce and Ideas of Militarism 17
2. Violent Exercise 61
3. Gorescarred Books 111
4. Domestic Forces 155
5. Barracks and Brothels 189
6. Reclamations 236
Afterword 259
Notes 263
Works Cited 275
Index 289

Foreword

"Militarism" is a term used exactly once in the Joycean canon, in a letter to the publisher Grant Richards about one of the chief external forces in Joyce's early career. "In his heart of hearts," said Joyce of the printer who objected to *Dubliners*, "he is a militarist," a term that has to be, like "epiclesis," as much a catnip word for Joyce critics as "paralysis" or "simony" is for the boy in "The Sisters." The word puts everything immediately into play. "Militarism" comes to stand for all forms of parochial belligerence, whether imperial or nationalist, and Winston provides nuanced readings of Joyce's connections with revolutionaries and pacifists in Dublin, Trieste, and Pola. Joyce's early essay "Force" makes a welcome appearance: the fact that the survival of Joyce's essay depends on its pages being co-opted by Stanislaus for his diary is beautifully presented as a figure for occupation itself.

Winston has a way of making his readings matter: a necessary review of the schoolyard origins of Joyce's loathing for militarism leads to a close analysis of the importance of Bloody Sunday in Joyce's revisions of "Cyclops," ending in modern-day Croke Park with a garrison game played on Gaelic sod. By treating Leo Dillon's subversive reading matter ("The Apache Chief") at the beginning of "An Encounter" as seriously as the work that Father Butler is actually teaching (Caesar's *Commentaries on the Gallic War*), Winston makes a neat and perfectly Joycean point about parallel colonial histories, and about the importance of all forms of intertexts. Winston nicely catches Joyce making the same argument through Dillon's teacher: "This page or this page? This page? Now Dillon, up! *Hardly had the day* . . . Go on! What day? *Hardly had the day dawned* . . . Have you studied it? What have you there in your pocket?" Both pages make their justifications for empire; Butler's rebuke is an elision of genre, language, race, and history.

A study of the sex industry in *Ulysses* then pays surprising dividends: the cost of Cissy Caffrey ("I'm only a shilling") is also the king's shilling, the horn of the cuckold is also the horney, or watchman, the frowsy whore is a "gunboat." Surveillance is the common denominator: for Joyce, binoculars are as valuable in the brothel as on the battlefield. Winston's binocular vision keeps our eyes trained on his subject while allowing us to survey Joyce's world from a new and highly provocative angle. The author, like Mulligan's drill sergeant, has sent us all "Back to barracks."

Time and again, I have been stopped in my tracks by the pervasiveness of Winston's theme, from the decanters on the Morkan sideboard standing like "sentries" to the snow that is "general all over Ireland." These martial undertones, like the "musketry of applause" escorting Aunt Julia, nicely hint at the political tensions below the surface of "The Dead," and provide the context for what Winston beautifully calls the "demilitarization process" of Gabriel Conroy. Of course Joyce was military minded; he could not be otherwise, coming from a country that gave the world both the Duke of Wellington and Lord Kitchener. Winston's papers are right: militarism is general all over Joyce.

Sebastian D. G. Knowles, Series Editor

Acknowledgments

So many individuals and institutions, grand gestures and small kindnesses have supported this project that trying to remember them all risks the near certainty of omitting some. What follows, then, is merely a last, best attempt.

First, thanks to everyone at the University Press of Florida, especially Amy Gorelick, whose initial inquiry helped me imagine a book, and Sebastian Knowles, who saw potential in my early drafts. Special thanks to Ann Marlowe for her careful and meticulous copyediting of the manuscript. Thanks also at UPF to Marthe Walters, Ale Gasso, and Shannon McCarthy, and to the former Joyce Series editor, the late Zack Bowen.

Like so many, I was already indebted to Brandon Kershner and Tom Rice for their magnificent contributions to Joyce scholarship; now I am grateful for the insightful advice they offered in their thorough reviews of the manuscript. Thanks as well to Claire Culleton for commenting on early versions of "Violent Exercise" and for indulging me in Irish sports talk.

My sincere appreciation goes to all International James Joyce Foundation colleagues in Europe, Asia, and "North Armorica," especially Vincent Cheng, Teresa Caneda Cabrera, Aida Yared, and Bill Hutchings. They have watched this project grow out of conference papers and articles; their responses and encouragement have shaped it in immeasurable ways.

I also wish to thank the National Endowment for the Humanities for the generous stipend that supported my seminar participation and library research. Particular gratitude goes to my fellow participants in the 2007 NEH seminar "*Ulysses* in Context": Kevin Dettmar (director), Margot Backus, Greg Erickson, Georgia Johnston, Joe Kelly, Anne MacMaster, Maria McGarrity, John McGuigan, Richard Murphy, Carrie Preston, Agata Szczeszak-Brewer, Erin Templeton, Janine Utell, Beth Wightman, and Teresa Winterhalter. They listened with interest and patience to many of the ideas that follow and offered thoughtful reactions at a crucial stage. For that, and for an unforgettable Dublin summer, I will always be grateful.

I wish to express my appreciation to Husson University for a faculty research grant, travel funding, and sabbatical that aided in completion of the project. A number of Husson faculty across the disciplines have demonstrated support; special thanks go to Professors Clifton Guthrie, Marek Sitarski, and Ken Lane, for collegiality and friendship that has also shaped these pages.

I am indebted to Amy Averre and her staff at Sawyer Library, Husson University, for constant effort in tracking down various sources. Thanks as well to the many librarians, archivists, and staff at the following institutions who hosted or otherwise assisted me in my research: Fogler Library, University of Maine; Bangor Public Library; O'Neill Library, Boston College; Cecil H. Green Library, Stanford University; Trinity College Library Dublin; University College Dublin Special Collections; National Library of Ireland; and National Archives of Ireland.

A part of "Gorescarred Books" appeared in earlier form as "Stephen's Schoolbooks" in *Études Irlandaises*. Thank you to Sylvie Mikowski and her coeditors for allowing it to be reprinted here.

Portions of "Domestic Forces" appeared in "Britain's Wild West: Joyce's Encounter with the Apache Chief" in *James Joyce Quarterly* 46.2 and as "Militarism and 'The Dead'" in *A New & Complex Sensation: Essays on Joyce's Dubliners*. Thanks to Sean Latham and Carol Kealiher at *JJQ*, and to Oona Frawley and Lilliput Press, for their sage editorial advice and kind permission to reprint.

"Barracks and Brothels" was originally published under that title in *Bloomsday 100* (University Press of Florida, 2009). Thanks to editors Anne Fogarty and Morris Beja for their encouragement of this project and for permission to reprint.

Special thanks to James Maynard, University at Buffalo Libraries, and to Louise Morgan, National Gallery of Ireland, for assistance with image reproduction rights.

Thanks to all my teachers of Joyce, Irish literature, and modernism, including Bonnie Kime Scott, Michael Coyle, Ann Nesslage, and the late John McGahern.

Finally, love and gratitude to my family for their kind interest and enthusiasm at every turn.

Abbreviations for Cited Works by James Joyce

CW   *The Critical Writings of James Joyce.* Edited by Ellsworth Mason and Richard Ellmann. New York: Viking, 1959.

D   *Dubliners.* 1914. Edited by Terence Brown. New York: Penguin, 1992.

FW   *Finnegans Wake.* 1939. New York: Penguin, 1976.

L   *Letters of James Joyce.* Edited by Stuart Gilbert (vol. 1) and Richard Ellmann (vols. 2 and 3). New York: Viking, 1957–66.

OCPW *Occasional, Critical, and Political Writing.* Edited by Kevin Barry. Oxford: Oxford University Press, 2000.

P   *A Portrait of the Artist as a Young Man.* 1916. Edited by R. B. Kershner. Boston: Bedford/St. Martin's, 1993.

SH   *Stephen Hero.* Edited by John J. Slocum and Herbert Cahoon. New York: New Directions, 1963.

U   *Ulysses.* 1922. Edited by Hans Walter Gabler et al. New York: Vintage, 1986.

ULR   "*Ulysses*: Episode Twelve." *Little Review* 6.7 (November 1919): 38–60.

Figure 1. Photograph of James Joyce, age six. 1888. By permission of the University at Buffalo Libraries.

Introduction

The painting *Military Manoeuvres* (1891) by Richard Thomas Moynan hangs in the National Gallery in Dublin. It depicts a group of around a dozen boys playing soldiers in the main street of a nineteenth-century Irish village. One wears boots, while the rest march barefoot in loose, ragtag formation. Several comprise a makeshift fife-and-drum corps using a wooden flute, penny whistle, wooden box, and milking can. A red rag tied to a tree branch flutters over the boys' heads, serving as regimental colors. The provisional pennant draws a viewer's eye from the center of the street scene to the sidewalk at left and the red coat of a British Army officer. Cap atilt, he strolls beside the boys with his lady on his arm and a stern expression on his face as he observes the juvenile procession. Several of the boys have turned to confront the officer, one even trumpeting mockingly through rolled-up newsprint. Opposite the officer, in the right foreground, the ringleader of the young band, wielding a broom and wearing a dragoon-style gold helmet, looks back impatiently at this sudden disorder in the ranks. Meanwhile, in the left foreground, a young peasant girl, feminine archetype of Ireland, stares at the boy with a look that suggests both quiet concern and emerging expectation.

The uncertainty of her countenance underscores the ambiguity of the scene. Is the boys' play-soldiering a gesture of sincere emulation or of mocking sarcasm? Will they grow up to be obedient colonial subjects or insurgent rebels? In either case, *Military Manoeuvres* represents the powerful hold of the British Army on late-nineteenth-century Irish society. At the same time, it suggests a nascent resistance to that imperial power, in a somewhat prophetic rendering of the rising generation that by 1916 would choose armed force in the wake of failed constitutional politics. Overall, Moynan's chain of interlocking lives and overlapping gazes depicts the pervasiveness of militarism in Ireland by the late nineteenth century.

2 · Joyce and Militarism

Figure 2. *Military Manoeuvres*, by Richard Thomas Moynan. 1891. By permission of the National Gallery of Ireland.

The writing of James Joyce similarly engages in its own complex response to the militarized condition of Irish life. One striking example occurs early in the dialogue of Butt and Taff from *Finnegans Wake* section II.3.[1] As the pair "endues paramilintary langdwage" of their own, their confabulation continually approaches but never quite achieves a full account of "How Buckley Shot the Russian General," Joyce's father's anecdote of an Irish soldier in the Crimean War who deliberated about whether or not to fire upon the enemy commander he spies in the vulnerable act of defecating on the battlefield. Buckley ultimately pulls the trigger when he sees the general "prepared to finish the operation with a piece of grassy turf." Richard Ellmann notes that "Joyce told the story to friends, convinced that it was in some way archetypal" (378). In exactly what way, however, the *Wake* never makes quite certain. Some regard it as "an account of resistance to totalitarianism" (Rice 140), while others read it as an inconclusive or even antiheroic narrative. Perhaps because the drinkers in HCE's pub have "heard it sinse sung thousandtimes" (*FW* 338.1–2), a fixed interpretation of the story is not possible or required. Or possibly, it is the story of warfare happening repeatedly throughout history. Nevertheless, as Richard Robinson observes, "we are never too distant nor too close to the lurking presence of the Crimean pairing" (171).

One thing Butt and Taff's recasting of the tale—as "How Burghley shuck the rackushant Germanon. For Ehren, boys, go brawl" (*FW* 338.2–3)—does suggest is the old story's new relevance to questions of Irish cultural identity, national independence, and armed force in the early twentieth century. To "go brawl" for Ehren/Erin necessitated a question of where and with whom. The revised German connection for Burghley suggests the decades of military rivalry between England and Germany that for Irishmen could prove an opportunity as well as a trap:

> "Conscribe him tillusk, unt, in his jubalant tubalence, the groundsapper, with his soilday site out on his moulday side in. The guberniergerenal in laut-lievtonant of Baltiskeeamore, amaltheouse for leporty hole!" (*FW* 338.17–20).

The imperative "Conscribe him tillusk" includes the hotly contested issue of British conscription in Ireland for the fight against Germany, against which, among others, Joyce's friend Francis Sheehy Skeffington rallied in the years leading up to the Great War. One hears Usk, the name of a Welsh town and river that suggests multiple imperial influences, ancient and modern. To conscript Buckley/Burghley or another Irishman to Usk/us is in a very real sense to bring him, like the Celtic kingdom of Wales, into the service of the British Empire. The historical reach of the place-name suggests its enduring military identity: Usk was the site of a legionary fortress at the western frontier of Roman Britain. Meanwhile, the fact that these orders are given in a German accent complicates the situation by conflating the military power of Britain in Ireland with that of its sworn enemy. It suggests both the strategy of German armed assistance to Irish independence—attempted unsuccessfully by Roger Casement in 1916—and the potential reality of a Prussified Ireland dominated by bellicose mercenaries. Regardless of cultural affiliation or historical context, each serves to reiterate the militarist mentality of the Buckley story being retold in the pub. Thus to "conscribe" the Buckley narrative into the *Wake* text itself is to invoke the longstanding tension of British imperial center and Gaelic periphery as well as the international military conflict of England and Germany as duplicate new versions of the same old story.

At stake as well in the barroom banter of Butt and Taff, quite literally, geographically, and tactically, is the land of Ireland itself. This occurs in the identification of the Russian general as "the groundsapper, with his soilday site out on his moulday side in," which associates the soldier's toilet activities in the Buckley story with the controversial Cartesian labor of the nineteenth-century British military in Ireland. The Ordnance Survey, a systematic mapping and renaming of the Irish landscape for purposes of taxation and military administration, was carried out in the early 1830s by army engineers and fortifications experts known as sappers. Therefore, the general's last act as "groundsapper" of using a clump of turf to wipe his "Bog carsse" (*FW* 339.6)—his big arse, or, even more portentously, bog carcass, as he will shortly become—suggests the British Army's soiling insult to the auld sod of Ireland.

That landmark moment in the colonization of Ireland is counterbalanced in the passage by one of liberation, notably in the mention of "leporty hole," which in the context of the Buckley anecdote suggests not only the general's posterior or his latrine but also, in the context of the Irish nationalist movement, Liberty Hall, Dublin headquarters of the national labor movement and, by Easter 1916, of the socialist Citizen Army serving under James Connolly, referenced shortly before by the phrase "Citizen soldiers" (*FW* 338.4). In this way the martial dialogue of the Butt and Taff episode ultimately conjoins Ireland's military-geographic conquest from without with its paramilitary insurgency from within. Joyce shows his disdain for armed force in the service of imperial hegemony or national liberation.

Each of Joyce's major works appeared in a year defined by major armed conflict in Ireland or Continental Europe. After much negotiation and long delay, *Dubliners* appeared in 1914, at the outbreak of the First World War. Critics often cite the Easter Rising and the publication of *A Portrait of the Artist as a Young Man*, both of which occurred in 1916, as parallel political and literary assertions of the coming of age of the Irish nation. The publication of *Ulysses* in February 1922 was less than two months after the Anglo-Irish Treaty, and just a few months prior to the Civil War. Lastly, when *Finnegans Wake* appeared in 1939, Joyce complained to Samuel Beckett about how it was being upstaged by the westward advances of the German army, which had already displaced Joyce and his family from Paris (Ellmann 741).

Yet more striking than the chronological correspondence of Joyce's books to such watershed military happenings is the texts' capacity for documenting and responding to the surreptitious and extensive reach of the militarist ideology that brought such events to pass. Joyce's fiction repeatedly demonstrates how the most telling impact of militarism stems from its capacity to dictate the needs and norms of life far from the battlefield. As this book will argue, Joyce's work continuously reveals the militarist presence in such diverse social realms and disparate cultural fields as education, athletics, marriage and family life, sexual commerce, and public space. As a predominant concern for Joyce, one of the shaping factors of his life and writing, militarism provides a frame for reading his fictional project through relevant historical events and contemporary political values.

* * *

Joyce began to broach this pressing subject and to "endues paramilintary langdwage" (*FW* 338.20) from his earliest literary output. In September 1898, newly matriculated at University College Dublin, Joyce submitted a theme for his English composition course that now seems prescient for both its style and its content. Posthumously titled by editors "Force" or "Subjugation"—the original title and other parts of the manuscript are lost—the essay interweaves in its surviving pages ideas as diverse as warfare and agriculture, hydropower and hunting, ethnicity and forestry. This panoply is not surprising, coming from the mind that would devise the stylistic complexities of *Ulysses* and invent the kaleidoscopic language of *Finnegans Wake*. Beside those texts, of course "Force"/"Subjugation" seems, while provocative, tantalizingly incomplete. In what remains—four fragments totaling just over 3,000 words—one can see the sixteen-year-old Joyce's earliest grappling with an issue that would become a major abiding concern throughout his career: physical force. Morris Beja notes how the "hatred of violence" espoused in the essay would remain a motif in subsequent of Joyce's political writings (48). Force, in its systematized cultural form of modern militarism, would also be an enduring subject for concern throughout his nearly four decades of writing fiction.

Through interrelated categories and a constant stream of examples, "Force"/"Subjugation" attempts an analysis of its topic in what amount to the realms of natural and social law. Bearing visible earmarks of Jesuit scholarship, the theme commences with an Aquinian distinction between righteous force (with its righteous outcomes) and unrighteous conquest, the latter inevitably leading to "ill-will and rebellion... unholy war, stamped with the stamp of ultimate conflict" (*OCPW* 4). Because "it seems barbaric to only consider subjugation, in the light of an oppressing force," Joyce expands from a strictly martial discourse to incorporate what he deems more positive and less oppressive cases wherein "subjugation by force" is "better used than for the vain shedding of blood" (4). These first instances include a series of unequal but benign relationships between man and the elements: tiller and field, gardener and vine, sailor and wind, miller and stream. In each pairing, the dominance of human technology over natural element points to a harmonious association and productive result.

This control of nature is immediately followed in the essay by man's subjugation of flora and fauna, a project deemed for the most part to be complete, although certain creatures and locales remain untamed such that "labour must be anew expended in hunting the savage tiger through the jungles and forests of India, and in felling the trees in Canadian woods" (*OCPW* 7). The allusions to British imperial regions are especially interesting in light of the later assertion that "subjugation is 'almost of the essence of an empire and when it ceases to conquer, it ceases to be'" (10). The quote comes from Cardinal John Henry Newman's sermon "The Christian Church an Imperial Power," in which the iconic cleric examines the geopolitical nature of the Church. In co-opting the words of Cardinal Newman, Joyce invokes the principal founder of University College Dublin, though whether in accord with or in challenge to his intellectual authority remains an open question. But Joyce's point about imperial subjugation is more clearly spelled out when the essay turns to the "important subjugation . . . of race over race" (7), a subtopic that generates a brief digression into the realms of eugenics and social Darwinism. The young Joyce regards the "negro," "red men," and "sluggish Maoris" as being among those who have experienced subjugation by the white man, their "predestined conqueror" (7). Although Joyce, in labeling slavery an "abuse of subjugation" (7), does prescribe limits to Euro-American conquest, he operates from what Richard Ellmann describes rightly, and somewhat understatedly, as a "less enlightened" view (70).

Not bogged down by issues of social or racial inequity, the essay takes up its ultimate position, one that advocates the use of force only to subjugate dubious personal qualities of modern urban life: "the fretful temper, the base interpretation, the fool's conceitedness, the fin-de-siècle sneer, the gossiping, the refusal of aid, the hurting word and worthless taunt" (*OCPW* 9). As Bonnie Kime Scott points out, this enumeration comprises "much of the hateful discourse of 'Cyclops,'" suggesting Joyce had tapped into a theme he was bound to revisit (57). Force of will (rather than physical force) is the best weapon for subverting hostile tendencies that, left unchecked, could lead to destructive violence. Once one becomes aware of the possibility of will power, subjugation of (not *by*) force suggests a means for societal improvement by dint of self-restraint: "all these are daily waiting for us to subjugate," concludes Joyce (*OCPW* 9). If there is a remedy to what Joyce would later have Bloom refer to as "Force, hatred, history, all that" (*U* 12.1481), it resides in sorting out, as Joyce the university student was attempting to do, proper from improper force, and learning to deploy one over the other in the correct moment and circumstance. If this occurs, the essay hopefully concludes, it will culminate with "Kindness over all the good, forever, in a new subjugation" (*OCPW* 11).

In this manner, what begin as "questions of moment and difficult to answer" (*OCPW* 4) are reduced to the level of the individual, as Joyce displays a budding tendency to parallel the international with the interpersonal. "Nations, like individuals, have their egos," he would state a decade later in the Trieste lecture "Ireland, Island of Saints and Sages" (*OCPW* 108). Overall, the university theme examines how force, whether physical or metaphysical, pervades the environmental, economic, social, and psychological realms. It exemplifies the essay in Michel de Montaigne's original humanistic definition of that genre as a modest attempt at understanding its subject—an attempt that raises important questions even if it never in fact resolves them. For Joyce, throughout the rest of his writing, force and subjugation would serve as effective frames through which to contemplate human nature, historical experience, and cultural interaction.

Crucial to the reception of Joyce's school essay is a notable variation in how editors have labeled it. This difference emerges first of all, as mentioned, in the two titles chosen for its publication. With this distinction, the two major editions of Joyce's critical and journalistic writing, one in the middle twentieth century, the other in the early twenty-first, proclaim different ways of reading and thinking about one of Joyce's earliest writings. In their 1959 edition of Joyce's *Critical Writings*, Ellsworth Mason and Richard Ellmann named it "Force"; four decades later, Kevin Barry assigned it the title "Subjugation" in his Oxford edition of Joyce's *Occasional, Critical, and Political Writing*. The Ellmann/Mason title and editorial note clearly invite us to read the 1898 essay as a kind of precocious prologue to Leopold Bloom's tense exchange with the bigoted Citizen of the "Cyclops" episode (*CW* 17). Ellmann reinforced such a recursive reading in his biography of Joyce, insisting "the essay on 'Force' expressed a hatred of violence which proved in

Joyce to be lifelong" (70). Despite his different title, Barry similarly remarks on the prophetic nature of the school essay, noting that it "proclaims the aversion to violence which Joyce, citizen of a country and of a continent immersed for much of his life in war, will always maintain" (ix). Barry justifies his retitling "in order to correspond more accurately to the essay's keyword and its theme" (290), a point borne out by a tally of its occurrences.[2] In support of Barry's choice, Brian Caraher sees the title "Subjugation" as able "to better reflect the thematic and stylistic recursiveness of the piece" (513).

Subjugation and force provide a useful study in etymological contrasts. "Subjugate" derives from the Latin *sub jugum*, "under the yoke," a reference to the ancient Roman practice of victorious legionaries placing the yokes of oxen around the necks of defeated enemy combatants. The action demonstrated to both victims and onlookers a sense of utter domination and clear subservience in the wake of defeat. In this regard, subjugation points toward the social eventualities of military conquest. Force, on the other hand—originating with *fortis*, Latin for "strong"—denotes physical power or strength without a necessary relational aspect or definitive historical context. Force is the immediate collision or physical impact, devoid of cultural ramifications or historical consequences. These differing connotations elicited by the title change demonstrate how scholars have come to reposition Joyce's work within the expanded matrices of postcolonial theory and cultural studies at the turn of the twenty-first century. In their conjunction and contrast, the two titles provide valuable guidewords for reading and thinking about the essay as well as snapshots of the ever-changing critical project in Joyce studies. Both are important keywords to understanding the continuum of ideas introduced in the essay. In fact, the two words also occur in direct conjunction or close proximity at several points in the essay, twice in the repeated phrase "subjugation by force," which might represent an alternative title. This idiomatic combination, forming a nexus of the ideological and the physical, the psychological and the political, contains the essence of militarism and its effects on early-twentieth-century culture and society. Not in the least redundant, "subjugation by force" speaks to the perceived and actual effects of force or the threat of force on a population. Whether exercised by revolution or counterrevolution, by state apparatus or individual, subjugation by force suggests a core pattern in human social and historical experience. The university essay itself represents Joyce's first foray into a topic that would remain central to his writing for decades to come. "Force" or "Subjugation" exhibits some of the remarkable and contradictory impulses Joyce would lend to the theme for years to come.

Whatever we might choose to call the essay, it is worth noting that its fragments exist owing not to the precocious ability of the writer or the masterful nature of his writing but to the paucity of resources in his family. Short on paper, Joyce's younger brother Stanislaus used the backs of several pages of the essay to continue writing his diary. There is an appropriate (and appropriating) irony to this tale of accidental preservation by which "Force"/"Subjugation" survived despite—or perhaps due to—a secondary occupying narrative. Figuratively, much the same could be said about Joyce's fiction, which both descries and relies on the administrative and military occupation of British colonial power for some of its most potent functions and complicated features. The manuscript's narrow escape is also fitting for an essay that deals with humankind's destructive tendencies and from a writer who was often preoccupied with the human potential for planning and carrying out forceful destruction. Indeed, the threat of systematic annihilation looms behind his famous boast that, were Dublin ever to be destroyed, it could be rebuilt brick by brick from the pages of *Ulysses*, a remark that might have emanated not only from genuine pride and self-admiration but also legitimate fears of widespread ruin.

Such fears were not unfounded. By the time *Ulysses* was published, Joyce, at forty, had lived in four heavily militarized societies: Ireland, Austria-Hungary, Italy, and France. He had witnessed anarchist bombings in Rome, had personal run-ins with police and military officials in Pola and Zurich, and fled the unprecedented destruction of the First World War. Any one of these events must have been remarkable and upsetting for one deathly afraid of firearms, dogs, and thunderstorms.

The fragmented state of the university essay offers an early snapshot of Joyce's thinking about the subjugating nature of force. As if foreshadowing his own long-term obsession, in the midst of the essay Joyce reflects how "often when a person gets embarked on a topic which in its vastness completely swallows up his efforts, the subject dwarfs the writer" (*OCPW* 7). What emerges from the broken segments that survive is nonetheless a continuous sense of the young writer's resolve to take on some of the most pressing questions in human history and international relations. The university essay initiates a working out of some of the problems that would be at the core of Joyce's literary project for decades to come.

The intellectual climate of University College offered Joyce ample opportunity for honing his views on the issue. His first year at UCD saw the rejuvenation of the Literary and Historical Society. William Dawson, one early member, describes its re-formation in sincere, if flippant, terms: "In 1897, Arthur Clery and Frank Skeffington ... by desire to hear themselves talk, and by a very genuine ambition to do something to impart a College atmosphere to what was then little better than a grinding academy, gathered one or two students together, and requested the President to give them permission and assistance to restart the Debating Society" (qtd. in Meenan 37). It was there that Joyce was exposed to at least one unflinchingly pro-militarist thesis. In February 1899 Hugh Boyle Kennedy, later chief justice of the Irish supreme court, presented a paper titled "The War Machine: A State Necessity."[3] No copy of Kennedy's speech survives; it is characterized briefly in the meeting minutes as "an able paper" which received a vote of thanks from those present, including Francis Skeffington (Hogan 173).[4] One can only imagine what the pacifist Skeffington, beyond his civil motion of thanks, really thought of Kennedy's position. Stanislaus recalls Father Finlay, a faculty advisor to the Society, commenting at the time how a better title for the non-bellicose Kennedy would have been "The Sewing-Machine, a Home Necessity" (124). Stanislaus says his brother's contribution to the debate following Kennedy's militarist argument "was an ironical modification of the eight beatitudes to suit the exigencies of the War Machine" (124). It would recur in *Ulysses*'s "Oxen of the Sun" episode as an alliterative enumeration of the "British Beatitudes! ... Beer, beef, business, bibles, bulldogs, battleships, buggery and bishops" (*U* 14.1453–54, 1459–60). The sardonic response, in voice and print, contains one of Joyce's most effective indictments of the entangled interests of imperial ideology, modern capitalism, and military power.

Over the ensuing four decades, Joyce would continue to deploy language to stem the rising tide of systematic violence in twentieth-century life. The historical causes and literary consequences of that enduring interest are the focus of this book. In that sense, it follows the lead of cultural and new historical readings that have recently helped redefine Joyce scholarship. Andrew Gibson and Len Platt frame the fundamental question that such approaches to Joyce should continue to ask: "What historical, political, and cultural specifics did Joyce really engage with?" (4). In the past two decades a number of scholars have illuminated the broader questions of national, postcolonial, and racial identity at stake in Joyce.[5] Their work has been of immeasurable value to readers looking to reconstruct cultural contexts and unearth long-lost details that help make sense of Joyce's fiction. They have brought reading Joyce into the folds of postcolonial scholarship on the one hand and Irish studies on the other. Doing so, they have illuminated many of the national and historical elements long obscured by the cosmopolitan-modernist vision that predominated through roughly the first half-century of Joyce criticism.[6]

Joyce and Militarism aims to fuse these oft-separated local and global perspectives. It is locally driven in the sense that, much like Joyce's fiction, it explores various aspects of Dublin life—education, recreation, sexuality, economy, domesticity, and urban space—and how each was affected by the escalating tensions of the Anglo-Irish conflict as it entered the modern phase of armed insurgency. At the same time, the study is Continental in orientation, considering the historical and ideological climate in which Joyce worked after he left Dublin in September 1904. To this end, it intends as well to examine some of the broader consequences of military culture on Joyce's life and writings. Robert Spoo and James Fairhall have provided insightful readings of Joyce's work in the context of the Great War.[7] This book will consider Joyce's writing in the less spectacular but no less prevalent shadows that militarism cast over Europe in the run-up to the First World War.

The heightened militarism of the decades preceding the Great War, especially in Germany and Britain, has been well documented as a motivating social and political factor of European life. For this reason, it is worth considering as one of the major contributors to the historical climate in and about which Joyce produced his fiction. His stories and novels are populated by literal and metaphorical images of what Deleuze and Guattari have termed the "war machine." In a fundamental sense, Joyce's writing reflects and rejects militarism, speaks of it and against it. Like the "war machine" itself, operating sometimes unnoticeably within diverse avenues of social, cultural, and economic enterprise, Joyce's literary response to the military presence is often subtle, entrenched, and difficult to detect at first glance. It is specifically inscribed as image, metaphor, allusion, theme, and motif; it assumes the shape of character and conflict, structure and setting, perspective and style. In all its subtlety, the martial element in Joyce is frequent and ubiquitous. Its consistency shows how Joyce turned his college composition topic into a lifelong writing assignment revealing the significant tug of physical-force ideology on the broader social fabric as well as the individual life.

* * *

Throughout this study, the term "militarism" is intended to refer to an ideology whose major premise is that the power and value of a society are realized primarily through the capability of its armed forces and, by extension, the potential of its population and economy to maintain those forces. This ideology might emerge as a set of overt tenets or underlying assumptions, of centralized policies or default actions, or of a combination of these. A militaristic society promotes the social, economic, even geographic reorganization of its citizens' lives for the goal of increased military capacity. In turn, military capacity might be tied to maintaining rule or usurping power within the state, or it might be expressly linked to goals of imperial and colonial expansion.

In either case, virtually every aspect of life in a militarized society becomes absorbed in the process of supporting the armed forces in their central role. Generally dictated from the top of the political structure, such martial orientation becomes evident throughout public service and government, private enterprise and commerce. It permeates academic and educational institutions, and it shapes artistic activity, mass media, and other forms of cultural discourse. Militarist ideology controls social structures, such as church, club, union, and guild, and it overtakes individual psychology, marital relations, and family dynamics. In effect, it enters all walks of life and excludes few, if any, resources for equipping, training, and sustaining the military as the major motive and controlling interest in society.

"Militarism" and "militarization" will both be used throughout this text. I have embraced the former for a title and primary term partly owing to its currency in Joyce's day. Like the word "terrorism" in our own time, "militarism" was generally used to refer exclusively to an enemy state, branding it a threat on the international stage while implying a dehumanizing state of its affairs internally. I also employ the word for the very reason historian John R. Gillis tends to shun it: "Like so many terms forged in the hot flame of public debate, militarism carries a meaning that is distinctly political and overtly ideological... It is a way of displacing responsibility and blame, and thus must be used with great caution" (1–2). Perhaps these are the same reasons Joyce appears to have used it with great caution in his writing, generally avoiding its direct mention while making its presence clear by structural and referential techniques.

In contrast to historians and political theorists like Karl Liebknecht and Guglielmo Ferrero, whose work he read in Rome in 1906, Joyce never uses the term directly in his published works.

Such paucity might suggest from the very start the difficulty or even impossibility of my argument. Yet Joyce's omission of the term has an effect of presenting its subtle intrusion into so many realms of early-twentieth-century experience. In essence, by showing rather than directly stating the pervasiveness of militarism, Joyce depicts what Deleuze and Guattari have theorized as its internalized and externalized manifestations:

> the war machine in itself... seems to be irreducible to the State apparatus, to be outside its sovereignty and prior to its law: it comes from elsewhere.... In every respect, the war machine is of another species, another nature, another origin than the State apparatus. (352)

The "war machine" assumes the powers and structures of the state but at the same time remains above them. As Joyce's fiction describes, it is an impulse translatable to numerous social and cultural levels; it transcends divisions of nation, culture, class, and political ideology.

Robert Spoo begins his critical study *James Joyce and the Language of History* with the confident metaphorical claim "The word history reverberates throughout *Ulysses* like the laugh of a ghost" (3). I cannot make the same bold assertion for the presence of my central term, since "militarism" is not a word Joyce employed often in writing. It appears in his correspondence, as I discuss in chapter 1, but not his fiction. Instead, militarism hovers as recurring concept rather than ubiquitous lexeme. Its ideological influence and material reflection appear across Joyce's writing through subtle incorporation rather than overt mention. To revise Spoo's simile, the idea of militarism reverberates throughout Joyce not so much like the laugh of a ghost but rather like the whisper of eyewitness testimony.

* * *

Joyce and Militarism begins with a general overview of the militarism debate as it pertained to politics and writing in the prewar years. The opening chapter, "Joyce and Ideas of Militarism," traces the emergence of militarism, as a term and ideology, in late-nineteenth- and early-twentieth-century Europe, examining the foreign and domestic crosscurrents of German militarism, British imperialism, Irish republicanism, and the international peace movement, which Joyce witnessed. The chapter discusses some of the major contemporary political theorists, such as Guglielmo Ferrero, who influenced Joyce's understanding of the subject. In addition, two of Joyce's classmates from University College, Francis Sheehy Skeffington and Thomas Kettle—the former a pacifist, the latter a soldier—became casualties of military action at home and abroad, as the three friends elected vastly different courses of thought and action during a period in Irish history that witnessed what Charles Townshend has termed "the militarization of politics" (28).

Chapter 2, "Violent Exercise," considers the connection between militarism and athleticism, by tracing the rise of school sports as a training ground for soldiering in both colonial and anticolonial contexts. The so-called garrison games of British public-school origin and the native Irish sports of the Gaelic Athletic Association (GAA) alike impressed on young practitioners distinct political perspectives and cultural values. Football matches were scheduled by the British Army as a means to community-building; hurling was used as cover for illegal drilling by the Irish Volunteers and Fianna Éireann, the Irish scout movement. Recurring references in *A Portrait* and *Ulysses* to these and other sports, including cycling and boxing, point to the politics of masculine and national identity at stake in the process of militarization.

The third chapter, "Gorescarred Books," takes its title from the history lesson taught by Stephen in "Nestor." The moment demonstrates recognition of the school curriculum as a vehicle for the indoctrination of adolescent males into the culture of the war machine. Stephen's role as unenthusiastic teacher of these dubious lessons is juxtaposed with his own schoolbooks, referenced in the opening chapter of *A Portrait of the Artist as a Young Man*, which themselves represent the impact of militarism on late-nineteenth-century reading and education. Other indoctrinating intertexts appear in the popular boys' papers that shape the discourse and effectively frame the adventure-story parody of the *Dubliners* story "An Encounter."

The next chapter, "Domestic Forces," commences with a look at home and family life in *Dubliners*, particularly "Counterparts" and "The Dead." It reads the literal and metaphorical militarism of those stories against the backdrop of imperial military occupation and armed resistance movements Joyce knew from his time in Ireland, Italy, and Austria-Hungary. Themes of domestic repression and physical abuse, generally at the hands of dominating father figures, are central to the collection. This notion of overbearing or corrupted patriarchy—on the levels of household and nation—persists in *Ulysses*'s overt critique of the English sociopolitical concept of the public police.

Chapter 5, "Barracks and Brothels," investigates the connection between soldiers and prostitutes in 1900s Dublin, and its particular effects on public health, residential space, and social control. Concentrating on streetwalkers, flashhouses, and their soldier clientele, in *A Portrait* and *Ulysses*, and *Finnegans Wake*, along with more tacit forms of prostitution in the residential spaces of *Dubliners*, the chapter looks at the interrelation of the military and sexual economies in the Dublin red-light district known as Monto. As it was a boon to military recruiting, authorities did little to curb the nighttime trade until the spread of syphilis and other sexually transmitted diseases presented a risk to troop safety and imperial security. Joyce's fiction leads us to think of soldier and sex worker as figures of surveillance and control both subject to the militarizing power of the state.

The final chapter, "Reclamations," considers how Joyce's work helped imagine the demilitarization of Dublin, through a process of reappropriation that continues a century later. Joyce's fiction commenced a re-visioning of public space, architecture, and monuments in early-twentieth-century Dublin. Commencing in the Martello Tower, a former army signal station and gun battery, *Ulysses* effects a symbolic reinvasion of Ireland from Joyce's Parisian exile. As twenty-first-century Dublin continues its own rapid redefinition of urban space, the city also redefines itself in relation to Joyce's public image and literary contribution. In this regard, the *Parable of the Plums* street theater event on O'Connell Street in June 2004, commemorating the one-hundredth anniversary of Bloomsday, offered a way of reclaiming Joyce and redefining Irish cultural identity for the new century.

Reading Joyce's response to the militarism of his time presents us, not least of all, with new ways of reading and responding to that of our own. In this regard, I hope *Joyce and Militarism* will contribute not only to the project of Joyce studies but to the broader contemporary relevance of literature and the humanities. Rita Felski asserts a current need for literary studies to escape its "crisis of legitimation" by making theories of reading equate with ways of reading, to make literature "usable" (B8). If literary criticism is to recalibrate itself with the concerns of contemporary readers, I can think of few greater issues for it to tackle in this decade than those of social, political, and environmental survival.

A number of critics have already made exciting moves in this direction. Margot Norris notes in *Writing War in the Twentieth Century* that "the polity and institutions responsible for inaugurating, promoting, pursuing, analyzing, and recording war explicitly extrude the job of registering the suffering caused by its vast machinery of injuring. This job—and the work of mourning it entails—falls largely to the work of art and to the work of culture" (32). Joyce's art contributed in no small measure to this work. It helps show us how the "vast machinery of injuring" can become rooted in the most seemingly innocuous aspects of daily experience: education, recreation, sexuality, media, and economy. Threads of militarism weave through the sparse stories of *Dubliners*, the fictional autobiography of *A Portrait*, the narrative innovation of *Ulysses*, and the stylistic experiment of *Finnegans Wake*. Joyce's characters live and move under surveillance through the contested spaces of a garrison city, whose population at times resists, at other times succumbs to, the militarizing control of the imperial state or the anticolonialist option of physical force.

Seeing such fictional representations can provide additional insight into the world Joyce sought to reflect and reform, as well as help us rethink the dangers of that world that endure a century on. In *The Sorrows of Empire*, Chalmers Johnson notes the overextended nature of the United States' military-industrial complex, which in 2002, one year before the American invasion of Iraq, had more than seven hundred overseas bases and installations. Johnson shows how such a vast socioeconomic system becomes self-perpetuating and nearly impossible to eradicate, both as physical and as ideological presence. Joyce sounded a similar warning almost a century ago, as his art examined the "machinery of injuring" in both its tangible and abstract forms (Norris, *Writing War* 32). In the first decades of the twenty-first century, the problems of force and subjugation are still, as the sixteen-year-old Joyce surmised, "questions of moment and difficult to answer" (*OCPW* 4). His work continues to remind us that, precisely owing to their inherent difficulty, they remain questions worthy of the asking.

1

Joyce and Ideas of Militarism

> His [the printer's] idea of gallantry has grown up in him (probably) during the reading of the novels of the elder Dumas and during the performance of romantic plays which presented to him cavaliers and ladies in full dress. But I am sure he is willing to modify his fantastic views. I would strongly recommend to him the chapters wherein Ferrero examines the moral code of the soldier and (incidentally) of the gallant. But it would be useless for I am sure that in his heart of hearts he is a militarist.
>
> James Joyce to Grant Richards, 5 May 1906

In the spring of 1906, James Joyce and Nora Barnacle, a year and a half out of Ireland, were adapting to their new life as exiles in Trieste. Their son Giorgio was born the previous summer, so to help make ends meet on Joyce's modest salary—he earned £80 per year teaching English at the Scuola Berlitz—since January they had shared a house with Alessandro Francini Bruni and his family on the edge of the city at 1 via Giovanni Boccaccio. Despite the auspicious street name, Joyce's literary progress had encountered a serious setback. *Dubliners* had for several months been under contract with the London publisher Grant Richards, but in the last week of April, publication was halted by a cautious printer who noticed a number of potentially controversial items that Richards and his reader had not. Well versed in British obscenity law, which held printers as well as publishers subject to legal action, the printer had objected specifically to numerous words and passages in the collection, but also, inexplicably, refused to print one story altogether. The returned manuscript bore pencil marks next to passages in several stories but none beside "Two Gallants," even though a letter from Richards singled out that story as the major stumbling block. The shady tale of nightlife on the streets of the Irish capital, concluding in a potentially suspect monetary exchange, had clearly rattled the printer's moral sensibility. Richards warned that the book could not go to press without significant changes to "'Two Gallants" and "Counterparts," leading Joyce to ask whether it was "the small gold coin in the former story or the code of honour which the two gallants live by which shocks him" (L 2:132–33). When no reply came, Joyce constructed one of his own; it focused not on the potential immorality of the stories but on that of their disapproving early reader.

In dismissing Richards's unnamed printer as "in his heart of hearts . . . a militarist" (L 2:133), Joyce deployed a strategic and revealing insult. The remark shows the sort of frustrated hostility Joyce frequently directed, rightly or wrongly, at those he perceived as obstacles to his success. Writing of the dispute decades later, biographer Herbert Gorman did not hesitate to demonize the "Moral British Printer" as an impediment not only to Joyce's career but to civilization itself (148–50).[1] In 1906 Joyce, eager to see his first book in print, could not afford to be so self-aggrandizing. Nevertheless, he tenaciously held his ground throughout the spring and summer, refusing to make the requested changes and ultimately causing Richards to withdraw the contract later that year. Joyce could not have known then he was at the start of a dispute that would delay publication of *Dubliners* for eight long years.

Yet Joyce's chilly diatribe against the printer suggests much more than the fervent ambition of a young writer seeking publication. As poignant counter to the printer's critique and censorship, it asserts a way of reading, so that, as Vincent Cheng in *Joyce, Race, and Empire* suggests, "the story is itself an attack on . . . a militaristic mentality" (113). To make such a mentality apparent to his publisher—and, indeed, to make the story available at all—Joyce mounts a defense for the story's inclusion and for the existence of *Dubliners* as the whole collection he imagined, by constructing a critical framework that explicitly demands moral recalibration of a (mostly) imagined reader who has apparently misinterpreted or otherwise overlooked this significant layer of the fiction. In this way, Joyce sets "Two Gallants," and his ripening fictional project overall, amid fundamental tensions and questions of martial ideology.

Beyond ad hominem attack or frustrated name-calling, his disparaging remarks about the printer essentially argue a place for *Dubliners* by elaborating a critical nexus of perceived readers, canonical texts, and literary correctives. Doing so, Joyce reveals his purpose of producing a literature that would transform its readers. The assumption that the printer—or, for that matter, any other resisting reader—must be "willing to modify his fantastic views" (L 2:133) in order to glean the proper meaning of the story implies a reformist, if not revolutionary, aim. In essence, anticipating Stephen Dedalus's remark, *Dubliners* will change the country by changing its subjects.

Joyce did not acquiesce to the major manuscript revisions or exclusions Richards requested; instead, he countered by asking printer and publisher to widen their notions of what constitutes legally publishable literature. He actively challenged their editorial resistance by redefining the criteria of the moral debate, replacing the issue of sexual indecency or linguistic vulgarity in the text with that of alleged bellicosity in its readers. In this way, Joyce's rhetoric deftly shifts the focus of controversy from the content of the stories to the moral makeup of their audience.

Joyce's rejoinder to Grant Richards and his printer is based, then, on the premise that literature shapes the values of its readers. Accordingly, the literature Joyce gives as example would seem to form a significant part of his argument. There has been much useful critical discussion as to which of Alexander Dumas's works Joyce had in mind as cause of the printer's myopic morality, but the specific identities of those texts are less important than the rhetorical offensive Joyce launches on behalf of his own.[2] It is the vague, blanketing pluralism of the authorial references that lends them a general strength. Joyce names no particular writings, only states that the novels of Dumas and a similar type of chivalric drama provide the source of a gallantry that, as R. B. Kershner notes, had carried both military and amatory connotations for centuries (*Joyce, Bakhtin* 79). Joyce emphasizes the martial half of this equation when he suggests the incidental connection from gallantry to the moral code of soldiering, but to pinpoint, say, *The Count of Monte Cristo* or *The Three Musketeers* would only dilute his claim that such values pervade those writings as much as they do any others of Dumas. One need not single out a particular book, play, or scene, when virtually all are shaped by militaristic values that in turn shape their readers. It is precisely the nonspecific, multigeneric nature of the statement that grants it the broader force of an ideological assessment or conclusion.

To be sure, Joyce's critical position rests upon a bold assumption concerning the printer's literary tastes and political values. Not knowing the man or his actual response to "Two Gallants," Joyce constructs him as a self-appointed critic and resisting first reader who, through his resistance, embodies the fundamental power of literature to influence both those who produce and those who consume it. Along these lines, Joyce proclaims that the apparent key to a story like "Two Gallants" lies as much in the text as in its readers' awareness of and ability to counteract the militaristic beliefs instilled by prior literary experiences (such as the novels of Dumas or cavalier drama). Conditioned by the ideology of such potent pre-texts, how could Richards's printer or any other early reader of *Dubliners* respond but with the resistance Joyce seems to expect, perhaps even wish to provoke in them? Indeed, it seems the very readers who would object to *Dubliners*' publication are precisely the ones Joyce most wants the book to reach.

This paradox of reader receptiveness extends from the London printer to the Irish readers that, as Joseph Kelly argues, were Joyce's actual "target audience" (16). Their firsthand experience of poverty, repression, English occupation, and Catholic ideology made the stories most resonant with those who lived daily amid such forces. At the same time, these cultural factors could also make the most poignant observations of the collection difficult for many readers in Ireland to accept. Later in the 5 May letter to Richards, Joyce appears to acknowledge this potential problem, imagining the printer among various types of Irish readers who would object to particular stories in the collection. These include a Dubliner, a "more subtle inquisitor," and Irish priests and boardinghouse keepers, who he suspects would "denounce," respectively, "Ivy Day in the Committee Room," "An Encounter," "The Sisters," and "The Boarding House." With such a range of potential readers in mind, Joyce concludes, "Do not let the printer imagine, for goodness' sake, that he is going to have all the barking to himself" (*L* 2:134). The hypothetical readers Joyce imagines alongside the printer present the various kinds of ideological opposition he expected *Dubliners* might and must encounter were it to fulfill its intended function of social reflection and reform. Thus the barking printer—at least according to the identity Joyce constructs for him—becomes one of several resisting readers Joyce anticipates for his work. His prior conditioning by the militarized values of popular literature prepares him to be reshaped by *Dubliners*.

If not his ideal printer, Joyce proceeds to refashion him as his ideal reader. In Joyce's view, the printer would make ideal editorial choices had he experienced as well quite another sort of pre-text for *Dubliners*, "the chapters wherein Ferrero examines the moral code of the soldier and (incidentally) of the gallant" (*L* 2:133). There has been some debate as to which chapters—and, for that matter, which of the three books Ferrero had published by 1906—Joyce might have meant, since as Susan Humphreys notes, "All three deal with war and militarism; not one has a chapter concerned exclusively with soldiers' morals" (240).³ Presumably any number of Ferrero chapters could serve as corrective for the militaristic virtues absorbed from the stylized violence of nineteenth-century popular literature. The most likely ones would have come from *Militarism*, the only one of Ferrero's books translated into English by 1906. Published in Italian as *Il Militarismo* in 1898, it offered a systematic and comparative historical study of how military thinking and policies were taking over civic, social, and cultural life in a number of European countries. The book achieved strong acclaim and a wide following in both academic and popular circles; it was translated into numerous languages, making its author something of a celebrity even beyond the Italian-speaking world. As this chapter will discuss, Joyce had great intellectual admiration for Ferrero's work and, in highlighting the growing presence of militarism in diverse realms of social and cultural experience, would proceed to convey through modernist literature what Ferrero was arguing through the budding field of sociology.

Situating *Dubliners* between his renunciation of Dumas and endorsement of Ferrero, Joyce effectively positioned his new fictional project between not just two particular writers and genres but two distinct ideological systems. Yet it is finally the precision of the insult that connects a simple publishing dispute to an urgent and contemporary political reality. "Militarist" was just one of several derogatory labels Joyce applied to Richards's uncooperative printer. (Others included "one-eyed printer" and "plain blunt man" (*L* 2:133).) But it was easily the most provocative and disparaging. More than just another personal jibe, it was a nod to the most pressing concern of contemporary European life. To call someone a militarist in 1906 was to invoke the most volatile global debate of the late nineteenth and early twentieth centuries.[4]

In London, where Richards would have read Joyce's letter, the epithet had special resonance, since Fleet Street journalists commonly fashioned imperial Germany as the dark specter of militarism during a decade of political tension that most saw as buildup to inevitable war. In their use of the term, many British newspapers reflected and activated the collective national consciousness by ironically co-opting a term of civil dissent that had originated in imperial Germany a generation earlier. The nightmarish results of galvanizing such patriotic fervor of course became painfully clear only after the Great War. George Orwell recalls the increasingly divisive sense of the word toward the close of the war, much of it along generational lines: "By 1918 everyone under forty was in a bad temper with his elders, and the mood of anti-militarism which followed naturally upon the fighting was extended into a general revolt against orthodoxy and authority. At that time there was, among the young, a curious cult of the hatred of 'old men'" (170).

A decade earlier, the emerging sense of "militarist" as a pejorative term for an outmoded worldview seems at once careful and presumptuous, clairvoyant and ironic, offering as it does a portal into the emerging social and historical background of Joyce's fiction. In sending the word quite literally back across the Channel, Joyce did not just argue with his publisher and insult his printer; he set the terms for critical reception of his work in the parameters of an international discourse that would continue to shape his fiction as it would shape his world for the next three decades.

Unfortunately, Joyce's response did not yield an immediate or positive resolution to the dispute. We can only speculate whether the unnamed printer ever heard or heeded Joyce's literary recommendation. Judging by the outcome, he probably did not. The negotiation over *Dubliners* lingered on, with Joyce grudgingly agreeing to changes in other stories so that he could keep "Two Gallants" intact. But on June 14 Richards insisted the story be left out of the book, leaving Joyce distressed at the prospect of excluding what he considered one of the collection's most important stories. Not mincing words, he told Richards he regarded the "omission as an almost mortal mutilation" of the book (*L* 2:142). He questioned once more the rationale and fairness of a system that for all intents and purposes made pressmen into penmen. While commiserating with Joyce's frustration about the legal power of printer over writer, Richards was firm in his decision. This kept the two at loggerheads through the summer, when Joyce and his family moved to Rome. By October, when Joyce at last agreed to suppress "Two Gallants" and "A Little Cloud," it was too late. Richards had already decided to pass on the entire project. The manuscript was returned, and *Dubliners* went into an eight-year limbo until Richards finally consented to publish it in 1914.

This snapshot of a tumultuous publication history shows Joyce's penchant for creative control, self-promotion, even personal grudge. But more important, the moment shows Joyce elucidating a place for *Dubliners* amid a contemporary strain of political debate. Joyce's defense of his manuscript in May 1906 suggests how, if *Dubliners* were to stay true to its goal of being for Irish readers a "nicely polished looking glass through which to view themselves" (L 2:64), that moral mirror must include as well an unobstructed view of the military ethos that permeated various aspects of Dublin life. Even in rather dire financial times, with publication itself on the line, Joyce hesitated to compromise this artistic and political integrity, stemming as it did from one of the continuous and inescapable concerns of his writing and his life.

Before Joyce made militarism a central issue of his fiction, he had experienced its ubiquitous presence and prevalent ideology through a range of intellectual influences, geographic realities, and personal relationships. He knew it firsthand while growing up in a colonized, occupied Ireland that was inching ever closer to a war for independence, and later, during an adult life in several volatile, contested regions of Continental Europe. Three of his close friends would be killed in combat or wartime violence; during their lifetimes, each of these men had been greatly affected by questions of politics and military might. For their part, Joyce and his family found themselves displaced by two world wars, and on several occasions in close proximity to the impact of state and non-state militarism, including syndicalist bombings in Rome, gunfire of civil war in Ireland, and encroaching armies of occupation in Trieste and Paris. And in the times and spaces where armed force was not a visible presence, the more surreptitious aspects of militarism gave a subtle but certain tug to various threads of the social fabric.

The deep-seated militarism of Irish and European life became a historical source, creative context, and dialogical adversary for Joyce's intellectual life. He encountered it as journalistic idiom, cultural stereotype, and academic debate; he felt it directly as social condition, local reality, and personal affliction. He made it a major subject of his reading, stocking his Trieste library with numerous works on military life and antimilitarist topics. From such investigations, Joyce's fiction came to describe and question how the martial ethos overwhelmed modern life on multiple levels.

Militarism was a relevant social issue and potent political dogma in each of the countries where Joyce resided. It shaped the atmosphere of daily life and influenced the process and product of his ongoing literary effort. If for Joyce that effort would focus consistently on depictions of life in the late-colonial Ireland he left behind in 1904, it was also informed by definitions of militarism originating from a central-European political discourse that Joyce was perfectly positioned to absorb.

Continental Currents

During the two decades when Joyce produced *Dubliners*, *A Portrait*, and *Ulysses*, the intellectual currents of the Continent flowed with competing and contradictory notions of militarism. There was heated debate within and across political camps as to the nature, causes, and consequences of militarism, all contributing to what Volker Berghahn describes as a "definitional muddle" that alternately treated the issue as a political-developmental model or a socioeconomic problem (10). This distinction generally fell along Marxist and liberal, Continental and British lines. From his time in Trieste and Rome, Joyce was ideally situated to write across this political and cultural divide. An expatriate Anglophone with socialist sympathies, he was attuned to key strains of antimilitarist ideology, which he effectively packaged and redeployed in fictional forms for English-speaking readers accustomed to seeing militarism as an essentially Continental phenomenon.

The word "militarism" appears to have entered English a generation before Joyce used it in his tirade against the reluctant London printer. Coincidentally, it made its linguistic flight from the same political conflagration whose embers were still smoldering in 1904 when Joyce arrived in Trieste. The *OED* attributes the earliest instance of the word to Giuseppe Garibaldi at the end of a highly publicized visit to Britain in the spring of 1864. In an open letter in the *Daily Telegraph*, the Italian revolutionary describes the British Army as "bright in glory, yet untainted with that disease of modern times, known under the sinister name of militarism" ("To the People"). With its blatant political overtones, Garibaldi's use of the term shows from the start how problematic it could be. He relies upon a fairly reductive distinction between armed "glory" and martial "disease," a binary that depends on no objective criteria, only whether the army in question belongs to one's admired ally or sworn enemy. "Militarism" was an abstract noun that, much like "terrorism" in the twenty-first century, could at once be used to dehumanize mortal adversaries and to project an at best feigned moral clarity on even the most clouded of political skies.[5] Meanwhile, the medical metaphor establishes another deceptive quality of the term, one that distracts from the physical horrors of military culture by calling attention to its abstract notions of honor. The analogy assumes a clear contrast between a presumably admirable activity of the human spirit and a wretched condition of the human body.

In the immediate political context, these simplified distinctions surrounding the term allowed the renowned guerrilla general to compliment his British hosts on having the right sort of armed forces in place. At the same time, such distinctions enabled Garibaldi to sidestep the inconvenient fact that either side in a military escalation or conflict could be labeled militarist by virtue of the fact that both adhere to a moral position that justifies the prevalence of the army and requires a complex arrangement of cultural and economic institutions to support it. In this case, as in many subsequent uses of the term, the overriding distinction between unconscionable belligerence and the morally defensible practices of a military organization represents a highly subjective gesture of political propaganda rather than objective, unbiased description. As typically derogatory labels, "militarism" and "militarist" sustain Garibaldi's assumption of a presumably recognizable distinction between the pervasive dominance and the proper place of armed forces in a society.

When Joyce hurled the word "militarist" across the Channel, he unwittingly reenacted Garibaldi's linguistic exportation of it to another English audience forty years before. For his part, Garibaldi had continued a Continental diffusion of the term that began in the first decades of the nineteenth century. While discussion of militaristic state policies or personal behaviors had existed for centuries, *militarisme* first occurred as a neologism in 1816–18 in the memoirs of Madame de Chastenay, a French revolutionary aristocrat who invented the word as a criticism of Napoleon's regime. Some four decades later the anarchist Pierre Proudhon used the word in his 1861 treatise *La Guerre et La Paix*, which railed against mainstream versions of human history that privileged war as a positive, energizing agent of human social progress. The word entered both French and German encyclopedias by the 1870s, and in that same decade, with the rise to power of Otto von Bismarck, it acquired a particularly significant presence. In the discourse of civil resistance that developed in the wake of unification and Prussian domination, the term acquired still greater momentum as the cornerstone of ideological debate; as Nicholas Stargardt observes of the period, militarism is "not only about institutions and power. It is also about culture and ideas" (5).

Garibaldi thus served as the linguistic conduit to English for a term that signified a deep fissure in the political landscape of Europe.

Whether or not Joyce knew about Garibaldi's use of the term, he was definitely cognizant of his historical presence. In the fractured state of Italian politics, to some Garibaldi was a freedom fighter, to others the consummate militarist. Living in the irredentist hotbed of Trieste, Joyce witnessed the course of Italian nationalism in the generation following Garibaldi's physical-force approach to Italian unification. In *Ulysses*, Leopold Bloom's thoughts naturally align the Italian revolutionary with the bellicose politics of Irish nationalist James Stephens: "Sinn Fein. Back out you get the knife. Hidden hand. Stay in. The firing squad. Turnkey's daughter got him out of Richmond, off from Lusk. Putting up in the Buckingham Palace hotel under their very noses. Garibaldi" (*U* 8.458–61). Members of Stephens's Irish Republican Brotherhood are caught between the brutal self-policing of that rebel organization and the capital punishment of British authority. At the end of the account, Garibaldi's name rests, rather ambiguously, as a possible influence on such coercive measures of military discipline, or an unattainable ideal of military achievement, as Don Gifford suggests, owing to his "quasi-successful efforts" in a national resistance movement (170). Even if he reserved the militarist label for the armies of adversaries, Garibaldi's popularity in Victorian culture has come to be considered as revealing "a profound British conviction in the justice of a liberal-nationalist form of militarism" (Summers 107). Whether Joyce/Bloom regards him, or James Stephens, as glorious hero or bellicose villain remains fascinatingly unclear.[6] On two points, however, Garibaldi was accurate: militarism was a defining characteristic of modern life, and it was a useful term of propaganda.

For Joyce a generation later, "militarism" remained a harsh term of political disparagement for unchecked and uncontrollable martial values, even when deployed for reasons of self-promotion or literary survival. It was, after all, invoked as his means to defend *Dubliners* from unfair assault or even all-out destruction, and ultimately to define a way of reading the stories and perceiving a prevalent aspect of the society they represent. Nevertheless, in Joyce's usage, the term sustains its original bias, maintaining as it does Garibaldi's same contradictory blend of ambitious self-definition and declared objectivity. Such objectivity is apparent, for example, in Joyce's characterization of *Dubliners* in July 1905 as his "general indictment or survey of the island" (*L* 2:96).

Still, in launching the invective at an English target, Joyce went against the grain of contemporary Anglo-Saxon discourse that chauvinistically reserved the term for the nation regarded as Britain's greatest rival and threat. The notion of German militarism became something of a journalistic and foreign-policy paradigm in England—and by extension Ireland—during the invasion scares and troops escalation of the prewar decades, to the extent that one word rarely appeared without the other. The *OED* records this national stereotype just four years after Garibaldi brought the term to the British press: an article in *Macmillan's* magazine claimed "Prussian officialism is supreme and . . . Prussian militarism as well."

The idea of "Prussianism" was only further advanced by an event that occurred in central Germany during the autumn Joyce spent in Rome. In October 1906 Wilhelm Voigt, an unemployed shoemaker who had served more than two decades in prison for theft and forgery, obtained piecemeal an army officer's uniform from several Hamburg tailors. Using a few commands he remembered from military service, Voigt managed to convince nearly a dozen soldiers from a nearby barracks to follow him to the town of Köpenick, near Berlin. When they reached the city hall, they took the mayor and town treasurer hostage and demanded as ransom the entire contents of the treasury. The soldiers guarded all exits to the building, while the local police obeyed Voigt's orders to cut all phone contact with Berlin. Escaping in civilian clothes, Voigt made off with more than four thousand marks, along with a receipt for the money signed in the name of his former prison warden. He was arrested ten days later and sentenced to four years.[7]

Accounts of the so-called Captain of Köpenick spread quickly. Across Europe, the anecdote became emblematic of the problem of modern militarism, which many regarded as a direct consequence of Prussian hegemony in the new Germany. The story was a source of great amusement to some, including Kaiser Wilhelm, who pardoned Voigt two years into his sentence. Others in Germany found the event deeply disturbing, noting how the cult of the uniformed soldier had entirely overtaken German society since Bismarck. Socialist and antimilitarist Karl Liebknecht described the "coup of the cobbler Captain of Köpenick" as a "catechism of militarist methods" and "six-hour examination" of the army and bureaucracy, as well as German subjection to Prussia, which "those under examination passed so brilliantly that even their teachers' hair stood on end in the face of this quintessence of their pedagogy" (91). Further afield, in Britain, many took it as confirmation of the stereotype they had affixed to German culture in the decades since the ascendance of Prussian power, including the editors of the *Illustrated London News*, who wrote in the 27 October 1906 issue, "For years the Kaiser has been instilling into his people reverence for the omnipotence of militarism, of which the holiest symbol is the German uniform." Many in the English media and political establishment saw this blind deference to military authority as a Teutonic trait that could never come to pass in the liberal economies and individualistic social climates of Britain and America. No matter that, in the run-up to war, realignment and mobilization of many sectors of British society would demonstrate that the potential for a society to become wholly driven by and for martial purposes was hardly unique to Germany.

By the decade preceding the First World War, "militarism" was a well-established pejorative. Confusion surrounded not so much what the term meant but who used it and in what circumstances. The growing pacifist movement claimed militarism, devoid of any specific national identification, as its ideological opponent. For instance, the 1913 pamphlet *Militarism: An Appeal to the Man in the Street* argued against the great social threat of the time as it took the forms of compulsory student drilling, scouting and other uniformed youth movements, conscription, and universal military training for the working class. It warned of the "professional militarist" who looked to convince people that preparing for war was somehow preferable to preparing for peace (6). Published simultaneously in London and Leipzig, the pamphlet sought to transcend nationalist fervor with an appeal to common sense and common ground. Its anonymous author reveals at least some affinity with Anglo-American liberalism in a colorful reference to British businessman Norman Angell's landmark 1910 study of economy and military power, *The Great Illusion*: "Mr. Norman Angell has proved up to the hilt that where a modern State succeeds in 'bringing its enemy to its knees' it is just cutting its own throat" (7).

Yet, with the exception of far-left publications, militarism remained a label most Britons reserved for the Kaiser. Conservatives and ardent nationalists frequently invoked the term in reference to the growing threat of Germany, ironically echoing the vocabulary of that country's very own tradition of civil dissent. These same voices were, like Garibaldi during his English visit, quick and careful to distinguish militarism from their own agendas, which in the Darwinian nomenclature of the period were often styled "social fitness" or "national efficiency." Typical in that vein was Arnold White's 1901 book *Efficiency and Empire*, which highlighted the looming threat of overseas powers against British imperial interests as reasons for making military preparedness the nation's top priority. With seemingly no awareness of the irony, White and others urged Britain to fashion itself as a greater military power in order to combat the scourge of German militarism.

The paradox reflected a global Great Powers dynamic guided by questions of military superiority and escalating arms races. Paul Kennedy describes the tenor of militaristic rivalry that underlay a superficially pacific period in international relations:

> Many clung to the liberal, laissez-faire ideals of peaceful cooperation. Nonetheless there existed in governing elites, military circles, and imperialist organizations a prevailing view of the world order which stressed struggle, change, competition, the use of force, and the organization of national resources to enhance state power. (196)

It was a drama whose principal players were Germany and Britain, with France and Austria-Hungary not far behind, all clutching to diminished imperial territories; in the East, Russia and Japan each stood to gain or lose in their own escalating regional tension. Expanded literacy, telegraphic and telephonic communications, and a growing mass media enabled millions to follow such developments on a daily basis for the first time. Thus in *Ulysses* the Dublin curate Larry O'Rourke can casually hypothesize, "Do you know what? The Russians, they'd only be an eight o'clock breakfast for the Japanese" (4.116–17).

There was a general sense as well, even in nonmilitary circles, that war was no longer confined to the battlefield. As never before, the military struggle played out on the domestic front in the social, economic, and cultural lives of citizens. Expansion of armies and navies became a universal project, for the first time involving the majority of citizens in many countries. Across Europe, large and small governments devised policies to foster and sustain the economics of state militarism. In the race to be among the major powers—or establish protection from them—manufacturing output intensified through an unprecedented partnering of state leadership and military entrepreneurs. Such "changes in the military-industrial productive base" were among the most important factors in reshaping the world order of the late nineteenth and early twentieth centuries (Kennedy 196). From London to Berlin, from Rome to Moscow, factories ramped up production of armaments, munitions, and other wartime supplies. An unprecedented connection between military and industry would determine the balance of power. Economic output and industrial knowledge came to be regarded as weapons themselves by many, including the British imperialist Leopold Amery, who wrote in 1904, "The successful powers will be those who have the greatest industrial base. Those people who have the industrial power and the power of invention and science will be able to defeat all others" (441). Military entrepreneurs established long-term contracts with government, drawing more civilians into an economic orbit around the expanding armed forces.

Changes to the industrial sector were paralleled by a reconfiguration of social and cultural life. Educational practices were altered to serve the military ends of the state. Schools and universities added drill and martial studies with the aim of turning out the cadet and officer corps. Art and music reflected the changes, sometimes by way of endorsement, other times in protest. Even leisure activities tended toward the military and paramilitary, as uniformed youth movements and adult militia organizations steadily gained in number and popularity. Their activities featured volunteer marching, drilling, and physical culture programs that became a common sight in cities and towns across Europe during the decades prior to the First World War.

Militarism was a uniquely modern and global transformation. To be sure, societies had focused on equipping themselves for war long before the modern era of empires, nation-states, and world wars. In some cases, as in ancient Sparta, warfare had even been the mobilizing center of the state. Yet armed force, whether as warrior class, citizen militia, or state army, had by and large not been the prime mover of social and political policies. A defining element of modern European life was the distinct possibility that martial ideology could come to completely dictate political agendas and, consequently, obscure cultural identity and social purpose. Therefore, intensive political and philosophical debate emerged around the term and in response to the rapid and, for many, the potentially disastrous changes it described. Volker Berghahn detects this watershed moment of political awareness in the West: "We may have had militaristic regimes in the ancient world or in the Middle Ages; but it was not until the seventeenth century that people began to show a political or academic interest in the position of the military in the emergent nations of the modern period" (7–8). Writers from England to Germany had long addressed the potential dangers standing armies posed to civil institutions.[8] But by the turn of the twentieth century, given the rapid, parallel expansion of the military and industry, militarism had emerged as a pervasive social system and central political problem for the industrialized nations of Europe.

Like the term itself, extended definitions and ideas of modern militarism originated in the political climate of central Europe. Berghahn summarizes two major theoretical strands related to the topic, distinguishing between "those analysts who saw it in a political and constitutional framework and those who examined it as a socio-economic problem," recognizing how, despite their different methodologies and political contexts, the two "approaches shared a common vision of a progressive movement towards an age in which armies would at least be closely controlled, if not abolished altogether" (10). By the turn of the twentieth century, British capitalists and German socialists alike sought to explain the paradox of military primacy in a supposedly free society with an unregulated marketplace. Marx and Engels had not made the effect of military organization on social, economic, or political life a major topic in their writings, but a number of theorists who added to their project had come to regard militarism in Prussian-dominated Germany as a direct outgrowth of laissez-faire liberalism. To varying degrees, Rosa Luxemburg and Karl Liebknecht defined militarism as an integral cause and inevitable consequence of capitalism.

Luxemburg first approached the issue as an internal party dialogue with Max Schippel in the columns of the *Leipziger Volkszeitung* in 1899. Schippel had argued against the arming of individuals and for maintaining standing armies on the basis that militarism provided a "necessary 'release' of economic pressure." In "The Militia and Militarism," Luxemburg offers her extended counterargument, reminding readers that Schippel's view confined itself to the status quo of industrial capitalism, failing to imagine the reconfigurations of wealth and class and, by extension, the military reorganization of society that socialism could bring. She proceeds to equate the militarist phenomenon with capitalist class struggle and the economic domination of the bourgeoisie:

> Militarism, which to society as a whole represents a completely absurd economic waste of enormous productive forces, and which for

the working class means a lowering of its standard of living with the objective of enslaving it socially, is for the capitalist class economically the most alluring, irreplaceable kind of investment and politically and socially the best support for their class rule. (chap. 2)

Emphasizing the military as the most rapid and profitable area of accumulating capital, Luxemburg noted how militarism in turn solidified social and political support for the capitalist elite. To be sure, Luxemburg was not an antimilitarist or pacifist calling for disarmament. She proposed the foundation of regional citizens' militias as an affordable alternative to maintaining a national standing army that ultimately served the interests of the few.

In 1907 in *Militarism and Anti-Militarism*, Karl Liebknecht offered a more broad-based treatment of the phenomenon, examining many of the subsets of cultural and civic life that had been affected by military predominance. While not strictly relegating militarism, as Luxemburg does, to the historical contexts of capitalism, he defines its capitalistic version as existing in two primary forms: "militarism for abroad," an international armed competition for resources and territory to feed the growth of capitalism, and "militarism at home," a domestic struggle against the potential for a liberating class consciousness that would threaten to undermine the system (22–57).

While Liebknecht broadly outlines these capitalist militarisms with examples drawn from Europe, Russia, and the United States, the majority of his analysis concerns itself with the paradigm of his own Prusso-German society, arguing generally that "Militarism has in fact already become the central sun in one dominant field" (42). Around that sun orbited such satellites as education, religion, police administration, and civil bureaucracy. He traces the military mindset outward from the German reserve units to the rest of society, noting how it is reinforced by economic policies and social privileges that give systematic advantages to the military caste. At the start of the chain, he likens the pedagogy of army training to the total indoctrination of religion and monastic life (59–78). He was arguably the first theorist to assert the strong link emerging between industry and the military, noting how capitalist magnates of munitions and supplies had attained the power to keep employees, municipalities, and the nation overall, dutiful and obedient to a militarized economy that provided work, profit, and purpose (85–90).[9]

Liebknecht introduced his work as a direct counter and corrective to Gustav Tuch's *Der Erweiterte Deutsche Militärstaat in Seiner Sozialen Bedeutung* (1886; The Extended German Military State in Its Social Significance), a seminal text of national efficiency that advocated a society whose educational, economic, and administrative activity centered on the army. Liebknecht regarded this militaristic manifesto as the academic equivalent of Wilhelm Voigt's infamous deception: "What the Captain of Köpenick did for militarism in the field of practice by his swindles was done by the invaluable Gustav Tuch at the end of the eighties in the field of honest theory" (41). Echoing Luxemburg, he viewed militarism as a strong symptom of liberal capitalism, though not exclusive to it. In teleological Marxist fashion, Liebknecht acknowledges militarism as a revolutionary obstacle and catalyst for Social Democracy, "whose prospects are the better the more militarism brings things to a head" (41). Beyond socialist circles, such class-based definitions of militarism were regarded as divisive and potentially dangerous. Pacifists, for example, saw the general socialist goal of replacing state armies with citizens' militias as no real alternative to widespread militarization: rather than diffusing military authority, such plans would only accelerate the march to global armed conflict.

In contrast to this Continental post-Marxist perspective, a liberal, primarily Anglo-Saxon discourse attributed militarism not to the material economics of class struggle but to the long-term process of human biological development.[10] Such a view, while also looking to the end of militarism, deemed it a primitive, outmoded trait, an evolutionary throwback still prevalent among certain nations and races but in the process of disappearance. Herbert Spencer's landmark treatise *Principles of Sociology* includes a chapter with an extended definition of the "militant type of society," which Spencer saw as characterized by a "process of regimentation which, primarily taking place in the army, secondarily affects the whole community" (2:573). Spencer describes a society in which all sectors of economic production and social organization are single-mindedly geared toward fortification or mobilization, so that even "the civilian is in a condition as much like that of the soldier as difference of occupation permits" (574). Following in the wake of Spencer, social Darwinists and adherents to eugenics ascribed martial qualities along racial lines. Such research raised questions of scientific validity as well as basic morality, but army authorities and imperial policymakers nevertheless gave it strong consideration in devising strategies of territorial conquest.[11]

While Spencer contrasted individual liberty with the enforced cooperation of militant society, by the following decade Angell's *Great Illusion* emphasized how the increasingly interdependent wealth of the global economy now ensured that military mobilization and territorial conquest would work to undermine rather than extend a country's political and financial power.[12] The book's lengthy subtitle, *A Study of the Relation of Military Power in Nations to Their Economic and Social Advantage*, underscored the coterminous connection between material affluence and martial puissance. Unlike the German socialists, Angell placed total faith in industrialism to overcome inequalities and present the solution to the crisis of global militarism through expanded, cooperative prosperity in a free market, a view that seems, in hindsight, "a touchingly idealistic and naïve view of the inherently peaceful nature of capitalist industrialism" (Berghahn 21). Far from being the causes of militarism, according to Angell, industrial development and free trade could be its best remedies.

For readers who interpreted class competition and expanded production as solutions rather than symptoms of the growing war machine, Angell's thesis was a welcome apology for unfettered enterprise as a means to world peace. Joyce's friend, the peace activist Francis Sheehy Skeffington, cites *The Great Illusion* as justification for the pacifist position in a free-market world: "One of the favourite arguments of 'Imperialists' and 'Militarists,' not so long ago, was, that by war territory could be 'won' and new 'wealth' gained. The economic theories of Norman Angell shattered this illusion, and it is now freely confessed that war is an economic evil" ("Psychology" 42). Skeffington shared the faith that as people awakened to the mutual benefits of individualism and free-market economies they would come to recognize the universal futility of arms escalation and total war.

Many British and French pacifists followed this liberal-capitalist line of reasoning. In liberal circles of Britain, Continental Europe, and prerevolutionary Russia, it became grounds for the international peace crusade of W. T. Stead and Tsar Nicholas, a movement referenced in *Stephen Hero* with Skeffington's fictional representation as McCann collecting signatures for the Tsar's Rescript of universal peace. For Stephen, and likely for Joyce, such a program was well intentioned but ill equipped for the magnitude of the problem, and even posed a potential source of distraction or confusion.

When McCann asks why Stephen will not sign, Stephen's excuse does not sound idealistic or moral but rather political and pragmatic: "If we must have a Jesus, answered Stephen, let us have a legitimate Jesus" (*SH* 114). If Joyce did not supply his signature to Skeffington's page or profess a belief in the economic, ethical, or religious underpinnings of the peace movement, the scholarly interests evidenced during his first years after university and out of Ireland made him less of an outlier than the scene suggests.

To Joyce in Trieste, the most immediate and influential theory of militarism came from the writing of Guglielmo Ferrero. By the time Joyce invoked him as a source of social and historical context for *Dubliners* and moral edification for its obstructionist printer, Ferrero had written *L'Europa giovane* (1897), *Il Militarismo* (1898), and the five-volume *Grandezza e decadenza di Roma* (1902–6). A copy of *L'Europa giovane* was among the books in Joyce's library in Trieste, but in 1906 *Il Militarismo* was the only one of Ferrero's books available in English translation. This publication timeline lends credence to Susan Humphreys's assertion (240) that it was the book Joyce had in mind when referencing the Italian historian. The work was translated as *Militarism* in 1899 and subtitled "A Contribution to the Peace Crusade," rendering its political intention even more transparent; as Ferrero noted in the preface, he had written the book "to contribute my quota to the grand work of pacifying civilized nations, entered upon by so many enlightened spirits" (i).

Militarism specifically discusses the function of war and martial culture in the evolution of Western civilization. While he claimed to write from a provincial Italian background, compared with the German socialist and English capitalist outlooks, Ferrero's treatment of the topic was both historically expansive and globally aware, which must have been part of its appeal for Joyce. Ferrero argues that military service and warfare, formerly justifiable means of cultural expression and social advancement, have been rendered outmoded and counterproductive, primarily by "the decay of all the triumphs which war, in its mysterious caprices, conferred on men and people" in previous periods (317). To support this thesis, the book marshals an array of economic details and historical case studies, with examples ranging from antiquity to modernity.

While Ferrero has been variously labeled socialist, liberal, and Italian irredentist, his extended definition of militarism is somewhat eclectic in its fusion of capitalist and post-Marxist components. Discussions of warfare in ancient civilizations precede treatments of the military-oriented societies of late-nineteenth-century Europe, suggesting the general persistence of the sort of primitive mindset described by Herbert Spencer. At the same time, in successive chapters on contemporary France, Italy, England, and Germany, Ferrero, not unlike Liebknecht or Luxemburg, posits militarism as not an inherent national or ethnic trait but a pan-European condition that can also be linked to localized class structures and economic interests. At times *Militarism* follows a great-men model of history, as in extended comparisons of the impact of such militant personalities as Napoleon and Attila. More often, though, the study concentrates on institutional structures and governmental policies as these play out across various societies.

In addition, Ferrero supports many of his claims with details of cultural conditions and military expenditures for every country studied, something that would have undoubtedly appealed to Joyce's love for minutiae. James seems surely under Ferrero's spell when, writing to Stanislaus from Rome in the fall of 1906, he includes the following statement not far removed from remarks concerning the Joyces' own household budget: "Japan, the first naval power in the world, I presume, in point of efficiency, spends three million pounds per annum on her fleet. Italy spends more than twice as much" (*L* 2:188).

Ferrero makes similar comments on the relative economic efficiency of the major powers discussed in *Militarism*. His chapter "Militarism in England and Germany" deliberately brings together the two rivals who each regarded the other at the time as overtly militaristic and aggressive societies. The juxtaposition alone goes against the grain of the contemporary jingoism and sensationalist journalism that had already set England and Germany on a collision course toward war. Ferrero begins by addressing the widespread misperception among English readers of Prusso-Germany as the most bellicose nation in Europe. Reminding readers that for the previous hundred years the only wars Germany waged were against the territorial incursion of Napoleon, Ferrero asks how such a nation could be considered to possess any "great passion for military glory" (276).

Still, Ferrero does note how Germany has become a military society in its civil organization, an elite class of army officials having secured positions at many levels of civil administration. He regards this state of affairs as the vestige of Prussian-led unification some three decades earlier: "In fact, the armor with which Bismarck invested her weighs heavily on the shoulders of

Germany, who cannot rid herself of it as she would desire, because modern militarism is an armor so curiously constructed that a people can easily don it, but once on, it is with difficulty cast off" (277). At the same time, he asserts the unlikelihood this military mindset will direct the entire course of society, owing to high degrees of public and journalistic pressure which make funding for military expansion or adventurism more difficult.

Looking at England, Ferrero finds a comparatively diminished version of militarism that, because of its widespread and deeper socioeconomic integration, might actually present a greater threat. He seems at once troubled and fascinated by the paradox that England has the smallest yet most expensive army in Europe. More than troop numbers and budgetary expenditures, however, Ferrero concentrates on the social assimilation of the army as representing a potentially greater problem: "And yet, of all European countries, England is the one where militarism is reduced to a minimum, because the military class does not possess a code of morality of its own, nor any special laws or manner of life" (280–81). This reference to a "code of morality" for English soldiers as indistinguishable from that of general society is likely what Joyce had in mind when he recommended that Richards's printer read "the chapters wherein Ferrero examines the moral code of the soldier" (*L* 2:133). It suggests the confluence of the soldier and civilian mindsets in England and anticipates the noticeable interdependence of martial and social values that recurs throughout Joyce's fictional portrayal of English-occupied Ireland.

In Ferrero's view, soldiers' lack of an independent moral sense suggests how English militarism, if comparatively minimal, is such only by virtue of the fact that soldiering has been normalized like all other occupations. Its reduced profile is both cause and consequence of the British army's being more residentially and socially integrated than those of other countries: "English barracks have lost much of that odious character, a cut between a monastery and a prison. They more and more resemble the traditional cottage, under whose roof English families live and work in all parts of the globe. It consists of small pavilions, surrounded by little gardens, and cheered by the green of vegetation, and by all manner of games, such as cricket, football, and lawn-tennis" (282). Ferrero's enumeration of the disparate areas of human experience subject to militarization—domestic life, sport and leisure activities, architectural and urban space—resounds across Joyce's work, as my subsequent chapters will discuss.

From his sequence of national-historical case studies, Ferrero concludes that "the duty of every well-meaning man to-day is to diffuse knowledge of the fact that war no longer serves the purpose it once served in the struggle for civilization" (316). In a statement whose metaphorical phrasing seems to anticipate some of Joyce's own figurative language, Ferrero reiterates his primary point: "It is our duty to free the eyes of the multitude from this veil of error which blinds them, by proclaiming the truth that war in Europe is to-day nothing but the ghost of dead injustices, which, like the bogies of fiction, return from time to time, but only to alarm" (317). As if answering this call to action and liberation, Joyce employed fiction to lift the same veil of error from Irish eyes and reveal the pervasive militarism of Dublin life. To that end, *Militarism* provided him not just a general outlook but a wholesale model for systematic analysis of the phenomenon in its diverse social and cultural manifestations.

Ferrero was clearly an intellectual presence as Joyce continued to write and seek publication during those foundational years in Trieste. As the *Dubliners* debacle lingered on through the summer of 1906, at which time Joyce took his family to Rome to pursue more lucrative employment, his correspondence mentions Ferrero with regularity and admiration for his antimilitarist leanings. A postcard to Stanislaus from Rome dated 19 August 1906 relates how these politics even surfaced one day at Joyce's job as a translator for the German bank of Nast-Kolb and Schumacher:

> I absorbed the attention of the three clerks in my office a few days ago by a socialistic outburst. One of them is German and he was ridiculing Lombrosianism and antimilitarism. He said when children cried they "should be caned," favored corporal punishment in schools, conscription, religion &c. I think he was surprised not to find an ally in an Inglese. (*L* 2:151).

Joyce seems to delight in undermining the German's assumption that an Anglophone would share his attitude on the subject, a dichotomy that recalls the penultimate chapter of *Militarism*. Moreover, the term "Lombrosianism" references Ferrero's colleague, coauthor, and father-in-law, Cesare Lombroso, who similarly espoused the antimilitarist agenda. Joyce notes Lombroso's direct relation to Ferrero in a letter on 13 November to Stanislaus and also requests, "If there is anything interesting (Ferrero etc) in the *Piccolo della Sera*, you might send it" (*L* 2:190).

So taken was he with Ferrero's work, Joyce also gave some extended expression of his fascination for the man himself.

> I will send you a picture postcard of Guglielmo Ferrero and you will admit that there is some hope for me. You would think he was a terrified Y.M.C.A. man with an inaudible voice. He wears spectacles, is delicate-looking and altogether, is the type you would expect to find in some quiet nook in the Coffee-Palace nibbling a bun hastily and apologetically between the hours of half-past twelve and one. (L 2:159)

Joyce's playful description hints at a deeper intellectual respect and a hope of emulating Ferrero in categories beyond physical meekness. There is no evidence that Joyce ever met Ferrero, but it was in Trieste that their paths drew nearest one another. Joyce was invited to write about Ireland for *Il Piccolo della Sera*, the Trieste-based irredentist newspaper to which Ferrero was also a contributor. In the first of his lectures the following April at the Università Populare, Joyce referred to Ferrero's new multivolume study of ancient Rome as a corrective to German versions of Roman history, tapping into the Italian nationalistic fervor of his Triestine audience (*OCPW* 109).

Part of what made Ferrero resonate with Joyce was likely the fact that he experienced Ferrero's work in immediate geographic proximity to the historical forces that it described. The first two cities in which Joyce and Nora lived after Dublin showed noticeable signs of militarization, starting with Pola, whose strategic position on the Adriatic Sea made it headquarters for the Austro-Hungarian navy. During Joyce's months there in the fall of 1904, most of his Berlitz students were naval officers. He noticed the constant presence of battleships in the harbor and came to regard the bleak port as "a naval Siberia" (L 2:69). Along with the display of armed force came constant reminders of violent political upheaval in the contested Adriatic region. In this regard, it bore a strong resemblance to the Ireland he and Nora had left behind. Joyce witnessed the dedication of a monument to the empress Elizabeth, assassinated six years earlier. Around the same time, anti-Italian riots erupted in response to similar ones in Innsbruck over the question of allowing law school classes to be taught in Italian.

With his transfer to Trieste, Joyce continued to experience life under imperial occupation, with the added element of a strong national independence movement. The city was home to a considerable navy base and cadet academy, and was a hub of naval shipbuilding. The shipyards were especially busy during Joyce's decade in the city, as the Austro-Hungarian fleet increased more than fourfold in the first decades of the twentieth century. This expansion mirrored a sizeable increase in sailor and troop numbers, which rose from 246,000 men in 1880 to 444,000 in 1914.[13] It would have been difficult not to notice the increased activity around the port and its direct effect on the social and economic life of the city during Joyce's time there.

Alongside the burgeoning presence of Austrian armed forces, Trieste was a hotbed of the Italian independence movement. As John McCourt writes, "On a political front, the imperial Austrian city with its indefatigable Italian irredentist spirit challenged and sharpened Joyce's ideas about socialism and nationalism" (4). The dichotomy duplicated certain aspects of the political culture Joyce had known in Ireland, providing a comparative model as he continued to write of Ireland. As in Dublin, differences in cultural identity and aspirations for political autonomy were complicated by a foreign troop presence. And like Irish nationalism, Italian irredentism was divided over questions of whether to pursue a socialist or a republican revolution, and whether to do so by constitutional methods or physical force. Its most militant proponents, including Giuseppe Garibaldi, advocated armed insurgency to achieve the unification of all Italian-speaking regions.

Joyce would become a direct witness to the militarized dimensions of Italian politics during his seven-month stay in Rome. His initial impressions of the Eternal City when he arrived in the summer of 1906 were dominated by the "funerary reality" of the Colosseum and other ruins, which triggered in Joyce vivid nightmares of dead bodies and political assassinations (Ellmann 233). These imaginative figments of ancient carnage were displaced by actual and modern brutality when anarchists detonated a series of bombs during the socialist congress in November. Joyce's job at the bank, which was located near the Piazza Colonna, put him in close proximity to the first of the explosions. It interrupted the tedious correspondence and translation work, though probably not in a way he might have wished. Not surprisingly, the first bomb blast was impetus for a postcard to his brother back in Trieste:

> Dear Stannie Tonight at 6:30 while I was sitting at my desk in the bank I heard a loud explosion and felt the house shake. A few minutes after I heard people running under the windows "Bomba! Bomba!" A bomb

had exploded at the Caffe Aragno which is at the corner of our palace. Have not yet seen the papers. The street is full of people and strewn with broken cups. Item. I am sick in my *cor cordium*. Nice country! (*L* 2:194)

When he did see the papers, Joyce would have learned the details of the bombing and its aftermath. Its target was Rome's central thoroughfare, the Via del Corso, during one of its busiest hours of the day. The *New York Times* reported: "At the time of the explosion the café was filled and the Corso was crowded with afternoon promenaders. A double line of carriages stretched in front of the place" ("Bomb Outrage"). Amazingly, all but one man escaped serious injury, but the chaotic wreckage of the café, marked by overturned furniture and shattered plate-glass windows, warned that the militarization of Italian politics could have deadly results.

Joyce's letter of 20 November to Stanislaus mentions two subsequent bombings that week, one in St. Peter's and the other in the Piazza di Spagna. By this time he seems less alarmed by the violence, or at least makes an effort to shrug it off with sardonic wit: "I hardly think these can be the work of anarchists. They are too clumsily made and do no damage" (*L* 2:196). Despite its jocularity, the letter notes a wider concern in the city about the potential effects a "serious explosion" could have during an upcoming visit by the king of Greece (*L* 2:196). In the Rome bombings, Joyce witnessed some of the first instances of political violence against nonmilitary targets, at the start of a century that would see an increased blurring of the line between soldier and civilian.

Militarism in Ireland

Through these Continental ideas and experiences, Joyce peered back at an Ireland that during and since his upbringing had undergone a militarization in its own right. In concert with the ideological forces of colonialism, religion, and nationalism, militarism had a pervasive and dogmatic influence on Irish life, its interrelation with these other ideologies accounting for much of its extensive reach. Despite—or perhaps because of—the Anglo-Irish divide, there emerged in Ireland during the first two decades of the twentieth century what David Fitzpatrick calls a "common rhetoric of militarism that transcended political divisions in Ireland" (379). It was at once an extension of the military escalation occurring both in Britain and on the Continent and a unique outgrowth of local circumstances. Militarism, in theory and practice, dominated the hierarchy of the British colonial administration and armed forces; it also suffused the nationalist and unionist organizations that sponsored cultural activities as diverse as language, music, and sports.

To some extent, militarism in late Victorian and Edwardian Ireland echoed a brand of British patriotism that had taken root during the years prior to the Great War, what Anne Summers defines as "Liberal, popular and independent forms of militarism [that] flourished alongside and indeed in opposition to militarism in its official forms" (105). These independent versions of militarism had begun thriving in the mid-nineteenth century amid public skepticism and distrust in the capacity of the Regular Army to protect the country from overseas threats. During the French and German invasion scares, many citizens took it upon themselves to join defense associations and receive military training. These included the Navy League, founded in 1895, which advocated for greater investment in the British fleet, and the National Service League, formed in 1901 to advance the cause of peacetime conscription. By the start of the Great War, the two organizations had a combined membership of 300,000.

The militaristic leagues comprised a financial and administrative complement to the Volunteer Forces, a nationwide system of local militias that had been a centerpiece of social life and recreation in many parts of the country for much of the previous half century. In the same open letter to the English public that identified militarism as the modern malady of European armies, Garibaldi commended the "rifle volunteers" as an ideal form of national defense, calling them "England's pride and my dream [for Italy]" ("To the People"). So-called "Saturday soldiers" participated in marksmanship competitions and military reviews that made Volunteering "the spectator sport of mid-Victorian Britain" (Cunningham 68). In Ireland, private and localized soldiering had taken the form of county militias and yeomanry dating back to the eighteenth century. These armed corps were less concerned with international invasion than with local security threats against the big houses of the Ascendancy class. Like the British Volunteer Forces, they conducted social events and recreational displays, including rifle-shooting competitions, drilling, and public parades. These occasions could be significant markers of class privilege and identity, as in Gabriel Conroy's account in "The Dead" of his grandfather Patrick Morkan's aspiration to "drive out with the quality to a military review in the Park" (*D* 208). Mr. Morkan's arc of social ascendance is paralyzed by the circular detour of the mill horse Johnny around the mounted statue of William of Orange, a revelation of the true political order behind the social posturing.

Along with such independent and vicarious activities, British militarism of course made itself felt directly in Ireland through authorized state policies that included enlarged troop numbers, expanded garrison facilities, and their associated ripple effects through economic and social life. While a large standing army had long been considered anathema to British political tenets, colonial authorities deemed it appropriate and necessary for Ireland. The Irish garrison was an ideal solution to multiple problems. It provided additional forces for policing Britain's closest colony and served as a staging ground for overseas expeditions. The garrison had been a regular feature of Irish life through much of the eighteenth and nineteenth centuries, but its numbers grew larger by the turn of the twentieth. The combined total of army, navy, and marines together with local militia and yeomanry troops was well over 25,000 by 1901, reflecting the British sense of the island as "theatre of operations as well as a source of recruitment" (Fitzpatrick 381). The numbers continued to increase during the Boer War and ultimately the buildup to fighting in Europe, amounting to a tangible change in places like Dublin, where the presence was strongest. In the first of three 1907 lectures at Trieste's Università Populare, Joyce points to this British militarism in Ireland when he argues that Queen Victoria's three-week visit to Ireland in April 1900 was

> certainly politically motivated. The truth is that she did not come but was, rather, sent by her advisers. At that time the English disasters in South Africa in the Boer War had made England the laughing-stock of the European press, and it was to take the genius of two commanders, Lord Roberts and Lord Kitchener (both of them Irish, born in Ireland) to restore the endangered prestige... In fact, the queen came to win the easy sympathy of the country and to increase the lists of recruiting-sergeants. (*OCPW* 117)

Noting an army presence that was as much about military public image and propaganda as security, Joyce refers rather contemptuously to "little English soldiers lining the route" presumably to guard their monarch from Irish aggression that might take the form of either "bombs or cabbages" (*OCPW*

117). By September 1914, his friend Francis Sheehy Skeffington would regard the growing garrison with somewhat less humor and more trepidation: "Dublin is full of soldiers,—evidently a much larger garrison than usual is to be kept here during the war. They are mostly raw recruits in training, but they may serve to overawe" (letter to *Critical Chronicle*). Whether scorned or feared, soldiers shaped many facets of Dublin life in the period, linked as they were to the socioeconomic condition of virtually every citizen in the capital. For better or worse, army officers and soldiers purchased the services of everyone from landlords to tailors to prostitutes. Along with bringing much-needed currency to the legitimate and illicit economies, the soldiers also brought verbal and physical abuse to the local civilian population. In *Ulysses*'s "Circe" episode, Privates Compton and Carr provide a little of each to the denizens of Bella Cohen's.

Militarism in Ireland was not limited to this official British variety. Unionists and nationalists alike founded organizations that promoted militaristic values and activities. These seeds of the modern paramilitary movement brought the conflict home to the masses, providing a chance for everyday citizens to become weekend warriors. In the North, the British Volunteering movement acquired a unionist following that approached 100,000. This Ulster Volunteer Force (UVF) was centralized in 1911 under the leadership of Edward Carson. Making no pretenses about the group's purpose, Carson brought in former British Army officers to train the growing membership. Much of this was more talk than action, due to a shortage of weapons and Carson's own policy "advising against pushing the make-believe aggression of the UVF into the realm of reality" (Jackson 237). The April 1914 Larne gunrunning put rifles in the hands of at least half of the members, though the group would remain more of a symbolic showpiece and social outlet than an actual fighting regiment.

During the same period, the Irish republican movement developed its own militaristic tendencies. Or, more accurately, it revived a martial element that had lain dormant for several decades. Amid growing disillusionment with the prospects for Home Rule, many nationalists advocated for a return to physical-force methods. The clandestine Fenianism of the preceding generation, led by such living legends as John O'Leary and Thomas Clarke, was reconfigured by the turn of the century in the secret, cell-based society of the Irish Republican Brotherhood. The IRB leadership, in turn, played a direct role in formation of the overt militia force known as the

Irish Volunteers. Led by Padraig Pearse, the master of St. Enda's Irish school, the organization began regular drilling in the countryside and public parading in the city. A successful gunrunning at Howth on 26 July 1914 had already shown they were more than just paraders, even if the Italian and German rifles they purchased were several decades old and tended to overheat on the firing range. By 1913 the Irish Volunteers were a full-fledged militia prepared for confrontations with northern paramilitaries and British regulars alike.

The Volunteers' socialist counterpart and ultimate partner in the Easter Rising, the Irish Citizen Army, emerged in the same decade out of a security force developed during the Great Lockout of 1913. As violence erupted between police and protestors during public street rallies, it became customary for union leaders such as Jim Larkin and James Connolly to move about the city under armed guard, a practice that soon evolved into the Citizen Army.

One view considers militarism an exaggerated or inaccurate descriptor of the republican politics that culminated in the fighting of Easter 1916. Charles Townshend refers instead to the "militarization of politics" in Ireland during the period: "Militarism is a strong word. As it was used in Europe at this time, notably by the critics of the Prussian-German monarchy, it meant the saturation of the entire political and social fabric by military values" (30). Yet the military ethos that extended to so many spheres of cultural-nationalist endeavor—including such disparate areas as education, athletics, art, music, and family life—strongly suggests that militarization was not confined to the political leadership. Like their unionist counterparts, Irish nationalists gradually subordinated their nation-building interests within a military mindset.

The opposing sides in the Anglo-Irish struggle were more alike than either would choose to admit. For political expediency, both vehemently denied their own militarist tendencies while pointing to the excessive belligerence of their opposition. Nevertheless, at both the unionist and republican ends of the political spectrum, the methods were remarkably similar. The strength of both the unionist and the nationalist following lay in an ability to bring military action and martial values into the otherwise normal lives of their membership. As Alvin Jackson observes, on both sides one key to mass recruitment and retention came from tapping into a deep-seated need for individual heroism in the service of the national cause:

> The UVF, like Fenianism, attracted immense popular support because it was simultaneously a military threat and a means of recreation. Both bodies provided bored, patriotic clerks and shop assistants and salesmen with a purposeful hobby; both bodies helped to cement family ties, and social and commercial connections. (109)

Beyond the ranks of comfortably middle-class adult males, this need for everyday people to feel themselves military adventurers and possible heroes seemed to resonate as well with some of the more marginalized segments of the population.

Women and adolescents were brought into the mix through like-minded auxiliary organizations. The female paramilitary group Cumann na Bann (Irishwomen's Council), founded in 1914, engaged in its own drilling and rifle exercises. By the time of the Easter Rising, its members did much more than carry tea and sandwiches or dress wounds of injured Volunteers, as many assumed. The refrain of their official anthem makes overt allusion to the group's strategic purpose and self-definition as sisters-in-arms to the Volunteers: "And they'll march with their brothers to freedom, the Soldiers of Cumann na Bann." Its first president, Countess Markeviecz, lived up to the image: she usually appeared in public in full khakis and carrying a pistol. The countess was among a number of Cumann na Bann members who saw action in the Rising; she reportedly shot a British soldier at close range in St. Stephen's Green.

Markeviecz, along with Bulmer Hobson, also played a major role in bringing adolescent boys into the militarized wing of the nationalist movement. In Britain, William Alexander Smith's Boys' Brigade and Robert Baden-Powell's Boy Scout movements were already established, the latter inspired by the actions of the young cadet corps Baden-Powell had witnessed firsthand during the Boer War at the siege of Mafeking. As counterpart, in 1909 Hobson and Markeviecz cofounded the Irish scouting organization, Na Fianna Éireann, to teach martial skills and values and to serve as a supporting band for the Volunteers in the coming conflict. The name, which translates as Warriors of Ireland, evoked the legendary Fianna band of Fionn Mac Cumhaill (Finn MacCool). An oath of declaration voiced the avowedly military purpose and identity of the organization: "I promise to work for the independence of Ireland, never to join England's forces, and to obey my superior officers." Scouts appeared in full uniform and functioned as street guards, messengers, and lookouts. By age sixteen they joined the recruitment pool for the Volunteers. Within the first decade a significant number of Fianna members graduated to the Volunteer ranks. Seamus Pounch, a lead scout from Na Fianna Éireann's inception through Easter 1916, recalled in his post-Rising witness testimony how the principal activities of the organization seem to have been as much about outward show as inward development:

> Many public displays of camping and field drill were served up, usually at big open air fetes, and rifle drill and bayonet exercises were performed with dummy rifles and sword drill with single sticks. Signalling and first aid displays were included. In all these events the Fianna displayed a keen knowledge and the public viewed Ireland's young soldiers in training for the eventful day when their knowledge and training would be put to the vital test of battle. (Pounch 2–3)

Pounch's rhetorical backward glance to an "eventful" future was accurate, as drilling and exercises eventually did lead to Fianna members taking part in volatile and potentially dangerous events like the Howth gunrunning or the Glasnevin funeral of repatriated Fenian leader Jeremiah O'Donovan Rossa. In the Easter Rising, Pounch and other scouts served right alongside the Volunteers, standing lookout and running messages throughout the city, some even seeing combat at several of the major garrisons, including the Jacob's biscuit factory and the General Post Office.

While Joyce was by no means averse to formation of an independent Ireland, he found these new directions of the nationalist cause to be troubling. His chief concern was that the nationalist movement had arrived at a perspective that was dangerously narrow-minded, oblivious to the levels of social and political reform the country truly needed to liberate itself. As Manganiello asserts, "The nationalists limited themselves to combating only one form of tyranny—that of the foreign conqueror. Joyce saw instead 'tyrannies of all kinds' holding Ireland captive, and it was precisely these tyrannies that he determined to oppose in his works" (66). Militarism, for its immense depth and broad reach, was an especially pervasive kind of tyranny. It directly involved people serving in military or paramilitary groups; it indirectly affected countless others through the cultural values and economic systems tied to the growing armed movements on divergent sides of the national question. A militarist outlook came to dominate education, mass media, religious discourse, and the political process, as Home Rule hopes were gradually eclipsed by the conviction that no alternative path to an independent Ireland remained short of armed insurrection. It colored the cultural-nationalist agenda, reshaping popular culture forms from athletics to music, from language and literature to visual arts.

* * *

Joyce's final visit to Ireland in the summer of 1912 enabled him to see firsthand the expanding scope of militarism there. This occurred during an excursion from Nora's hometown of Galway to the Aran Islands that, as Ellmann notes, realized Joyce's prediction in "The Dead" of at last coming to share in the primitive identity of the West (336). Joyce's attention on that Aran trip seems to have been on much less quaint or bucolic things, as evidenced by the essay published a few weeks afterward, on 12 September, in *Il Piccolo della Sera*. One of his more fascinating and overlooked critical writings, "The Mirage of the Fisherman of Aran: England's Safety Valve in Case of War" juxtaposes one of the last outposts of traditional Irish culture with modern Europe's march toward war. It commences and concludes with Joyce and his unnamed travel "companion" (Nora?) studying a pamphlet and map that tout a scheme for developing Galway harbor for commercial and defensive purposes in preparation for the seemingly ineluctable military showdown.

A recent circumnavigation of Ireland by the German navy had led the author of the pamphlet titled "Galway as a Transatlantic Port" to assert the "absolute Imperial necessity" of developing the commercial port and of constructing coastal fortifications on nearby Mutton Island (qtd. in *OCPW* 342). As Kevin Barry observes, "The booklet emphasizes the eventuality of war" (*OCPW* 342) in order to make its case for the vast port-development project. The Galway Harbour Scheme, as it was called, embodied the quintessential total-war strategy, ironically countering the threat of German militarism with a similar integration of transportation, commerce, and defense. Joyce perceives such a collusion of military resources and commercial capital at work, noting how the pamphlet "makes a heartfelt appeal to the British Admiralty, to the railway company, to the chamber of commerce, and to the Irish populace. The new port would be a safety valve for England in the event of war" (*OCPW* 203).

Joyce's response to this dangerous collusion is immersed in history as well as irony. His title suggests from the start the highly unrealistic promise of the harbor development proposal by likening it to a thousand-year-old legend of the paradise of Hy-brasil. Like the fantastically elusive western island, such a vision for Galway is hopeful but illusory. In its place, Joyce supplies a nonidealized portrait of Aran life. He frames the contemporary portrait of Inishmor with three examples of historic foreign intruders in Ireland—the Spanish Armada, the British garrison, and "the Danish hordes that burned the city of Galway in the eighth century" (*OCPW* 205). The trio of national-historical references sets the current military threat amid a broader historical context; its blend of favorable and destructive visitors creates a sense of ambivalence about foreign invasion that leaves open the question of what a potential German occupation might mean for Ireland.

What is certain is the broader point that even an ostensibly remote outpost of traditional culture is not immune to modern militarization. Joyce shows how already, four years before the outbreak of hostilities, the total-war strategists have the most placid corner of Ireland in their sights. One is far from the idyllic portrait Synge had penned of the same islands only five years before. As the boat steams back to the mainland, Joyce closes the essay on an ironic note that adds a final emphatic rejoinder to the proposed port development and militarization project. Looking once more at the prospectus map in the half-light of the return journey, he sees the lines of the transatlantic shipping routes as a flowering lily and branching terebinth tree (*OCPW* 205). In their original context of *Ecclesiasticus* 24, these biblical metaphors described the voice of divine wisdom flourishing and spreading among the people of Israel. Joyce's concluding images and their subtext bring into question whether such wisdom is in fact the true impulse behind the proposed courses to peace and prosperity.

The Galway Harbour Scheme remained on Joyce's mind several years later as he wrote *Ulysses*. It appears twice in the novel, first in "Nestor," where Stephen notices it among other selected details of Mr. Deasy's letter to the editor about foot and mouth disease:

> May I trespass on your valuable space. That doctrine of *laissez faire* which so often in our history. Our cattle trade. The way of all our old industries. Liverpool ring which jockeyed the Galway harbour scheme. European conflagration. Grain supplies through the narrow waters of the channel. (*U* 2.324–28)

Deasy, like the promoters of the Harbour Scheme in 1912, argues that Galway is a safer landing place for the British food supply than the "narrow waters of the channel" (English, North, or St. George's), where German ships could easily attack British vessels. Like his recommendation for the contemporary livestock market, Deasy's reflection on the failed Galway Harbour Scheme of 1858–64 combines protectionism for Irish industries with concerns for national security as he prescribes abandoning the prevailing neoliberal policies of an unregulated marketplace in favor of a defense-centered economic strategy. Even the polite rhetorical opening—"May I trespass on your valuable space"—betrays the military-industrial impulse underlying Deasy's policy.

At the end of the day, the Galway Scheme literally resurfaces amid the sea stories of D. B. Murphy, who alludes to the fate of one ship in the Halifax-Galway line, the *Indian Empire*, which "ran bang against the only rock in Galway bay when the Galway harbour scheme was mooted by a Mr Worthington or some name like that." Murphy goes a bit further than Deasy, suggesting that bribery and an inside job of sabotage were behind the 1858 incident: "Ask the then captain, he advised them, how much palmoil the British government gave him for that day's work, Captain John Lever of the Lever Line" (*U* 16.964–68). John Orrell Lever was in fact not a ship's captain but the Manchester-based owner of the *Indian Empire* and other vessels of the original Galway Scheme (Gifford 548). Probably Lever's investment in the project accounted for his rise to political prominence in Galway, which he represented as borough MP from 1859 to 1865, a period corresponding almost precisely with the years of the Galway Harbour Scheme of 1858–64. Murphy mistakenly conflates the original scheme using Lever's ships with its 1912 revival by Robert Worthington, a Dublin railroad contractor (Gifford 547–48), which is still eight years in the future. The anachronism allows Murphy to play up Anglo-Irish tensions and hint at internal conspiracy surrounding the Harbour Scheme. Despite his historical inaccuracies and possible rumormongering, Murphy advances the broader point that Joyce makes in "Mirage of the Fisherman of Aran": private capital ventures and economic opportunities are necessarily and dangerously subsumed by national military interests.

Fallen Friends

On an individual level, militarism in Ireland directly impacted the lives of several people who were close to Joyce. Three friends from his University College days, George Clancy, Francis Sheehy Skeffington, and Thomas Kettle, perished in the violence of war. They were men whose movements Joyce followed even after leaving Dublin, mentioning them in his letters home and corresponding with their widows and families. All three devoted their lives to Irish independence, but each worked toward that end from a drastically different vantage point: Clancy via militant nationalism, Kettle via enlistment in the British army, and Skeffington via pacifism. They formed the basis for several key characters and ideological positions in Joyce's work; their enduring significance for him was perhaps due to the distinct differences they had with Joyce and with each other.

Clancy, a nationalist with strong interest in the Irish language, founded a branch of the Gaelic League at University College Dublin. His passion for hurling and other traditional sports made him the model for the sexually repressed athlete Davin in *A Portrait*. After graduating from UCD in 1904, he was hired to teach at Joyce's former school, Clongowes Wood College, where he stayed just a brief time before illness obliged him to return to his hometown of Grange, County Limerick. Indeed, his poor health conflicted with his athletic interest thoughout his life, but it did not hinder his energies in other areas. He taught Irish language classes for the Gaelic League, and he joined and trained with the Limerick branch of Irish Volunteers at its founding in 1913. Like many other members, he was rounded up and imprisoned following the Easter Rising, though he had not been directly involved in the fighting. His popularity within the Gaelic League and the Volunteers led to his candidacy for mayor of Limerick, a position to which he was elected in 1921. Shortly afterwards he was assassinated by British Black and Tan auxiliary forces in their intentional targeting of republican leaders during the War of Independence.[14]

While Joyce approached militarism somewhat tangentially through the cryptic medium of avant-garde fiction, Francis Sheehy Skeffington addressed the issue in more overt tones as journalist and peace activist.[15] The two had met at UCD in the newly revived Literary and Historical Society, where military policy and peace diplomacy were among the issues members debated. An outspoken idealist and advocate for pacifism and equal rights for women, Skeffington became, as noted, the model for the peace-petitioning McCann in *Stephen Hero* (and MacCann in *A Portrait*). Joyce by then referred to his friend with the sarcastic moniker "Hairy Jaysus," presumably in reference to his lengthy beard as well as steadfast principles. Joyce wrote to Stanislaus inquiring whether Skeffington was still registrar at University College—he ultimately resigned over the institution's refusal to answer his call for complete access for women—and to note he was "working in Hairy Jaysus at present" (*L* 2:81). Joyce's letter includes the passage from the novel that introduces the character based on Skeffington, one notable for presenting a bewildering contradiction to his peers, in large part by espousing antimilitarist values while cultivating an aggressive, hypermasculine appearance:

> there was a serious young feminist named McCann—a blunt brisk figure, wearing a Cavalier beard and shooting-suit, and a steadfast reader of the *Review of Reviews*. The students of the college did not understand what manner of ideas he favoured and they considered that they rewarded his originality sufficiently by calling him 'Knickerbockers.' (*SH* 39)

Skeffington did in fact favor knickers over trousers much of his life, including his wedding day and commencement ceremonies. Since his youth in Ulster, he was also an avid reader of W. T. Stead's *Review of Reviews*, the preeminent journal of the pacifist movement.[16] Stead's peace activisim, including a meeting with the tsar, led in the 1890s to his establishing the international Peace Crusade, to which Guglielmo Ferrero later dedicated the English translation of *Militarism* and which organized the Hague Peace Conferences of 1899 and 1907. Skeffington, and the characters drawn from him, were virtually synonymous with the European antimilitarist movement.

The contrast between Stephen and McCann suggests something of the strange but not unfriendly relationship between Joyce and Skeffington. Their differences on the question of militarism had less to do with morality than with pragmatic politics and public image. If they agreed about standing by their principles, even in the face of adverse public opinion, they differed in their strategies. Joyce showed little patience and great cynicism for what he regarded as Skeffington's self-righteous stance, at times voicing harsh doubts as to his friend's sincerity:

I am sure however that the whole structure of heroism is and always was a damned lie and that there cannot be any substitute for the individual passion as the motive power of everything—art and philosophy included. For this reason Hairy Jaysus seems to be the bloodiest impostor of all I have met. (*L* 2:81)

Skeffington would spend much of his abbreviated life warning of the imminent danger of armed force in Ireland. His pamphlet "A Forgotten Small Nationality" documents the move toward military drilling by the Ulster Volunteers, followed by growing numbers of republicans in the South under the aegis of the Volunteers and the Citizen Army. He voices his objection to the Larne and Howth gunrunning episodes while the promise of a peaceful transition to Home Rule lingered, then finally sat suspended, at the outbreak of war on the Continent.

Nor was Skeffington's pacifism sidelined by his own nationalist sympathies. Readers of his *Irish Citizen* newspaper on 22 May 1915 found his open letter to Thomas MacDonagh of the Irish Volunteers. Knowing that nationalist Volunteers might take Britain's seemingly inevitable slide into the war as Ireland's opportunity for armed insurrection, Skeffington expressed grave concern over the global trend of military escalation he saw taking shape in Ireland:

> But, you will say, Ireland is too small, too poor, ever to be a militarist nation in the European sense. True, Ireland's militarism can never be on so great a scale as that of Germany or England; but it may be equally fatal to the best interests of Ireland. European militarism has drenched Europe in blood; Irish militarism may only crimson the fields of Ireland. For us that would be disaster enough. ("Psychology")

He closes with a cautionary note to the Volunteer commandant that is eerily prophetic about the danger of being "led by the military spirit. Now we realize it. And we must never fall into that abyss again.... Think it over before the militarist current draws you too far."

Perhaps of greatest interest to Joyce was Skeffington's turn to fiction to address the past and current militarism of Ireland. His novel *In Dark and Evil Days*, completed in 1907, was published posthumously in 1916, within months of *A Portrait*; Joyce obtained a copy for his Trieste library shortly after (Gillespie and Stocker 216). The historical novel follows the events of the 1798 United Irishmen rebellion through their impact on the Kyan family, County Wexford farmers who are reluctantly drawn into the action. The title comes from a line of John Kells Ingram's 1843 commemorative poem of the 1798 Rising, "The Memory of the Dead," to which Joyce also alludes in "Wandering Rocks" when Tom Kernan thinks of the ill-advised cause of the United Irishmen: "Course they were on the wrong side. They rose in dark and evil days. Fine poem that is: Ingram" (*U* 10.789–90). Like his journalism, Skeffington's novel, while sympathetic to the national cause, did not rattle the saber like Ingram's song or Joyce's Citizen by posing the provocative question "Who fears to speak of '98?" (*U* 12.481). As Skeffington's widow Hanna recalled in her introduction to the novel, he was a "fighting pacifist" who sought a nationalist direction that was "militant but not militarist" (xiii, xxi).

In Dark and Evil Days clearly does not fear to speak of '98 on its own terms. It depicts the United Irishmen rising in terms of its brutal human costs and moral dilemmas, rather than the patriotic sacrifices or military glory of Ingram's poetic tribute. Skeffington has some characters, like Esmond Kyan, grapple with the decision to take up arms against the British. The novel consistently emphasizes the harsh physical realities and bloodshed of war over any sanitized descriptions. At times this can and does tend toward the predictable and polemical. The opening passage, for instance, immediately conveys the book's blatant antimilitarist argument in a sentimental and melodramatic style that might have been a model for Joyce's overblown parody in certain moments of *Ulysses*:

> It was a bright spring day in 1798, and the plains of Wexford, as yet unstained by military massacre, breathed out all the fragrance of the youthful year in response to the caressing rays of the sun. Sweetly sang the mating songsters on every tree and edge, but nowhere, surely, more sweetly and contentedly than in the pleasant grove that stood close by Kyan's farm. For here all around spoke of peace, plenty, and content; the young corn and the fresh meadow-grass rustled with life over the gently undulating plain that stretched away beyond the eye's range to the distant sea on one side, on the other to the mountain chains that fringe the county from Blackstairs to Croghan Kinsella, while hard by flowed the swift Slaney, no trace of blood yet sullying its dark waves. (1)

Despite its occasional purple prose and somewhat formulaic plotline, *In Dark and Evil Days* does approach more nuanced moral terrain concerning questions of revenge, justifiable force, and the limits of pacifism, as for example when Esmond, after the destruction of his home and the murder of his parents by British troops, abandons his pacifism to join the United Irishmen under local leader Dermot Fitzgerald. In this way the novel manages to explore the debate of constitutional and physical-force Irish nationalism that still lingered a century on.

At times Skeffington put down his pen and took to the streets for the antimilitarist cause. Under the Cat and Mouse Act, he was arrested and released multiple times for speaking out in rallies against British conscription. Indeed, this very willingness to take a public stand against civil disorder and military violence helped shape the circumstances of his premature death. During Easter Week, in attempts to prevent looting and injuries from the fighting, as well as trying to assist a wounded British soldier, he was arrested and imprisoned in Portobello Barracks. Two days later his captor, Captain John Bowen-Colthurst, ordered Skeffington to be shot by a firing squad. He was buried in the barracks without any notification to his family.

After his death, Hanna Sheehy Skeffington contextualized her husband's story in a lecture and essay aptly titled "British Militarism as I Have Known It." She spoke of the inquiry led by Major Sir Francis Vane in which Bowen-Colthurst was deemed mentally unstable and temporarily relieved of his command, though not stripped of his rank. As Vane would comment concerning the investigation, the incident seemed to go beyond the alleged insanity of one individual; rather, it seemed to relate precisely to that social and political problem to which Skeffington had dedicated his energies and career:

> Militarism, which is the vulgarization of Patriotism, is an universal vice (to talk of Prussian Militarism is as stupid and illogical as to talk of English or Irish Catholicism) for we find as much of this sentiment to-day daily expressed in London or in the Kildare Street Club in Dublin, as in any Military coterie in Berlin or Dresden." (qtd. in "British Militarism" 20)

Within months of Skeffington's death, news reached Joyce in Zurich of another University College classmate who had become a casualty of war. On 25 September 1916 he wrote to Hanna's sister Mary:

Dear Mrs. Kettle,
I have read this morning with deep regret in the *Times* that my old school fellow and fellow student Lieutenant Kettle has been killed in action. I hope you will not deem it a stranger's intrusion on your grief if I beg you to accept from me a word of sincere condolence. (*L* 1:96)

Thomas Kettle died near Givenchy, France, in the Battle of the Somme, the first major English operation of the war. Considered one of the most brilliant minds of his generation, Kettle had taken an oddly circuitous route to combat. His career was marked by success in a number of roles, including lawyer, editor, professor, and journalist. He was a founder, with Francis Sheehy Skeffington, of the Irish Socialist Party. The political comrades also shared a family connection, having married the sisters Mary and Hanna Sheehy.

Most emblematic of Kettle's political life was his affiliation with two different armies: he served in the original Irish Volunteers but died wearing the uniform of a British officer. If to some these seemed politically incongruous roles, to Kettle they were logically defensible positions amid the tumultuous political realities of contemporary Europe.

As with some of his other relationships, Joyce's connection to Kettle appears to have suffered during his exile, though not for any specifically personal reasons. In a September 1906 letter to Stanislaus, he lays the blame mostly on himself: "As for a possible friendship with Kettle it seems to me my influence on my male friends is provocative. They find it hard to understand me, and difficult to get on with me even when they seem well-equipped for these tasks" (*L* 2:157). Nevertheless, Joyce memorialized Kettle in his fiction with a certain fondness and respect, inscribing Kettle several times in the pages of *Finnegans Wake*. Two references allude directly to his wartime fate. Joyce suggests the difficulty of comprehending Kettle's military choice—"those ars all bellical, the highpriest's hieroglyph of kettletom" (*FW* 122.7)—as well as the sense of unalterable destiny it seemed to signify: "kettle auction like the soldr of britsh he was bound to be and become" (*FW* 362.10–11).

Kettle's position on Irish nationalism and the Great War changed dramatically while he was on a mission for the Irish Volunteers to establish a German gunrunning operation through Belgium. He came to see how German violence and hegemony in that small Catholic country spelled a similar threat for Ireland. It would be in the best interests of Ireland, Kettle thought, to join with England against German encroachment rather than, as some Irish nationalists hoped, to use the global crisis as Ireland's opportunity to cast off the yoke of British colonialism. He returned to Dublin convinced that the moment demanded Irishmen heed the British clarion call in order to defend the rights of small nations; Home Rule—a hope still harbored by many in Ireland's republican movement—would depend on earning British trust by way of a shared military commitment. From potential collaboration with Germany against Britain, Kettle had shifted to the polar opposite view of joining the war against Kaiser Wilhelm as the best option for Irish independence. After an organizational split of the Irish Volunteers in 1914, Kettle followed the majority of members into the ranks of Lord Kitchener's New Army. That autumn, the newly appointed secretary of war became a ubiquitous image on recruiting posters from London to Dublin; under his mustachioed visage, glaring eyes, and pointing finger was emblazoned the slogan "Your Country Needs You." The fact that the image appeared in newspapers and on billboards on either side of the Irish Sea did not appear to complicate the message for the Irish republicans now opting to serve in the British Army; it was even bolstered by the fact that Kitchener himself hailed from County Kerry. Tom Kettle and scores of others like him trusted that the British legislative promise of Home Rule would surely be fulfilled following a war that many, though Kitchener was not among them, expected would be over by Christmas. Kettle was commissioned a lieutenant in the Ninth Dublin Fusiliers and within a matter of months found himself in the trenches of northern France.[17]

Kettle outlined the reasons behind his choice in *The Ways of War*, a 1917 collection of essays written while he was first a visiting journalist and later a voluntary combatant on the Western Front. Like Skeffington's novel, the book was posthumously published and was among a number of titles on war and military topics that Joyce owned in Trieste.[18] Its chapters range from political arguments to descriptive, sometimes even humorous, trench-life vignettes, such as "Rhapsody on Rats." The compilations generally reflect Kettle's overall purpose of convincing Irish readers that the war on behalf of small nations, namely Belgium and Serbia, is necessary and justified.

The book's anchor essay, "Why Ireland Fought," commences with fairly nuanced arguments about the causes of the war that reflect Kettle's academic training and earlier economic scholarship.[19] Still, it ultimately falls back on a definition of militarism that, in line with Anglo-American rhetoric of the period, bills it as a uniquely Prusso-German phenomenon: "We have seen committed, under our own amazed eyes, the greatest crime against civilization of which civilization itself keeps any record. The Blood-and-Ironmongers have entered into possession of the soul of humanity" (*Ways* 58). The reference to Bismarck's infamous "Blood and Iron" speech to the Prussian parliament in 1862 suggests a German origin of militarism that Kettle soon makes more definite and explicit: "There was indeed before the war one people in Europe, but only one, whose leaders preached war as a national duty and function" (63). Compared to Liebknecht or Ferrero, Kettle remains quite moderate in his opinion about the extent to which the militarist mentality has infused the overall fabric of German society. He sees it rather optimistically as a problem confined to the ruling elite and not infecting the entire social hierarchy:

> How far the militarism of his rulers had penetrated to the common man in Germany must remain something of a question. Personally, I do not think the peasant who knelt by the wayside crucifix in the Tyrol, or the comfortable, stout farmer in Bavaria or Württemberg, or the miner in Westphalia, or any typical Rhinelander wanted to dip his hands in blood. He bore with rulers who did so want. (63–64)

While conceding that Britain and France are not "sinless" in their own histories of imperial conquest, Kettle ranks them ahead of Germany in having "begun to cleanse themselves" and found ways to work out "the democratic formula," concluding that in the long run "the triumph of Prussia must mean the triumph of force: the triumph of the Allies must mean the triumph of law" (71). This distinction between rampant militarism and appropriate military action acquires a decidedly nationalist hue. Kettle's earlier socialism appears suspended or dormant as he seems to accept that Europe must set its house in order along lines drawn of international conflict. Nor, given the extent of the hostilities, does he place much faith in Norman Angell or the "arbitration movement" to which Skeffington and the Hague peace conferences had subscribed: "Europe, we said, was a monstrous contradiction in terms—an armed peace. There is no contradiction now, it is a manual of pure logic after Krupp. The Norman Angell evangel to the money-masters has failed" (109).

No matter how clear it was in his own mind, the decision to put on the British uniform remained a source of great anxiety for Kettle. He came to realize by the summer of 1916 that the formerly unpopular rebels of Easter Week were likely to be praised as liberators of Ireland, while those like himself who trusted in Britain's hollow Home Rule promise would at best be derided as fools, at worst labeled traitors. While Kettle viewed siding with Britain as the surest path to Irish independence and European peace, *The Ways of War* reveals his unceasing need to clarify the appropriateness of that choice. Such clarification ultimately hinged on the distinction between the righteous military mobilization of the Allies and the evil "Prussified" militarism of the enemy. Even neutrality was, in Kettle's view, not a route to peace but "a decision of adherence to the evil side" (72).

Recent assessments have tended to downplay the influence of militarism as a motivating factor in Kettle's decision, echoing his assumption that distinguished German militarism from the presumably more noble military effort launched against it. For example, Senia Pašeta emphasizes several deeply personal struggles, including the early loss of his brother and an ongoing battle with alcoholism, as the real fights of Kettle's life, a pretext to the sincere outrage he felt at witnessing the wartime atrocities on his 1914 visit to Belgium.[20] To be sure, such a psychological portrait of Kettle's choice is valuable, if only for reasons of biographical accuracy. Yet it also runs the risk of tacit sympathetic acceptance of the reductive militarist definition on which Kettle predicated his thinking. That his decision was grounded in the essential paradox of fighting one brand of militarism with another—of becoming part of the war machine in an attempt to halt its progress—cannot be ignored. For Tom Kettle, and for countless others who made the deliberate decision to fight, that possibility never entered into the equation. They saw themselves as military men waging a valiant war against militarism; they did not consider any political or moral inconsistencies that might arise from such a designation.

At the end of his condolence letter to Mary Kettle, Joyce included as well a solemn, if belated, acknowledgment of the death of her brother-in-law: "May I ask you to convey to your sisters (whose addresses I do not know) my sympathy with them in the losses they have suffered? I am grieved to hear that so many misfortunes have fallen on your family in these evil days" (*L* 1:96). The allusion to Skeffington's antimilitarist novel respectfully grants the last word to "hairy Jaysus" in literary and complimentary terms.

It juxtaposes Kettle's death with that of his brother-in-law but refrains from the contemporary rhetoric of heroism or self-sacrifice that marked many wartime condolence cards. Their deaths are "losses" and "misfortunes"; the historical moment itself ("these evil days") is the singular agency. Leopold Bloom experiences a similar loss of his schoolmate Percy Apjohn "killed in action, Modder River" during the Boer War (*U* 17.1251–52). Joyce seems to acknowledge the impact of losing these old friends who, despite opposite responses to European militarism, became in the prime of life two of its innumerable casualties.

* * *

From 1882 to 1922, the period of Joyce's upbringing and education and his foundational years of writing and publication, militarism was among the most pressing and potent realities in Irish and European life. It left its imprint on the political, economic, social, and cultural realms, and was linked directly to the growth of modern industrial capitalism and the expansion of colonialism. Writing about Dublin from his Continental exile, Joyce was never far from the largest armies in history moving to and from the fiercest combat of all time, or from the paramilitary acts of terrorism or armed insurgency by non-state entities. As he devised his new fiction, Joyce was touched by the currents of militarism and antimilitarism that flowed from political, intellectual, and personal sources.

Joyce's works demonstrate how he was mindful of the catastrophic experience of war. As the subsequent chapters in this book will discuss, those works also show Joyce attuned to the transformative social and cultural ideology that shaped the conditions of conflict long before the first shots were fired. Yet, unlike classic war novelists such as Ernest Hemingway or Erich Maria Remarque, Joyce was not so much concerned with reflecting the traumatic action of the battlefield or its aftermath as with revealing its perennial causes. He located these among the subtle methods by which modern nations had subordinated every aspect of life to serve an all-encompassing "war machine."[21] While many in the English-speaking world at the time pointed across the Channel to the scourge of German militarism, Joyce pointed back, revealing how this condition of modern life reflected equally in the cracked looking-glass he held up to British Ireland, if anyone cared to look closely.

2

Violent Exercise

> You say you don't see much in it all—nothing but a struggling mass of boys, and a leather ball which seems to excite them all to great fury, as a red rag does a bull. My dear sir, a battle would look much the same to you, except that the boys would be men, and the balls iron; but a battle would be worth your looking at for all that, and so is a football match.
>
> Thomas Hughes, *Tom Brown's School-Days*

> If you are practiced in the hurling field, in the football field, at the chessboard, it will be little trouble to you when the time comes for the freedom of your country to handle a rifle.
>
> P. C. Kelly, GAA Executive Council member, 1886

Athletics and militarism move in practical lockstep through Joyce's fiction, occurring frequently in the contested arenas of cultural ideology and national identity. Joyce situates sports—of the British garrison and traditional Irish varieties—in definite and complex roles that play out most pointedly in portrayals of educational practice and social discourse. These range from the football and cricket scenes in the schooldays segments of *A Portrait* to the barroom banter about Gaelic sports and shoneen games that leads to the volatile conclusion of *Ulysses*'s "Cyclops" episode. In each instance, sports come to represent the militant values they helped foster on both sides of the Anglo-Irish divide. The British Army had long used sports for a variety of purposes, including physical training, leisure entertainment, and community relations. By the late nineteenth century, some physical-force nationalists exploited the Gaelic athletic revival to military ends, seeing the movement as an effective vehicle for troop recruitment, group cohesion, and covert drill. Drawing from a broader ethos of muscular Christianity and national efficiency, English imperialism and Irish nationalism revealed a similar ironic tendency to carry out the destructive violence of the war machine by cultivating the healthful habits of followers. Even the seemingly individualized aspirations of the physical culture movement, literally embodied in *Ulysses* by the figure of strongman Eugen Sandow, could be subject to the manipulating political agenda of militarism on either side.

The chapter "Rugby and Football" in Thomas Hughes's 1857 novel of English public-school life, *Tom Brown's School-Days*, articulates what is probably the most famous analogy of playground competition and battlefield combat, in a narrative tone that seems intended to draw readers into a shared veneration for both. The goal is not so much a detailed understanding of football as a general investment in "the broad philosophy" that enfolds it (94). That philosophy is grounded in a casual comparison that readily substitutes men for boys and cannonballs for footballs. With unwavering assurance, the narrator leaps past any possible moral objection to the analogy and straight to the assumption that football heroics and the spectacle of combat are both innocent of any deleterious effects and simply "worth your looking at" (94).

Just like the sports culture it describes, *Tom Brown's School-Days* seems intent on influencing young readers through its evocative metaphors and exuberant tone. The playing field is anything but level amid the agile rhetoric of a narrator who feigns a gentlemanly dialogue of equals ("My dear sir"), all the while maintaining his didactic superiority over the imagined reader. What we witness in the novel is a rhetorical form far more compelling than any propaganda pamphlet or recruiting poster could ever be. Hughes's popular novel reflects the larger military purpose behind the school-games phenomenon of the last half of the nineteenth century.

If not a direct call to arms or cause of war, *Tom Brown's School-Days* instilled in several generations of English boys the public-school athletic ideal and suggested the greatness to which sports might lead in life after school. The novel became as substantial on a cultural level as the economic crises, diplomatic brinksmanship, and escalating troop numbers that were drawing the major European nations to war. Tom Brown's pluck, fortitude, and leadership on the rugby pitch were regarded by many as skills directly transferable to the challenges of empire-building, most specifically on the battlefield and in the barracks. Moreover, he appeared at a moment when increasing literacy rates and mass production of books made his story extremely accessible and widely available to readers throughout the empire. The book thus attained unprecedented influence on multitudes of adolescents who received through its elevated treatment of sport an equally glorified attitude to war. Its popularity both originated in and reinforced a fast-growing movement of regimented school athletics that easily extended to patriotic duty and military service, diffusing through popular literature from imperial center to colonial periphery what J. A. Mangan calls the "games ethic" of the Victorian public school.[1]

A half century after its first publication, *Tom Brown*'s linkage of athletics and warfare maintained its validity with devastating and deadly consequences. On 1 July 1916 Captain Wilfred Percy Nevill, age twenty-one, led the East Surrey Regiment's 8th Battalion into the Battle of the Somme, commencing British action in the First World War. From a visit home earlier that summer, he had brought back a number of footballs, one of which bore the inscription "The European Cup. The Final. Bavarians vs. British." Nevill and fellow officers had decided this substitution of national athletic glory for the horrors of combat would be just the thing to coax the men over the top after many suspenseful and sedentary weeks in the trenches. At 7:27 a.m. the officers sounded an opening whistle and kicked off toward the German lines. Several officers and men dribbled the footballs a mile and a quarter into enemy territory. Prizes had been announced for those who could stay nearest to the footballs. Nevill, for one, did not live to hand them out: he was killed later that day attempting to negotiate German barbed wire outside the village of Montauban.

On that single day, the British lost 20,000 men. By the end of the summer offensive, the losses totaled 415,000, including a large number of Irish who had opted to join the fight. Among them was Joyce's friend and university classmate Tom Kettle. The French would lose some 200,000 men, while across the lines more than half a million German troops perished. Many of them also followed football—-as "broad philosophy" if not tangible object—all the way from their own schooldays to No Man's Land. The opening stanzas of a poem titled "The Game" glorify the athletic-warrior parallel exploited by Nevill and his regiment:

> On through the hail of slaughter,
> Where gallant comrades fall,
> Where blood is poured like water,
> They drive the trickling ball.[2]

That opening day of the Battle of the Somme, Nevill's analogy achieved what he intended, encouraging thousands of infantrymen to enter battle as though they were merely stepping onto the football pitch. At the same time, it effectively and tragically collapsed any original distance between the tenor and vehicle of *Tom Brown's* original playground-battleground metaphor.

Despite its distinctive cultural identity and opposite political agenda, the revival of traditional athletics in Ireland during the same period evoked the same deadly parallel as the imperial discourse of British sports. Gaelic footballers and hurlers were actively recruited by the Irish Republican Brotherhood, and later the Volunteers, to join their growing ranks. In turn, the sports were encouraged for the physical conditioning and covert training they offered members. From the outset, the sports revival hinged on an expectation that athletic training was integral to a militarized Irish masculinity. Gaelic Athletic Association cofounder Michael Cusack, model for the Citizen of "Cyclops," solidified the connection in an account of his own indoctrination to the sport, writing in his regular athletic column for the *United Irishman* newspaper, "Having a mind to make up, I made it up. I resolved to be a Fenian. To be a Fenian, I should be a hurler. I became a hurler and a Fenian. This was the beginning of my manhood" ("Gaelic Athletic Association: Hurling").

Cusack's remarks echo an established tenet of the Irish sports movement as a direct vehicle for nation-building through armed liberation. Addressing an early meeting of the Gaelic Athletic Association in Mullagh during the spring of 1886, P. C. Kelly, an Executive Council member from Galway, deemed the traditional sports of hurling and Gaelic football, and even the intellectual tension of chess, fitting preparation for armed combat "when the time comes for the freedom of your country" (qtd. in Mandle 67). Such direct parallels between Gaelic games and military action led British police to respond with bans on Irish sports in order to disrupt the unit cohesion and corporeal training of practitioners. Nevertheless, before the first shots were fired in the Easter Rising, sports had become a locus of armed struggle in modern Ireland.

Joyce's fiction explores the close affiliation between athletic and martial culture on both sides of the national divide. His representations of British and Irish sports alike critique the indoctrinating role each had in a highly militarized society. Regardless of political ideology or national affiliation, sports comprise, to quote Leopold Bloom, a "violent exercise" (*U* 12.892), in bodily activity, social relations, and cultural imagination. Sports in Joyce often function within the historical contexts of British occupation and the concurrent call to arms of the Irish independence movement. Despite their obvious antagonism toward each other, British imperialism and Irish nationalism alike exploited the social capital of athletics and physical culture in order to recruit, train, and embolden followers in the use of armed force. By parodying the militant patriotism and physical brutality of sport, Joyce challenges the core values of the Victorian sports movement that shaped the political landscape in each direction.

Garrison Games

Tom Brown's School-Days in particular and the public-school games ethic in general were fixed on the assumption, rooted in classical values, that sports form the basis for bodily strength and soldierly prowess. "Sports, manliness, and militarism have been associated for centuries. In ancient Greece, which the Victorians and Edwardians revered, equal prominence was given to the athlete and the warrior" (Moss 30). Merging with the strong currents of the midcentury evangelical movement, the neoclassical athletic ethos formed the core of "muscular Christianity," which recommended the development of bodily strength as complement to spiritual stamina and restraint from physical indulgence. In secularized, political terms, the burgeoning cult of athleticism also deemed physical fitness essential to national defense and patriotic duty. This came about in large part after recruiting centers in several of Britain's industrial cities found a majority of applicants physically unfit for military service during the Boer War.[3] Spurred on by the military, a growing number of individuals, organizations, and government ministries rapidly subscribed to Herbert Spencer's dictum "To be a nation of healthy animals is the first condition of national prosperity." From journalism to education, influential voices echoed Spencer's axiom with a pragmatic call for compulsory sports and exercise in the schools of Britain and the colonies. After the tragic British losses in South Africa, by the turn of the century many would equate national health with national force.

The growth of public athletic interest in Britain became tied directly to maintaining well-conditioned troops for overseas engagements and domestic defense in a time of mass public invasion scare concerning the troop escalations of France and Germany. In 1901 in *Efficiency and Empire*, Arnold White emphasized the primary role of sports in enhancing overall public health for military recruiting purposes, and ultimately, national survival: "The production of sound minds in healthy, athletic, and beautiful bodies is a form of patriotism which must be revived if modern England is not to follow ancient Babylon and Tyre" (121). White's chapter titled "Physical Inefficiency" suggests athletics as an antidote to the rapid urbanization and resulting decay of the British population, which could be blamed for the recent military defeats in South Africa:

> Unlike the Boers, we create a fighting machine out of a small and carefully chosen *corps d'elite*. The maintenance of British interests could not be entrusted at random to men from the great towns.... A quarrel between two nations, one of which lives mainly in the open air, and the other mostly in streets and tenement houses, suggests the reconsidering our own attitude towards the unfit. (95–96)

White lamented the state of a British athletics that, like military service, was limited mainly to the aristocratic and leisure classes (107). If they were only encouraged and accessible across social strata, sports could be harnessed as a means to producing a stronger pool of soldiers and officers. Such arguments had a direct hand in the diffusion of the physical-culture curriculum from elite institutions to the national schools.

For decades the top-tier British public schools such as *Tom Brown's* Rugby had been at the forefront of such a defense-minded sports movement. It manifested itself in the campus primacy of football—both association football (soccer) and rugby—and cricket, team sports that provided vigorous physical training while they instilled a collective, regimented mentality in their participants. Other scholastic sports followed, including running, field hockey, swimming, gymnastics, racquets, squash, fencing, and fives (a handball game), yet football and cricket retained their dominant hold. Intramural competitions were held at public schools throughout the British Isles, and "foreign" or "out" matches were played among a number of schools and clubs. From around 1860 there began a steady increase in organization, record keeping, and rules structures, so that by the last decade of the nineteenth century "A huge games-playing machine was ultimately constructed, efficiently serviced and periodically improved" (Mangan, *Athleticism* 74). This machine was deemed ideal for developing the physical and mental prerequisites of military service.

As the latest addition to the Victorian curriculum, sports were regarded by a number of educators as the most essential activity for molding youth into obedient officers or well-conditioned functionaries. Athletic training prepared them to do the work of empire, whether defending against invasion at home or posting to distant and inhospitable locations. As preparation for imperial service, Hely Hutchinson Almond, headmaster of Loretto School near Edinburgh, emphasized football and hunting over reading and writing (Mangan, *Games Ethic* 28). Almond was one of a number of leading educators who, for similar reasons, made organized football and other sports a curricular mainstay in the last half of the nineteenth century. By the early part of the twentieth, the educational emphasis on sport for military ends would come to have profound effects beyond the public-school campus.

In Britain's national schools, a physical education program soon served a dual purpose of exercise and military training. From 1871 to 1906 drill in British elementary schools became a physical and patriotic training piece, in large part as a direct response to its implementation in the Prussian school system (Mangan and Ndee 71). As educational budgets increased and the danger of a troop shortage appeared to have been averted, primary schools in Britain began to replace drill with the team sports that had been popularized by the public schools. But the physical culture movement in the decade before the Great War remained geared to the same end of instilling regimentation, discipline, and camaraderie in many boy athletes soon destined to become new soldiers.

* * *

The same year Percy Nevill and his fellow officers so literally and athletically kicked off the Battle of the Somme and collapsed the playground-battlefield metaphor of Hughes's novel, Joyce included in *A Portrait of the Artist as a Young Man* his own response to the public-school sports ethic.[4] *Tom Brown's School-Days* advances the familiar proverb—often attributed to the Dublin-born Duke of Wellington—that the fate of the British Empire was to be determined on the playing fields of Eton (or, in Hughes's case, Rugby); *A Portrait* conveys something else taking shape on the playing fields of Clongowes by depicting its protagonist's nascent resistance to the militarist ethos of British public-school athletics. Stephen's evasion of the indoctrinating brutality of British garrison sports in an Irish boarding school embodies a colonial renouncement of imperial militarism that shows his first signs of silence, exile, and cunning.

The opening chapter of the novel features rough-and-tumble football descriptions as a dominant part of Stephen's schooldays that initiate a provocative counterthrust to the celebratory athletic rhetoric of Tom Brown. Joyce's depictions of football and cricket critique the militarism that suffused organized sports and other aspects of the school curriculum. As Kershner notes, the Clongowes segment is neatly framed by athletic activities, starting with football and closing with cricket (*Joyce, Bakhtin* 171). The fresh perspective it affords on both garrison games in turn helps to reinforce Stephen's emerging sense of the social and political hierarchies those sports carry with them. Andrew Gibson sees this bounding of the chapter in British sports as articulating nothing less than the "institutional formation of a colonial subject" ("Stubborn" 91). Beyond colonialism, the Clongowes sports curriculum described by Joyce reflects the deep-seated militarism of British garrison games as a normalized component of education in nineteenth-century Ireland. As a Jesuit college in Ireland, Clongowes had a unique institutional history, but in many ways it emulated the general curricular trend that emerged from the Victorian games movement in Britain.

Like Tom Brown's, Stephen's schooldays begin with football. It is not themes or books but sport that marks the watershed event of the protagonist's school career. But unlike Hughes's schoolboy hero, Stephen feels an instant repulsion for the game:

"The wide playgrounds were swarming with boys. All were shouting and the prefects urged them on with strong cries. The evening air was pale and chilly and after every charge and thud of the footballers the greasy leather orb flew like a heavy bird through the grey light" (*P* 20). A systematic and threatening violence is established in the beelike image of the footballers, while the early darkness and coldness of the setting provide additional discomfort to the strange and brutal contact of the game. The comparison of the flying football to "a heavy bird" seems the avian incarnation of Dante's earlier nursery-rhyme threat that Stephen apologise, "O, if not, the eagles will come and pull out his eyes" (*P* 20).[5] Alongside the menacing physicality of the pitch, the intensely regimented nature of the game contributes as well to Stephen's sense of dread, as the shouts of players and prefects set the chaotic whirl of the scrimmage amid the context of an authoritative social fabric ruled by actual or threatened physical force.

In marked difference to the athletic favoritism of *Tom Brown*, Joyce's limited-omniscient narrator represents football in sympathetic perspective with one of its unwilling participants. Tom Brown's natural aptitude and love for the game contrast with Stephen's desire to escape from the hostile playground environment. Lacking the inherent skill or active engagement of Tom Brown, Stephen shuns the physical aggression. His response, twice emphasized, is to feign participation while trying to escape notice: "He kept on the fringe of his line, out of sight of his prefect, out of the reach of the rude feet, feigning to run now and then. . . . He crept about from point to point on the fringe of his line, making little runs now and then" (*P* 20, 21). Like a soldier looking simply to survive in modern mass warfare, Stephen looks to blend in, not stand out.

Equally significant as this description of the football ground is Stephen's gaze at what lies beyond it. When he looks away from the chill and fray of the playground, Stephen longingly pictures its counterpart in the orderly light and comfort of the castle: "The sky was pale and cold but there were lights in the castle . . . It was nice and warm to see the lights in the castle" (*P* 22). As at several other moments in the chapter, a parallel and repetitive syntax underscores an entrapped ideological perspective. Andrew Gibson argues how Joyce's depiction of Clongowes reflects the enhanced competitiveness of Irish education in the Victorian period as contributing to the labyrinth of "formations" and "counterformations" in which Stephen finds himself ("Stubborn" 88–91).[6] Rather than "look beyond the sports field," one might look to Stephen's own meaningful gaze beyond it, so as not to overlook specific local facts and historical factors directly invoked in Joyce's narrative of Stephen's recollection (91).

More than just the warm escape from football and sanctuary of evening study hall, the interior of the castle recalls for Stephen the school legend of Hamilton Rowan tossing his hat beside the moat as a decoy to English soldiers. The military anecdote of the United Irishmen hero outsmarting and singly evading his group of pursuers intermingles with the scene on the football pitch in which Stephen also relies more on brains than brawn. Like Stephen "caught in the whirl of a scrimmage," the outnumbered Rowan also used his cunning and imagination to flee a mob of "flashing eyes and muddy boots" (*P* 22). While Stephen's mental escape might be considerably less dashing, it still suggests his "first youthful success at defying oppressive authority" (Cheng, *Joyce, Race* 73). The success, however, much like that of Rowan himself, proves limited and temporary, as the liberating potential of individual imagination ultimately runs up against the structured social reality of school life, bringing Stephen back to where he started on the cold and brutal football pitch.[7]

Thus despite his own attempt at evasive maneuvers, Stephen is encircled by the militarized scripts of athletics and local history that Clongowes sanctions for its students. Like the physical barriers of the campus—embodied in the square ditch and the haha where Rowan cast his hat—the narrative structures surround Stephen and his contemporaries with ideals of manliness and physical culture. Robert Spoo notes, "At this stage of his development, Stephen is more a symptom of his culture than an exception within it; he is assimilating its values and narrative structures rather than questioning them" (*Language* 41). Such values and structures leave him circumscribed not just by the great-men theory of history, as Spoo contends, but more specifically by a dominating historiography of martial action and physical force (40–43). The doubling irony of cultural discourses suggests further evidence of Stephen's entrapped status. In this case, the minimal difference between a military legend and a garrison game seems to reinforce the fact that the chances for escape are remote. As with Wells's entrapping joke about a fellow who does or does not kiss his mother good-night, it is difficult to know which, if either, represents a viable discursive pathway out of what Andrew Gibson terms the "intricate ambivalences of the labyrinth" ("Stubborn" 89).

A Portrait develops a critique of the Victorian public-school games ethic in large part by questioning the relevance of its military-imperial values transferred to an Irish context. Joyce's depictions of sports at Clongowes are therefore most effectively viewed against the historical diffusion of a physical education movement intent on transferring core principles of the British school curriculum to colonial locations. In *Athleticism in the Victorian and Edwardian Public School,* J. A. Mangan describes the inception of compulsory sports programs as no less than an ideological phenomenon tied directly and explicitly to the ongoing growth and maintenance of the armed forces: "By the end of the nineteenth century . . . English playing fields were recognized training grounds for imperial battlefields" (138). For educators interested in developing the martial mindset and physical fitness of their pupils, the athletic aspect of secondary-school life became an essential complement to the academic. Sports like the Rugby School version of football could reinforce classroom lessons and even go further by providing hands-on physical experience that many considered ideal preparation for the challenge of the battlefield.

The belief in military applications for sport had much to do with the rapid expansion of funding for athletics in education that started around midcentury. Increasingly this formed part of a growing response to a crisis in national health and military recruitment during the final decades of the nineteenth century and the first decade of the twentieth. Clongowes experienced the innovation and diffusion of athletic culture through its affiliation with its English Jesuit mother school, Stonyhurst. While sports programs at Stonyhurst initially preceded those of other elite public schools by several decades, the school ultimately increased its own athletics programs and facilities largely as an attempt to compete with the rapid capital expansion taking place at more prestigious Protestant institutions.[8] Such development stemmed mainly from contemporary marketing and economic competition, through efforts to keep pace with the growing trend in British public schools; still, they were supported by aspects of the traditional Jesuit curriculum that emphasized physical training and military regimentation. These date to Society founder and former soldier Ignatius Loyola, who received his divine calling while recuperating from injuries suffered at the siege of Pamplona in 1521.[9]

A statue of the saint in full body armor still stands guard just inside the reception hall of Clongowes Castle today, suggesting something of the contradiction surrounding his historical identity. Initially, Loyola's military career was a point of departure rather than an exemplar for the life of the new order. He had discovered his spiritual calling as a way to escape the violence of the secular world. Therefore his original Jesuit program kept physical education as one minor facet of the traditional curriculum, secondary to the academic program Loyola outlined in the *Ratio Studiorum*. Loyola was "not himself enthusiastic about games, but he realised the need for some species of exercise for students after long hours of work" (Costello 115). In theory, at least, the nineteenth-century Jesuit colleges sought to sustain Loyola's original perspective on the place of athletics. Stonyhurst's director of studies Reverend Michael Maher wrote in 1907 that sports was never an end in itself at the school but instead a means for developing qualities of "subordination and co-operation" (qtd. in Mangan, *Athleticism* 64).

Yet the unprecedented funding and expansion of athletic programs in the decades prior to Maher's remark show how sports themselves were anything but subordinated to the academic curriculum. Capital outlay and investment in sports facilities at Stonyhurst and Clongowes reflected the heightened importance of the playing field. In line with its non-Jesuit counterparts, Clongowes increased its athletic grounds from two to thirty acres between 1845 and 1900; the same period showed Stonyhurst gradually develop not only comparable facilities but also rituals and symbols of sport emulating and rivaling the Protestant schools (Mangan, *Athleticism* 71, 65–66). Like Stonyhurst, Clongowes made substantial investment in athletic facilities beginning right around the time Joyce attended the school. The facilities improvements reflect the decidedly West British influence the Jesuits brought to Clongowes, preferring cricket and rugby to hurling and Gaelic football (Sullivan 26–27). The year prior to Joyce's arrival at the school, 1887, saw construction of the indoor swimming pool and leveling of the Higher Line cricket ground; the college built a gymnasium in 1902 and erected the cricket pavilion a decade later, reflecting increased participation and spectatorship. They were not merely a venue for character-building activity but the veritable centerpiece of school life. The school scenes of *A Portrait* demonstrate how the school games ethic, transcending sectarian differences, had also come to dominate the elite Jesuit colleges by the final decades of the century.

Overall, Clongowes and Stonyhurst paralleled the capital investment and curricular expansion of sports at Protestant public schools like Rugby, Harrow, and Eton. Doing so, they played a significant role in the diffusion of athletic values from imperial center to colonial periphery. But if the public-school sports ethos was to a great extent a uniform phenomenon across Britain and Ireland, it was not without certain variations due to the sectarian or geographic isolation of some institutions. Both were factors in the case of Stonyhurst and Clongowes. The two schools absorbed much from the broad influence of the British physical culture movement while fashioning specific, localized versions of the games being played throughout Britain. Peter Costello notes the shared athletic legacy of the elite Jesuit colleges: "when Clongowes was founded from Stonyhurst, the same games, in the form of Stonyhurst cricket and Gravel football, were brought to Kildare" (115). Through the middle decades of the nineteenth century and up to Joyce's years at Clongowes, "gravel" was played regularly from late September to the Grand Match held on St. Patrick's Day. Its name derived from the fact that it was played on a loose stone surface behind the castle to give relief to the grass athletic fields in the autumn and winter months. The game "bore a broad resemblance to soccer, but the ball (small, hard, not perfectly spherical and made on the premises) could be struck by the closed hand ('boxed') when in flight" (Costello 115). It could not be carried or thrown. The goalposts, nine feet wide and twenty-five feet high, were set at opposite corners of the pitch in a diagonal arrangement. As there was virtually no limit to the number of players, games could become chaotic and violent. One participant called them "a lawless scramble . . . where anything was allowed except carrying the ball" (qtd. in Costello 115).

Despite this impression, the complete "laws" for gravel, along with the following description of "boxing the ball," appear in the *Clongowes Record* for 1888. Both are noteworthy for their overt use of martial terms, including references to "enemy" opponents and an "assailing party" of forward offensive players:

> If the ball were got into the enemy's semicircle, or home court, and kicked over the touchline by the home team the other side were entitled to a "box." That is, one of the assailing party standing just beside the goal post with the ball in his left hand was entitled to box it with his right into play. On such occasions (comparatively rare ones) what a packed mass of panting humanity was squeezed into that semicircular enclosure! (1)

Besides boxing the ball, the rules for gravel football define such game techniques as "forcing" and "charging" and "repelling charges," all rigorous and combative displays that had more to do with making contact with one's opponents than with putting the ball in their goal.

The violence of Clongowes's home-fashioned sport, like that of warfare, was wrapped in a powerful display of pageantry and pseudo-military symbolism. The annual St. Patrick's Day "colour matches" began with a parade of the two teams, each displaying their flags of red and green, quite obvious representations of Ireland and Britain. The "choice of colours, or rather the right to have the green," was determined by competitions in the days leading up to the match (Hosty 131). Each side then affixed their flag to the top of the goalposts and during the course of the match lowered it a few feet each time they allowed a goal. Thus the football field was draped in a glorified version of mimic warfare, as the boys assumed an athletic battle of national identities on the Kildare playing fields.

Gravel football was phased out by the turn of the century, though not before Joyce had a chance to play the game, and apparently not because of its violence. For it was replaced by the even more aggressive rugby football starting in the 1888–89 school year—the year of Joyce's arrival—with the first outmatch being played that spring against Lansdowne, as noted in the *Clongowes Record*. As rugby took precedence that year, "gravel was relegated to short play-hours after breakfast and occasional very muddy days," as appears to be the case in *A Portrait* (Corcoran 153). The gravel football Joyce describes would have likely been among the last played at the school. And while many contemporary games emphasized group regimentation, none surpassed football—be it gravel or rugby—for its ability to simulate the esprit de corps, emotional fears, and physical hardships of combat. Frederick Temple, one Rugby headmaster, "had a reputation for never stopping a scrummage 'short of manslaughter'" (Mangan, *Athleticism* 120). Even the tamer association football had come to be recognized for its battlefield utility, as would become evident at the Battle of the Somme.

Such militaristic underpinnings to football remained in students' heads well beyond their time at school. Patrick Hosty, a student from 1882 to 1884, recalled decades later the violence of "Old Clongowes football": "Every boy worked hard to get his place on the team—many a broken knee and torn hand were got in the 'earning' of it—he was proud when he got it, and worked like a Trojan to keep it. Every member of the team was most loyal to the Captain, and the utmost good fellowship prevailed amongst the members of the team" (130–31). Avid footballers like Hosty could try for a place on the team that represented the college in out-matches. But even those students with little interest in the game, like Joyce, had at least some exposure to it through the regular practice scrimmages and house matches. The latter sometimes pitted a single residence hall—often of first- and second-form students—against the rest of the student body in a kind of ritual athletic hazing. It was probably for this reason Hosty begins his account somewhat defensively: "To those who have not been initiated into the intricacies of 'Old Clongowes Football' my advice is, do not judge harshly of it. It was a most fascinating game to watch, and the perfection to which some of the players brought the art of 'forcing' was astonishing" (Hosty 130). His rhetorical tone is not unlike that of the *Tom Brown* narrator, defensively and then enthusiastically convincing his readers of the value and power of football.

Ever the staunch advocate of Clongowes football, Hosty may or may not be the model for the character of that name in *Finnegans Wake* I.2 credited with composing "The Ballad of Persse O'Reilly," which invokes the martial and athletic associations of its setting, Phoenix Park. From the outset the *Wake* geography imbues the park with pugilistic and martial overtones of Anglo-Irish conflict: it is the site where the sleeping HCE's "tumptytumtoes" (*FW* 3.21) emerge from the earth, "their upturnpikepointandplace is at the knock out in the park where oranges have been laid to rust upon the green since devlinsfirst loved livvy" (*FW* 3.22–24). The park is a place of rest—and rust—not only for the Dreamer but for all the antagonistic histories of Unionist orange and Nationalist green, the upraised pikes of 1798 and other Irish rebellions, the forts and barracks of British military occupation, the erected monuments of British military leaders, all of which materialize in the park beside the River Liffey, Dublin's first love. By the next chapter, Hosty's subversive *rann* recasts the story of HCE's sexual sin in the Park in postlapsarian terms that range from Humpty Dumpty to Napoleon: "Our heavyweight heathen Humpharey / Made bold a maid to woo / ... / The general lost her maidenloo!" (*FW* 46.33–36). The heavy alliterative pun, with its subtle reference to the Battle of Waterloo, anticipates the similar heft of "Wellinton's monument" as site of HCE's unpardonable action (*FW* 47.7). In Wakean fashion, Hosty's ballad conjoins medieval and modern incursions, from the Vikings to the British Black and Tans (*FW* 46.12–16), pointing to the timeless repetition of military aggression in Ireland and suggesting such activity is something akin to sexual violation.

The Phoenix Park setting for "The Ballad of Persse O'Reilly" evinces the multiplicity of that locale's roles as army facility, war memorial, and sporting ground. The latter function was a particular flashpoint of political debate around 16 June 1904, as my look at "Cyclops" later in this chapter will discuss. In this regard, besides the Wellington Monument, reference to another park landmark, the Magazine Fort, a munitions storehouse overlooking the cricket and football grounds, situates the ballad narrative at the nexus of sports and warfare. Both the vocabulary and the arrangement of Hosty's ballad emphasize the corporeal and munitional meanings that resonate "By the butt of the Magazine Wall, / (Chorus) Of the Magazine Wall, / Hump, helmet and all" (*FW* 45.4–7). In one particular episode of the 1916 Rising, the Magazine Fort existed at the confluence of football and warfare. While most of the action of Easter Week focused on the GPO and the city center, the magazine became a strategic target for thirty members of the Irish Volunteers and Fianna Éireann who, disguised as a football team from the nearby playing fields, disarmed the guards and took control of the arsenal. They would abort their plan to blow up the fort, but not before the incident had demonstrated the easily transferable roles of soldier and footballer.

James Joyce and, by extension, Stephen Dedalus are considerably less enthusiastic about football than Clongowes alumni like Hosty, if not downright averse to the game. Stanislaus notes simply how Joyce "disliked football" (61). Eight years prior to the publication of *A Portrait*, Joyce directly expressed his disaffection for the game when he wrote to Stanislaus from Rome in December 1906: "I suppose it is because I never played football or was treated only slightly to your captain of fifty's regime that I can't turn out that kind of poetry" (*L* 2:199). "That kind of poetry," as Richard Ellmann notes, referred to "Napoleon," an elaborate ode by George Meredith documenting the rise and fall of the French field general, while the "captain of fifty's regime" suggests the homosocial hazing for which British boarding schools were legendary. Joyce's sardonic remark thus links Meredith's military poem with the aggressive sports regime of public-school education, in what appears to be Joyce's first shot at a physical-culture establishment that would remain in his sights over the coming decades. Rugby football reappears in tandem with army training in *Ulysses*'s "Oxen of the Sun" episode, where the two discourses become so verbally enmeshed as to be practically interchangeable: "Keep the durned millingtary step. We fall. Bishops boosebox. Halt! Heave to. Rugger. Scrum in. No touch kicking" (*U* 14.1462–63). Drill sergeants' orders and referees' commands merge amid a saturated fray of martial references that range through history from ancient Persian campaigns, American Civil War song lyrics, and newspaper headlines about Russo-Japanese naval battles.

The fact that Clongowes adopted British garrison games also suggests something of the social and professional expectations of the Catholic upper middle class in Ireland. Daunted by the football pitch, Stephen attempts to meet the social pressures of the elite school in other ways: "You told the Clongowes gentry you had an uncle a judge and an uncle a general in the army" (*U* 3.105–6). In an Ireland he will later regard as full of imposters—"beware of imitations" (*U* 3.483)—Stephen invents high-status subaltern identities for himself and his family. Nevertheless, his reluctant participation in British sports suggests a possible social trajectory away from being "a servant of two masters" (*U* 1.638). Possessing neither the class status nor the athletic proclivity of his Clongowes peers, Stephen experiences the games from a distance, as it were, even when he steps within the lines of the playing field.

This psychological distance extends to the other major school sport when Stephen must watch cricket practice without the aid of his glasses. (They are broken by another violent athletic impact when he is struck by a passing cyclist on the cinder path.) Despite his visual and mental detachment, Stephen manages to derive some sensory pleasure and tranquility from the springtime game. In exercising his aesthetic and poetic skills, he seems to be learning to devise a way out of the labyrinth:

> But there was no play on the football grounds for cricket was coming: and some said that Barnes would be the prof and some said it would be Flowers. And all over the playgrounds they were playing rounders and bowling twisters and lobs. And from here and from there came the sounds of the cricketbats through the soft grey air. They said: pick, pack, pock, puck: like drops of water in a fountain slowly falling in the brimming bowl. (*P* 48)

The emergence of a new poetic language effectively negates football and welcomes cricket. In contrast with the generally laconic scene of football, the passage nearly overflows with alliteration, personification, rhyme, and simile. Even the forceful names associated with football—Rody Kickham, Nasty Roche, and Cecil Thunder—are now replaced with pastoral ones like Barnes and Flowers that emphasize a regenerative, vernal hope.[10]

Still, even such springtime respite is not without its dangers. Soon another linguistic association foreshadows the sting of contact Stephen will feel from his unjust corporal punishment by Father Dolan: "In the silence of the soft grey air he heard the cricketbats from here and from there: pock. That was a sound to hear but if you were hit then you would feel a pain" (*P* 51). Like the word "belt"—"That was a belt round his pocket. And belt was also to give a fellow a belt" (*P* 21)—"pock" presents another duality, as soon after, just as cricket bat is replaced with pandybat, imaginary pain is replaced with real. The lyrical bubble of narrative is burst by another experience of repressive injustice and physical discomfort. Only after the friendly meeting with Father Conmee is justice served and faith restored, as evidenced in the return to the poetic description of the cricket ground:

> The fellows were practising long shies and bowling lobs and slow twisters. In the soft grey silence he could hear the bump of the balls: and from here and from there through the quiet grey air the sound of the cricketbats: pick, pack, pock, puck: like drops of water in a fountain falling softly in the brimming bowl. (*P* 62)

As the harmony of Stephen's perception restores itself, it remains tied to his emerging poetic techniques through renewed alliteration, rhyme, and syntactical balance. Still, this is not a simple case of overblown pathetic fallacy. Rather, Stephen is discovering the power of language as a means of escape from the systematic regimentation and physical dangers of athletics.

While less physically brutal than football, cricket was not devoid of patriotic rhetoric and martial indoctrination. In one sermon to students at Marlborough School, headmaster F. W. Farrar proclaimed in melodramatic fashion the preparatory and consolatory promise of playing cricket:

> Perhaps as you faint on the arid plains of India, perhaps as you toil in the dingy back streets of great cities, amid haunts of poverty and crime—may come the memory of sunny cricket grounds where once you played. Like a draught of clear water in the desert—like that sparkling cup which his warriors brought to David from the well which he had loved in boyhood—you will drink of the innocent delights of these schooldays. (qtd. in Mangan, *Games Ethic* 372)

To Farrar, cricket was a vital wellspring from which future officers and functionaries might draw hope to sustain the work of empire amid the toughest foreign conditions or against the most terrible odds. His allusion to the Old Testament battle of David and Goliath neatly interweaves military and religious impulses of the broader imperial project, while strategically recasting the representatives of the empire as underdogs in a deterministic struggle that depends on the individual fortitude acquired on the school cricket grounds.

Replete with such imperial connotations, cricket became a sign of British conquest in cultures as distant and diverse as India, South Africa, and the West Indies, where soldiers constructed grounds and taught natives how to play. The sport had made its way across the Irish Sea even earlier, in 1792. Its strong association with the army, viceregal court, and Anglo-Irish Ascendancy class led to its declining popularity by the founding of the Free State, but from the mid-nineteenth century at Clongowes, cricket inspired even greater interest than football. In 1849 Clongowes students first played the sport according to its official rules, though less organized games probably took place in earlier years. By the end of the century the school had developed a renowned cricket program on what W. P. Hove called the "most splendid ground in Ireland" (qtd. in Costello 117). During the 1880s the Clongowes side regularly defeated opposing clubs consisting entirely of adults.[11] A number of these were definitively military squads, such as the Curragh Brigade and Dublin Garrison clubs. Such triumphs no doubt held great meaning, and not just because of the age discrepancy of the competitors.

The significance of colonial subjects competing with soldiers at their own game would not have been lost on participants or spectators, Joyce among them. As Stanislaus records, his brother "still took an interest in the game when he was at Belvedere, and eagerly studied the feats of Ranji and Fry, Trumper and Spofforth" (61). Of those notables, Ranji, a star from India who set records playing for England, appears in the Museyroom of *Finnegans Wake*, appropriately within the context of nineteenth-century India's anticolonial insurgency.[12] Cricket is also referenced in a moment of potentially serious sectarian conflict in "An Encounter," when the silver badge of Mahony's cricket cap leads a group of children to misidentify him as Protestant (*D* 14). Like Stephen's experience of the cricket ground, these depictions also show how even the comparatively tranquil sport manifested military overtones similar to football's.

In this way readers exit Clongowes as they enter it, through a British garrison game. This framing of the opening chapter with sports conveys some of the earliest signs of a cultural discourse from which Stephen will devise his escape. The engirding athletic narrative reflects the new prominence of sport, especially in the nineteenth-century school, which stressed the link between individual physical fitness and national military preparedness.

The pairing of athletic and martial training follows Stephen into his adolescent years at Belvedere College as part of the "new and complex sensation" of his family's move to Dublin (*P* 67). Following the lead of Clongowes, Stonyhurst, and other elite schools, Belvedere enhanced its own sports facilities and curriculum in the final decades of the nineteenth century. Owing to its comparative spatial and financial constraints as a newer institution in an urban location, Belvedere could never match the expansive playing facilities of Clongowes. There was no space for field sports, but the school built a new gymnasium in 1883 and under the charge of a former army officer, Sergeant Major Wright, implemented a "physical culture program" that included muscle-building exercise with dumbbells, coordination drills with Indian clubs, and gymnastic routines on the parallel and horizontal bars (Sullivan 87). That program is very much on display in the Belvedere Whitsuntide pageant described in chapter 2 of *A Portrait*, in which Joyce includes the detail that the gymnastics team is led by a "plump bald sergeantmajor" who seems to typify the militant and hypocritical quality of the athletics program (*P* 73). This reflects a standard—and to many unconscionable—contemporary practice of employing former army officers as physical education teachers in British and Irish schools: "These ex-drill sergeants bellowed at young children in exactly the same way that they would have done on the barrack-square when drilling enlisted men. Consequently, many educationists felt that these drill sergeants were entirely the wrong kind of people to be delivering programmes to children" (Mangan and Ndee 74).

Originators and proponents of such programs saw them as a way to inculcate values of discipline and prepare many students mentally as well as physically for military service. The practice persisted well after the First World War, as critics voiced growing disapproval in newspaper editorials and larger publications. The 1926 pamphlet "Militarism in Our Educational Institutions" highlights such employment arrangements as the surreptitious militarization of schools: "There is no military instructor, but drill is conducted by the gymnastic instructor, an ex-army sergeant, and by masters who were officers during the war" (Smith 5).

Joyce's depiction of Belvedere echoes this same phenomenon of former military officers with new pedagogical responsibilities. Short of marching and drilling, Stephen and his classmates function under the indoctrinating pressures of a military-educational complex. The lack of fitness Joyce grants his fictionalized sergeant-major seems both a good-natured jab at his own former instructor and a broader criticism of a curricular hypocrisy that conjoins physical health with destructive hostility. The Whitsuntide pageant develops such contrast even further in a series of links between athletic and military details. Against the walls stand "companies of barbells and Indian clubs," while the gymnasts are said to resemble "a flock of geese," a covert allusion to the Irish soldiers serving in foreign armies who came to be called Wild Geese (*P* 73, 74). (Stephen will later deride his athlete friend Davin by calling him "one of the tame geese" for his aspirations to join the French Foreign Legion (*P* 159).) From his vantage point outside and apart, Stephen can make out the sounds of the pageant, which suggest his growing awareness of and distancing of himself from its cultural overtones. As if witnessing a collision of armies in the darkness, he hears the "brazen clashes of the soldiers' band" followed by "a noise like dwarf artillery . . . the clapping that greeted the entry of the dumbbell team on the stage" (*P* 75). It is little wonder the display of fortitude and combative associations triggers the recollection of a previous beating by classmates on Clonliffe Road.

As Stephen returns to the chapel, he hears—in terms that speak as much of moral emptiness as sonic resonance—the "hollow rattle" of dumbbells (*P* 74). The phrase provides a bridge to Stephen's recognition of Belvedere's growing investment in physical culture: "When the gymnasium had been opened he had heard another voice urging him to be strong and manly and healthy and when the movement towards national revival had begun to be felt in the college yet another voice had bidden him be true to his country and help to raise up her fallen language and tradition" (*P* 82). He acknowledges the sports movement as "yet another voice" of ideology or propaganda. Personal fitness is equated with national health, mimicking the call of imperial educators, military recruiters, and now Irish nationalists. In *Ulysses*, Bloom looks to emulate the early physical-culture guru Eugen Sandow as a means to self-improvement, but even such an individual aim, as will be discussed, was not without its nationalist and militarist overtones. For Stephen the related call of the new fitness culture merely blends with the discourse of fathers, teachers, and classmates into the "din of all these hollowsounding voices" (*P* 82). The description suggests the inability of these cultural, athletic, or paternal voices to move Stephen. Just as it did years before on the Clongowes football pitch, his position remains as ever one of passive evasion and intelligent resistance. In still another echo of athletic discourse, the verb "urging" circles back to the football ground where prefects "urged them on with strong cries" from the sideline (*P* 20).

The echoes carry forward into *Ulysses*'s "Nestor" episode, in which the adult Stephen Dedalus hears the students of Mr. Deasy's school preparing for the playground: "Hockeysticks *rattled* in the lumberroom: the *hollow* knock of a ball and calls from the field" (*U* 2.153–54; emphasis added). The repeated language of the gymnastics pageant suggests Stephen's continued disdain for the militarizing role of school athletics, not to mention his profound fears for this particular group of students.[13] The playground scene directly follows a history lesson on Pyrrhus and the battle of Asculum, thus likening the contact of hockey to that of ancient combat.[14] For Stephen, now as teacher and adult, the playing fields say more about historic destruction than about manly preparation:

> Shouts rang shrill from the boys' playfield and a whirring whistle.
> Again: a goal. I am among them, among their battling bodies in a medley, the joust of life. . . . Jousts. Time shocked rebounds, shock by shock. Jousts, slush and uproar of battles, the frozen deathspew of the slain, a shout of spearspikes baited with men's bloodied guts. (U 2.313–18)

Here sport elides with warfare, boyhood with manhood, as the present-day game dissolves into timeless imagery of the carnage of battle. In his temporary role as teacher, Stephen's youthful suspicion turns to prophetic reflection of the more devastating eventualities that flow from this association; as Robert Spoo observes, "Stephen's students are both hockey players and infantrymen, schoolboys and victims" ("Nestor" 145). To be sure, within a decade they would be of the right age to join Thomas Kettle and other British troops in the first advances of the Battle of the Somme.

The battlefield metaphor transcends cultures and historical epochs, in "Time shocked rebounds, shock by shock" (U 2.316). At the same time, vivid details of carnage allude to the warrior culture of medieval Britain as an enduring and influential discourse casting its violent shadow all the way to the modern schoolroom. Vincent Cheng, noting the alliterative patterns in the passage, argues effectively how the sound and sense of the description mimics that of Old English verse: "The entire passage attempts, and succeeds, precisely at evoking the sort of battle description which the harsh, guttural sounds and stresses of Anglo-Saxon poetry are most often associated with" ("Twining Stresses" 397). In this regard, the daily ritual of field hockey at Mr. Deasy's school bears a direct link to British warrior culture past and present.

As at Clongowes Wood, at Belvedere and the Dalkey school there emerges a discursive labyrinth linking athletics to armed conflict. All three institutions, with their direct links to muscular Christianity and military patriotism, reflect the colonial diffusion of the public-school games ethic in the educational curriculum. Nevertheless, the British garrison games represent only a fraction of the athletic culture of Victorian and Edwardian Ireland. As influential as they were on the cultural life of the country, they also found a militarized counterpart in the revival of sports as a nationalist cultural form.

Insurgent Athletics

If British imperial education and its colonial offshoots found sports a viable mechanism for producing able-bodied officers and infantry, they were not alone. The late-nineteenth-century revival of traditional sports in Ireland had both ideological and pragmatic purposes for the physical-force wing of Irish republicanism. Coming from within rather than without, it was as much a militarized cultural form as British garrison games were, and in many ways a direct response to them. Joyce's fiction reflects how nationalists exploited the cult of athleticism to advance their own military purpose. A strain of native athletic discourse runs through *A Portrait* and *Ulysses*, posing a challenge to Stephen's and Bloom's views of individual and national identity, and ultimately conveying Joyce's own response to the Gaelic Athletic Association ethos of racial purity and armed militancy.

The chief organizational vehicle behind the Irish sports revival was the Gaelic Athletic Association (GAA), launched in 1884, two years after Joyce's birth. The GAA was, in David Fitzpatrick's words, "the most overtly militarist" of all sporting clubs in the country (383). It advocated a return to ancient sports as a means for developing the physical capability and self-determination of the Irish people, in particular young boys and adolescents. At the core of the GAA ethos was a belief that young men could decide the future of the country through a revitalization of traditional games and a purification of the male mind and body on which rested the foundation for military action. If not overtly stated in the founding meeting at Thurles, the military connection nonetheless emerged in subsequent self-generated publicity of the organization, delivered primarily through the pages of cofounder Michael Cusack's short-lived but vocal newspaper, the *Celtic Times*.[15]

Hurling and Gaelic football reports in the *Celtic Times*, for their constant combat metaphors, read a lot like wartime propaganda pieces. For example, the account of a Gaelic match between Feach and Killiney in February 1887 likens the Killiney defensive strategy to a siege mentality: "The Killiney men after this guarded their citadel more closely and in trying to save it from the besieging Feach's forfeited many a point" ("Killiney v. Feach" 3). Such parallels between sporting ground and battlefield invoked, sometimes directly, other times implicitly, Ireland's legendary band of Fenian fighters, elevating even the most routine club matches into extraordinary, epic showdowns. To this end, game summaries were even interfused with heroic verse, as in the following couplet commending the parity of football competitors in a match that took place on the Phoenix Park polo ground: "That stern joy that warriors feel / In foemen worthy of their steel" ("Goldsmith").

GAA sports were depicted as having longstanding connections with ancient Gaelic martial culture, particularly the legendary heroes who first revealed their warrior prowess as boy hurlers. Indeed, in a GAA hurling column for *The United Irishman* newspaper, Cusack commences with an elusive statement as to the origins of the game: "I have been asked over and over again when the Hurling was first started in Ireland. I am unable to answer" ("Gaelic Athletic Association: Hurling"). Nevertheless, Cusack proceeds to answer the unanswerable question at length by tracing the sport's evolution from the ancient Tailtean games to the storytelling traditions of the Fenian Cycle. Documented evidence is less important in this regard than a belief in folk traditions that confidently locates the sport in "the days of Fionn and Oisin, and Oscar and Diarmuid O'Dubhne" while leaving no doubt as to the dual identity of the warrior-hurlers, and no question as to who reigns supreme: "Fionn, the Commander-in-Chief of the Fenian hosts, is believed by many to have been the greatest hurler of his time" (ibid.). The updated martial title for the leader of the Fianna reiterates the blatant parallel.

Similarly, in a chapter titled "The Military Athletes of Ancient Ireland" in *The Ethics of Boxing and Manly Sport* (1888), the Fenian writer John Boyle O'Reilly stressed the outgrowth of Gaelic sports from Irish training in arms, starting with the Fianna: "The militia of ancient Ireland is highly interesting in the history of athletics. Its members were tested athletes to a man, and their preparation and competition for enlistment were most arduous and remarkable" (189). This juxtaposition of Irish warfare and sport is reinforced by an immediately subsequent chapter on the history of hurling, which reminds readers how Fionn Mac Cumhaill and Cuchulain both trained at the sport as children (197–98). O'Reilly also includes an excerpt from the Ossianic tale "The Pursuit of Diarmaid and Grainne" describing an epic three-day hurling match. The translation of the tale wraps up with a noteworthy appeal to national unity and territorial supremacy as achieved through athletic prowess: "Now the whole of the Tuatha Dé Danann were all that time, without our knowledge, on either side of Loch Lein, and they understood that if we, the Fenians, were united (all) the men of Erin could not win the goal of us. And the council which the Tuatha Dé Danann took was to depart again and not play out that goal with us" (197). Many revivalists seized upon and amplified such connections, with an interest in using sport to raise national consciousness and numbers of fighting men.

Alongside their mythic associations, the territorial acquisition and defense strategies of Irish field sports were readily transferable to the notion of fighting for the soil of Ireland. In this way the Gaelic games mirrored the tactical value of soccer and rugby, even while their distinctive rules, equipment, and styles of play unequivocally proclaimed national independence. Their degree of original invention as opposed to geographic diffusion and innovation is still a matter of debate, especially in the case of Gaelic football.[16] Nevertheless, a strong native sports movement at least succeeded in shaping a public perception that the games were profoundly and authentically Irish. As with language, religion, or music, many counted on an independent tradition in sport to make national independence something of a foregone conclusion. Unlike those other cultural forms, Gaelic athletics were also considered a direct means to martial training and armed insurgency.

In this regard, the public discourse of the Gaelic games movement emphasized the same close association between masculine athleticism and warfare that had been exploited by British educationalists. Some Irish nationalist proponents of physical culture also made arguments for school fitness programs in the interests of national health and military development. In a 4 February 1904 column titled "Native Athletics in the Schools," the *United Irishman* newspaper urged the adoption of Irish sports as a solution to the same public-health crisis identified by British military and civilian authorities in the preceding decade in the vast number of unfit recruits for the Boer War. The *United Irishman* columnist blamed the problem on urbanization, a process characterized as practically synonymous with Anglicization: "As the rural people emigrate to the cities and vice versa, the defects of city life are propagated amongst those otherwise immune, and the all-round physique of a people deteriorates." With an increasing number of people moving between countryside and the crowded centers of Dublin and Belfast, cultural nationalists came to regard English urban and industrial development as threats to Irish health, most notably in the transition many people made from agricultural labor to more sedentary forms of urban employment. A bedrock of Gaelic games was seen as the best way to prevent any further erosion of a cultural identity that fused collective physical health and a strong work ethic with a tradition of military service: "The sports which have produced generation after generation of soldiers and hardy toilers have become a part of our heritage and a portion of our lives," and giving them up would, according to the columnist, "expose us to all the evils of modern decay."

Joyce's representations of the GAA in *A Portrait* and *Ulysses* challenge these sports-based notions of manliness and Irish identity. Read against the public persona of the traditional games movement as expressed in the nationalist press, his depictions of Irish athletic discourse reveal the hypocrisy of promoting a new national health through bellicose physicality. This paradox becomes evident in the final chapter of *A Portrait*, where hurling is linked to the military calling of Davin, Stephen's friend and classmate who epitomizes the GAA ethos: "Side by side with his memory of the deeds of prowess of his uncle Mat Davin, the athlete, the young peasant worshipped the sorrowful legend of Ireland" (*P* 158). Vincent Cheng considers Davin part of Joyce's general attempt to complicate the revivalist discourse concerning an authentic Ireland rooted in the rural peasant identity and at odds with the urban and cosmopolitan.[17]

A key component of that identity was the Gaelic sports movement, which Davin evokes on several levels. His very name recalls Maurice Davin, a cofounder and first president of the GAA, while his rabid appreciation for hurling in all its violent glory seems perfectly aligned with his future plans for a career in the French Foreign Legion (*P* 158–59). As he recalls the competition—"between Croke's Own Boys and the Fearless Thurles and by God, Stevie, that was the hard fight" (*P* 159)—Davin's language is a nearly perfect actualization of the Gaelic athletic movement; its vibrant idioms and excited syntax might have been lifted straight from Cusack's *Celtic Times* or another nationalist sports page. He gives an excited description of the violence of the game, in particular, a narrow escape from serious injury to his cousin by a brutally wielded hurley: "One of the Crokes made a woeful wipe at him one time with his camaun and I declare to God he was within an aim's ace of getting it at the side of the temple" (*P* 159–60).

At once well-molded GAA product and promoter, Davin evinces precisely the brand of hypermasculine athletic passion that Gaelic games proponents hoped to instill in young disciples.

For all Davin's excitement, however, it is difficult not to read this playing field–battlefield connection against the earlier scenes of Clongowes football, and in that juxtaposition find the implicit point that the GAA has replicated and maybe even surpassed the most militant aspects of the imperial games-playing machine. Irish sports have undeniably shaped Davin to such a degree that his "rude Firbolg mind" engages Stephen in a sort of mental hurling match, as it draws Stephen's mind "towards it and flung it back again ... by the force of its delight in rude bodily skill" (P 158). Furthermore, the fact that Davin "had sat at the feet of Michael Cusack, the Gael" (P 158) implies the sort of loyalty to the Gaelic sports movement that further emphasizes athletic parochialism to the detriment of individual intellect. Joyce depicts Davin as not only of an athletic bent but destined to follow in the Wild Geese military tradition. Presumably it won't be such a drastic change from that obsequious position beside the GAA founder to taking orders in the French army.[18] Either type of servility, regardless of its physical fortitude, seems the antithesis of the self-realization, intellectual liberty, or free artistic expression that Stephen regards as the truer sort of cultural independence.

Not all physical-force nationalists agreed that traditional sports offered a direct, fail-safe means to an armed campaign. Some even voiced concern that the Gaelic athletic movement, rather than being a training ground for armed action, could actually divert youthful energy from waging a successful fight. The games themselves could be divisive and distracting; rather than recruiting and exercising a national militia, sports might sap the strength of young men or, even worse, turn them against each other by fostering regional or local rivalries. Such a cautionary view of athletic militarism emanated particularly from northern Protestant and feminist voices within the nationalist movement who tended to be less inclined to go along with the Catholic iconography that often underlay GAA rhetoric.

One outlet for such a dissenting version of nationalism was Alice Milligan's Belfast-based magazine the *Shan Van Vocht*.[19] A May 1896 editorial voiced concerns that "the unbridled passions of players will inevitably develop into violence where the softening influences of a brotherhood do not exist among the contestants" ("Gaelic Athletes" 88). Too much emphasis on individual glory or regional team success, the author argued, threatened to undermine loftier goals of national liberation: "Should the National idea be not kept constantly before the minds of our young Gaelic men, the energy employed in the cultivation of Irish muscle may be diverted into unworthy channels, from which the fruits of this magnificent organization would spring up as rank weeds" (88–89). Instead of strengthening the physique and galvanizing the spirit, as so many hoped, it seemed the sports threatened to drain the vital energy of young Irishmen and divide the people in general against each other. To avoid such a predicament, the *Shan Van Vocht* writer concluded that football and hurling should maintain their place as sports but be distinguished from the republican military strategy, remaining for those who play them "trifling considerations compared with the cohesiveness and discipline of a great National force" (89).

The possibility that militant athleticism might ultimately prove a distraction rather than an aid to becoming a nation once again is underscored in *A Portrait* by the meandering form of Davin's account. As he sets out to tell Stephen about his seductive encounter with a mysterious peasant woman, Davin gets waylaid by the incidental details of the hurling match. Only at his friend's prompting does he come back to his original narrative thread. When at last he does, it still seems unclear whether the muscular Catholicism of the Gaelic athletics movement has not in fact shielded his eyes from the authentic version of Ireland the woman might represent. Indeed, her assertive sexuality is reminiscent of the early-Irish goddesses of territorial sovereignty.[20] Nonetheless, Davin remains puzzled and somewhat fearful of the woman's sexual invitation, rather than drawn to her emblematic significance. Probably more accustomed to chaste Kathleen ni Houlihan and other desexualized feminine icons of Catholic Irish nationalism, Davin shuns this carnal and Celtic archetype; his rejection of her advances amounts to a symbolic rejection of the early Irish earth goddess or Sovereignty figure, who, according to Proinsias Mac Cana, "symbolized not merely the soil and substance of territory, but also the spiritual and legal dominion" over it (94). Davin's traditional athletic fetishism becomes an obstruction rather than an opportunity for national communion and symbolic repossession.

A curious parallel emerges as well between the bare-breasted woman offering herself from the cottage doorway and the homoerotic—yet safely athletic—nudity of Davin's cousin, "stripped to his buff that day minding cool for the Limericks" (*P* 159). From his ideologically determined position as GAA disciple, Davin speaks comfortably about the hurling match but falters at the woman's transgressive desire and the alternative, sexualized notion of traditional Ireland it represents. In such a Catholic and nativist mentality, the close parallels of athletic prowess and military fortitude depend on a renunciation of sexualized cultural archetypes. In this regard, Davin's outlook contrasts sharply with Stephen's *non serviam* attitude toward athletics, religion, and national revival. His opposition is reiterated in his eventual abandonment of the hope to be with Emma Clery and voiced as well in terms that are antithetical, not to mention antagonistic, to athletic culture: "She could love some clean athlete who washed himself every morning to the waist and had black hair on his chest. Let her" (P 202). The strong physicality of sublimated sexuality hints at the muscular Catholicism of Davin and the GAA. In each case, the symbolic goal of national and/or sexual union is deferred rather than achieved through the culture of traditional athletics.

In this regard *Portrait* counters the "voice" of the Gaelic sports movement that Stephen heard previously at the Belvedere pageant. Moreover, the novel goes on to implicate that voice for its role in the increasing militarization of Irish nationalism through the Irish Republican Brotherhood (IRB) and its eventual larger offshoot, the Volunteers. The final reference to Davin in Stephen's journal conflates his Gaelic sports interests with clandestine planning for revolutionary violence: "3 April: Met Davin at the cigar shop opposite Findlater's church. He was in a black sweater and had a hurleystick. Asked me was it true I was going away and why. Told him the shortest way to Tara was *via* Holyhead" (P 216).

Davin remains associated with hurling but now in a decidedly urban and highly politicized location. The "cigar shop" is undoubtedly the one established by the Fenian veteran Thomas Clarke, who returned to Ireland in 1907 and opened a tobacco shop at 75A Great Britain (later Parnell) Street, on the corner directly across from Findlater's Church and just a block west of Belvedere College.[21] After a long forced exile for his role in republican violence, Clarke needed a way to earn a living and a dynamic social location for his continued involvement in physical-force politics; the tobacco shop offered both and "served as the public front for his subterranean activities" (Foy and Barton 3). The place became a kind of unofficial headquarters for the Supreme Council of the IRB, the chief architects of the Easter Rising. By the time of the Rising and publication of *A Portrait*, Clarke's tobacco shop had been a well-known meeting place of militant nationalists for nearly a decade.[22]

The tobacco shop is featured in *Stephen Hero* as a "circle" of the "separatist centre" and the place where Madden (the prototype for Davin) mixes paramilitary recruiting with nationalist sport: "Cooney's tobacco-shop where the members sat every evening in the 'Divan' talking Irish loudly and smoking churchwardens. To this circle Madden who was the captain of a club of hurley-players reported the muscular condition of the young irreconcilables under his charge" (*SH* 61). The presence of the hurley sticks in this symbolic and strategic location reinforces the core paradox of physical-force nationalism—that, like violent sport, it simultaneously promotes and endangers national health. Incidentally, Joyce's use of the term "hurley" instead of "hurling" would in and of itself have rankled the more ardent GAA members, since the term applies not just to the stick or *camaun* but to a modified, low-contact version of the sport from which Cusack and others sought a return to its warrior-game origins.

Stephen and Davin have thus chosen opposite ways to approach the same goal of restoring Irish sovereignty, one through constructive, imaginative art, the other through destructive physical violence. The nationalist athletic movement made some overtures to reconcile these contradictory impulses. In a May 1899 *United Irishman* column Cusack, writing under his Gaelic pseudonym Micèal, likens refined hurling skills to the compositional talents of Tolstoy. "Hurling: A Fine Art" includes tireless portrayals of virtually every aspect of the game, from on-field collisions to raucous crowds of spectators. But by the end of the article, Cusack's vivid descriptions achieve for hurling a more convincing affiliation with the martial than the literary arts. The resemblance is most apparent in a rather lengthy digression from an account of a match in Ossory, County Kilkenny, which tangentially relates how the village "is named after an English woman, the minions of whose sister conceived and carried out the infamous slaughter at Mullaghmast." In 1578 the British military in Ireland, collaborating with local landed gentry, had executed a number of prominent Gaelic chieftains and their families by luring them to a banquet in Mullaghmast, County Kildare. The elaborate ruse belonged to broader efforts by the Tudor government to expand the Pale of Settlement following the Kildare rebellion of the 1530s (Carey 305). Several hundred people were killed in what came to be called the Massacre at Mullaghmast. The not-so-implicit hope that well-trained hurlers can eventually avenge such historical atrocities on the same grounds reminds readers of what's at stake even in comparatively minor provincial matches. Even the influenza suffered by one player, "Citizen Foley," is denounced as a "prostrating foreign complaint," a new pathological euphemism for the old metaphor of the English occupiers as strangers in the house. The column concludes with a far less subtle, and decidedly nonartistic, pronouncement: "Get on the war path!"

In the North, F. P. Burke would adapt Cusack's metaphor when urging the boys of Belfast to join a new-formed hurling club, commencing his plea with a highly politicized challenge: "At a time when the Gaelic Athletic Association is being revived all over Ireland, will the young men of Belfast allow the present deplorable conditions of apathy and indifference towards purely national movements to continue?"; the answer, Burke contends, would have a great effect on "the position to be occupied by the youth of this city in the unceasing struggle between the Celt and the Saxon" (186). The unabashed military analogy kicks off a series of parallels stressing the connection of hurling with warfare across Irish history and pseudo-history, from celebrated past to turbulent present. This timeline includes the great hurling match supposedly played between the Firbolg and the Tuatha Dé Danann just prior to the battle of Magh Tuireadh in 1272 BC; hurling as the sole regimen of physical training for the Fenians ("the most famous body of athletes and warriors in Pagan Ireland"); and the United Irishmen Rising of 1798, which "showed that wielding the 'caman' was no mean practice for wielding the pike" (186). Burke concludes with a direct drill-sergeant command that his young readers "Fall into line immediately" and join the hurlers' ranks, or else risk failing the country by surrendering this form of "distinctive nationality" (186). For Burke as for many other nationalists, the boys were already a part of the struggle; their choice of recreation was more than a simple matter of how to spend idle hours.

The protagonist of *Stephen Hero* confronts such arguments when he engages Madden in a sarcastic Socratic dialogue:

—I suppose these hurley-matches and walking tours are preparations for the great event.
—There is more going on in Ireland at present than you are aware of.
—But what use are camàns?
—Well, you see, we want to raise the physique of the country. (*SH* 62)

For Madden as for most physical-force nationalists, the literal and symbolic, the individual and national bodies, become indistinguishable. Stephen's response adheres to the militarist truth he sees through the transparent veil of traditional athletics when he suggests Madden and his compatriots follow the more practical route of attending British militia camps, at government expense, to return home fully trained in weapons and drilling. In the GAA view typified by Madden, Irish sports not only fostered self-confidence and physical fitness, they provided the perfect cover for secret drilling of paramilitary forces. Under the guise of sport, large groups of boys and young men could assemble without suspicion for physical training and strategic planning. The GAA club system, organized across Ireland at the county level, provided as well an ideal recruitment pool for nationalist soldiers. A decade later, toward the height of the Volunteer movement, D. P. Moran's *Leader* newspaper twice "urged the starting of local companies, asking 'Why should not every Gaelic Athletic Club, for instance, turn out as Volunteers?'" (qtd. in Townshend 39).

Ulysses undercuts such militant republican expectations for hurling during the fourth parody segment of "Cyclops," where the overblown enumeration of revolutionary leaders, military commanders, and assorted characters includes "The Man in the Gap," a double entendre signifying both the goalkeeper in a hurling match and a strategic defensive position of combat infantry (*U* 12.186).[23] The equivocal nature of the term suggests how, on both symbolic and pragmatic levels, republicanism via the Gaelic sports movement articulated a pathway of physical force to Irish independence. As British authorities became aware of the strategy, Irish sports and even certain of their equipment—hurling sticks in particular—were outlawed by the police in many locations across Ireland.

The Irish sports ban in Phoenix Park becomes a specific topic of conversation in "Cyclops" when the drinkers recall that Dublin MP Joseph Patrick Nannetti is on his way to London to question the House of Commons about it. A brief exchange between Nannetti and George Wyndham, Chief Secretary for Ireland, was reprinted in the *Freeman's Journal* on 16 June 1904, suggesting the currency of the debate. Nannetti requests that the Sluagh na h-Eireann be permitted to practice Gaelic games in the Nine Acres, since polo matches are permitted there but, under police order, space for playing other sports remains restricted or unavailable, even on Sundays when the grounds are generally unused. Wyndham responds that, while some limited space has been set aside for polo and cricket, this has not been without some public protest; he does not name Gaelic sports outright but claims "other games" are generally disruptive and damaging to the grounds ("Public Rights").

In the shifting style of "Cyclops," the issue is relayed through pub-stool banter followed by a parody of parliamentary minutes that conflates the Gaelic sports question with the seemingly unrelated concerns of foot and mouth disease, English coercion policy, and police violence (*U* 12.858–79). The mock House of Commons debate culminates with a reference to the riot that occurred during a Land League anti-coercion rally in Mitchelstown, County Cork, in 1887. In setting up his defense of a police barracks, Lieutenant "Pasha" Plunkett of the Royal Irish Constabulary shouted to his men the infamous command "Don't hesitate to shoot" (*U* 12.877; Gifford 202). Consequently, two men were gunned down among the crowd of protestors. Joyce's juxtaposing the event with the deliberation on the native sports question at Westminster shows how civil discourse and civic violence are separated by the thinnest of margins.

This association of sports with constabulary violence has a more direct and contemporary resonance as well. About fourteen months prior to the publication of *Ulysses*, the period when Joyce was busily revising and expanding "Cyclops," the RIC again deployed deadly force against a civilian crowd, this time in the immediate context of Irish games. On Sunday, 21 November 1920, following a series of IRA attacks on British intelligence officers and policemen, RIC Black and Tan auxiliary forces opened fire during the All-Ireland football final at Croke Park. The attack killed twelve spectators and Tipperary captain Michael Hogan, and injured dozens of others in the crowd.[24]

Joyce's late revisions to "Cyclops" in 1920–21 include several references to police and military violence that fall in the midst of the sporting conversation. If not direct allusions to Bloody Sunday, these in the very least reflect the increased martial violence of the Irish War of Independence. Before submitting the *Ulysses* typescript to the printer in the late summer of 1921, as Michael Groden points out, Joyce made a number of changes to the version of the episode that had been published in the *Little Review* from November 1919 to March 1920.[25] These late changes include references in the public execution scene to "a posse of Dublin Metropolitan police" (*U* 12.534) and "big strong men, officers of the peace and genial giants of the royal Irish constabulary" (*U* 12.655–56), somewhat ironic descriptions, considering the casualties at Croke Park the previous autumn. These additions to "Cyclops" contribute to the amplification of its gigantism, as Groden describes. Moreover, they comprise a heightened paramilitary presence that aligns with the episode's prevalent discourse of Gaelic athletics and nationalist politics, mirroring the ideological clash that led to Bloody Sunday.

The fact that Croke Park had itself become a flashpoint for military-civilian violence lends a unique and local significance to a reading of "Cyclops." Constructed atop rubble carted from O'Connell Street after the Easter Rising, the stadium was as much a symbol of nationalism as the games played on its pitch. Joyce was well aware of the violent upheaval at home as he revised "Cyclops" and prepared to write the final episodes of *Ulysses*. In June of 1920 he wrote to Ezra Pound that "the disturbed state of Ireland" was reason enough not to carry out plans to return there to finish the novel (*L* 3:469). Its inclusion of police and paramilitary activities in opposition to a militant revival of traditional Irish athletics became one way of representing the profound cultural depth and breadth of that disturbance.

"Cyclops" elsewhere integrates, and ultimately equates, sporting feats with martial action. At the center of the episode is the Citizen, based of course on Davin's old mentor, GAA founder Michael Cusack. Cusack's earlier portrayal in *Stephen Hero* as a "very stout black-bearded citizen" (*SH* 61) presiding over Gaelic League meetings was direct and indicting as to his alignment of sports with nationalist violence: under his lofty supervision and encouragement, "bodies of young Gaels conflicted murderously in the Phoenix Park with whacking hurley-sticks, thrice armed in their just quarrel since their revolution had been blessed for them by the Anointed" (*SH* 62). In *Ulysses*, the critique of Cusack and his militant discourse evolves into a deflating parody of the Citizen and the GAA ethos in the sports discourse and mock violence at Barney Kiernan's.

Citizen Cusack, as he was known in the Gaelic athletics movement, develops here into a highly ironic personification of militant nationalism, primarily through a purposeful accumulation of falsified athletic and historical records. Cusack would have been fifty-seven in June 1904, and, perhaps owing to the years gone by, his athletic career is misremembered by Joe Hynes, who dubs him "champion of all Ireland at putting the sixteen pound shot" (*U* 12.881–82). As Gifford notes, the real champion and record holder for this event was not Michael Cusack but Denis Horgan (342). Cusack never won the all-Ireland but did in fact place first in the sixteen- and twenty-five-pound shot events at a Dublin Amateur Athletic Club competition (de Búrca 7). Whether an honest mistake or exaggerated flattery, Hynes's flawed fact occurs in the same breath as his equally erroneous claim that the Citizen was "The man that got away James Stephens" (*U* 12.881). Athletic prowess and militant nationalism are so closely associated in the public consciousness that legendary deeds in each category become misattributed to the same overblown personality by the barstool historians in Barney Kiernan's.

Such historical error needs a compliant audience if it is to become acknowledged as historical truth. These exaggerated triumphs are immediately perpetuated by Alf Bergan's eager questioning and Bloom's affirmative response: "Is that really a fact? . . . Yes . . . That's well known. Did you not know that?" (*U* 12.887–88). The Citizen's false modesty at a falsified accomplishment—"I was as good as the next fellow anyhow" (*U* 12.884–85)—is met with Hynes's validating and punning reply: "Put it there, citizen . . . You were and a bloody sight better" (*U* 12.886). A glorified, if distorted, recollection of sport is coupled with a disfiguring act of violence.

Beyond its inflated accomplishments, the Citizen's athletic resumé reveals the hypocrisy of his response to the questions of nationhood formulated in "Cyclops." For in competing at the shot put he in fact practices a militarized, Anglicized version of a traditional Irish and Scottish test of strength. The modern name of "shot put" for the ancient event in fact derives from munitions, a result of British Army athletes in the mid-nineteenth century substituting a sixteen-pound cannon shot for the traditional fourteen-pound fieldstone used in the Tailtean and Highland games. Hynes uses the term "putting the sixteen pound shot" (*U* 12.882), while the narrator refers to the event in its ancient Irish name as "putting the stone" (*U* 12.890). In its substitution of manufactured ordnance for pastoral equipment, putting the shot gave a British army spin to a traditional Irish pastime. British soldiers used the event for physical training, and in so-called friendly competitions and exhibitions before the Irish public it could serve as a clear reminder of the potent arsenal at their disposal. For instance, the sporting columns of the *Cork Examiner* for 30 May 1904 list "putting the shot" among the several featured athletic events during the annual training of the Tipperary Royal Garrison Artillery Militia ("Tipperary R.G.A."). This reequipping and renaming of the sport was emblematic of the British occupation in general.

In the politically charged athletic discourse of "Cyclops," the shot put speaks to a reality of cultural cross-pollination in athletics. Doing so, it begins the process of undermining the Citizen's cherished misconception of Irish sport as a pure, de-Anglicized cultural form. The word "shot" recurs in the parody of biblical prose that marks the final phrase of the episode: "like a shot off a shovel," eliding the Citizen's ballistic behavior with Bloom's heavenward ascendance (U 12.1918). In that closing passage, the *Little Review* inadvertently printed "short" in its serialized publication of the episode (ULR 60). Joyce corrected it to "shot" the following year in his first-edition typescript of the novel for Sylvia Beach, elucidating the parallel between the Citizen's athletic background and belligerent tendencies.[26]

The Citizen's athletic history reveals the inherent GAA problem of categorizing sports or other activities along strict racial and cultural lines. His own participation in the shot put suggests, if not a violation, then at least a compromise of Gaelic Athletic Association regulations which, besides advocacy of Irish games, featured a wholesale ban on non-native sports. Rule 42 forbade members from participating in association football (soccer), rugby, cricket, field hockey, and other "foreign games." Track and field athletics, including the shot put, were never specifically banned, nor were they encouraged. Still, categorizing (and excluding) sports based on national or cultural affiliation is no easy task. In this regard, the hybrid reality of athletics resembles music, language, and other dynamic attributes of national identity that accumulate across *Ulysses*. Like so many aspects of culture, sports are never as pure in origin as the Citizen or the GAA might imagine them to be.

This becomes apparent when one sets the athletic discourse of "Cyclops" in the context of the founding mission of the GAA. Central to the organization's focus on traditional Irish sports was its ban on foreign ones, which originated in the correspondence of Cusack and Archbishop Thomas Croke that became, for all intents and purposes, the constitution for the new governing body of Irish sport. Such exclusionist thinking was extended two decades later by the GAA with the passage of motions that excluded not just Irish athletes from foreign games but foreign athletes from Irish ones. Of special interest were members of the military and constabulary, who were banned from future participation in Gaelic football or hurling by the January 1903 GAA congress.[27]

Croke's letter to Cusack in December 1884 to accept the position of first patron to the GAA resonates with the divisive nationalist sporting ethos of "Cyclops." It offers a catalog of "manly exercises" that Croke encouraged for Irish athletes. The archbishop's enumerative distinction of Irish from foreign games, echoed in the sports talk at Barney Kiernan's, was adopted as a founding statement for the new organization:

> Ball-playing, hurling, football kicking, according to Irish rules, "casting," leaping in various ways, wrestling, handy-grips, top-pegging, leap-frog, rounders, tip-in-the-hat, and all such favourite exercises and amusements amongst men and boys, may now be said to be not only dead and buried, but in several localities to be entirely forgotten and unknown. And what have we got in their stead? We have got such foreign and fantastic field sports as lawn-tennis, polo, croquet, cricket, and the like—very excellent, I believe, and health-giving exercises in their way, still not racy of the soil, but rather alien, on the contrary, to it, as are, indeed, for the most part the men and women who first imported and still continue to patronise them. (qtd. in O'Hegarty 612)

Croke emphasized a strict Gaelic/foreign dichotomy of Irish sporting culture that became the foundation of Rule 42. Bloom's identified favorite, "lawn tennis," is notably first on the list of sports he discourages, and its favorable mention becomes a catalyst for the Citizen finally losing his temper.[28] Even so, the archbishop does concede a certain value to the sport later in his letter—"there is something rather pleasing to the eye in the 'get up' of a modern young man who, arrayed in light attire, with parti-coloured cap on and racket in hand, is making his way, with or without a companion, to the tennis ground"—though he makes it clear this is still a poor substitute for Irish pastimes (qtd. in O'Hegarty 612). Most notably, Dr. Croke's guidelines do not include the Citizen's preferred event, shot-putting, or even track and field events in general, an omission that recalls a fundamental difference between Croke and Michael Cusack in the early history of the GAA. From the start, Michael Cusack's vision for the GAA was as much anti-English as it was pro-Irish. He had been particularly interested in reviving track and field athletics in which he felt Irish athletes could be more competitive with their English counterparts. In the late 1870s he began to push for a revival of "what he called pure athletics" including the return of "weight and jumping events" in which he judged Irish competitors might excel against English opponents (de Búrca 8). According to Archbishop Croke's criteria, the Citizen's own claim to athletic fame risks being at least as "foreign and fantastic" as Bloom's preferred sport, and perhaps even less "racy of the soil."

The sports authorities at Barney Kiernan's reveal the internal fault lines and inevitable contradictions of a native athletics movement whose self-definition purported unequivocal categories of nation and race. In this context, the escalating tension between the Citizen and Bloom is framed by the cultural difference in the ensuing talk of "Irish sports and shoneen games" (*U* 12.889). The debate translates into real political stakes, underscored in the parody Gifford describes as "the minutes of a meeting written up as disguised advertisement of a social or political organization" (342). The organization in question is the same group backing the MP Nannetti in his questioning of the House of Commons about the ban on Irish sports in Phoenix Park; its name translates as Army of Ireland, reinforcing the identification of Gaelic sports with military drill. Archbishop Croke had recommended a public relations campaign for the GAA movement that would enlist the support of "national journals," and Joyce's parody captures the unmistakable style of elevated diction and biased reportage typical of cultural-nationalist publications: "A most interesting discussion took place in the ancient hall of *Brian O'Ciarnain*'s in *Sraid na Bretaine Bheag*, under the auspices of *Sluagh na h-Eireann*, on the revival of ancient Gaelic sports and the importance of physical culture, as understood in ancient Greece and ancient Rome and ancient Ireland, for the development of the race" (*U* 12.897–901). The alliance with the Gaelic League and Irish language movement is also apparent in the overblown representation of "the wellknown and highly respected worker in the cause of our old tongue, Mr Joseph M'Carthy Hynes" (*U* 12.907–8).

The rhetoric of Hynes's "eloquent appeal" echoes the familiar strains of like-minded advocates "for the resuscitation of the ancient Gaelic sports and pastimes" whose association with the "manly strength and prowess" of Finn MacCool and Fianna warrior culture are ostensibly reason enough for their revival (*U* 12.908–11). Meanwhile, Bloom's medical-scientific view of sports for individual wellness is all but written out of the journalistic account, in favor of the coded blend of heroic military tradition with sanctioned athletics that was a central tenet of physical-force nationalism. It also points to another contradiction. The Citizen has proclaimed himself a Sinn Fein man, but in this regard he mistakenly claims armed militancy for

Arthur Griffith's organization, which in fact supported civil disobedience above either constitutional reform or military action. The inconsistency extends with the Citizen's misappropriation of the Young Ireland ballad "*A Nation Once Again*, in the execution of which the veteran patriot champion may be said without fear of contradiction to have fairly excelled himself" (*U* 12.917–19). The real "fear of contradiction" appears to lie within the chauvinistic cultural views, not to mention the dubious athletic history of the "veteran patriot champion."[29]

Inaccurate as it may be, reference to the Citizen as All-Ireland champion at the shot put ultimately transmogrifies into his equally exaggerated act of throwing the biscuit tin at Bloom:

> Begob he drew his hand and made a swipe and let fly. Mercy of God the sun was in his eyes or he'd have left him for dead. Gob, he near sent it into the county Longford. The bloody nag took fright and the old mongrel after the car like bloody hell and all the populace shouting and laughing and the old tinbox clattering along the street. (*U* 12.1853–57)

In the Homeric architecture of the novel, the hateful gesture undoubtedly casts the former shot-putter in the role of Polyphemos hurling a boulder at the fleeing Odysseus and his crew.

Alongside its mythic and athletic echoes, the hurling of the Jacob's tin is also fraught with historical association, in that it nods to one of the more practical, if peculiar, details of the Easter Rising. As they mustered on Easter Monday, members of the Citizen Army and Irish Volunteers were issued homemade tin-can bombs. The rudimentary hand grenades were fashioned from milk cans and, in some cases, from Jacob's biscuit tins. These were abundantly available to members of Thomas MacDonagh's Third Battalion of Irish Volunteers who turned the immense biscuit factory on Bishop Street into their garrison headquarters. As Seamus Pounch, a member of the Third Battalion at Jacob's, recalled, "The weapons we had were mixed and represented every class of gun and revolver used by Volunteers; to this was added tin-can bombs to be used in case of a close attack from roof and windows on enemy troops" (11). Placed along the pavement surrounding the factory, Jacob's tins also served as a makeshift alarm system to alert the Irish Volunteers of a nighttime attack (Foy and Barton 92). Therefore, those occupying Jacob's were in fact constantly listening for the sound of an "old tinbox clattering along the street" (*U* 12.1857). Despite a perceived need for these precautions, things remained relatively quiet at the factory, owing both to its distance from the city center and to the sheer immensity of the complex, which isolated the garrison from the streets outside. Apart from a few minor skirmishes, the Third Battalion at Jacob's never saw action, and, as Charles Townshend remarks, most of its members "stayed in the biscuit-filled mausoleum for the rest of the week, waiting for an attack that never came" (181). Turning the familiar product and location into resources in the fight against British power in Ireland had, like the Rising itself, a certain symbolic resonance but minimal tactical impact.

In this regard, the presence of the Jacob's biscuit box in "Cyclops" embodies the futility of the Easter Rising and hypocrisy of a militarized nationalist politics. The last gesture of the one-man Citizen army conveys the futility of the homemade munitions and of the narrow-minded nationalist program that produced them. It is even more incongruous given the cultural background of Jacob's biscuits: W & R Jacob was just the sort of Irish-owned enterprise the Citizen would be prone to favor, given his discourse on native industry (*U* 12.1241–55).[30] The biscuit tin is further transfigured in the mock-journalistic account of Bloom's funeral to an ornate, Gaelicized symbol of wartime casualty: "a silver casket, tastefully executed in the style of ancient Celtic ornament, a work which reflects every credit on the makers, Messrs Jacob *agus* Jacob" (*U* 12.1823–25). Rural scenes and other traditional art on Jacob's boxes in fact made them not just consumer container but popular collectables in the period, prime examples of an early commodification of Irish identity. This conversion of consumer good to cultural artifact is undone by its refashioning as ordnance and, to even darker effect, its transition from armament to coffin.

The Citizen's hurl of the biscuit tin thus deflates revolutionary facts to a reductive absurdity. The action also extends his career in a sporting event not approved by the GAA administration of which he is a part, suggesting the confused, hypocritical tendencies of a movement whose own narrow vision turned the national athletic revival into a recruiting pool for the Volunteer movement. In this way "Cyclops" contextualizes the Easter Rising as one particularly pointless and bloody long-term result of the Gaelic games movement. There has been significant disagreement as to whether the GAA originated as a nonrevolutionary cultural-nationalist athletic organization or as an outgrowth of the physical-force nationalism led by the IRB.[31] Joyce's literary critique asserts a direct connection of sports with violent nationalism, which, if not wholly advocated by Cusack, was nevertheless set in motion by his revival of national athletic passions.

The link between the GAA and physical-force nationalism became clear early on, as the armed wing of the modern independence movement, the Irish Republican Brotherhood, made quick inroads into the athletic organization. Cronin has noted how from its "very first meeting the G.A.A. was infiltrated and, at various times, controlled by the forces of the I.R.B." (81). Three of the seven attendees of the inaugural convention were IRB notables: John Wyse Power, Joseph K. Bracken, and F. R. Moloney. Two years later, the Brotherhood further entrenched itself in the GAA when at the 1886 meeting in Thurles, several IRB men attained prominent positions on the Executive Council.

In opposition to such militarized athletic discourse in "Cyclops," Bloom extols a version of physical culture tied to inward corporeal health instead of competitive external struggle. His view of physical fitness aspires to the promotion of individual well-being rather than destructive self-sacrifice. Bloom is, after all, a man who owns a copy of Eugen Sandow's *Physical Strength and How to Obtain It*, even if he has only "intermittently practiced, subsequently abandoned" the book's regimen of exercises (*U* 17.512–13). "Ithaca" recalls something of the promotional copy for the Sandow exercise program, noting it was "designed particularly for commercial men engaged in sedentary occupations . . . to bring into play the various families of muscles and produce successively a pleasant rigidity, a more pleasant relaxation and the most pleasant repristination of juvenile agility" (*U* 17.514–18). Yet these "pleasant" commercial promises and their bourgeois context tend to obscure the contested reality of the physical-culture enterprise and its most famous proponent.

* * *

Eugen Sandow's upbringing and career demonstrated his own conflicted relationship with things military. He was born Friedrich Müller in 1867 in Königsberg, East Prussia, and his childhood coincided with the unification of Germany and the distinct martial tone of Bismarck's Prussification. One early exchange between the young Sandow and his father recounted in *Strength and How to Obtain It*—Bloom adds the word *Physical* to the title— revolves around the question of how the male body fits within the social and military goals of the modern state. During a visit to a Florentine art gallery, where Sandow "was struck with admiration for the finely developed forms of the sculptured figures of the athletes of old," his father emphasized how "these were the figures of men who lived when might was right, when men's own arms were their weapons, and often their lives depended on their physical strength" (Sandow 85, qtd. in Plock 116). His father's explanation distinguishes between physical fitness for personal aesthetic and for national defense.

For many Germans, such a distinction was of little or no consequence. Since the early nineteenth century, the German states had cultivated the physical fitness movement for military purposes. After a decisive defeat of German forces by Napoleon in 1812, a national system of gyms known as *Turnvereine* was established to improve young men's strength and conditioning for military service. Ironically, Sandow trained at one such facility before emigrating at the age of eighteen to avoid compulsory military service (Chapman 7). After some time in a circus and on the theatrical circuit, he came to London, where his performances played to the strong patriotic and military sensibilities of the time. One display of strength from Sandow's show at the Hippodrome in September 1900, titled "Tommy Atkins Supporting the British," had Sandow, decked out in Boer War khaki, acting as the human girder for a bridge crossed by cavalrymen, horses, and supplies, while an orchestra played "Rule Britannia" (Chapman 118–19). Vike Plock notes: "Like Bloom, who is stigmatized on grounds of his racial identity in 'Cyclops,' Sandow's Germanic background made him the target for verbal assaults from contemporaries" (115). This likely had something to do with the unbridled patriotic spectacle he provided audiences in his adopted country.

Such support went beyond performance and metaphor: Sandow became a consultant to the British Army on fitness issues and in 1914 received a lifetime Royal Warrant as instructor in physical culture. As R. B. Kershner describes, his commercial success resulted in large part from responding to a unique social climate: "Certainly Sandow as an individual was only one beneficiary of an overdetermined cultural complex in Edwardian Britain that associated physical fitness and strength with beauty, health, heroism, intelligence, progressivism, moral force, and even domestic virtue. He further benefited from *fin-de-siècle* British malaise and especially from the fear that the British race was in a process of physical degeneration that would leave them helpless before the Germans" ("World's Strongest" 682–83). Thus the German immigrant helped assuage the period's two major British anxieties of national physical decrepitude and inevitable German invasion.

Bloom's reading of Sandow of course emphasizes self-improvement rather than aggressive patriotism; the goal of physical exercise is to build oneself up, not cut others down. Like Stephen, he will not serve the ideologies of national efficiency or muscular Christianity. This demilitarized perspective is denounced by the "Cyclops" narrator, who derides Bloom for his opinion of sports as a means to self-improvement and individual well-being: "of course Bloom had to have his say too about if a fellow had a rower's heart violent exercise was bad" (*U* 12.891–93).[32] But Bloom's purely medical assessment of the topic has little to do with what his listeners want to hear. Therefore, when Alf Bergan rejoins the conversation, he appropriates Bloom's phrase to very different effect: "Talking about violent exercise, says Alf, were you at that Keogh-Bennett match?" (*U* 12.939–40). The conversation reverts to the baser function of sport in an even more highly politicized and nationalistic form, the symbolic warfare of a military-civilian prizefight.

The Pride of the Ring

By the end of "Cyclops," the cultural-nationalist affiliations of sports give way to the most belligerent and basic of athletic forms. It is finally through boxing, specifically the Keogh-Bennett fight parody, that Joyce makes the discourse degenerate, as patriotic pretense and nationalistic sentiment from both sides become subordinated to a larger militarizing tendency. The dynamics of boxing in *Ulysses* take on well-documented political, social, even biographical implications.[33] In the Keogh-Bennett match the competing discourses of Gaelic athletics and garrison games converge. Despite the privileged position of traditional Irish games in the conversation at Barney Kiernan's, boxing comes to dominate the barroom banter. It is not among the GAA-approved pastimes, and was noticeably absent from the list of sports in Archbishop Croke's acceptance letter, but amid the general obsession with fixed national and racial categories, boxing is a contested cultural form. In fact, if boxing had a national identity in the early twentieth century, it was decidedly a British one. Despite the multicultural origins of the sport, England had come to regulate prizefighting in the eighteenth and nineteenth centuries to such a degree that across much of Europe the sport was more precisely referred to as "English boxing."[34]

When Bergan alludes to the brutal outcome of the match, "Queensberry rules and all" (*U* 12.958), he recalls such British hegemony over the sport, suggesting an ideological sparring that goes above and beyond the pugilistic. This did not stop some advocates of Irish athletics from laying their own claim to the sport on moral and military grounds; it might even have been a major impetus for such claims, as mastering one's colonial master in the athletic arena could be taken as a portent of greater political and military triumphs. Discussed earlier for its back chapters on hurling and ancient military training, John Boyle O'Reilly's *The Ethics of Boxing and Manly Sport* (1888) is of course primarily a book arguing the merits of that sport with a rhetoric that constantly reveals its author's strong affinity for military life and physical-force nationalism.[35] Invariably O'Reilly's discussions of boxing yield to extended accounts of Irish achievements in the sport, as in a chapter focused on Dan Donnelly's December 1815 defeat of the English champion George Cooper at the Curragh. Given his background and readership, O'Reilly's argument for pugilistic training and overall physical fitness as essential to individual and national self-defense comes across as a slightly veiled call to Irish arms:

> It is of little importance, perhaps, whether or not a grown man can play cricket or row a boat; but it is of very great importance, no matter how cheap pistols or post-chaises may be, that, in case he were called on, for personal or patriotic duty, to swim or climb for a life, to fight for a child or a woman, to defend his country in the field, he should be ready with a strong body, a stout heart, and a trained hand and mind to raise him over difficulty and danger. (4)

If his tone is more overtly militaristic, O'Reilly's logic echoes the familiar Anglo-Irish sports dichotomy of Croke's GAA acceptance letter. Reflecting his army training and revolutionary politics, his criteria for the value of sport hinge on its direct application to military action or what he terms "personal or patriotic duty."

This was precisely what James Joyce disliked about the sport. Stanislaus recalls how, along with rugby and wrestling, Joyce detested "boxing... which he considered a training not in self-control, as the English pretend, but in violence and brutality"; he notes his brother included the account of the Keogh-Bennett match "not to express personal bias but to associate violence and brutality with patriotism" (62). From its very first reference, the Keogh-Bennett prizefight suggests antagonism and conflict, as Bloom learns that Blazes Boylan profited from a bet on the "boxingmatch Myler Keogh won again that soldier in the Portobello barracks" (*U* 8.801–2). Boylan's association with the fight is likely one reason Bloom might prefer to talk of lawn tennis or other sports than boxing (Ledden 630). The first sustained allusion to the Keogh-Bennett fight occurs in "Wandering Rocks," where it offers a brief study of the psychological and political ramifications of the bout. Passing a shop window, the newly orphaned son of Paddy Dignam spies an advertising poster for the fight featuring "the two puckers stripped to their pelts and putting up their props" (*U* 10.1131–32). Richard Brown suggests the young Dignam speaks in "his own Edwardian idiolect" (85); it is an idiolect clearly influenced by the idioms and alliteration of the sports page.

Young Dignam is the ideal audience for the poster and consumer of its ideology, as suggested by his instant mimicry of alliterative sports journalism. For a moment, he notices his own mourning reflection in double from the side mirrors that frame the milliner's window, a psychological duality that mirrors the poster of dueling fighters. But any prolonged introspection is avoided when his focus returns to the poster.

Like Davin's enthusiastic description of hurling, Dignam's response is one of transfixed fascination, as his monologue begins to alternate with the poster's promotional language, establishing public rhetoric in relation to individualized consciousness: "Myler Keogh, Dublin's pet lamb, will meet sergeantmajor Bennett, the Portobello bruiser, for a purse of fifty sovereigns. Gob, that'd be a good pucking match to see. Myler Keogh, that's the chap sparring out to him with the green sash. Two bar entrance, soldiers half price. I could easy do a bunk on ma" (*U* 10.1133–37). Young Dignam's reading of the poster previews the sports-column parody of the same fight that takes over in "Cyclops" (*U* 12.960–87). The seamless integration of mass media (advertising and newspaper) language and interior monologue suggests the dialogical intrusion of public sports discourse within individual consciousness. This discursive struggle, yet another duplication of the fighters on the poster, speaks further to the internal fractures of Dignam's life, most notably the loss of his father. Even the ticket rates ("Two bar entrance, soldiers half price") evince the two-tiered military-civilian reality of Dublin life. Meanwhile, the terms of the payout hint of the tension of imperial rule versus national self-determination, in that the men fight not for pounds but for "sovereigns."

When the Keogh-Bennett fight resurfaces in "Cyclops," its depiction expands on the notion of sports as surrogate ideological and national struggle. As in "Wandering Rocks," readers experience the pugilistic event on two levels, through barroom banter and then journalistic parody. This discursive division parallels the growing fractiousness between Bloom and the Citizen, about to erupt as physical hostilities. On the heels of bitter identity politics, the analogy of conflict effects an ironic realignment of nationalities, granting Bloom unquestionably Irish status as the lovable Myler Keogh while recasting the Citizen as the metonymic British military power of Percy Bennett, the antithesis of his Irish nationalist values. From its opening phrase, the sports-column description of the fight invites "historic" interpretation recalling the militarization of Anglo-Irish relations that in a little over a decade would explode into armed conflict:

> It was a historic and a hefty battle when Myler and Percy were scheduled to don the gloves for the purse of fifty sovereigns. Handicapped as he was by lack of poundage, Dublin's pet lamb made up for it by superlative skill in ringcraft. The final bout of fireworks was a gruelling for both champions. The welterweight sergeantmajor had tapped some lively claret in the previous mixup during which Keogh had been receivergeneral of rights and lefts, the artilleryman putting in some neat work on the pet's nose, and Myler came on looking groggy. (*U* 12.960–67).

The hyperbolic sports journalism, as much as the Anglo/Irish, military/civilian matchup, emphasizes the one-sided nature of the Easter Rising, in which British troop numbers and firepower greatly overbalanced those of the Irish Volunteers and Citizen Army. The pugilistic "fireworks" represent not only the metaphorical action of the match but the actual smoke and flames of Easter Week, including the pounding of British artillery on the General Post Office and other rebel posts as well as the widespread conflagrations that resulted from bullets and shells striking a chemicals warehouse and other flammable targets.

Joyce's late revision process for "Cyclops" shows his intensified focus on the militaristic metaphors of the boxing scene. In his final changes to the episode during 1920–21, Joyce expanded the Keogh-Bennett sports-column parody from 809 to 889 words. Among his significant additions were the series of monikers to emphasize Bennett's soldier identity: "welterweight sergeantmajor," "artilleryman," "soldier," "redcoat," "military man," "Battling Bennett," and "Portobello bruiser."[36] The last of these is a reference not just to the southside Dublin neighborhood but to the infamous barracks that shared its name. During the 1916 Easter Rising, Portobello became one of the primary detention centers for captured Irish rebels and anyone else deemed suspect or treasonous by British military authorities, including, as noted, Joyce's own friend Francis Sheehy Skeffington.

Along with such military details, the Keogh-Bennett fight parody alludes to the powerful and controversial spiritual symbolism that surrounded the Easter Rising. The blood-sacrifice theory of the 1916 rebellion considers how the planners exploited Catholic sentiments and iconography, convincing the national militias of the Christ-like act of laying down their lives for the cause.[37] While Easter Week offered Irish Volunteers and Citizen Army at least something of a tactical advantage to compensate for their inferior equipage, training, and numbers, the death-and-resurrection cycle of the holiday had a powerful significance from the start. The religious dogma of the Volunteer movement and the timing of its great event assured followers of the spiritual meaning of their actions and, if it came to it, their deaths. In this regard, the nickname of Myler Keogh, "Dublin's pet lamb," evokes the Christian view of Jesus as Lamb of God; the metaphor likens the Crucifixion to the animal sacrifices of Hebrew tradition, suggesting the prefiguring continuity of Old to New Testament that Bloom will profess in historical terms when he reminds the Citizen "Christ was a jew like me" (*U* 12.1808–09). The image of rebel blood-sacrifice comes through also in the colorful metaphor of Bennett having "tapped some lively claret"—that is, having made wine from the blood of Dublin's sacrificial lamb.

Joyce's proleptic literary revision of the Rising halts the bloodletting, however, by having the Keogh-Bennett outcome turn out to be the exact opposite of the crushing defeat of Easter 1916. From the narrow-minded perspective of the cheering mobs at the fight or the drinkers in Kiernan's pub, it offers a wishful instance of athletic victory as national triumph. In the broader framework of sports in Joyce, however, it represents the pinnacle in the militarization of Irish athletic culture. In the Keogh-Bennett fight, any cultural meaning of sports is reduced to a level of proxy warfare and nationalist fervor. Its caricature of national identities and armed struggle presents Joyce's indictment of patriotic militarism for its hijacking of athletic discourse. By incorporating the most militant of sports in a match of army/civilian and British/Irish affiliations, Joyce illuminates the role of boxing as a militarizing cultural form.

The Keogh-Bennett segment thus offers strong criticism of the violent direction in which the nationalist sports movement was headed in 1904—or, in Joyce's backward glance from 1919–21, where it had arrived. It is a mirror for the questions of physical force and pacifism that confront Bloom and the Citizen.

More than the incidental contact of hurling or football, the direct blows of boxing are the closest thing to military action that sports can provide. Yet one cannot escape the fact that boxing, Queensberry rules and all, is at least for those in Barney Kiernan's still very much a justification of bodily pain and sacrifice, for the alleged purposes of national progress or self-improvement. Keogh-Bennett is, in the end, less about the national affiliations of the competitors than about the evolving cultural identity of the sport itself. At stake is not just whether David can defeat Goliath, or a Dublin civilian beat a British soldier, but whether Irish cultural autonomy realized through sporting pastimes will pursue a militarized or a peaceful course. The fact that boxing supplants the Irish athletic interests proclaimed so vehemently in Barney Kiernan's suggests that, even if Myler Keogh wins the battle, the ideology of boxing has won the greater war to dictate cultural forms. If athletes and spectators trade in Irish sports and shoneen games for the regulated violence of boxing, they succumb not only to a colonizing cultural activity but to a military mindset poised to overtake sports and recreation as well.

This function of games as surrogate combat or vicarious warfare shows blatant disregard for one of the fundamental nursery lessons of *Finnegans Wake*: "Since alls war that end war let sports be leisure and bring and buy fair. Ah ah athclete, blest your bally bathfeet! Towntoquest, fortorest, the hour that hies is hurley" (*FW* 279.5–9). The elision of a Shakespearean title and American presidential speech conflates the comedy of the Elizabethan stage with the tragedy of another kind of more recent and deadly European theater, famously described as "the war to end all wars."[38] The playing fields of public schools and the revival of national sports that marked the buildup to the wars in Europe and Ireland had, as Joyce shows in *A Portrait* and *Ulysses*, been characterized by an inability to simply "let sports be leisure." Joyce's rhyme suggests how this potent threat might finally be countered through the cultural integration represented in the embracing linguistics of the *Wake*.

The overlap of apparently disparate cultural fragments resounds in the mock athletic cheer ("Ah ah athclete, blest your bally bathfeet!") conjoining a child's Irish language primer with Anglo-Saxon alliterative verse. Along with the merger of languages comes a fusion of geographical references—the Irish name for Dublin, *Baile atha Cliath*, and the English (formerly Roman) city of Bath—that imbues athletics with a heightened sense of historical fluidity and universality. This cosmopolitan vision of sports is vastly different from the muscular Catholicism espoused by Davin or the "clean athlete" Stephen imagines will marry Emma Clery (*P* 202). The idea of athletics as a potential unifier of nations persists in a conflation of English and Irish pastimes: the phrase "the hour that hies is hurley" combines the primary equipment of hurling with a loose, alliterative echo of a term from cricket. (In *A Portrait* the boys are "practising long shies and bowling lobs and slow twisters" (*P* 62) at Clongowes cricket ground). Like Shem and Shaun, the warring factions might possibly be moved to a provisional peace through an evolving patchwork of shared linguistic, geographic, and cultural forms, sports not the least among them.

Postscript: Croke Park, 2007

Ireland has perhaps at last attained at least a kind of tentative, fraternal accord between its divided athletic traditions. The notion of sports as a militant cultural activity can seem outmoded or counterintuitive at the beginning of the twenty-first century, an era when such global athletic marketing powers as the International Olympic Committee or FIFA promote sports as peaceful cross-cultural engagement. While cultural allegiances and class differences still guide regional sports participation and affiliation, a once-strict segregation of British and Irish athletics appears to be on the wane. With its 2005 repeal of Rule 42, the Gaelic Athletic Association finally lifted its ban on "foreign" games, permitting international rugby and soccer competition on the hallowed nationalist ground of Croke Park. In Celtic Tiger fashion, it was a change propelled more by economics than ideology: the south Dublin stadium at Lansdowne Road was slated for a massive renovation, and the GAA venue offered the only alternative for Dublin to host an upcoming international rugby tournament. Nevertheless, it presented an opportunity for Irish athletics to break with a rigid and divisive past.

In February 2007, Ireland played England before a sold-out crowd in Croke Park as part of the Six Nations tournament. It was the preliminary program as much as the match itself that raised concerns. The singing of "God Save the Queen" for the first time in the GAA ground caused tense anticipation and some angry reaction. Some die-hard Associaton members and Gaelic sports followers planned game-day protests outside the stadium. One of them, former all-Ireland footballer J. J. Barrett, removed his and his father's medals from the GAA museum, saying he could not "reconcile the provocative words of 'God Save the Queen' being sung in the very stadium where Michael Hogan and others died at the hands of crown forces on Bloody Sunday" (Berlin); Barrett did not comment on the fact that the Irish national anthem contains its own share of fighting words, including a closing reference to the "Saxon foe."

In the end, both "God Save the Queen" and the match were played without incident and with a generally warm reception from the opposing players and fans. (It probably helped that Ireland won by a score of 43–13.) More than one commentator regarded the event as ushering in a new era in the politics of sport in Ireland. The discovery of common athletic ground between former territorial enemies extended to one more area of popular culture the process of demilitarization that had begun to unfold in Ireland with the 1998 Good Friday Accord. If not an outright end to history or conflict, a garrison game played on Gaelic sod signified at last the chance to envision for Ireland, as did Joyce, a way to let sports be leisure.

3

Gorescarred Books

> Culture is a sort of theater where various political and ideological causes engage one another. Far from being a placid realm of Apollonian gentility, culture can even be a battleground on which causes expose themselves to the light of day and contend with one another.
>
> Edward Said, *Culture and Imperialism*

At the start of *Ulysses*'s "Nestor" episode, Stephen leads the students of Mr. Deasy's school through their ancient history lesson. The topical focus on this presumably typical morning is not the Golden Age of Pericles or the splendor that was Rome but the narrow and costly triumph of King Pyrrhus over Roman forces at Asculum, a syllabus selection that emphasizes the enormous price of war, even for its winners. After all, it represents the advent of the term "Pyrrhic victory." Moreover, this portrait of the schoolroom emphasizes the interrogative pedagogy and textual authority that were typical of the day:

—I forget the place, sir. 279 B.C.
—Asculum, Stephen said, glancing at the name and date in the gorescarred book.
—Yes, sir. And he said: *Another victory like that and we are done for.*
 That phrase the world had remembered. A dull ease of the mind.
(*U* 2.11–15)

While Stephen, reluctant teacher, teases out the answers from the pupils with his own halfhearted look at the book, the stupefying classroom drill gives over to a transhistorical vision. The image of teacher quizzing students transmogrifies into that of field commander interrogating subordinates: "From a hill above a corpsestrewn plain a general speaking to his officers, leaned upon his spear. Any general to any officers. They lend ear" (*U* 2.16–17). Indeed, in the clipped cadences of the question-answer format, in the students' constant repetition of "sir" after each response, the classroom discourse resembles a martial interview. Even student surnames like Armstrong and Sargent help complete the segue from modern schoolroom to ancient battlefield. There emerges a perspective not typically realized through the stultifying pedagogical procedures of rote memorization and authoritative interrogation. At the very least, it reflects Stephen's conflicted attitude about serving an educational system primarily geared to transforming young boys into future soldiers. As Declan Kiberd notes, "The boys from such a colonial school could hope for nothing more—either military/naval service, or becoming apprentice Yoricks, fellows of infinite jest, at the London court" (58).

The famously proleptic development of *Ulysses*—written during and after the Great War but set in the previous decade—anticipates the paradox by which Paul Fussell famously defines post–World War I literature: "Every war is ironic because every war is worse than expected.... Irony is the attendant of hope, and the fuel of hope is innocence. One reason the Great War was more ironic than any other is that its beginning was more innocent" (7, 18). Innocence, hope, and irony abound in "Nestor" as the episode takes its shape at the nexus of schoolroom order and historical chaos.

Joyce's composition of the episode during the peak of the fighting in Europe underscores this juxtaposition, since as James Fairhall notes, "Corpsestrewn plains and Pyrrhic victories, in 1917, were topical subjects" (165).[1] Schoolboys are made to reflect upon the facts of ancient battles as they are groomed for future ones known only too well to *Ulysses*'s author and first readers: "The teaching of Roman history, along with the practice of field sports, had fed a cult of manly prowess designed to counteract the enfeebling acts of the prolonged peace before 1914. But Joyce, writing this episode in Locarno in 1917, knew what the 'back kick' of aerial bombardment could wreak" (Kiberd 59). As Europe awoke from its historical nightmare, the early days of the century must have seemed all the more halcyon and remote in hindsight. Stephen seems eager for the students to escape at least from history as schoolroom subject, even if he knows none of them can escape from history as the confines of human experience. His Blakean vision of history's end—"the ruin of all space, shattered glass and toppling masonry, and time one final livid flame" (*U* 2.9–10)—suggests as well the apocalyptic potential of the modern weaponry unleashed in the new century.

For their part, the students voice a preference for a fanciful tale from

Stephen rather than a deadening account of military history. But instead of the entertaining ghost story they desire, they are treated to Stephen's baffling riddle of the fox, which, according to Spoo, suggests the act of writing amid the episode's broader tension of art and history (*Language* 95). The puzzle seems to offer a welcome respite and refuge from the marching boots of history, creative pause in a curriculum geared more to indoctrination than to introspection. Nevertheless, in a few moments the boys will take to the hockey field to simulate the decisive, irreversible action of the battlefield. Their school regimen, like their historical fate, seems ineluctable and imposed.

The complications of history and pedagogy are grounded in Joyce's re-visioning of the Homeric roles that undergird the episode. In the third book of *The Odyssey*, the visit to Nestor concerns a youth who seeks a direct, unadulterated historical truth from his elders. Telemakhos journeys to the mainland in search of accurate and reliable news of his father; the lord of Pylos tells him all he knows about the siege of Troy and the Akhaian homecoming, and all he has heard since, noting he has "no reason to keep it from you" (Homer III.198). For additional information, Nestor advises a visit to Menelaos, promising the Spartan king "will tell you history and no lies" (Homer III.354). Joyce's revision complicates this idea of history as credible, received knowledge from a trusted source, since Mr. Deasy tells Stephen little history and plenty of lies. Stephen, in turn, perpetuates the authoritative discourse of school text and classroom, even while he acknowledges the powerless situation of his students as akin to the historical experience of colonial Ireland: "For them too history was a tale like any other too often heard, their land a pawnshop" (*U* 2.46–47). The moment reveals "Stephen's remorse of conscience . . . as a teacher of history . . . forced to conspire with the very nightmare he so dreads" (Spoo, *Language* 90). It is no surprise that his days at the Dalkey school are numbered, as even the narrow-minded, gaiter-clad headmaster is quick to acknowledge. In the brief episode, Stephen plays first old Nestor and then young Telemakhos. Each is a flawed version of its original, particularly when Stephen's uncertain classroom authority is supplanted by the more self-assured but less trustworthy Deasy.

Yet, notwithstanding these powerful, changing roles, the ultimate focus of the educational process is not so much on pedagogical as textual authority, in the form of the unnamed book of classical history. Even as—or possibly because—the "gorescarred book" lacks a title and identity, it exerts a power over teacher and students alike. In keeping with Stephen's unspecified transhistorical vision, the tattered text is more than a simple record of facts. A symbolic embodiment of human history, it functions as a kind of universal sign-book whose description is at once metaphysical reminder and physical proof of history as a turbulent, unending process of armed struggle.

The potency of the classroom portrayed in "Nestor" stems at least in part from the way in which youthful innocence is already threatened by violent ideology. In this sense, it exemplifies Fussell's notion of lost innocence as something of a foregone conclusion in the educational system of the prewar decade. At Mr. Deasy's school, and presumably many others like it, the generation that would in the next decade experience the terrible beauty of Easter 1916 and the unprecedented casualties of the Somme is being prepped for military conflict by learning to see history as a glorified fusion of battlefield and book. Spoo (*Language* 93) goes so far as to suggest that the history text is likely one of the catechistic primers Stephen studied at Clongowes—Richmal Mangnall's *Questions* or the Peter Parley books. This seems possible, in light of the similarly rigid pedagogy; yet, given Joyce's omission of the title, the precise identity of the book seems altogether less significant than its function as sympathetic reminder of the wounds of conflict its pages describe.

What is certain is how the students at the Dalkey school are being indoctrinated into rote procedure and imitative gesture, rather than critical questioning or creative ingenuity. The school curriculum treats them not as emerging citizens but as future soldiers, doomed to absorb and repeat the nightmarish violence of history. They will take their unthinking roles in the human historical cycle that is symbolized in Armstrong's home address, "Vico road, Dalkey" (*U* 2.25), rather than understand its destructive pattern and steer their future away from its danger.[2] In this sense, Stephen's pupils function as mere repositories for a dominant European narrative of history as conflict. Intellectual potential, enlisted in the service of armed struggle, is reduced to a type of submissive mimicry.

For this reason, the history lesson triggers Stephen's recollection of the library of Saint Genevieve, in Paris, where "By his elbow a delicate Siamese conned a handbook of strategy" (*U* 2.70–71). The mysterious figure represents an exchange of tactical military knowledge that, as a product of Far East colonization, was well under way by the early twentieth century. European imperial designs in East Asia suggest the "delicate Siamese" might be an official visitor, or else a double agent, sent to glean the technical and tactical knowledge of the West. After quietly recording his data, the Asian scholar will presumably return home to bolster imperialist ambitions or support insurgent nationalism. Whichever the case, his ambiguous intellectual labors appear to serve the transnational military ambitions shaping the new century. The "handbook of strategy" resurfaces in *Finnegans Wake* as one of the many military relics described by "janitrix" Kate on the Museyroom tour: "This is the jinnies with their legahorns feinting to read in their handmade's book of stralegy while making their war undisides the Willingdone" (*FW* 8.31–33). The revitalized volume conjoins modern science and history of warfare with ancient belief in traditional astrology, effectively underscoring their shared origin. In this dissemination of knowledge, the reading material in HCE's back-garden privy extends the rote scribal activity of the Paris library and the Dalkey classroom.

At Mr. Deasy's school, the notion of mimicry is particularly evident in the case of young pupil Sargent timidly rewriting mathematical sums in his copybook. His prophetic name suggests the inevitable march to the trenches that he and many of his classmates would make in the ensuing decade. As Sebastian Knowles suggests, "in an episode filled with gorescarred books, military debacles, and schoolboy battles, Sargent's name foreshadows the death of these children ten years later" (7). At the same time, he functions as a counterpart to Stephen in *A Portrait*, practicing his own act of resistance by writing on the flyleaf of his geography primer. In contrast to Stephen's bold literary declaration of independence and self-awareness, however, the aptly named Sargent simply follows the orders of his superior, writing what has already been written. Like those of the feeble transcriber in the Paris library or Kate in the Museyroom, Sargent's role is one of receiving and replicating information, rather than generating or synthesizing. The copybook and the act of copying are themselves duplicated several times in quick succession, as the pupil explains:

— ... Mr. Deasy said I was to copy them off the board, sir.
—Can you do them yourself? Stephen asked.
—No, sir. (*U* 2.135–38)

The exchange, resembling that of any general to any officer, reveals the shortcomings of an educational curriculum based in uncritical obedience to cultural memory and chain of command. Clearly the pedagogical emphasis is on following orders rather than learning to think for oneself. It clashes greatly with what we know of Stephen's sense of the educated mind as one that aspires to creativity, originality, and a politics of *non serviam*.

To be sure, the militarized schoolroom is not without its certain small acts of resistance. Moments before, another student, Armstrong, steers the lesson away from the ancient battle by sonic association: "Pyrrhus, sir? Pyrrhus, a pier" (*U* 2.26). Notwithstanding his curiously martial surname, Armstrong suggests humanity at its most vulnerable, as the delicate crumbs of figroll adhering to "the tissue of his lips" sweetening his "boy's breath" constitute a portrait of youthful frailty and filial tenderness (*U* 2.24). At the same time, that he comes from a well-to-do family with an older son serving in the British navy (*U* 2.24–25) suggests the high social regard for a military career and a possible destiny for this sensitive schoolboy.[3] The phonic transfiguration of the ancient general with the Kingstown breakwater suggests at least the sort of imaginative flight to safety through language with which Stephen can identify. Whether naïve or intentional, the inherent humor and creativity of the diversion spare the class from more of the same tedious lesson. By extension, one wonders if these playful schoolboys might perhaps be saved from joining in history's inevitable march to the battlefield. Soon after, the "hollow knock of a ball" calling them to hockey practice suggests otherwise (*U* 2.154).

At the same time, the sympathetic depiction of frail Armstrong conveys its own passive resistance to the militarization of youth. Armstrong's response—whether a well-intended effort or a calculated ruse—draws an outburst of "Mirthless high malicious laughter" (*U* 2.27) that Stephen takes as proof against naïveté. Already it seems these boys have become not just indoctrinated subjects but complicit agents in the sordid ways of the world: "Yes. They knew: had never learned nor ever been innocent" (*U* 2.35–36). It seems virtually impossible to shield them from the brutal facts of history. They are uneducated minds, yet experienced actors, a negation of both sides of the Blakean binary of innocence/experience.

* * *

A progression of gorescarred books wends its way through Joyce's portraits of childhood and adolescence, indicating how a code of militarized masculinity had come to dominate Irish education and juvenile reading at the turn of the twentieth century. From sanctioned schoolbooks to sensationalist periodicals to canonical literature, these intertexts are an interpellating force in the lives of adolescent readers. For all their diversity of genres, authors, and contexts, they contribute to a uniform message of martial culture and masculine identity realized through reading practices of childhood and adolescence.

Reading was both a highly encouraged and a heavily monitored activity for boys growing up in the late nineteenth century. Its depictions of adolescent life, attitudes, and ideals contributed in almost a single generation to a new sense of identity attached to the years between childhood and adulthood. Novels and stories by writers such as Captain Marryat, Thomas Hughes, and Rudyard Kipling helped to pioneer tales for and about adolescence. Readily affordable juvenile periodicals rose rapidly to prominence, reaching even greater numbers of readers. In their study *Juvenile Literature and British Society, 1850–1950*, Charles Ferrall and Anna Jackson argue that the emergence of "juvenile" literature in the late 1850s was essential for the invention of adolescence during the Victorian period (5). Juvenile literature, mainly in its two major genres of school stories and adventure stories, played a strong role in disseminating English public-school ideals to the masses of middle- and working-class readers. As the definitive intellectual pastime for youth culture, reading served as an outlet for imaginative recreation and as an index of social competition.

Juvenile books and magazines reflected the shifting social and political climate of Victorian Britain and Ireland. This was particularly the case in the decade leading up to the Great War, when topics and content saw a broad shift from religious virtues to nationalist overtones. As Ferrall and Jackson remark, "just as muscular Christianity reacted against an infantilizing and emasculating evangelical piety, so the succeeding generation of imperialists and nationalists rejected muscular Christianity" (10–11). Prior ideals of childhood morality made way for manly stories of action and self-sacrifice, from the school playground to the overseas adventure. In his introduction to *Imperialism and Juvenile Literature*, Jeffrey Richards observes in British children's fiction of the period "an active agency constructing and perpetuating a view of the world in which British imperialism was an integral part of the cultural and psychological formation of each new generation of readers" and notes a particular shift to "aggressive militarism" in the popular boys' fiction of the late nineteenth century (3, 5). Joyce remarks and responds to this shift, relating its effects on the formative experiences of reading and school education in his fictional portrayals of boyhood and adolescence.

More than a decade before his depiction of Mr. Deasy's schoolroom, Joyce focused on the indoctrination of adolescent males by schoolbooks and popular texts. In the boyhood stories of *Dubliners*, acts of reading frame questions of pedagogical authority and social control. The potent influence of reading is evident through a concert of allusions—to magazine stories, classical history books, and nineteenth-century canonical literature. *A Portrait of the Artist as a Young Man* explores the interrelation of armed imperialism and colonial education, mainly through Irish students' reading of British and American textbooks. Stephen's schoolbooks demonstrate the intrusion of militarist discourse into the contested space of the young colonial mind. These indoctrinating intertexts assert the influence of militarism in boys' lives as popular discourse and curricular ideology; its incursion on the intellectual terrain of young subjects-in-formation reflects a comprehensive cultural strategy of the modern war machine.

Britain's Wild West

The indoctrinating influence of juvenile reading is apparent in the childhood stories of *Dubliners* through a series of intertexts. When old Cotter remarks in "The Sisters" on the potentially deleterious influence of the late Father Flynn, he emphasizes the pliant susceptibility of youth: "It's bad for children . . . because their minds are so impressionable. When children see things like that, you know, it has an effect. . . ." (*D* 3). Whether for censorious morality or simple lack of words, he stops short of revealing the nature of that effect; it is left to the narrator and the reader to draw their own conclusions from Joyce's ellipsis. Himself pondering the significance of Cotter's cryptic remark, the narrator expresses what might well be the mindset of the reader: "I puzzled my head to extract meaning from his unfinished sentences" (*D* 11). The exchange is prologue to questions of discursive adult authority and adolescent identity. It suggests that reading and interpretation are already major activities of the boy's developing intellect. The ensuing stories of childhood incorporate canonical literature and sensationalist periodicals as these engage with malleable young minds. Suffused with martial masculinities, these popular intertexts represent an influence that becomes as morally dubious as the adult authorities of home and school.

Allusion to a trinity of boys' papers in the opening lines of "An Encounter" establishes the initial literary touchstone and creative inspiration for Joe Dillon's gang, not to mention countless readers of the time. Even more than the paternal figures at each end of the story, Father Butler and the old josser, these framing textual authorities serve as the boys' most potent influences. Launched in 1893–94 by the brothers Alfred and Harold Harmsworth, the *Union Jack*, *Pluck*, and the *Halfpenny Marvel* featured tales of detection, warfare, exploration, and adventure targeting an adolescent male readership. With a significantly lower price, the new Harmsworth boys' weeklies purported to have a higher moral standing than such predecessors and competitors as the *Boy's Own Paper* and *Chums*. In a memoir of working-class London, Frederick Willis recalls the Harmsworth halfpenny papers specifically for their affordability, since "It was a great social step from a halfpenny to a penny" (qtd. in Springhall 108).

The new publications claimed to provide a healthy moral alternative to the suspect content of current boys' papers, known as penny dreadfuls. The editor's preface to the first issue of the *Halfpenny Marvel* therefore touted its superiority to such publications:

> The police-court reports in the newspapers are alone sufficient proof of the harm done by the "penny dreadfuls." It is almost a daily occurence with magistrates to have before them boys who, having read a number of "dreadfuls," followed the examples set forth in such publications, robbed their employers, bought revolvers with the proceeds, and finished by running away from home, and installing themselves in the back streets as "highwaymen." This and many other evils the "penny dreadful" is responsible for. It makes thieves of the coming generation, and so helps fill our gaols. Parents, if you see your children reading "penny dreadfuls," take them away and give them the "HALF-PENNY MARVEL" LIBRARY books instead. (qtd. in Springhall 111)

Apart from the price, however, Harmsworth's new publications differed little from the twice-the-price competitors they hoped to supplant. As A. A. Milne noted, "Harmsworth killed the 'penny dreadful' by the simple process of producing the ha'penny dreadfuller" (qtd. in Carpenter 53).

The basic format for each weekly issue was one complete story of around 20,000 words, set in two or three columns across thirteen to sixteen book-sized pages. Front-page promotional copy for early numbers of both *Pluck* and the *Halfpenny Marvel* billed them as "A High-class Weekly Library of Adventures at Home and Abroad, on Land and Sea," a slogan echoed in the narrator's assertion in "An Encounter" that "real adventures ... do not happen to people who remain at home: they must be sought abroad" (*D* 12). If the boy somewhat distorts the original press copy (to suggest adventure is possible only abroad and so justify the "day's miching" with Mahony), the imitative aspect is clear, as it is with the simple fact of Dillon's gang reenacting the content and characters they meet in the papers.

The matter and tone of the story papers resurface in the very language the narrator uses to describe the imaginary warfare in which he and his friends engage, spurred on by the content of the Wild West stories in particular. His description of their play seems lifted straight from the diction of the western adventures, marked as it is by tactical phrases of warfare: "carry it by storm," "fought a pitched battle on the grass," "never won siege" (*D* 11). The technical vocabulary describing the stylized violence of the backyard battles reflects the direct influence the Wild West library of Joe Dillon has on the boys. Recreation is re-creation, in both a literal and a literary sense.

The sensitive-minded narrator very much prefers the intellectual adventure of reading to the violence of recreation, as he counts himself one of the "reluctant Indians" in the group (*D* 11). There is an odd mixture of brutality and civility inherent in the very notion of boys who meet in the back garden for "arranged Indian battles" with the same nonchalance one would display in organizing a social outing. A primitive/civilized contrast is suggested by the fact that Joe Dillon wears "an old tea-cosy on his head" when he masquerades as an Indian warrior (*D* 11). Like the pith-helmeted Englishman stopping for high tea in hostile territory, the moment carries a sense of Oxbridge gallantry in even the most allegedly uncivilized locale—in this case, Dublin's North Side. The fact that Joe Dillon will grow up to become a priest reinforces this ironic dichotomy; so does the very ambiguous nature of the story's title, with its suggestion of both social and armed engagement. In their reading and recreation, Joe Dillon and company exist along a complex interface of British and Irish, civilized and savage, imperial and colonial.[4] Such ethnic contrasts and hostile interactions were a perennial feature of the popular magazine stories the boys are reading.

Each of the boys' publications referenced in "An Encounter" began with its particular thematic focus, but all three published stories that were closely aligned with the conservative political interests of British expansionism and global military triumph. Their stories often relied on a formulaic structure in which British heroes struggled and excelled in harsh settings, usually far-flung battlefields and other challenging outposts of progress. From exotic locales like South Africa and Afghanistan to rugged peripheral regions like the Canadian wilderness and the American West, settings for the Harmsworth magazine stories made explicit reference to imperialist politics of expansion. The *Halfpenny Marvel* included the early stories of detectives Sexton Blake and Nelson Lee, and S. Clarke Hooke's tales of Jack, Sam, and Pete, a trio comprised of an Oxford graduate, an American trapper, and a Zanzibar Negro, "who roamed the world clearing up international crises" (Springhall 113). *Pluck* featured stories dealing in themes of British military action in contested colonial regions like Africa, central Asia, and the Indian subcontinent. A brochure for the *Union Jack* described that paper as containing "stories relating to many phases of the British Empire . . . how we obtained our various colonies and stories of England's prowess on land and sea, and of her great naval and military heroes" (qtd. in Springhall 113). Its pages were replete with heroic battles and frontier adventures, which generally depicted British triumphs over native cultures. The general content of the Harmsworth boys' magazines gradually shifted from distant colonial conflicts to those emerging closer to hand: "War was brought nearer home towards the end of the century in a spate of invasion stories presenting the attempts by France, Germany, and Russia, alone or in collusion, to catch Britain unawares, steaming in from the continent, sneaking through the Channel Tunnel, or floating in on Zeppelins" (Carpenter 52). Indeed, the cover of the *Boys' Friend* paper for 12 June 1909 showed the ominous German airships hovering in the London skies above the sensationalistic caption "The Peril to Come!"

The *Union Jack* editor was G. A. Henty, himself one of the most prolific and renowned writers of Victorian boys' fiction. Henty specialized as writer and editor in works that were "less literary than pedagogical" (Rault, 168, trans. Nelson); they were "teaching tools meant to illustrate the glories of the British constitution or the role of the British navy in establishing the Empire. By reading about what English boys have done in the past to make England great, modern boys will learn how to act in the future to keep her so" (Nelson 107).

Such patriotic paternalism cohered naturally with the policies of the Tory Unionist party, under whose banner Alfred Harmsworth launched an unsuccessful parliamentary bid in 1895. Harmsworth undoubtedly saw military recruitment as an ulterior motive for his boys' papers, just as he would later use his greatest media acquisitions, the *Daily Mail* and the *Times*, to rally public support for British entry into the First World War. Media fortune and renown led to a peerage for Harmsworth in June 1904, when he was created Baron Northcliffe.

Like his publications, Harmsworth/Northcliffe himself was known for making bold proclamations about the inevitability of the coming conflict. During a visit to Canada in 1909, he noted that German shipbuilding and armaments manufacturing were approaching levels that both Britain and Canada should begin to monitor and emulate. Canadians, he told reporters, should be asking themselves "why it is Krupp's works have increased the number of their hands to more than 100,000, nearly the population of Winnepeg" ("Germany to Fight"). Such warmongering words eventually made his prediction come true, leading to the famous claim by the *Star* newspaper that "Next to the Kaiser, Lord Northcliffe has done as much as any living man to cause the war."

Envisioning a strategy of warfare that included agencies of civilian government, he used his media influence to help establish a Ministry of Munitions, first headed by David Lloyd George. Paul Fussell notes how Northcliffe "assumed full charge of government propaganda" (87). In 1916 he published *Lord Northcliffe's War Book*, a collection of essays intended to inspire Anglo-American cooperation in the war effort. The book delivers a glamorous and sanitized account of the war at every turn. In one essay, for example, Northcliffe glorifies the Continental battlefield for the general public by exploiting the same analogy used by Percy Nevill to urge his men over the top in the Battle of the Somme: he characterizes English tank crews as "young daredevils who, fully knowing that they will be a special mark for every kind of Prussian weapon, enter upon their task in a sporting spirit with the same cheery enthusiasm as they would show for football" (94). The following year, in recognition of his services leading the British war mission to the United States, he was granted the title of viscount.

Joyce displays a continuing interest in Harmsworth through overt references in his later fiction. For instance, in *Ulysses*, appropriately in the newsroom setting of "Aeolus," the media tycoon's modest Dublin origins are mentioned in direct connection with his penny papers when he is referred to as the "Chapelizod boss, Harmsworth of the farthing press" (*U* 7.732–33). The Harmsworth/Northcliffe name resounds as well in *Finnegans Wake*, in both mythical and mundane association with questions of creation and destruction, war and peace. It occurs, for example, in contrast with the Genesis imagery of God's covenant with Noah: "Our pigeon's pair are flewn for northcliffs" (*FW* 10.36). Moreover, as "Homesworth breakfast tablotts" (*FW* 458.23), the publications themselves are recognized as dietary staples of media culture. Such homey status for the Harmsworth tabloids does not preclude their being sources of media propaganda or emotive misinformation. For instance, the notions of correct intellectual development and informational accuracy are likened to proper nutrition when HCE "pours a laughsworth of his illformation over a larmsworth of salt" (*FW* 137.43–35). In other words, taking such media doses too lightly might bring the world its share of sorrow and tears (Fr. *larmes*). At other moments Northcliffe/Harmsworth appears amid wordplay highlighting his tendency to subordinate journalism to the parallel interests of waging war and profiting from the trade in wartime information. Indeed, "them newnesboys pearcin screaming off their armsworths" (*FW* 363.6) suggest how the selling of newspapers itself comes to embody—or disembody—the same loud and violent acts of war their pages portend.

Alongside tales of detection and soldiers' and sailors' adventures, the Harmsworth boys' papers published many Wild West adventure stories of the sort favored by Joe Dillon and crew. Often celebrating the exploits of upper-class Englishmen on the North American frontier, such stories were calculated to instill in young British readers an unbounded pride and confidence in their nation and its ruling class. As one edition proclaimed, "these [boys'] journals aimed from the first at the encouragement of physical strength, of patriotism, of interest in travel and exploration, and of pride in our Empire" (qtd. in Springhall 109). How does the story translate for a young Irish audience, such as the boys of *Dubliners*? As Brandon Kershner states, "The popularity of Wild West stories in cultures such as that of middle-class Dublin deserves some analysis in itself" (*Joyce, Bakhtin* 35). What is really at stake when the boys read the *Halfpenny Marvel* and imitate their intercultural hostilities? A look at the Wild West story Joyce references in "An Encounter" provides context for understanding the role of popular magazines in promulgating a militarism that worked in tandem with a contemporary ethos of colonial subjugation and racial difference.

Cultural and textual encounters begin when Father Butler catches Leo Dillon with an issue of the *Halfpenny Marvel* while Dillon and the class are supposed to be reciting their Roman history lesson. The *Marvel* issue in Leo's possession, titled *The Apache Chief*, looks to be straight from his brother Joe's collection mentioned at the outset of the story. Terence Brown tenuously describes it as "a story in *The Halfpenny Marvel*, dealing, one supposes, with the Amerindian wars" (D 246), while Jackson and McGinley merely note the term *apache* is "French slang for urban hooligan or street arab" (13b). The actual source text suggests somewhat more complex interpretive possibilities. The allusion initiates an artful parody of the boys' papers and raises questions about the indoctrination of their young readers to glorified notions of racial conflict and national violence.

The basis for the allusion is "Cochise the Apache Chief," featured story in the *Halfpenny Marvel* of 25 June 1895. While Father Butler attributes the story in Leo Dillon's possession to "some wretched scribbler" (D 12) writing for drink, "Cochise the Apache Chief" was in fact written by Paul Herring, a regular contributor to the *Union Jack* and the *Halfpenny Marvel*.[5] Although the Harmsworth boys' weeklies published a steady stream of western stories, Joyce's decision to single out "The Apache Chief" might well be deliberate with respect to chronology: Its publication about seven months after the Joyce family's move to North Richmond Street coincided with the end of James's second spring at Belvedere College and occurred in close proximity to an actual day of truancy for James and Stanislaus. That day, as Stanislaus notes, was the experiential source for "An Encounter."[6]

Herring's tale constructs an episodic sequence of manly feats and incredible adventures, all grounded in a vocabulary of ethnic essentialism, imperial bias, and physical force. This ideological blend serves in general to reassert British superiority over a former colony (America), its landscape, climate, natural resources, and primitive peoples. "An Encounter" parodies many literary devices, racialist assumptions, and geographic features of "The Apache Chief," giving them a mock-heroic urban-Irish twist that underscores how young Dubliners become subject to the propagandist fiction of British story papers. Numerous elements of the original tale, including martial violence, wilderness adventure, and male camaraderie, are co-opted and satirically reduced in Joyce's retelling, demonstrating the incongruence of that narrative for childhood and for colonial Ireland. This interplay of texts ultimately helps construct what Marjorie Howes and Derek Attridge have termed the "semicolonial" perspective of Joyce's fiction, conveying, with respect to issues of nationalism and imperialism, "a complex and ambivalent set of attitudes, not reducible to a simple anticolonialism but very far from expressing approval of the colonial organizations and methods" (3).

The title "Cochise the Apache Chief" is somewhat misleading, as the tale's true focus resides less with the real-life Indian leader than with a fictional English protagonist. Nevertheless, an editor's footnote about Cochise insists on the historical veracity of the tale: "This character is not an invention, but a real one. Cochise, the last of the great Apache war-chiefs of modern times, was at this period in his youth" (Herring 1). Feigning scholarly credibility, the editor goes so far as to cite an unnamed "American authority" who states, "There were formerly three principal war-chiefs of the tribe, under whose direction all hostile parties were marshaled: Mangus Colorado, Cochise, and Delgadito. Of these three, the only one now living who exercises any control over them is Cochise, a tall, dignified Indian" (3). The footnote purports authority on multiple levels: of Apache chiefs over unruly followers, of white historiography over Indian history, of newspaper editors over impressionable young readers. As in "An Encounter," questions of textual verity and ideological control are already at stake in this attempt to make fiction pass for history.

The real focus and shape of the story are more accurately forecast by its subtitle, "The Perils and Adventures of Dudley Fraser and his Chum in the Wilds of Arizona," which provides the first hint that the story will have more to do with British fantasies than Apache realities. Dudley Fraser is an Oxford-educated Englishman who proves himself against the physical hardships and cultural challenges of the American frontier. Having sold his gold-prospecting claim at Cedarwood Camp, he has decided to try his hand at ranching in Arizona. Alongside what pal Yankee Nat calls a "U-niv-er-sit-y eddication," Dudley displays his remarkable mastery of virtually every skill necessary to survival in the lawless and wild American West (Herring 3). His refined language and manners constantly outwit or outmatch those of his coarse American inferiors, as do his physical prowess and general toughness. In a series of incredible episodes (usually rooted in equally implausible coincidences), Fraser bests a gang of outlaws, rescues and befriends Cochise, kills an attacking bear, takes up cattle ranching, defeats a vengeful vaquero, is captured and nearly executed by the Apaches, is freed by Cochise, assists Cochise in defeating his Apache rivals, strikes gold, and meets and soon marries his conveniently English sweetheart, Alice, sister of his chum Phil Stanton.

This checklist of amazing adventures is emulated in the series of less-than-heroic incidents for Mahony and the narrator in "An Encounter." Just as they play Indian warfare at home, they attempt in their trek across Dublin to re-create the substance and style of the adventure story.[7] When we consider the boys as reenactors of "The Apache Chief," many moments in their day suggest the mismatch of the idealized Harmsworth narrative with the ordinary Dublin setting. In Britain's Wild West, they confront a string of social threats rather than mortal dangers. For instance, the many intercultural conflicts and interactions of Herring's story are relived in the row with street children, the experience of "foreign sailors" on the quays and exotic passengers on the Liffey ferry, and, finally, the encounter with the old josser. Even Dudley Fraser's triumph over the deadly bruin is mimicked through Mahony's pursuit of the cat across the field in Ringsend. Of the river crossing, for instance, the narrator recalls, "We were serious to the point of solemnity, but once during the short voyage our eyes met and we laughed" (*D* 23). The oxymoron and shattered mood undercut any attempt at a heroic tone to rival that of "The Apache Chief." In overall contrast to Dudley Fraser, the successful imperial adventurer who acquires land, love, and wealth abroad, the boys fall short of any tangible success in their misadventure. They do not even reach their planned destination of the Pigeon House, a failure that seems appropriate in this unwarranted attempt to emulate a worldly, British manliness in childlike, colonized Ireland. The fact that the location, a former navy fort, had been the target of an unsuccessful plot by Irish nationalists in 1881 adds to the sense of deflated drama.[8]

Read and then refashioned in the paralyzing milieu of Dublin, the heroic feats of Herring's story are reduced to miniaturized or metaphorical renderings, as the boys' imaginations fuel a sense of adventure and action that is never realized. The changed setting for adventure parodies another key element of the *Halfpenny Marvel* tale by substituting the slavish, confining qualities of urban Ireland for the harsh and boundless sense of America. Belvedere College stands in for the lawless mining settlement of Cedarwood Camp as, early in each story, the place represents the attempt to impose civil order on an uncouth and unruly populace. Dublin's "noisy streets flanked by high stone walls" and "groaning carts" (*D* 23) replace the "solitary plains" where "under a scorching sun" Dudley Fraser rides his tireless mustang as all the while he pines for England, his "dear old homeland" (Herring 3). This favorable reference to the mother country reinforces the notion of British superiority that already plays out among the characters in the story.

Thinking toward England also offers Dudley hope of eventual departure from the harsh American setting, while the boys of "An Encounter" cannot expect similar deliverance. Additionally, the "surging stream," site of a hair-raising canoe chase and Cochise's vengeful killing of Texas Jake in the narrative finale, contrasts with the dull, commercial waters of the Liffey, which the boy narrator nevertheless scans for a hint of the active or exotic (Herring 14). He momentarily thinks he finds it among the sailors on the quays, but this proves illusory: "I came back and examined the foreign sailors to see had any of them green eyes for I had some confused notion . . ." (D 23). Along with the telling ellipsis, the boy narrator's failure "to decipher the legend" on the stern of the "graceful threemaster" suggests a breakdown in reading and interpretation through a palimpsest of cultural affiliations (D 23). The boys will face an element of perilous social adventure in the encounter with the old josser, but this presents a different sort of peril from what Dudley Fraser and chum encounter in the wilds of Arizona.

The ways in which "An Encounter" appropriates "The Apache Chief" demonstrate how even children's literature can become an instrument of political domination and military indoctrination, assuming its role in what Louis Althusser terms the ideological state apparatus.[9] Ironically, much like the schoolroom in which it is discovered, "The Apache Chief" ultimately serves a rigid, highly structured function for the students, despite the contention of Father Butler and other detractors that the "penny dreadfuls" wielded a corrupting influence completely at odds with formal education. While appearing to engage juvenile readers with a discourse of unruliness and disorder, "The Apache Chief" effectively serves the propagandistic purpose of the British Empire in Ireland by diverting the energies and indoctrinating the minds of young consumer-subjects. It does so by programming boys' reading and recreation according to common standards of British imperial ideology that celebrated virtues of manliness, modernity, and Englishness, set in oppositional relation to the non-English, savage, and premodern. In this sense, the politics of reading elaborated in "An Encounter" embody what Seamus Deane terms the Irish colonial problem of "derivativeness."[10]

If the choice of roles in the western tales seems limited, so are the boys' overall literary options. This becomes apparent from the moment Father Butler discovers *The Apache Chief* in Leo Dillon's possession: "This page or this page? This page? Now Dillon, up! *Hardly had the day* . . . Go on! What day? *Hardly had the day dawned* . . . Have you studied it? What have you there in your pocket?" (*D* 11). Their standoff represents not just a spar between authoritative pedagogue and idle pupil but a meaningful clash of reading choices—curricular and canonical on the one hand, subversive and popular on the other. Or so it seems to Father Butler in his quick assessment of the story. If he could give more than a cursory glance to the content of "The Apache Chief" before labeling it "rubbish" and banning it from Belvedere, he might find it could bolster rather than undermine his Roman history lesson. Indeed, the Wild West tale conveys a justifying message for empire akin to the one Leo Dillon would find in Julius Caesar's *Commentarii de bello gallico*, were he to complete his assigned reading.[11]

Caesar's commentary on the Gallic campaign is in essence a manual of military strategy, conquest, and colonization: a gorescarred book par excellence. Its opening line, "Gaul is a whole divided into three parts," suggests tactical analysis and division, and resonates with a pattern of three that persists across "An Encounter" and across *Dubliners* overall. Moreover, according to Caesar, one of the three peoples in Gaul is "called in their own tongue Celtae, in the Latin Galli" (3). As synonymous terms, Celt and Gaul build an analogy of Ireland as Britain's unsettled Celtic fringe.

Of further relevance is the fact that Britain in Caesar's time played the same subordinate role to the expanding Roman Empire. Significantly, Caesar's military operations in Gaul did not just involve the region of that name but also included the initial incursions of Roman military forces to Britain. Book IV of the *Commentarii* describes the first stage of the conquest by identifying the prime strategic value of the island: "Caesar was intent upon starting for Britain. He understood that in almost all the Gallic campaigns succours had been furnished for our enemy from that quarter" (Caesar 205). The ensuing pages relate the arrival of Roman ships near the cliffs of Dover. The vessels, carrying the renowned Tenth Legion and other forces, came under intense attack by the Britons as soon as the regiments tried to disembark. According to Caesar's account, four days of fighting ensued before the Britons surrendered to the overwhelming numbers and superior technology of the Romans (211–17).

Joyce's incorporation of Caesar completes a triple parallel of westward imperial expansion: of Rome into Britain, Britain into Ireland, and the United States into Native America. The submerged conceit recalls the more overt comparison in Conrad's frame narrative of *Heart of Darkness* that parallels Kurtz's ensuing narrative of the Congo with a description of the Roman invasion of Britain: "Land in a swamp, march through the woods, and in some inland post feel the savagery, the utter savagery, had closed round him" (5). If somewhat more subdued and less direct, Joyce's allusion to Roman legions contributes to a similarly ironic reflection on the eternal repetition of military and cultural conquest.

Although Father Butler and the Belvedere faculty would probably never admit it, Caesar's *Commentarii* is not so different from *The Apache Chief*. Notwithstanding distinctions between memoir and story, high culture and low, the two texts share in the remarkable ability to legitimate for young readers the activities of generals, warriors, and conquerors. The conflicting texts become conflated ones from the moment Father Butler barks his rebuke to Leo Dillon with its telling grammatical slippage: "This page or this page? This page?" (*D* 12). Devoid of any visual cues, repetition of the demonstrative pronoun has the effect of eliding *The Apache Chief* and Caesar's *Commentarii* both verbally and conceptually. The elision bespeaks the utter lack of literary options or ideological alternatives for the students. It suggests as well a collapsing of genre distinctions (popular fiction and military memoir), language (English and Latin), and history (American and Roman). Anglo-American Manifest Destiny becomes closely aligned with Roman conquest; both, in turn, parallel the state of British-occupied Ireland. The ironic implication emerges that the kernel of Father Butler's lesson might be as easily gleaned from a forbidden magazine as from a sanctioned schoolbook.

The charges Father Butler levels against *The Apache Chief* do not at all question its subject matter, style, or literary intention. They merely rest on his unfounded supposition that "the man who wrote it . . . was some wretched scribbler that writes these things for a drink" (*D* 12). This presents no critique of the story itself but merely a speculative ad hominem attack. While Father Butler might rail against the genre or its alleged author, he safely skirts any text-based argument about its literary meaning or imaginative function, presumably because he has never read the story, having just discovered it in Leo Dillon's possession. It is clear that he holds the general prejudice of the period against the *Halfpenny Marvel* and similar publications. As a literary critic, the boys' teacher shows himself inferior to the narrator, whose own judgment on the merits of the magazines at least weighs such aspects as morality and intent. He recognizes the potential for the Wild West adventures to open "doors of escape" but notes his preference for American detective stories (*D* 11). By contrast, Father Butler's criticism rests not on rational close reading but on rash social assumptions, particularly concerning the magazine's potential to displace the canonical reading of the class syllabus. His need for pedagogical control precludes open-minded reading and thwarts critical analysis.

If the *Halfpenny Marvel* finally poses a real risk to its younger readers, Joyce's story never overtly states as much. Rather, by setting Father Butler in opposition to a culture of juvenile reading, "An Encounter" raises the question of what does or does not constitute an immoral text. In this sense, Joyce's story involves itself directly with the contemporary opposition to the penny dreadfuls from critics who deemed them morally dubious or corruptive influences. Indeed, the phrase "penny dreadful" itself originated in public perceptions and reformist declamations of the moral dangers that stories of outlaws and adventure posed for young readers: captivated by the murderers and thieves depicted in many tales, these readers would presumably run away from the safe moral confines of home and school to embark on lives of crime and debauchery.[12]

Playing to such concerns, the debut issue of the *Marvel* even went so far as to sound the death knell for its higher-priced competition: "No more penny dreadfuls! These healthy stories of mystery, adventure, etc., will kill them."[13] To this end, Harmsworth papers ran fictitious testimonials from appreciative headmasters, clergyman, and parents lauding the moral uprightness of the publication. For example, the cover page of the *Halfpenny Marvel* for 13 May 1896 featured the following "Schoolmaster's Letter of Recommendation":

> The Manhood Schools, Birdham, Chichester, March 2nd, 1896—Dear Mrs. Boughton, I have looked through the two numbers of the Marvel Library and as far as I can judge from these numbers, there is nothing objectionable in them, and they appear well suited for youths to read. If they succeed in doing what they profess to be attempting to do—"kill the penny dreadful"—they will be doing an excellent work.

They are remarkably cheap, and it is wonderful how the books can be produced at the price. Yours faithfully, A. J. Nixon, Schoolmaster.

In reality the Harmsworth publications reproduced the same sort of unsavory plots and dubious characters as their penny competition, something the publishers themselves and the vast majority of readers understood. As R. B. Kershner observes, "Ironically for a magazine generally regarded as cheaply sensational, *The Halfpenny Marvel* claimed the intent of counteracting the influence of unhealthy sensationalism aimed at children" (*Joyce, Bahktin* 33). Concerns such as those voiced by Father Butler in "An Encounter" about the moral state of the stories and authors featured in the magazine were anticipated by Alfred Harmsworth himself when he suggested for the *Marvel* the alternative title *Boys' Weekly Reader*. As he told his brother, "It sounds respectable and would act as a cloak for one or two fiery stories" (qtd. in Springhall 111).

Other marketing efforts in the Harmsworth penny papers reflected their publisher's ardent pro-military stance in a period of increasing invasion scares and anticipation of war. As Kevin Carpenter describes, "The inadequacy of Britain's defences against the German military build-up was heavily underlined in Harmsworth's newspapers and boys' magazines" (55). Fostering national unity and military recruitment were an ideological focal point and clear ulterior motive for the boys' papers as they were later for the *Daily Mail* and the *Times*. Indeed, the *Halfpenny Marvel* issue that features "The Apache Chief" contains a bold-font running footer on several pages promising its young readership information on "HOW TO JOIN THE NAVY. SEE "PLUCK" on Saturday" (3). The subsequent page carries the teaser "SHIPS OF THE NAVY. PLUCK is giving a picture each week of one of the Ships of the British Navy. They will be a fine collection when complete" (4). Both naval promotions function as tie-ins to the serial story "Under Nelson's Flag, or The Wooden Walls of Old England," which begins on the final page of the issue. Other advertising in the Harmsworth boys' papers even catered to the ballistic impulses of their young readers, with many issues including notices not only for toy guns but for actual firearms.[14]

For his part, the narrator of "An Encounter" is not against the Wild West stories, yet neither is he an enthusiastic supporter of the genre. Unlike Father Butler, he has actually read them, and discounts the tales for no better reason than that he prefers the detective stories "traversed from time to time by unkempt fierce and beautiful girls" (*D* 12). This preference would probably not be reassuring, maybe would be even more alarming, to Father Butler and others who disapproved of the penny papers on moral grounds. In hindsight, the narrator recalls succumbing to the peer pressure of physical-force culture; he seems to understand the powerful effect the stories can have on their readers when, from his retrospective narrative viewpoint, he recalls being among those less eager to participate in the mock warfare the stories inspire.

As the narrator is well aware, the boys' reading of Wild West stories has the potential to galvanize both collective identity and physical violence: "A spirit of unruliness diffused itself among us and, under its influence, differences of culture and constitution were waived. We banded ourselves together, some boldly, some in jest and some almost in fear: and of the number of these latter, the reluctant Indians who were afraid to seem studious or lacking in robustness, I was one" (*D* 11). Vincent Cheng regards the moment as a prime example of the carnivalesque, an opportunity in the energy of misrule "for people to accept each other as separate and different and free, and not as hierarchically overdetermined" (*Joyce, Race* 84). This is a useful reading of the boys' play, especially given the ultimate absence of historical agency and racial difference in "Cochise the Apache Chief," whose title character is permitted little beyond the role of token minority and stock character—a far cry from the Apache political dissident and warrior who stood up to American policies of westward expansion and Indian resettlement. The Harmsworth story pays lip service to the idea of authentic history, but only, like Father Butler, in an effort to keep up appearances and to exert authority over readers. To be an unwilling actor in the back-garden wars suggests at least a nascent resistance to the narrative of the Harmsworth stories and the greater shadows of militarized imperialism and native nationalism the tales represent. This invites readers to see a certain irony in the fact that Caesar's Gallic campaign memoir represents no less a threat than *The Apache Chief* as far as the students' moral instruction.

If Joe Dillon's story library represents an initiation to knowledge, its imaginative range extends to include the parallel wild-west territories of North America, Ireland, and Gaul, which function as a somewhat interchangeable geographic threesome. Emanating from the distinct genres of boys' magazines, Roman history, and the English novel, they nonetheless reiterate a story of colonial occupation by ideological and physical conquest. In this way the three elevated literary figures function as ironic counterparts to the three lowbrow magazines, *Pluck*, the *Union Jack*, and the *Halfpenny Marvel*. Just as the Harmsworth publications sanctimoniously set themselves above their penny-dreadful competitors, so three mainstays of nineteenth-century letters, Thomas Moore, Sir Walter Scott, and Edward Bulwer-Lytton, are granted a dubious moral high ground over the popular boys' papers.

There are varying arguments as to the potential significance of specific works by these canonical writers in relation to the boys' suspicious yet under-described encounter with the old josser. Since Lord Lytton is mentioned both individually and as part of the triad, he has generated the most critical discussion, even though Sir Walter Scott's name, along with a specific title, *The Abbot*, recurs in the opening of "Araby." Kershner suggests how Lytton's *The Last Days of Pompeii* "has considerable significance for 'An Encounter'" owing to its themes of sadomasochism and pedophilia (*Joyce, Bakhtin* 40–41). Considering the boys' reading in relation to the literary constraints of the social purity movement, Katherine Mullin (43–44) prefers a broader range of Lytton's works, including *Richelieu* and *Eugene Aram*, which Joyce references, respectively, in "Aeolus" and "Penelope" (*U* 7.617, 18.656). Both are compelling candidates, considering the inconclusive, yet surely corruptive, nature of the old man's unprintable actions before the boys.

Given the prominence of names over titles at this end of the story, some biographical consideration can shed light on "An Encounter" as well. In view of the Indian-battle and Wild West themes in the story, it is worth noting that Edward Bulwer-Lytton served a brief but notable term as Secretary of State for the Colonies in 1858–59. In that role he focused particularly on the development of British Columbia, primarily through the design and administration of programs for exploiting the natural resources of the area and implementation of some harsh policies for the forcible removal and resettlement of indigenous peoples in far western Canada.

As colonial secretary, Bulwer-Lytton oversaw the settlement of British Columbia and the opening of the territory to mining. Establishing truces and trade with the Indian tribes of the region—in effect, taming the landscape and peoples of western Canada—was deemed crucial to the survival and profitability of the British colonial presence there. Correspondence between Secretary Bulwer-Lytton at Downing Street and James Douglas, colonial governor in Vancouver, shows implementation of a governance plan dominated by typical mercantilist concerns over industrial access, military security, social cohesion, and commercial regulation. The most significant action in the latter category occurred in February 1859 when Bulwer-Lytton revoked an 1838 Crown grant of exclusive trading rights with the Indians of British Columbia to the Hudson's Bay Company, thus opening the colony and its economy to large-scale immigration and competitive commercial enterprises.

Bulwer-Lytton's colonial administration was not averse to the use of force in promoting its interests in the region. In a dispatch dated 19 May 1858, Douglas requested British naval enforcement of customs duties in the area of the Couteau gold mines. Within three months he would petition Bulwer-Lytton for a military force to be sent expressly for the purpose of patrolling the gold districts. The potential for illegal mineral extraction and smuggling seemed to reside with both European immigrants and Indian inhabitants of the region, as Britain sought to control its new wild west. Moreover, the threat of Indian insurrection against English colonists was cause for alarm. For his part, Bulwer-Lytton recognized the dangers but, considering the already overextended forces of the empire, recommended another military alternative: raise a homegrown army. He sent the following reply on 16 September:

> It is certainly much to be desired that you possessed a force adequate for the protection of the Revenue laws of the country, but it is totally impossible for Her Majesty's Government to provide you with such a force from England. The most that we can do is, to supply you with suitable and well-recommended public officers, whose experience and capability will enable them to assist you in raising a force in the Colony itself, capable of preserving order, and causing the law to be obeyed. (n.p.)

With respect to the Indian question, Bulwer-Lytton recommended a village resettlement plan to control area tribes. Douglas concurred that such a long-term solution would prove more effective policy than a military presence and also could benefit the safety of the Indians themselves, whom he saw as being in moral as well as physical danger: "with such settlement, civilization would at once begin; that law and religion would become naturally introduced among them, and contribute to their security against aggressions of immigrants." Elsewhere the correspondence between Bulwer-Lytton and

Douglas assumes that settlement and assimilation into British colonial society would enlighten Indians morally and spiritually, and thus spare them from "degradation . . . oppression and rapid decay." Of no small interest, however, was the taxation that could be levied on a settled Indian populace and added to the colonial treasury.

None of this should be ignored if we are to assess the broader range of meaning that reference to Lord Lytton can bring to Joyce's story. It is the name of not just a literary figure but a colonial administrator who commanded real encounters with reluctant Indians in Britain's other Wild West. "An Encounter" excavates the Wild West trope to its very foundation: the narrator and his companions playing at Indian wars not only derive a children's game from their reading but also settle into the very role imagined for them in the discourse of British and American imperialism that constantly played itself out in the pages of the Harmsworth juvenile story papers. While the language and content of their play emulate what the boys read, the unchanging result of the war games echoes the tragic pattern of Irish colonial history: "however well we fought, we never won siege or battle and all our bouts ended with Joe Dillon's war dance of victory" (*D* 11). In its fatalistic assessment of recurring defeat, the narrative might be that of Irish as well as Native American history. The fact that all of the boys play Indians fighting against each other suggests an even deeper tragedy of the colonial experience: the dissolution and internecine combat of a conquered people. Their mimic warfare shows colonized subjects turning against each other in the confined, pressurized spaces of what anthropologists Brian Ferguson and Neil Whitehead term the "tribal zone."[15]

In this regard, the high culture that Lytton, along with Walter Scott and Irish balladeer Thomas Moore, represents, while it appears the polar opposite of the Harmsworth boys' papers, in fact moves toward the same ideological purpose. Popular juvenile reading inculcates the same cultural values and political assumptions encountered in a supposedly more respectable brand of literary fiction. As someone who has become paralyzed by social prohibitions and limits on reading choices, the old josser represents the same kind of limited reader and decrepit mind the boys are in danger of becoming. A second literary mentor for the boys—and a somewhat ironic echo of Father Butler—he displays a lapse of intellectual guidance for Mahony and the narrator. Wherever he turns, whether newsstand or school curriculum or adult library, he finds a common denominator of colonizing texts beset by codified violence. In the end, the story is not only an encounter between age and youth, perversity and innocence, but also between young readers and limited reading choices, as the intertextual references ultimately collapse distinctions of genre, readership, and nationality.

What boys are reading and the circumstances in which they read construct a supplemental narrative in "An Encounter." The story posits a direct connection between juvenile reading and militarist ideology in Ireland through reference to curricular texts from the schoolroom and popular tales from Fleet Street. In either case, no matter where the central characters turn—whether at play, at school, or in truancy—they do not fail to encounter writings steeped in the glorified tones of imperial adventurism and nationalist glory, served by armed force. The authors, writings, and cultural discourse alluded to throughout the story, despite differences of social background and historical era, constitute narratives of militarized masculinity. The popular magazine adventure stories, classical wartime memoir, and nineteenth-century canonical fiction comprise a set of literary landmarks by which the unnamed boy narrator must navigate as he goes to encounter the reality of his experience, if not for the millionth time, then probably not for the first.

Stephen's Schoolbooks

Joyce's depictions of childhood and school life in *A Portrait of the Artist as a Young Man* show Stephen Dedalus, like the young boys of *Dubliners*, come of age amid the martial discourse of local legends, standardized texts, and popular fiction. Well before the twenty-two-year-old Stephen teaches from the "gorescarred book" in "Nestor," he experiences school texts and campus culture that are saturated with notions of militarized masculinity. On the heels of nursery rhymes and songs, local anecdotes become the first history lessons of Stephen's life. After this, *A Portrait* represents the prevalence of American and British school primers in Irish classrooms, a textbook imperialism that poses questions of cultural domination, physical force, and individual and national self-definition. Joyce's nod to such textbooks demonstrates what David Livingstone terms the "contested enterprise" of Anglo-American geography at work on the formation of young colonial subjects.[16]

Clongowes in Joyce's day was steeped in a history of military conflicts and heroics. These ranged from Celtic legends to nationalist history, including the United Irishmen Rising of 1798, all part of a past that students absorbed from the local landscape and culture. As Kevin Sullivan notes in *Joyce Among the Jesuits*, "that past was deep and rich around Clongowes" (20). The long-suffering history of the area included the role of the castle in oppressive English military campaigns. Sullivan ruminates on the blend of historical and mythic martial elements that defined the campus and its environs:

> the walls had been pummeled by Cromwell's cannon, and . . . long before Cromwell the once powerful Eustaces—now but a dim memory—had stood medieval guard on these *frontures des marches de guerre* that stretched miles north and east and south of *silva de* Clongowes. Beyond history, most remote memory of all, was legendary Queen Buan, asleep now in her grassy mound beside the castle walls. All this was the past of Clongowes Wood and was with the years to become part of the lore of successive generations of young Clongowians. (21)

Two particular military legends of Clongowes feature in the opening chapter of *A Portrait* as potent influences on Stephen. The first is the tale of eighteenth-century nationalist Hamilton Rowan pursued by British soldiers into the castle that later became the main campus building. A friend of Wolfe Tone, Rowan was wanted for his role in planning the 1798 United Irishmen Rising. He fled across the fields from his home in nearby Rathcoffey, a location itself counted among "Places of historic interest" for Clongowes faculty, students, and alumni over a century later (Bradley 154n136). The account handed down to Stephen and his classmates emphasizes attributes of courage, pluck, and grace under pressure, typified in the gallant gesture of Rowan tossing his hat out the window and onto the haha in the midst of his getaway (*P* 22). It is significant that Stephen learns this legend in a context that reifies notions of class hierarchy and social standing: "One day when he had been called to the castle the butler had shown him the marks of the soldiers' slugs in the wood of the door and had given him a piece of shortbread that the community ate" (*P* 22). Rowan's story is quite literally spoon-fed to Stephen and his classmates, as tangible evidence of the story combines with a social gesture of communion. Like the Sallins church service, where Stephen notes the damp-corduroy-and-turf smell of the peasants, the ritual enables the Clongowes student to partake in community while maintaining a measure of class separation from it.

Another school military legend centers on Anthony Browne, last proprietor of Clongowes Castle before its transition to Jesuit boarding school. His full name and title suggest his Continental provenience, with a coincidental Joycean ring: Maximilian Ulysses, Reichsgraf von Browne, Baron de Camus and Mountany. Browne was a marshal in the Austrian army in the Seven Years' War who, as Stephen learns, "received his deathwound on the battlefield of Prague far away over the sea" (*P* 30). The fatal injury occurred as he led a bayonet charge against the advancing Prussian forces of Frederick the Great. Along with Prince Charles of Lorraine, Browne commanded more than 12,000 troops at the Battle of Prague; his death and long service in the Austrian army were commended by naming the 36th Regiment after him in 1888, a name it carried until disbanding in 1918.

At the moment of the marshal's death, his white-clad likeness was said to have been witnessed moving about the castle. Michael Devitt's account for the Kildare Archaeological Society in 1902 is likely close to the version Joyce would have heard at Clongowes two decades before:

> Concerning the Marshal's death, a curious story is found recorded in the family papers. While he was fighting abroad, Clongowes was occupied by his sisters, two Misses Browne. At that time one of the rooms opening into the hall of the mansion was used as an ironing room, and in ironing days, the necessary fire made it an attractive resort for the servants of the house. On one such day the door of this room as well as the hall door happened to be open, and the servants gathered together were astonished to see an officer in white uniform enter the hall and ascend the stairs. They noted that his hands were pressed to his breast, from which blood was flowing; and when they had sufficiently recovered their presence of mind, they hurried upstairs to where the Misses Browne were occupied with some needlework. The ladies, on being questioned, replied that they had seen nothing; but on hearing a full description of the apparition, unhesitatingly said that it must have been their brother, and that he must have met his death on the field of battle. (213)

The Browne ghost story enters Stephen's nightmares after he is shoved into the cold water of the ditch, and his feverish thoughts even reimagine his own parentage according to the same elite social and professional standing: "His father was a marshal now: higher than a magistrate" (*P* 30, 31). Like Joyce and countless other Clongowes students, Stephen internalizes these campus tales endorsing virtues of manly fortitude, martial prowess, and glorious self-sacrifice. They offer students not just arcane historical facts but moral exemplars inscribed most literally and vividly on the campus, like the bullet scars on the castle door. They constitute lessons in shared values acquired through communal reading.

Such vivid narratives no doubt contributed to the military mystique so tangible and apparent in the architecture of a school described by Joyce's early biographer Herbert Gorman as "a Norman stronghold built for imminent wars . . . strangely transformed into an Irish Jesuit college" (24). Many nineteenth-century pupils undoubtedly relished the fortified campus atmosphere and its associated legends. As Richard Ellmann describes, "Clongowes Wood, with its elms, large grounds, and storied (if rebuilt) medieval castle, roused its pupils to thoughts of grand action and great suffering" (29). Indeed, a number of alumni did go on to attend officer academies or pursue army careers. One of the most renowned was Thomas Francis Meagher, who matriculated in the 1850s. Following deportation to Tasmania for involvement in the Young Ireland movement, he escaped to America, where during the Civil War he enlisted in the Union Army and rose to the rank of brigadier general while commanding the "Fighting Irish" Brigade of Irish-American infantry regiments from New York, Massachusetts, and Pennsylvania.[17]

Joyce's own classmate P. R. Butler, a future lieutenant colonel and son of a British general, would have found his penchant for soldiering well cultivated by the Clongowes environment and curriculum. Butler's chief recollection of Joyce consists of a poetry recitation in which each student read a poem "chosen for its real or fancied appositeness to his own character," and while Butler opted for "The Charge of the Light Brigade," the young Joyce, in contrast to Tennyson's paean to battlefield sacrifice, chose a meek pastoral lyric titled "Little Jim" (Ellmann 30). Even fiercer opinions about reading—Lord Tennyson, in particular—occur when Stephen voices a preference for Byron over Tennyson and receives a brutal beating for it (*P* 79–80).[18]

But well before they can argue about their poetic preferences, Stephen and his classmates are exposed to the historical discourse of school texts. Alongside athletics and local legends, these constitute the most influential ideology depicted in the Clongowes chapters. Formative reading commences with the dogmatic narratives and pedantic primers of the Class of Elements. On the way to Father Conmee's office, Stephen ponders how his quest for truth (in the matter of his unjust "pandybatting") parallels an experience "done before by somebody in history, by some great person whose head was in the books of history," books he then identifies as "Richmal Magnall's Questions" and "Peter Parley's Tales about Greece and Rome" (*P* 53). As Victorian school texts used widely throughout Britain, America, and their overseas possessions, these "books of history" reveal some of the social assumptions and indoctrinating biases underscoring male education in late colonial Ireland. Significantly, these books are suffused with the perspectives of nineteenth-century Britain and America that consistently profess the cultural superiority and military might of these two national powers. For Stephen and other young Irish readers, this ethos of imperial militarism poses challenges to individual and national identity.

First published in 1833 in Philadelphia, *Peter Parley's Tales About Ancient and Modern Greece* underwent numerous reprintings, ensuring its use in English-speaking classrooms throughout the world from the mid-nineteenth to the mid-twentieth century. Its American author, S. G. Goodrich, adopted a pseudonym and narrative persona appropriate to the book's didactic purpose—one readily apparent in the anecdotal style and footnoted study questions for each page. Kevin Sullivan notes how with the Peter Parley series Goodrich "seems to have monopolized the juvenile trade during the middle decades of the nineteenth century" and "introduced his young audience to every land under the sun and, more than that, to the sun itself and to the moon and the stars and the whole of the known and parts of the unknown universe" (44).

Despite such far-reaching, imaginative claims, the book never ventures too far beyond an American orbit. The preface to the 1864 edition of *Parley's Tales* identifies "an audience of boys and girls about ten or twelve years of age," right around the average age of a student at Clongowes Wood, though a few years older than Stephen. Goodrich also readily assumes these potential readers to be American, justifying his practice of explaining ancient mythic and historical events through allusions to celebrated happenings in U.S. military history. He clarifies as much in an introductory comment that underscores both contemporary comparisons and intended audiences: "if I have illustrated the adventure of Hercules and the Nemean Lion by a reference to Putnam and the Wolf; if I have brought Athens and Sparta into homely comparison with our own republic, and subjected even Jupiter to the test of our yankee morality; I beg the critical reader to consider two things; first, who I am, and second, who I am talking to."

In light of this editorial disclaimer, American ethnocentrism seems to define the book's construction of global geography, which from the first page establishes a book-as-voyage metaphor whereby an imaginative journey to the Greek past commences notably in the New England present: "Suppose we enter a ship at Boston, and when all things are ready, proceed to sea" (9). An East Coast U.S. bias persists as the narrator relates the provenance and topography of Greece: "Athens is almost exactly east of Washington in the United States, and is at the distance of about five thousand five hundred miles"; "the greatest extent" of Greece is "considerably less than New England"; and "Mount Olympus... is about seven thousand feet high, therefore somewhat taller than Mount Washington in New Hampshire" (14, 15, 17). With every city, mountain, and dimension grounded in North American points of reference, one can sense the marginalizing effect the volume might have on even the most worldly of Irish students.

This geographic orientation soon encompasses political and military perspectives, as the narrative offers an account of Greek antiquity with frequent digressive references to U.S. military history, including the Revolutionary War and westward expansion. Some seem naïve assertions of arrogant patriotism, as for instance the claim that Greece's successful overthrow of Turkish rule in 1821 followed directly from the translation of Benjamin Franklin's *Poor Richard's Almanac*: "Dr. Franklin's Poor Richard... read with delight by the Greeks; their minds became expanded, the detestation of their oppressors grew stronger in their bosoms, and many a heart began to beat with a desire for liberty" (190–91).

Peter Parley's Tales has a strong impact on Stephen, evident from his interpretation of its opening illustration: "Peter Parley himself was on the first page in a picture. There was a road over a heath with grass at the side and little bushes: and Peter Parley had a broad hat like a protestant minister and a big stick and he was walking fast along the road to Greece and Rome" (*P* 53). The description allegorizes America's unswerving political and religious dominance, in part conveyed by the affiliation with Protestantism, a religion also associated with Ireland's British colonizers and Ascendancy class. Even while the United States proffered much in the way of political and economic aid to nineteenth-century Irish nationalism, its image in the mind of at least this colonial schoolchild conveys qualities of religion and authority more akin to the country's Anglo-Irish ruling elite.[19]

With *Peter Parley's Tales* as a principal intertext, *A Portrait* asks its own readers the implicit question how an American geo-historical perspective might affect a young Irish reader and British subject. Like young Dubliners reading Wild West stories and Roman history, the Clongowes student assigned *Parley's Tales* finds himself in the twice-removed position of learning about classical history and topography through an American lens. Asked to read the wars of Persia and Greece or Athens and Sparta in "homely comparison" with the American Revolutionary War, Stephen and his classmates are forced to learn geography and contemplate history through an intimidating comparison of two unknowns. One is hard pressed to find any material within the pages of *Peter Parley's Tales* that could forge a familiar or direct connection for an Irish student. On the contrary, brought into the context of late-colonial Ireland, the book's unbounded pride in American military triumphs and decolonization from British rule only seem to illuminate Irish failures to achieve the same.

The second schoolbook Stephen recalls along the corridor to the headmaster's office is the one he calls "Richmal Magnall's Questions" (*P* 53). The allusion contributes an additional level of significance, principally through its unyielding articulation of a pro-British imperialist influence on Stephen's developing geographical and political awareness. The book epitomizes the inherently British bias in colonial Irish education. British schoolmistress Richmal Mangnall first published her *Historical and Miscellaneous Questions for the Everyday Use of Young People* in 1800. It quickly became a standard history and geography textbook in British schools and went through numerous editions and reprintings up to the last quarter of the nineteenth century. Joyce memorializes the book in that era as another of the assigned readings for the Class of Elements at Clongowes. An 1829 edition of Mangnall was part of Joyce's library in Trieste, attesting to his ongoing interest in it while he wrote *A Portrait*.[20]

Mangnall's *Questions* sought to provide its young readership a general account of the major political, scientific, and literary currents of European history. The basic structure of the book implies that English history, in particular, has its roots in antiquity, clear evidence of Mangnall's own late neoclassical education. The opening chapters, treatments of ancient Greece and imperial Rome, followed by a lengthy section devoted to British history, aim to legitimate a British imperial perspective in much the same way that *Parley's Tales* does for America. Next, monarchical histories of Britain and France precede the book's longest section of "celebrated characters," those encyclopedic entries Stephen undoubtedly imagines as he pictures "some great person whose head was in the books of history" (*P* 53).

Not surprisingly, Mangnall's version of British history often leans toward a justification of its contemporary imperialist agenda. Historical summaries explain and justify British foreign policy during each period, often in patronizing tones. For instance, the account of the eighteenth century states that "the foundation of British power in India was also laid and reared in this century" (19), metaphorical terms that combine vocabularies of architecture ("foundation") and parenting ("reared"). The rhetoric aims to naturalize the colonial power struggle by comparing it to processes of social and biological development. By contrast, Mangnall's description of the American Revolution refers to shaking "off the yoke of Great Britain" (22). Nevertheless, the military connotation of the metaphor does as much to fasten British history to the enduring greatness of imperial Rome as it does to celebrate American self-determination.[21]

Mangnall's rare allusions to Ireland, while made in connection to Britain, echo neither the Indian nor the American example. The Irish references differ mainly in the fact that they give no sense of Irish nationalism as a conscious, motivating force in the history of the two countries. Instead, following the general trend of imperialist and unionist historiography, mention of Ireland comes merely as a subset to discussion of Britain. Therefore the first event noted for the nineteenth century is "the union of Great Britain with Ireland and the first imperial parliament" (19). The account refers briefly to the Irish Parliament, the only other mention of Ireland being a reference to the seventeenth-century Cromwellian campaigns. Sectarian-based nationalism is the main determinant in this simplified history: "What was the Irish massacre? A conspiracy of the Roman Catholics in Ireland, to murder all the English and Irish protestants residing there" (119).

Mangnall's *Questions* and *Parley's Tales* exhibit biases that promulgate, respectively, British and American ideologies of military might and cultural expansion. Through recourse to traditional models of classical and European history, these imperial textbooks seek to normalize and justify the international political order. The books demonstrate how, for Irish students in the late nineteenth century, "British and American geography comfortably subserved interests of nationalistic self-absorption both at home and abroad" (Livingstone 216). Joyce's schoolbook allusions reposition the budding Irish national consciousness as growing up between the competing hegemonies of imperial might. Doing so, they underscore the problematic nature of education in a colonial setting.

Whether referencing imperialist classroom texts or local histories of anticolonial resistance, *A Portrait* depicts a system of education that offers scant hope for boys to envision possibilities for their lives outside the imposing historical narratives of imperial militarism. Sanctioned glorification of violence and an overall paucity of imaginative alternatives continue to express the closed circuit of violence and violent reading discovered in "An Encounter." Yet, while the young narrator of that story had little access to "portals of escape" in his reading choices and literary role models, the experience of Stephen Dedalus shows at least the potential of pursuing a different course.

For even as the narratives and intertexts of *A Portrait* seem to replay the same potent and inescapable influences, Stephen has issued his initial response to his schoolbooks. Frustrated with his lesson in American place-names, Stephen inscribes on the flyleaf of his geography book (*P* 27):

> *Stephen Dedalus*
> *Class of Elements*
> *Clongowes Wood College*
> *Sallins*
> *County Kildare*
> *Ireland*
> *Europe*
> *The World*
> *The Universe*

Some critics have read Stephen's act of writing with a view to the psychological and intellectual ramifications of the developing character's insightful realization and self-positioning.[22] But the moment extends beyond the cognitive self-development or growing awareness of its young protagonist: *A Portrait*'s publication in 1916 of course coincided with another written assertion of cultural independence, the Proclamation of the Irish Republic.[23] Most notable is the fact that Stephen omits from his list any mention of the United Kingdom—thereby subverting (knowingly or not) the authority of the 1801 Act of Union of Ireland to Great Britain—and thus demonstrates how learning geography in a colonized setting becomes inevitably and inescapably political.

The issue was already very much on the minds of Irish cultural nationalists. In September 1899 an editorial titled "Learning Geography" appeared in the *United Irishman* newspaper of Arthur Griffith's Sinn Fein movement. The article, published under the pseudonym Calraide, traced the misinformed studies of "Tom," an "average" Irish schoolboy who has learned geography with an English emphasis—to the near total exclusion of Ireland: "The book he got to learn had about forty pages in it, and thirty-five of these were taken up with England" (Calraide 2). In the National School curriculum, even other British colonial regions besides Ireland take on unfairly disproportionate roles, as Tom comes to know "as much about India or Africa as about Ireland." The writer expresses concern that ultimately such biased and limited education will bring the student to have "but a confused notion of the world in his head" (Calraide 2).

Along these lines, Marjorie Howes describes Stephen at this point in his *Bildung* as "struggling with competing ways of transforming the local affiliations he has lost into membership in a national community" (70). As a literary manifesto locating the formation of national identity in the sensibility of the most vulnerable colonial subject, the schoolchild, Stephen's scribbled list does no less than transform an authoritative space of the colonizer, the school textbook, into a locus of negotiable geographic terms.

Like a journalist or political revolutionary, the artist Stephen contests and reconfigures those terms through his act of writing. His inscription exhibits a fundamental interrelation of colonial education, decolonization, and the assertion of a liberating national geography. Edward Said has noted the role of the "great colonial schools" as loci of imperialist power that taught the "bourgeoisie important truths about history, science and culture ... [in which] millions grasped the fundamentals of modern life, yet remained subordinate dependents of an authority based elsewhere than in their lives" (223). We might consider Stephen's act of reading and textual revision as one of his earliest steps toward circumventing such authority and declaring his own independence from it and, in the process, realizing himself as a spatial center; he does so, not surprisingly, in terms that are specifically imaginative and geographic.

Stephen's nascent act of resistance writing can be seen as directed toward school texts like *Parley's Tales* and Mangnall's *Questions* that impose upon students a mindset of subordination to imperial and martial values. What might be regarded, then, as Stephen's earliest literary effort offers a reply to such limiting geographic and militaristic perspectives. As *A Portrait* progresses into Stephen's adolescence, the potential for individual agency and liberation from such forces will appear in its most vulnerable light.

Playing Soldiers

Early in his time at Belvedere, Stephen forms a friendship that revolves around emulating the appearance and protocol of nineteenth-century field generals:

> He became the ally of a boy named Aubrey Mills and founded with him a gang of adventurers in the avenue. Aubrey carried a whistle dangling from his buttonhole and a bicycle lamp attached to his belt while the others had short sticks thrust daggerwise through theirs. Stephen, who had read of Napoleon's plain style of dress, chose to remain unadorned and thereby heightened for himself the pleasure of taking counsel with his lieutenant before giving orders. (*P* 65)

Stephen's role-playing with Aubrey shows books, as much as parents or schoolmasters, as an authoritative influence in boys' lives: he makes his own choice based on what he "had read of" the French emperor and his sumptuary style. Joyce shows the boys as avid consumers and conscious imitators of martial ideals and aesthetics gleaned from books. Such impersonation of historical heroes seems a relatively harmless kind of play. Soon after, however, an especially traumatic moment in Stephen's artistic development comes when a debate about reading choices escalates to a less-than-playful kind of military posturing.

The idea of literature as a context for violent engagement is borne out most vividly when the conflict over what to read takes on the guise of a civil disturbance, suggesting a harsh lesson about the freedom of discourse and critical expression. This occurs when three Belvedere classmates corner Stephen on Clonliffe Road and hold something of a mock military tribunal concerning his literary preferences. From the moment of their approach, the boys are an intimidating physical presence, their words, positioning, and movement mimicking those of an army detachment on street patrol:

> —Halt!
> He turned and saw three boys of his own class coming towards him in the dusk. It was Heron who had called out and, as he marched forward between his two attendants, he cleft the air before him with a thin cane, in time to their steps. Boland, his friend, marched beside him, a large grin on his face, while Nash came on a few steps behind, blowing from the pace and wagging his great red head. (P 79)

Growing up in a garrison city, the boys appear to have absorbed the customs and comportment of its occupying forces. The narrator suggests as much, referring to Heron's companions as "the two lieutenants" (P 80). Prior to the encounter, Stephen is described in soldierly terms as having "marched from home to the school" (P 78). Now he becomes a virtual prisoner of war. This might seem humorous play, if the playful approach did not turn suddenly to hostile interrogation. In a conversation marked by intellectual competition and class tension, the four boys "speak about books and writers, saying what books they were reading and how many books there were in their fathers' bookcases at home" (P 79). Eventually, Heron's choice of Captain Marryat and Tennyson over Stephen's elected favorites, Cardinal Newman and Lord Byron, turns the intellectual parrying in a more violent direction. For all its child's play, the encounter comes to resemble the mental coercion and corporal brutality of martial law, especially considering that part of Heron's motivation stems from his apparent obligation to the English master, Mr. Tate, who a few days earlier accused Stephen of committing heresy in his weekly essay. In national-allegorical terms, Heron and his fellow thugs assume the guise of imperial power or its local subalterns: they resemble British Army soldiers, RIC officers, or plainclothes G-men functioning as a forceful delegation of authority.

The Clonliffe Road incident renders Stephen a tortured internee of these self-proclaimed authorities. He is subject at once to the "cuts of a cane" and the blows of a cabbage stump—ad hoc weapons that suggest, incidentally, a dual symbolism of Anglo-Irish Ascendancy and Gaelic peasantry (P 79). Like the "Half door, hall door" pairing of peasant cottage and upper-class Big House in W. B. Yeats's *Purgatory* (537), no social class or station is immune to the inevitable conflict of Irish history. Neither is Stephen, as, trapped by his attackers, he is eventually forced against a "barbed wire fence" (*P* 83). Stanislaus recalls this specific detail, in his account of the real-life "tussle" that inspired the scene,

> as neither invented nor exaggerated. He [James] must have been thrown heavily against barbed wire, for my mother had to mend the rips in his clothes so that he could go to school the following morning. It was one of the unpleasant memories of Millbourne Lane. (73–74)

In *Ulysses*, Bloom's thoughts momentarily arrive at the peculiar urban legend that "It was a nun they say invented barbed wire" (*U* 8.154). In fact, barbed wire originated in the mid-nineteenth-century American West; its enclosing function was first intended for territorial control of agriculture and livestock, but soon transferred to military uses. The British Army made successful use of it in South Africa during Kitchener's campaign against the Boers. By 1914 the new technology had become a potent image of armed conflict, territorial control, and mass killing on an unprecedented scale; as Nigel Fountain notes, its primary advantages were that it could endure heavy artillery fire and ensnare soldiers "like fish in a net."[24]

Alongside this harsh physical reminder, the particulars of Stephen's brutal interrogation are worth considering. In the category of prose, the preferred author of Heron and his lieutenants is Captain Frederick Marryat, a choice that undoubtedly bolsters their association with the Victorian cult of manliness and military ideals. His influence seems to shape not just the critical opinion of Heron and his lieutenants but their violent enforcement of it. A career naval officer, Captain Marryat authored in his retirement several notable works of juvenile fiction that typically dealt in themes of high-seas adventure, imperial conflict, and military triumph. The books saw numerous reprintings from the mid-nineteenth to the mid-twentieth century, finding an audience of millions of young readers. While these novels in no way conceal the harsh realities of shipboard life and wartime, they generally serve up glorified depictions of the Royal Navy.

Two Marryat works relevant to *A Portrait* are the early novels *The Naval Officer* (1833) and *Mr. Midshipman Easy* (1836). As biographies of Royal Navy sailors, they suggest British military counterparts to Joyce's Irish *Künstlerroman*. They had a major following among juvenile readers, a vast number of whom would later fill the ranks of the same navy they read about in the stories. Marryat did not in fact set out to write literature for boys. As

R. B. Kershner points out, "Only after Captain Marryat's *Mr. Midshipman Easy*, intended for an adult audience, had been adopted by schoolboys did he venture into the field of fiction for children" (*Joyce, Bakhtin* 168). Ultimately Marryat's fiction came to serve a dual function of entertainment and indoctrination.

The Naval Officer; or, Scenes and Adventures in the Life of Frank Mildmay follows the making of a naval officer from an aborted school career to high-seas adventure and combat duty in the Napoleonic Wars, followed by a hero's return to Britain and a promising marriage and family life. Like the boys in "An Encounter," the young Frank Mildmay eschews the adult authorities of school and family life to chase after glamorized notions of adventure. For him this means running away from an oppressive boarding school to enlist in the navy at fourteen. Once there, he discovers an even harsher climate of abuse and corruption. But the benefits of male camaraderie, patriotic duty, and military adventure soon outweigh any momentary shocks suffered at the coarse hands of fellow midshipmen or enemies in combat. Any negative experiences along the way merely reinforce the nobility of the sailor's life, for Mildmay in particular and the British navy overall. Perseverance and triumph over the temporary setback or unkind treatment only contribute to a fuller picture of the successful officer who, like his country, strives for perfection in an imperfect world.

The Naval Officer tends to uphold a status quo imperial militarism as a vehicle to shape the moral and physical condition of British manhood, not to mention the world in general. The following passage, recounting the narrator's role in repelling a French siege in Catalonia, typifies Marryat's glorified vision of warfare and chauvinistic exaltation of British superiority:

> Groans, screams, confusion, French yells, British hurras rent the sky! The hills resounded with the shouts of victory! We sent them hand-grenades in abundance, and broke their shins in glorious style! I must say that the French behaved nobly, though many a tall grenadier and pioneer fell by the symbol in front of his warlike cap. I cried with rage and excitement; and we all fought like bull-dogs, for we knew there was no quarter to be given. (90)

A triumphant end for the cause of Empire will always justify the means. Likewise, the conclusion of the novel trumps any of the potentially deleterious effects of navy life, when the protagonist's return to his designated social milieu and a proper marriage ultimately justify the harsh realities or moral compromises he found along the way.

Mr. Midshipman Easy (1836) was an adult novel by Captain Marryat that also became popular with young readers. It provides some additional insight into the militaristic and corporal violence seen in *A Portrait*. Like *The Naval Officer*, *Mr. Midshipman Easy* is a biographical novel, tracing an aristocratic boy's unlikely route to navy life; its special appeal for younger readers no doubt emanated from its focus on the boy-hero's progression of adventures along the path to manhood. Most relevant for their connection with Heron and his lieutenants in *A Portrait* are two early chapters that satirize educational reformers and opponents of corporal punishment. Nicodemus Easy, father of the protagonist, refuses to enroll his son at any school that permits flogging with a birch, on the grounds that it is "not only contrary to the rights of man, but also in opposition to all sound sense and common judgement" (13). He follows with a litany of rhetorical questions touching on the psychological, theological, and pedagogical implications of flogging. In essence, these suggest a parody of arguments against bodily discipline and punishment that concludes with a mocking portrait of their source: "And Mr. Easy threw himself back in his chair, imagining, like all philosophers, that he had said something very clever" (14). Soon after, Mr. Easy undermines his own progressive philosophy when he beats his son for upsetting an urn of boiling liquid and scalding him. The entire episode seems intended to deride and deem hypocritical those who would question traditional wisdom, and go so far as to spare the rod and spoil the child.

The debate lingers into the protagonist's schooldays when the decision is made to enroll Jack Easy at the academy of Mr. Bonnycastle, a headmaster who promises he does not include birch flogging in his curriculum. What he does not tell Mr. and Mrs. Easy is that he does possess a significant collection of canes that provide an even more menacing form of corporal punishment. Bonnycastle boasts of the more thorough coverage and result his system achieves: "I can produce more effect by one caning than twenty floggings. Observe, you flog upon a part the most quiescent; but you cane upon all parts, from the head to the heels" (21). He continues with a detailed physiological description that contrasts the pain and after-effects of flogging with those of caning, proving the latter to be the superior technique.

The issue of corporal punishment in schools receives humorous treatment but ultimately strong endorsement from Marryat. It is no surprise, then, that his literary followers two generations on will be such cane-wielding interrogators as Vincent Heron. Stephen's earlier experience in his unjust pandybatting at the hands of Father Dolan demonstrates the unjust, abusive nature of such disciplinary measures. This seems an easily discarded minority opinion, however, in a time when so much of the discourse of education and popular culture favored the use of force in schoolroom discipline and social coercion. At odds with such a militarized educational and cultural environment, it is no wonder Stephen the teacher in "Nestor" experiences grave misgivings about perpetuating such a violent ideology and its related actions.

The popularity of Marryat's naval fiction reflected an ethos of physical discipline and self-sacrifice through military service that came to dominate youth culture in the Victorian and Edwardian periods. Drawing on many of the same aspects and energies of muscular Christianity and patriotism, it emphasized self-improvement, mental discipline, and rigorous exercise as means of individual secular devotion to a greater national good. The period saw the advent of military drill in schools and the rise of uniformed youth organizations such as the Boys' Brigades and the Lads' Drill Association, as well as Boer War veteran Robert Baden-Powell's Boy Scouts, whose original slogan read not simply "Be prepared" but "Be prepared to die for your country." Such groups emphasized preparation for the action of battle that boys were already reading about in their school texts, popular novels, and penny story-papers. Ferrall and Jackson observe this "democratization of sacrifice" as one of the hallmarks of juvenile fiction during the prewar years (35).

Indeed, the notion of sacrifice infused social and literary discourse to such a degree that one of the most renowned custodians of nineteenth-century culture came to emphasize the subordinate role of arts and letters to the military purpose of the state. During an 1865 address, John Ruskin told the Royal Military Academy at Woolwich:

> No great art ever yet rose on earth, but among a nation of soldiers because the creative, or foundational, war is that in which the natural restlessness and love of contest among men are disciplined, by consent, into modes of beautiful—though it may be fatal—play: in which the natural ambition and love of power of men are disciplined into the aggressive conquest of surrounding evil. (qtd. in Ferrall and Jackson 35)

Ruskin's remarks establish soldiering and armed conflict as competitive outlets and necessary struggles, without which a country or society cannot produce worthwhile art. His oxymoronical notion of a "creative war," while conceding the potential risk of death, nevertheless spurs the "young warriors" on to action for the sake of promoting the cultural life of the nation (ibid.). Such a pronouncement from the most influential critic of the day provides a clue to what guided mainstream British attitudes to art, literature, and popular culture. Ruskin's labeling of combat experience as a form of "play" is noteworthy, not least for its hinting at a sense of extended adolescence or delayed adulthood that was often encouraged by Victorian education. Ruskin presents play as a functional precursor to art, essential to the development of an individual and a society's artistic imagination and self-definition.

Four decades later, Joyce shows the behavioral effects that boys' curricular and popular literature could have on their readers. Ruskin's sense of the warring impulse as a foundation for creative play is inverted in Joyce's depictions of boys who play at war after reading about it in books. Like Joe Dillon's gang in "An Encounter" arranging back-garden battles or the North Richmond Street boys in "Araby" who "ran the gantlet of the rough tribes from the cottages," the imaginative recreation of Stephen and his schoolmates shows some sure signs of their indoctrination by militarist ideology acquired through reading (D 11, 22).

Even prior to the Great War, some peace advocates and education reformers sought to warn the British public about the dangerous, antithetical blend of school and militarism. Many had begun to recognize how the process of militarization extended far beyond the training and equipping of armies, by specifically targeting school-age boys to fill the future ranks. In response to invasion scares, uniformed drill had become a part of the British schools, even down to the primary level. In 1923, antimilitarist pamphleteer Rennie Smith protested the insinuation of martial ideologies and practices into the national school curriculum: "Oil and water don't mix. Neither do militarism and education" (1).

A Portrait, *Dubliners*, and *Ulysses* sound the alarm as to the militarization of boys' lives through the power of reading, whether through official academics or popular texts. Joyce's depiction of schoolrooms and reading as sites of military indoctrination anticipates Edward Said's definition of culture as a "theater" of ideological engagements and "battleground" of contentious politics (xiii). For the Irishman Joyce, and for the Palestinian Said, battlefield metaphors do not remain so for long: insofar as cultural discourses and literary texts shape historical actions, they are quite often precursors to combative realities. If culture represents a violent terrain of ideological engagement, then schoolbooks and popular magazines are some of its arms and ammunitions. For Joyce's schoolboys, caught between the propaganda of the newsstand and the schoolroom, cultural clashes have pyrrhic consequences, as "Nestor" describes. While Said's discussion in *Culture and Imperialism* privileges the novel as a literary medium for colonial and anticolonial discourse, Joyce's fiction presents multiple genres squared off in ideological engagement with readers and in competition with each other. Canonical fiction, popular periodicals, classical writing, and contemporary textbooks all bespeak a recurring focus on militarized content. Vying for limited political and intellectual space, these diverse texts all similarly convey the imperial ideals of the Victorian and Edwardian eras, as well as the manly and martial codes of behavior that upheld them.

In his portrayals of male upbringing and adolescent reading, Joyce references popular and curricular writings as meaningful indicators of how a generation of boys was directed by school and media culture to emulate militarized masculine identities. Diverse in genre and content, these texts form a complex network of cultural authorities worthy of additional attention and analysis by readers of Joyce today, when not only juvenile literature and popular magazines but movies, television, video games, and rapidly proliferating online media have an even greater reach for military public-relations and recruitment.

Joyce's gorescarred books argue consequences for boys' reading that rival those of the athletic culture discussed in the previous chapter. His adolescent readers and their military intertexts, in their various pedagogical contexts, outline a role for juvenile reading as a social and psychological influence that is sometimes coercive, other times subversive, but always close at hand. His portraits of young characters show the socializing potential of reading and writing; the texts they read run the gamut from school primers and canonical literature to serialized fiction, the so-called penny dreadful of the newsstand. Each suggests a sanctioned or suspect contribution to the socialization of young men. Some of the stories are expressly encouraged, some are vehemently prohibited. Still others are utterly unknown by the parental, church, or school authorities charged with the moral instruction and guidance of their young readers. Beyond mere local color or narrative furniture, the variety and abundance of boys' reading materials in Joyce weave a rich tapestry from the militarist threads of education and popular culture.

4

Domestic Forces

> By the public police and economy I mean the due regulation and domestic order of the kingdom; whereby the individuals of the state, like members of a well-governed family, are bound to conform their general behaviour to the rules of propriety, good neighbourhood, and good manners.
>
> William Blackstone, *Commentaries on the Laws of England*

> A squad of constables debouched from College street, marching in Indian file. Goosestep. Foodheated faces, sweating helmets, patting their truncheons. After their feed with a good load of fat soup under their belts. Policeman's lot is oft a happy one. They split up in groups and scattered, saluting, towards their beats.
>
> *Ulysses* 8.406–10

Leopold Bloom's lunchtime encounter with a squad of Dublin Metropolitan Police constables in "Lestrygonians" makes overt reference to some of the potential abuses and inherent dangers of police power. When Bloom walks past the officers just after their midday meal, he sees the constables as a concoction of martial and gastronomic language that underscores their role as a domestic—and domesticated—force of law. Their animal presence seems a far cry from English legal scholar William Blackstone's definition of the police as "due regulation and domestic order" intended to reinforce "propriety, good neighbourhood, and good manners" (161). Dynamic wordplay associates the DMP detachment with activities of eating and soldiering, underscoring the rather blurred distinction between police presence and military occupation. For example, the verb "debouched," a tactical term referring to the movement of infantry from narrow terrain into wider battle space, suggests in bodily terms (it's French for "unmouthed") the precise counter of the healthy ingestion and civilized dining that Bloom seeks. Moreover, "marching in Indian file" (*U* 8.406–7) the police emulate the formation British soldiers learned in seventeenth-century North America and brought to other colonies, including India and Ireland. Parade-ground maneuvers then mingle with culinary consumption in the ominous term "Goosestep" (*U* 8.407). An allusion to the notoriously intimidating marching style of the nineteenth-century Prussian guard, the word might be something of an exaggeration for the movements of well-fed Dublin policemen. Nevertheless, the extreme image from Bismarck's Germany suggests real concerns about civil rights, social order, and police power—theoretical and actual—in colonial Ireland.

By 1904, Prussian-dominated Germany was the paragon of a military-based society, not only for civil dissidents in that country but for many across Europe and the British Isles who regarded German invasion as a foregone conclusion to heightening international rivalry. A dangerous creeping of militarist ideology into civil affairs and police administration was observed by Karl Liebknecht in Germany, where he warned that the police had become a key satellite orbiting the "central sun" of militarism.[1] While the DMP were not in the habit of goose-stepping down Dublin streets, Joyce's deployment of the term turns a passing description of policemen into a striking political critique. The image is replayed in *Finnegans Wake* with "the act of goth stepping the tolk of Doolin, drain and plantage, wattle and daub, with you'll peel as I'll pale" (*FW* 332.10–11). As the Germanic historical scope widens to incorporate both the ancient Goths and modern "Gestapose" (*FW* 332.7), references to "peel" and "pale" nonetheless retain the connection with British military and police administration in Ireland under Secretary Robert Peel. Tom Rice has shown us Joyce's concerns with the rise of totalitarian police states in conjunction with the emergent technologies of radio and television.[2] That Dublin Metropolitan Police might be included in that category and regarded even as metaphorical goose-steppers suggests that a militarized police state had already begun to take hold in Ireland, despite the clearly prescribed limits of police under English statutes.

Defining the role of police for English society in 1769, Blackstone drew upon a classical metaphor of state governance. Book 4 of his *Commentaries on the Laws of England* characterizes police power in the familiar, and *familial*, terms of the home. The king—and the hierarchical delegation of his authority—was father, his subjects the dependent wives or children in need of his care and control. Blackstone associates the "public police" to "due regulation and domestic order," thereby extending the centuries-old vision of king as national paterfamilias (161). From a legal concept of royal authority, the police became the institutionalization of that authority, assuming the literal embodiment of personnel charged with its enforcement. Theory and practice effectively conflated king and father, state and family: police and patriarchy came together by metaphorical association as well as practical implementation.

Blackstone was not so much inventing a new theory as reiterating for English society a definition of political economy articulated a decade earlier by Jean-Jacques Rousseau. The French social philosopher invoked the term for its ancient Greek root *oikos* (house), extending the longstanding parallel of state government with household governance. Blackstone brought the concept into a specifically English and monarchical context, emphasizing how the king's authority to police the nation both originated from and resembled the rule of a patriarch over his wife and children. In the house of state, the inherent power of the father-king, or *patria potestas*, was realized in the abstract notion and actual organization of the public police.

In Ireland, occupation politics gave additional significance to the public police and domestic order. The 1801 Act of Union codified the sense of paternalism at a national level by establishing a secondary role for Ireland within the United Kingdom. As John Bull's other island, Ireland was formally rechristened a dependent colony and subordinate kingdom to Westminster; Irish subjects, long deemed unruly children by popular English racial stereotypes, saw their national identity still further compromised. In the ensuing decades, establishment of police forces in Ireland along English guidelines was among the most visible and paternalistic effects of the new Union. Despite concerns even from the architects of union themselves about blurred distinctions between the police and the military, almost from the beginning these domestic forces served as an adjunct or paramilitary to the army in Ireland.

Policemen traverse Joyce's fiction with a regularity that seems to simulate their real-life comings and goings through Dublin streets a century ago. At that time, as Kim Devlin notes, "Dublin and other Irish cities constituted the most heavily policed zones in the United Kingdom" (45). Rarely do policemen patrol Joyce's pages alone; rather, they tend to occur in appropriate conjunction with the very image of authority that served as conceptual basis for the police function: the father. In this regard, Joyce's writing considers the power of the father that originated in Greco-Roman political economy and became the basis for the nineteenth-century science of police. As police theory migrated from the Continent to Britain and Ireland, and as a national constabulary was established, each operated from a central metaphor of paternal discipline and familial correction. This connection lurks behind the police-father parallels of *Dubliners* and *Ulysses*. Its presence in both texts not only depicts the reality of early-twentieth-century Ireland as modern police state, it encourages readers to question the function of patriarchal physical force as a method of household governance and social coercion.

Through recurring association of paternal figures with the militarization of policing and family life in Ireland, Joyce mounts parallel critiques of the public police and *patria potestas* in colonial Ireland. He alludes, for instance, in "Grace" to how sound knowledge of policing does not guarantee domestic tranquility in either a familial or a national sense. The constabulary clerk Martin Cunningham wields a "blade of human knowledge, natural astuteness particularised by long association with cases in the police courts," yet despite being part of the official apparatus for policing the life of the state, Cunningham's "own domestic life was not very happy" (*D* 156). The same could easily be said of colonial Irish subjects experiencing the coordinated brutalities of the British police and military presence. Other fathers in *Dubliners*—including Mr. Doyle in "After the Race" and Farrington in "Counterparts"—exist in various and complicated relationships to the police and the garrison. So doing, they reflect the challenges of distinguishing military from police power and of upholding the ideal principles of public policing defined by Blackstone and espoused by Peel. By the close of the collection, only Gabriel Conroy in "The Dead" offers some hope for reconfiguring the patriarchal role in Dublin. *Ulysses*, through Bloom's perspectives on abusive or corrupt police authority, suggests the potential for demilitarizing the paternal power of the state and reforming the harmful patriarchy it exerts over the lives of its subjects.

Paternal Order of Police

The transmission of *patria potestas* from individual to national household gave rise to the science of public police in European legal philosophy. Police originated in the classical Greek notion of the single house, or *oikos*, from which the word "economy" was derived, initially to mean general household welfare rather than its modern sense of fiscal commerce. As part of the public economy, before it identified an official force of men, the term "police" signified the patriarchal authority of the royal householder over the extended household or citizenry of the state. "From the perspective of police, the state is the institutional manifestation of a household. The police state, as *paterfamilias*, seeks to maximize the welfare of his—or rather its—household" (Dubber 3). Centuries before it became an actual and tangible force of officers, the public police emerged as a contested concept in European legal science and political theory, with the idea of the public police referring to a branch of royal power distinct from law. Thus the power to police evolved into the political economy of the European nation-state, but as it assumed the physical form of officers and patrols, there emerged a contradiction between protection and state control.

Police authority and coercion by force, by the early-modern era, emerged as counterpoint to rule by law. For instance, in the Enlightenment political philosophy of John Locke, the concept of police exists in counterbalance to the law under which all members of society exist in equal freedom and autonomy. The vertical notion of police, by contrast, emphasizes the subject nature of the citizenry by sustaining the classical notion of citizens as inferior members of the royal household. "After Locke, governing through law must be legitimate—and for him, that meant consensual. Governing through police, by contrast, came to be held to a lower standard, of minimum competence; it must be not so irrational as to draw the householder's fitness into question" (Dubber 47). Ireland, by the early nineteenth century, saw the scale tipped away from rule by law and toward police governance.

The militarization of law enforcement was a calculated strategy of British rule in Ireland. From the mid-nineteenth century, the constabulary and metropolitan police forces were developed to augment the needs of the British Army in Ireland. This achieved what Elizabeth Muenger describes as the "institutionalized ambiguity in the relationship between the army and the two branches of the Irish police" (81). Joyce includes both branches in his fiction: the unarmed, neighborhood-based DMP and the paramilitary RIC, whose Black and Tan auxiliaries were notorious for their violence against civilians during the War for Independence. Following the Constabulary and Dublin Police Acts of 1836, each had become an integral part of British efforts to maintain domestic order and political power in Ireland.

Nor is Joyce's militarization of police power and the *patria potestas* limited to British imperialism in Ireland. A subtle but certain household brutality applies as well to the Irish nationalist movement when, soon after Bloom passes the goose-stepping constables, his thoughts turn to the traditional

Irish repast of "Michaelmas goose" (*U* 8.468). The image suggests that the republican movement, in advocating violent means to Irish independence, might also be devoured by its own paramilitary mindset. Bloom references the pragmatic and menacing discipline of the new physical-force wing of Irish politics led by James Stephens and others: "Sinn Fein. Back out you get the knife" (*U* 8.458–59). The same instinct for self-preservation that Karl Liebknecht located at the core of German state militarism can lead to dangerous emulation, and not just by Sinn Fein but even by the most peaceful of individuals, given the right circumstances.

Therefore Bloom suddenly envisions the plump and lazy policemen themselves becoming easy prey, like fattened geese or pastured livestock: "Let out to graze. Best moment to attack one in pudding time. A punch in his dinner" (*U* 8.410–11). Similarly, in *Stephen Hero* "the great cow-like trunks of police constables [that] swing slowly round after him as he passed them" inspire a "deep-seated anger" on Stephen's part (*SH* 146). Having acknowledged the animal quality and potency of the police, Bloom seems poised to strike back and match their force with his own. Leaving the Burton lunch counter to seek out the more humane and moral confines of Davy Byrne's, his thoughts of the police take a stark, Hobbesian turn: "Eat or be eaten. Kill! Kill!" (*U* 8.703).[3] The modern paterfamilias reacts in turn to the paternalistic police presence.

While this lunchtime moment offers up policemen in humorous animal parody, it also conveys their escalating tensions with the civilian population, as evidenced by Bloom's subsequent recollection of violent action by the Dublin Metropolitan Police against crowds at a Boer War street protest a few years earlier. The constables move in great numbers, with reinforcements, for as soon as the first group has passed, "A squad of others, marching irregularly, rounded Trinity railings making for the station. Bound for their troughs" (*U* 8.411–12). By "marching irregularly," the police assume not just an unusual or arrhythmic gait but an official British Army designation: as irregular, rather than regular troops, they reflect the subaltern, paramilitary status of the police in Ireland that evolved, on the one hand, in emulation of the eighteenth-century British metropolitan constable-and-watchmen system and, on the other, from the longstanding rural tradition of local militias (Muenger 81–83). Bloom's perspective suggests the fundamental anxiety and lingering conflict over the distinction between police and the military in Ireland dating back nearly a century to Robert Peel and the reform of law enforcement in the country.

Joyce begins to explore the conflicted nature of Irish policing as early as *Dubliners*, where a series of fathers exist, like Bloom, in varying relation to police. More often than not, the difference between domestic order and disorder for these fathers depends upon their social or economic ties to Dublin law enforcement or military administration. In some cases, the connection to army or police barracks can be socially or financially profitable; at other times, it is morally degrading or even mentally destructive. In the worst cases, it inspires physical abuse against other members of the family.

The first reference to police in *Dubliners* conjoins law enforcement with food and household economy of a different sort than Bloom notices in "Lestrygonians." Police are the foundation for paternal wealth in the story "After the Race," as the father of Jimmy Doyle is a butcher who has been "fortunate enough to secure some police contracts" (*D* 36). This seemingly innocuous detail of a background character nonetheless sets police and paterfamilias in complementary and potentially controversial relation. It calls into question the very basis for the Doyles' financial profile and social aspirations, starting from the multivoiced phrase "fortunate enough" (*D* 36). The construction begs the question whether it was good luck or sufficient cash, or some combination of both, that won Mr. Doyle his commercial advantage. Additionally, the undisclosed story of exactly how and from whom Doyle senior secured his contracts raises questions about whether bribery, favoritism, or undue influence might possibly have played a role. While there is no certain malfeasance, there is also no clear agency or definite identity on the police end of the deal. The narrative style of *Dubliners* tends in general toward the minimal, but in this instance verbal thrift suggests secrecy and therefore questionable legality. The fact that such a dubious transaction involves the police—the very ones meant to uphold, not evade, the law—is certainly grounds for concern.

The police and Mr. Doyle have much in common besides their business deal. Both also exercise paternal authority and domestic responsibility. Mr. Doyle aims to "secure" not just meat contracts but his family's future, by way of his son's Cambridge education and upward mobility. For their part, the police are charged with the security of the greater household of the state, or as Blackstone describes it, "the due regulation and domestic order of the kingdom" (161). The fact that Mr. Doyle has possibly gotten ahead in business as the result of payoffs to corrupt police officials only renders his and their authority the more dubious. The complicity suggests how both the Doyle family and Dublin overall are at some risk due to the actions of these actual and symbolic heads of household. Presumably, neither the police nor Mr. Doyle is above whatever means it takes to achieve domestic security, revealing that the basis for it, whether in family or city, already exists somewhere within the shadow of a moral doubt.

As an extension of his paternal role, Mr. Doyle's occupation, along with his politics, reinforces his police affiliation. Butchers and policemen operate in a paradoxical moral terrain that sanctions violence in pursuit of the presumably greater good of middle-class comfort and public order. To that end, each employs techniques of brute physical force and treads a fine moral line that depends as much on the changing nature of the law as it does on the regulatory vagaries of his own conscience. That he "had begun life as an advanced Nationalist" but "modified his views early" (*D* 36)—in enough time and to such degree to enter into profitable alliance with the enemy—demonstrates how for Doyle, if not all bourgeois Dublin householders, paternal power trumps patriotic idealism.

A decade before Joyce was writing *Dubliners*, Joseph Conrad's *Heart of Darkness* posited the same two occupations as normative poles of security and civility in British life. In one impatient aside, Marlow wonders whether his story of savagery in the Congo is even intelligible to those who have grown up amid the bourgeois stability of London:

> "Absurd!" he cried. "This is the worst of trying to tell. . . . Here you all are, each moored with two good addresses, like a hulk with two anchors, a butcher round one corner, a policeman round another, excellent appetites, and temperatures normal—you hear—normal from year's end to year's end." (84)

In effect, butcher and policeman represent the social parameters of the modern metropolis; they are the cornerstones of state paternalism, providing the safety and sustenance that allow the "normal" life of European modernity to carry on. At the same time, however, the norms that butcher and policeman represent and protect also threaten to supplant human agency. Such a trade-off of security for intellectual autonomy, Marlow acknowledges with some frustration, helps make civilized living possible even if it might impede his listeners aboard the *Nellie* from understanding the full implication of his narrative.

For Joyce, by contrast, the heart of darkness is not confined to some distant colonial trading station of the Belgian Congo; it exists right at home in the social and economic commerce of urban Ireland. Joyce's butcher and policeman suggest not a normative softening of the social order but the corrupt tendencies that underlie Dublin life. Despite their official responsibilities concerning the physical security and general welfare of the population, they often exist in a corrupt power structure that enables both to exercise their paternalistic power in forceful and, at times, severely injurious ways.

While this butcher partners with police in questionable commercial activities, others in his professional fraternity inflict a more direct social harm. "The Boarding House" commences with a butcher who wields the tool of his trade as a direct weapon of patriarchal violence. Mrs. Mooney, the daughter of a butcher, married her father's foreman, and "One night he went for his wife with the cleaver and she had to sleep in a neighbour's house" (*D* 56). Fortunately, Mr. Mooney's attack culminates in legal and not literal separation; nevertheless, this husband's violence is enough to dismember a household and family structure, with lasting effect. His action severs the very same civility and normalcy that Conrad's butcher and policeman serve to protect, demonstrating in effect that the distance between social stability and destructive force can be as narrow as the butcher's blade. The distinction between physical and legal power, household governance and state authority—whether to intimidate or to protect—can be just as fine. In this regard, patriarchal and governmental powers cast parallel, menacing shadows of domestic violence. Brutal actions and dubious dealings thus emerge from under the legitimate guise of state or familial authority.

Joyce's pairing of Dublin fathers and police effectively traces Blackstone's concept of the police to its origins in the household governance structures of ancient Greece and Rome. Classical economy, the science of household management, granted the paterfamilias total authority, from financial to physical, over all members of the household or *domus*. Ideally, the power of the father was intended for the benefit of the entire household; his right to discipline could only be checked by state authority in cases where the punishment had been carried out with malicious intent or in which it threatened rather than benefited the entire household, and, by extension, the rest of society.

This mirroring of the household in national governance established long-reigning cultural and linguistic reflections. Father and country came to be expressed in virtually identical terms, reinforcing the concept of paternal power at the levels of state and family. Thus Julius Caesar was the first of some two dozen Roman emperors to bear the seemingly redundant honorific *pater patriae* (father of the fatherland). On the other side of the coin, being an imperial subject was analogous to being a woman or child dependent in the greater *domus* of the state. As multiple households united over time to form the basis of ancient city-states and later, medieval kingdoms and modern nation-states, the *patria potestas*, especially in its physical form, was duplicated and specified in the expanded authority of emperor or king.

Along these lines, the Kingstown location of Mr. Doyle's first butcher shop in "After the Race" forges a subtle allegorical link concerning his microeconomic relation to state authority (*D* 36). Like the police contracts, Kingstown associates Mr. Doyle with the paternalism of the Crown and British governance in Ireland. That his son comes to the same town years later to gamble aboard a yacht at best suggests, much like his incomplete Cambridge education, shifting allegiances and tenuous authority. Terence Brown notes that Kingstown replaced the name Dun Laoghaire "in 1821 to record George IV's departure from Ireland on the royal yacht after a brief visit" (*D* 257n7). At the historical nexus of disputed sovereignty and territorial aggression, its renaming in effect altered the social contract without full consent of the citizenry.[4] Like Mr. Doyle's business with police, or Britain's Act of Union with Ireland, the very name of Kingstown functions along questionable contractual lines. The parallel is reinforced by the inherent pun generated by the story's title, as "After the Race" gradually comes to signify not just the evening following the motor derby but the impulse for the "gratefully oppressed" Irish, including even the prosperous Doyle family, to model themselves after the values of the British race (*D* 35). Notwithstanding the potential moral shortcomings or legal compromises of his commercial connections, Mr. Doyle profits from the British police state; other men and their families in *Dubliners* fare less well financially or socially. Joyce shows several who exhibit the enormous psychological toll of living under the coordinated pressures of police surveillance and army occupation.

In the Shadow of the Barracks

Writing to Stanislaus from Rome in the fall of 1906, Joyce expressed his open disdain for violent patriarchy; at the same time, he emphasized a need to contemplate the broader causes and conditions behind domestic abuse:

> I am no friend of tyranny, as you know, but if many husbands are brutal the atmosphere in which they live (vide Counterparts) is brutal and few wives and homes can satisfy the desire for happiness. In fact, it is useless to talk about this any further. I am going to lunch. (*L* 2:192)

If he found the subject too futile or tiresome for further discussion, his fiction did not abandon the argument. Joyce's parenthetic pointing suggests the unpublished *Dubliners* manuscript as a space for realistically considering the circumstances and causes of household brutality. The story collection consistently circles back to the representations of domestic abuse and patriarchal tyranny. If Stanislaus did take his brother's advice and take a close look at the story, he would not have had to read very far to discover that a vital part of the "atmosphere" shaping tyrannical husbands and brutal fathers is the paternalistic cruelty of a militarized state. A century on, readers continue to find in "Counterparts" a fable of domestic violence.[5] The story's causal connection of the harsh brutality of the father to the repressive paternalism of the state should also not be overlooked.

The progression across "Counterparts" from metaphorical to concrete violence suggests how the external infrastructure of state coercion ultimately assumes a volatile dynamic at the household level. The brutal atmosphere within the typical middle-class Dublin home is merely a reflection of the militarized colonial control happening in the world around it. Symbolic atmospheric aggression is evident from the story's very first phrase: "The bell rang furiously" (*D* 82). Even before characters interact, an aggressive vocabulary dominates the law office of Crosbie and Alleyne. Mr. Alleyne's "furious voice" echoes the angry sound of the bell, the first sign that authoritative anger, like legal documents, will be readily duplicated (*D* 82). As Joyce's most oppressed and oppressive head of household, Farrington is a beleaguered scrivener who copies not just legal documents but bullying behavior by bringing his workplace frustrations home to his wife and children. The hostility of office machinery and environment soon leads to the metaphoric skirmish of patron and employee, described in the ongoing figurative language of battle. Twice Farrington employs a slang term for detonation—"*Blast him!*" (D 82); "*Blast it!*" (D 86)—and he displays his explosive personality at several stages, as for instance when a "spasm of rage gripped his throat" and, soon after, when he "longed to . . . bring his fist down on something violently" (D 83, 86). Such hand-to-hand combat escalates into recurring gunfire when Mr. Alleyne "shot his head up over a pile of documents" and "he shot up his head again" (D 82, 83). Consequently, such battlefield conditions have Farrington behaving like a fighter in enemy territory. Sneaking out to the pub during work hours, he dives into a doorway for fear of being spotted, and following his midday tipple he "retreated out of the snug as furtively as he had entered it" (D 84). In the return to the office chain-of-command, the narrator even mocks formal military ritual when the aroma of perfume "saluted his nose" (D 85).[6] The atmosphere of his workday is suffused by emotional volatility and combative interaction.

By the end of the story, what follows these metaphors of systematic armed attack is anything but metaphorical: Farrington takes a stick to his child. The moment appropriately copies the violent action of several other fathers in *Dubliners*. As Gerald Doherty observes, "Child bullying is just one further link in a long chain of reduplication" (98). In "Ivy Day in the Committee Room," for example, the old caretaker Jack takes care of his son with questionable methods: "Only I'm an old man now I'd change his tune for him. I'd take the stick to his back and beat him while I could stand over him—as I done many a time before" (D 116). In "Eveline," the title character's enduring childhood image of her father notably associates him with the terror of pursuit and forced removal of the neighborhood children at play: "Her father used often to hunt them in out of the field with his blackthorn stick" (D 29). The bullying action evokes the traumatic race memories of the mass evictions that decimated the Irish population a half century earlier: the children's displacement and dispossession from the field recalls the forced, sometimes violent, evictions of Irish tenants by land agents, army, or constabulary. Still another violent patriarch appears in "Grace" with Mrs. Kernan's sad description of her husband's actions: "There were worse husbands. He had never been violent since the boys had grown up and she knew that he would walk to the end of Thomas Street and back again to book even a small order" (D 155). The apologetic account suggests a fall from grace antedating the story; it also affords a brief hint of the coping mechanism by which many victims—out of fear, denial, or both—rationalize their suffering and even defend their abuser.

"Counterparts" provides the best answer to why all of these men come to behave as abusively as they do. The overlapping social, economic, and cultural tensions indeed seem to have their impact. Mark Spilka reads Farrington as becoming a child batterer to work out his frustration at finding himself "at the bottom of several status ladders—commercial, religious, national, regional, athletic" (189). Yet in addition to the social and office politics of the story, one telling detail looms largest in the atmosphere that shapes this abusive father. It appears only briefly in the movement from metaphorical to actual violence, but it affords a glimpse of state paternalism that suggests the most important underlying cause of Farrington's own brutal fatherhood.

Just prior to his attack on his son, the narrative depicts Farrington on the street near his home. There, just steps from his door, a force much greater than overbearing bosses or barroom rivals towers quite literally over his domestic surroundings. Joyce's tone and syntax convey its undeniable presence: "His tram let him down at Shelbourne Road and he steered his great body along in the shadow of the wall of the barracks. He loathed returning to his home" (D 93). Doubling idioms and dense grammatical layering contribute a sense of the domineering architecture that weighs heavily on Farrington's consciousness. The phrase "let him down" carries both the literal meaning of disembarking and a figurative sense of disappointment. Indeed, Farrington seems continually let down by his situation and the lack of prospects for changing it. Appropriately, the phrase underscores his lack of agency and renders him an unmoving block of freight to be off-loaded from the streetcar. When the inebriated copyist does take tentative charge of his movement, it is with a marked disconnection or loss of control over his own body, which becomes an ungainly vehicle that must be "steered . . . along in the shadow of the wall of the barracks." The triple prepositional phrase seems to embody not just the thickness of the barracks wall itself but the complex social and psychological partitions it represents.

The street location means this particular wall belongs to Beggars Bush, a British military facility dating from the early nineteenth century. From March to August of 1904, Joyce lived in a house at 60 Shelbourne Road, across the street from the Beggars Bush barracks wall (Igoe 173). Where

Farrington is deposited by the tram, Shelbourne Road parallels the northeast side of the barracks compound for about 500 feet. The orientation means the twelve-foot-high wall does in fact cast a shadow over the road and sidewalk most days of the year and most times of day. That shadow would have been particularly great, in a physical and moral sense, in the early evening of February when Joyce has Farrington returning home. Living in the shadow of the barracks suggests then a fundamental cause of Farrington's domestic abuse if not a potent symbol of the overwhelming British presence, and, by extension, Ireland's inability to take charge of its own domestic order. Down to each neighborhood and house, the barracks represent a constant paternal state presence always looming right outside the door, usurping the autonomy of home and nation that should appropriately fall to the Irish themselves.[7]

Farrington is of course not the only Dubliner to feel overshadowed by barracks. Through most of the city, imposing police and army barracks had been features of life for more than a century and seemed poised to occupy not just city streets but residential spaces. Molly Bloom acknowledges as much in "Penelope" when she laments her own nocturnal isolation and anxiety at 7 Eccles Street: "I dont like being alone in this big barracks of a place at night I suppose Ill have to put up with it" (*U* 18.978–79). The remark—which could well apply to Dublin as a whole—suggests the deeply entrenched presence of the police and army: it renders domestic and military/police space virtually indistinguishable, a socioeconomic reality that will be discussed in chapter 5. Unlike Farrington, whose divided consciousness duplicates the destructive armed presence in his own family life, Molly finds ways to endure the militarization of her own household. She keeps things metaphorical in a way Farrington cannot. This might have something to do with her own actual experience outside of Ireland and as part of the British military community: she is, after all, the daughter of a sergeant major and grew up beside the barracks in Gibraltar, loving soldiers rather than fearing them. She is not a father whose essential agency and masculine identity are overwhelmed or undercut by the patriarchal attitude of the state.

Forefathers and Metaphors

The paternalism of occupied Ireland extends across *Dubliners* to confront the ultimate paterfamilias of the collection, Gabriel Conroy. The head of household in "The Dead" offers hope for breaking the cycle of patriarchal brutality by resisting the militarized atmosphere and redefining paternal identity for Ireland. Gabriel contends with the same paternal pressures and domestic forces that broke Farrington and others before him. Midway through "The Dead," a steady stream of metaphors depicts even the most festive and familial occasion of the Christmas season as a virtual battle zone. Already we have seen guests participate in dances named after British Army units—"Lancers were arranged" (D 187)—and heard the placid singing of Aunt Julia encouraged by an "irregular musketry of applause" (D 193). Such martial symbolism becomes even more apparent, and abundant, in the dinner-table description, a remarkable narrative centerpiece whose enumeration of food and drink belongs more to the realm of quartermaster than caterer. In this regard, the Morkan table incorporates the motifs of occupation politics and domestic violence from prior stories in the collection.

A series of metaphors dominates the table setting, equating military force with patriarchal ideology. The two principal entrees, ham and goose, are set at "rival ends" and supported by "parallel lines of side-dishes" (D 197). In her convincing reading of the culinary origins and post-Famine significance of the feast, Bonnie Roos notes how this configuration represents "internal Irish disputes intensified by what lies between them" (117). The diverse geography of the products on the table is not just reference to the current colonial situation but to Ireland's long history of foreign invasion and armed struggle. In this regard, Joyce's sustained martial conceit suggests how a culture of force is not confined to a single colony, country, or epoch, but transcends locality, linking distant periods and places in the decanters of port and sherry that stand as "sentries" to a "pyramid of oranges and American apples" (D 197). These allusions to ancient Egyptian and contemporary U.S. power situate the Anglo-Irish conflict amid a broader index of transhistorical comparisons.

Similar geo-culinary associations arise from the dish of "Smyrna figs," another exotic item imported to middle-class Dublin from a location that resonates with historical and literary echoes of armed conquest and control (D 197).[8] Originally named for a warrior queen, the city remained a contentious site for centuries, owing to its position in the eastern Mediterranean at the imperial nexus of Persian and Greek, and later Christian and Muslim, civilizations. Most notably, it served as a stepping-stone for Alexander the Great as he extended his empire into Asia Minor and beyond. Like Dublin,

Smyrna became a permanent naval station and fortified garrison outpost. Its thick walls of brick and stone made Smyrna among the most heavily fortified cities of the classical world, a sense captured perhaps in Joyce's description of the figs as a "solid rectangle" (D 197).[9] Along literary lines, Smyrna was long recognized as the birthplace of Homer as well as the less celebrated Quintus, whose own epic war poem *Posthomerica* eponymously "followed after Homer" at both the chronological and narrative levels, not unlike what Joyce would begin to do within a few years in *Ulysses*.[10]

Other items on the Morkans' menu establish more subtle double entendres of military personnel, matériel, or strategy. For instance, "a round of spiced beef" sits alongside the ham, and a dish of pudding "lay in waiting" (D 197). Additional support in the coming attack comes from "three squads of bottles of stout and ale and minerals, drawn up according to the colours of their uniforms" (D 197), of which the prominent red labels and "transverse green sashes" imply, respectively, British Army regulars and physical-force Irish nationalists, who were already well engaged in recruitment and covert drilling at the time Joyce was writing the story. If we take the term "smallest squad" to refer to the inferior number rather than size of the soldier-bottles, then red outnumbers green in the table setting much as British regiments outnumber Irish ones in the coming fight. Alternatively—or additionally—it could signify that well-fed soldiers or policemen loom larger in physique than their republican opponents, which would accurately reflect the realities of malnourishment and depopulation that dominated Ireland for the half century following the Famine. Such dark recollections seem far from the security and abundance of the holiday board, to be sure, but nonetheless maintain their place in the traumatized cultural memory.

A volatile family gathering was familiar territory for Joyce. Readers of *A Portrait* will recall Christmas-dinner animosity between Dante and Uncle Charles concerning nationalism, the Church, and the undoing of Charles Stewart Parnell; the interplay of familial tensions and national politics in that scene, as in much of the novel, had a strong autobiographical basis. But "The Dead" literally brings more to the table than just a clash of personalities or ideologies. Rod Mengham remarks of the scene how "a vocabulary of militarism overrules any naturalistic priorities that might have been engaged in the straightforward descriptions of objects on a table" (78). Many of the products on the Morkan holiday table are both realistic and emblematic, economic roots of the very military tensions they represent. They reference global commerce and conflict, including the actual conditions of colonial militarization right outside the door of the house on Usher's Island. As dynamic vehicles in the sustained martial conceit of "The Dead," they effectively collapse the normal safe distance between literal and figurative.

Even before the dinner table is set, the opening line of the story prepares readers for such dangerous grammatical slippage. Lily, the caretaker's daughter, is not "literally run off her feet" (D 175); rather, we can assume the remark to mean she is working ceaselessly to greet guests and assist with catering. But the telling misuse of the adverb—in which "literally" means its opposite, figuratively—initiates an effective blurring of concrete and abstract meaning from the start, as if to prepare for the fluid comparisons of the table menu. In this regard, bottles and side dishes resembling squadrons and sentries do not simply offer artful descriptions; they provide (and provoke) accurate reflections of the pressures on home and hearth that develop in an occupied colonial city with a growing armed resistance movement. The metaphorical militarism on the dinner table suggests the broader militarization of the domestic realm, experienced in the formalized rituals of a social gathering as well as the more intimate interactions of parenting and marriage.

In this sense, "The Dead" draws readers to central issues of the household and state in which male power and identity are shaped by the culture of military occupation. While not a soldier himself, Gabriel is a member of a society whose code of male behavior is very much derived from the culture of warfare. David Morgan notes the overt construction of male gender identity in the military subculture of contemporary western societies: "Of all the sites where masculinities are constructed, reproduced, and deployed, those associated with war and the military are some of the most direct" (165). Such a socializing context was well in place for early 1900s Dublin. Therefore, the demilitarization of Gabriel's domestic life necessitates the deconstruction and dismantling of his patriarchal inheritance.

In their seminal work on the origins of patriarchy, Richard Lee and Richard Daly locate its rise in conjunction with emerging class hierarchy and collective preparation for warfare in later agrarian societies and early-modern nation-states: "Male domination is one part of a complex of power relations fundamental to the maintenance of a class society; the other two parts are social inequality and militarism" (30). The classical western notion of the male-centered household (Gr. *domos*, L. *domus*) evolved into the civic arrangement of Greek city-state, Roman Empire, and medieval kingdom.

With the rise of the nation-state in the eighteenth and nineteenth centuries, the national order came to reinforce the intrafamilial relationships. Lee and Daly suggest that this connection originated in Roman society: "Patriarchy can best be understood as the reproduction of state hierarchy within the family. A well-known example of this is the *patria potestas* of the Roman Empire: the emperor rules the empire, the father rules the home and the family" (Lee and Daly 41). The governing of individual households and of national households were mirror images and parallel processes. At each level, domination is rooted in the domestic, historically and etymologically. From medieval to modern Europe, from Latin to English, "domestic" came to be synonymous with matters of home, as in "Put a stop to domestic violence now," and of nation, as in, "The prime minister's domestic policies will be of great importance to voters."

With this in mind, we can read "The Dead," among other ways, as Gabriel's search for the *patria potestas* appropriate to his historical and cultural conditions. A well-intentioned desire for domestic mastery characterizes Gabriel's role as husband and father. Compared to other patriarchs in *Dubliners* he is a "model paterfamilias," but he is still guilty of "petty paternal tyrannies masked as solicitude and practiced on the bodies of wife and children" (Norris, *Suspicious Readings* 223). Rigidly, if lovingly, he polices the life of his family. As Gretta reports, he has started making her wear galoshes, "forcing" their daughter Eva to eat stirabout, and having their son Tom wear shades over his eyes and work out with dumbbells (*D* 180). Like Farrington, Gabriel's corporal control over his family is a symptom of his subjugated status in British-occupied Dublin.

Although it does not approach the same level of corporal violence, it nevertheless mimics in household and family life the overbearing paternalism of police or garrison. As Vincent Cheng notes, Gabriel is "a well-meaning patriarch who is *almost* a domestic tyrant . . . a qualified representation by Joyce of a potentially oppressive patriarch in symbolic collaboration with the ruling masters of the English colonial empire" (*Joyce, Race* 134). It is domination with perhaps only the best intentions, but domination all the same. In his assuming the patriarchal seat at the head of his aunts' table, the alignment of colonial power, military might, and domestic domination is particularly apparent. Gabriel's own epiphany on this Feast of the Epiphany will have much to do with reimagining his own paternal power.

The Morkan holiday party resembles contemporary Ireland in such a reconfiguring of domestic power and identity. Gabriel, like many of his countrymen, faces increasingly complex choices about cultural identity, political loyalty, and, ultimately, physical force. One potential answer arrives in the fervent nationalism of Miss Ivors. Her cultural program, while on the surface a safe, bourgeois pastime of Irish language classes, Celtic jewelry, and summer excursions to the Aran Islands, nonetheless reveals its own inevitable pull toward violence. To start, the narrative frames their encounter with vivid military wordplay. While the two are partnered in the lancers, a dance named for one of the main British regiments stationed in Ireland, Miss Ivors's interrogation of Gabriel is likened to a regimental advance: "He did not know how to meet her charge" (D 188). Her parting insult that he is a "West Briton" (D 190) comes on the heels of verbal sparring that began in the aggressive metaphor of her greeting: "I have a crow to pluck with you" (D 187). The traditional English idiom equates social dispute with a violent domestic chore.[11] In the context of Irish revival, this assertive conversational opener enfolds a more menacing association: the Morrigu, the legendary Celtic war goddess, was often said to appear in the guise of a crow or raven. This battlefield association is reinforced by Miss Ivors's very name: Ivor is a conflation of the Old Norse term for warrior or battle-archer and the Old English word for bow or yew, the tree from which the Welsh longbow was first fashioned. The heterogeneous etymology undercuts the very sort of rigid and artificial nationalist program Miss Ivors would have Gabriel pursue.

In this way, Joyce inscribes drawing-room politics with notions of armed action, demonstrating how the physical-force wing of Irish republicanism emulates, literally and figuratively, the militarism of its enemy the British Empire. Yet militant nationalism offers an insufficient model by which Gabriel, and by extension Ireland, might reimagine and reorder domestic life. Meanwhile, the Anglo-Irish subalternity behind Gabriel's masculine outlook does not offer much in the way of improvement, as it remains confined to a traditional and debilitating patriarchy. Gabriel regularly writes reviews for the pro-unionist *Daily Express* about such English poets as Robert Browning, whose quotation he plans to include in the after-dinner tribute to the Morkan sisters (D 188–189, 192). The speech itself comes to emphasize "the tradition of genuine warm-hearted courteous Irish hospitality which our forefathers have handed down to us and which we in turn must hand down to our descendants" (*D* 204). The remark, however well intended, recontextualizes the holiday party and Irish domestic space in general along patriarchal lines, negating the fact that this evening is almost entirely the cultural and economic production of women.

A hope of liberation emerges in Gabriel's account of the misadventure of Patrick Morkan with Johnny the horse, which begins to revise and challenge the unquestioned allegiance to paternalistic tradition. In telling the story of his grandfather—in Gabriel's words "a very pompous old gentleman"—he begins with a purposeful and bombastic declaration: "Out from the mansion of his forefathers . . . he drove with Johnny" (*D* 209). The very same elements Gabriel celebrated in the dinner-table speech—patriarchy, courtesy, and domesticity—now become subjects of mockery. Johnny's comical and ultimately subservient behavior of walking repeated circles around the statue of King William renders Patrick Morkan even less aristocratic than he had hoped. Gabriel's derisive retelling of the story seems to underscore his grandfather's social arrogance rather than his social mobility. Gone are the idealized notions of Irish household and family, as well as the traditional deference to "forefathers," the very same word that appears in Gabriel's speech without the sarcasm it acquires in his storytelling.

The recurring terminology but altered connotations mark a measureable change in Gabriel, one that undercuts the traditional authorities of patriarchy and Irish domestic space, all through a narrative that rests upon shifting class dynamics and assumed military identities. After all, in wanting to "drive out with the quality to a military review in the park," Patrick Morkan seeks vicarious participation in the Dublin garrison, but instead finds a frustrating lesson in power relations of horse and rider (*D* 208). Gabriel's retelling of the story shows his growing awareness of a connection between domestic life and armed occupation that has been under critical interrogation since the opening lines of the story. It suggests the hope that Gabriel might avoid the paralyzing situation and actions of his forefathers by relocating himself in a demilitarized family narrative and national tradition.

The worst brutalities of that tradition are seen in two artistic allusions in the story entwining political and domestic violence; each suggests the most violent and tragic potential of a militarized domestic masculinity. "The Lass of Aughrim," the traditional ballad sung by Bartell D'Arcy at the end of the evening (D 213), parallels the rape and subsequent death of a young woman with the Galway village that was the setting for the 1691 defeat of the Jacobite armies by William of Orange. Military and sexual violence, personal and political betrayal, are virtually inseparable components of the story told in its verses. Meanwhile, the embroidery of "the two murdered princes in the Tower" (D 186) frames another cultural moment that conflates family with state violence. In this case, the work of art itself is feminine and domestic, as it was completed by Aunt Julia herself, albeit in subordinate imitation of the original work. When Gabriel refers to Irish hospitality rhetorically and euphemistically as "a princely failing" (D 204), it is difficult not to think on the ruptures of nation and royal household during the divisive monarchy of Richard III. These tragic histories, representing the disastrous mistakes in affairs of state and family, become crucial to the conclusion of the story as Gabriel attempts to understand the violence of history and rise above it (D 186).

In the room at the Gresham Hotel, a language of attack and defense brings the military motif of patriarchal force to a psychological level. The simple act of securing the door suggests the use of a firearm: "Gabriel shot the lock to" (D 217). In a relatively short space, a series of figurative verbs—"conquer," "assailed," and "seized" (D 218, 221)—all suggesting combative violence, lead to Gabriel's "riot of emotions" (D 224). The potential to demilitarize Irish domestic life and masculinity centers on Gabriel's ability to master his own impulse for patriarchal control, particularly evident in his violent desire toward Gretta, "to be master of her strange mood... to crush her body against his, to overmaster her" (D 218). Repetition of the verb "master" expresses the internal challenge for Gabriel to overcome the destructive impulse, to resist imitating the tradition of his forefathers, which was itself merely a flawed knockoff of the military and social customs of the British colonial masters.

An optimistic reading of the end of "The Dead" finds a measure of success for Gabriel in meeting this challenge. His emotional journey westward in the final paragraph suggests a learned sympathy for Gretta's past experience and present longing. His internal monologue in the closing lines strikes a note of discursive closure that his bombastic dinner speech could not. The epiphany suggests not least of all Gabriel's ability to transcend the hostilities of social order and political identity. As John Paul Riquelme suggests, "Rather than giving in to administrative control by abandoning the will that might resist, Gabriel begins to leave behind his own willfulness, which has tended to perpetuate social hierarchies of domination" (125). Doing so, he transcends the urban environment that is saturated by the more brutal forces and policing impulses of male identity.

The ultimate test of militarist ideology occurs not on the historical battlefields of Allen, Aughrim, or the Boyne referenced in the text, but in the mental terrain that leads characters toward or away from combativeness. Gabriel Conroy, as Dublin citizen and father, makes his own choice to resist the call to violence from both imperial and nationalist quarters.

He emerges between the pillars of British and Irish militarism, represented by the Wellington Monument and Molly Ivors respectively, to forge an alternate path. He is an exception in this regard to the patriarchal rule reflected in many of the preceding stories in *Dubliners*. As Margot Norris observes, "Gabriel is the antipode to the shiftless, ineffective, and sometimes brutal family men who people Joyce's texts" (*Suspicious Readings* 223). In the end he does not succumb to either impulse but finds a transcendent vision in his imaginative westward glance, suggesting the hope of a redefined paternal power and a renewed national life. It is a hope that readers can hear in the final, affirmative weather forecast and military pun: "Yes, the newspapers were right: snow was general all over Ireland" (*D* 225). The snow, long a decisive factor in military operations, exerts a metaphorical—and metaphysical—superiority over the landscape.[12] Indeed, this is hinted at earlier in the story when a major symbol of British militarism in Ireland, the Wellington Monument, "wore a gleaming cap of snow that flashed westward over the white field of Fifteen Acres" (*D* 203). General Snow overwhelms even this most potent personification of imperial and patriarchal conquest, showing that the most hardened social and cultural elements are not beyond the realm of pacification.

Soldiers and Constables

The paternal notion of police espoused in Blackstone's *Commentaries* translated in the early nineteenth century into more established systems of policing for Ireland; along with the garrison, to which they functioned as an auxiliary force, the police were among the most visible signs of British dominance. The emergence of official police forces in Ireland was intended to replace the function the army had exercised over civil society for decades.

Robert Peel, among others, spoke of the need to distinguish the constabulary from the soldiery. Still, despite clear intentions in some quarters to demilitarize the domestic life of the island, the police in Ireland maintained an image and function that duplicated the British military presence.

In *Ulysses*, we hear concern about this in Bloom's comment to Stephen on the policing function of the military in Ireland, specifically the dangerous policy of "equipping soldiers with firearms or sidearms of any description liable to go off at any time which was tantamount to inciting them against civilians should by any chance they fall out over anything" (*U* 16.83–85). Bloom has had firsthand experience of such police power and brutality, as evidenced by his recollection of a street rally "the day Joe Chamberlain was given his degree" (*U* 8.423) at Trinity College. Public protest against the colonial secretary and architect of Boer War policy reached a crescendo on 17 December 1899 in a street demonstration led by the Transvaal Committee that was violently disrupted by Dublin Metropolitan Police ("Mr. Chamberlain's Visit"). Merging his memory of the event with the squad of lunchtime constables in "Lestrygonians," Bloom recalls the police order to advance upon the crowd—"Prepare to receive cavalry. Prepare to receive soup" (*U* 8.413)—and his narrow escape from the charging "horsepolice" by taking cover in a nearby pub: "Lucky I had the presence of mind to dive into Manning's or I was souped" (*U* 8.425–26). The sustained culinary metaphor pivots abruptly on the notion of bodily harm, underscoring how the protective force of the police can turn quickly and uncontrollably into a destructive threat.

From the outset, the expansion and centralization of police power in Ireland was framed by this contradiction. Baronial police (Barneys) and county police (Charleys) operated in rural districts through much of the eighteenth century, while the Dublin Watch maintained close surveillance over the capital. Overseeing the watch was Henry Charles Sirr, Town Major of Dublin at the turn of the nineteenth century and "the head of as brutal and bullying a secret police as the times could produce" (Landreth 62). Heading up intelligence operations against the United Irishmen in 1798 and Robert Emmet in 1803, Major Sirr became "notorious for his ruthless use of informers and for the brutality of the police he led" (Gifford 275). In one instance, following arrests based on an inside tip, Sirr had troops follow the informer home and execute him just before he reached his own front door. Not surprisingly, such treatment did not instill very much public cooperation or trust in local law enforcement. In this regard, the first Dublin police force was little more than a tyrannical homegrown complement to the British Army.

The move toward police reform in the ensuing decades was more an attempt to free up regulars for overseas deployment than to demilitarize law enforcement in the country. At the same time, growing civilian-military tensions following the 1798 and 1803 risings convinced Dublin Castle of the importance of preserving the public peace through a reformed police system. The 1814 Police Bill paved the way for constabulary units throughout the country. It established the Irish Constabulary (the honorific "Royal" would be granted by Queen Victoria in the 1860s) throughout the country in its own network of heavily armed and fortified barracks. By 1836 the Dublin Metropolitan Police (DMP) was established as a separate entity to patrol the capital from its own network of barracks and station houses. Despite their separate jurisdictions, both forces were headquartered at Dublin Castle and thus in close proximity and communication with each other and with British military command. Both forces had an official auxiliary role to the army and assumed many of the most interactive and volatile of domestic duties formerly assigned to soldiers, such as local surveillance and crowd-control operations. In contrast to the European science of police expressed in the enlightenment ideals of Locke or the social contract of Rousseau—or, for that matter, the pragmatic definition of Blackstone—police power in Ireland emanated from the imposed authority and martial coercion of the colonizer.[13]

The police in Ireland were almost the single-handed creation of Robert Peel. Secretary for Ireland from 1812 to 1818, Peel came to be known as the father of modern policing. The slang terms for constables derive from his name: in England they are still known as "bobbies" and in Ireland by the less friendly moniker "peelers." Beyond nicknames, Peel influenced how the public police in Britain and Ireland moved from legal concept to administrative reality. He was instrumental in establishing the constabulary, and, in Dublin, London, and other major cities, the metropolitan police. The procedural guidelines for police ethics attributed to him, still known as the "Peelian principles," remain core tenets of criminal justice education and law enforcement practice in Ireland, Britain, and North America.[14] Perhaps the most famous dictum traditionally ascribed to Peel—and still practiced by police departments today—is the idea of an inseparable and equal relationship of the people and the police: "The police are the public and the public are the police." Whether the realities of policing in Ireland approached this idealized social symbiosis is quite another matter.

Peel himself was divided on the controversial issue of how or whether to distinguish military from police powers in Ireland, as evidenced in some of his conflicting statements about army and police identities. From their founding, Peel envisioned the Irish Constabulary as a military-style force when he advocated for former officers and soldiers to fill the ranks at all levels. Writing to Military Under-Secretary Sir Edward Littlehales in June 1814, he conveyed his sense of ideal IC officers and men: "I have no doubt that some of the brigade majors will make good police magistrates, and I am sure we shall be very glad if Sir G. Hewett [commander of forces in Ireland] will recommend us good constables from the military" (Peel 152). Peel had introduced the Police Bill just days before as part of the Peace Preservation Act. Addressing Parliament in support of the bill in the final week of June, he stressed the public-relations difficulty of using uniformed soldiers to suppress civil disturbances (Gash 179). An Irish police force run by former soldiers would have a more pacifying effect, dissociated as it was from the army in the public mind, Peel reasoned. His argument was convincing, and the Police Bill passed unopposed on 1 July.

Peel still maintained a conveniently vague distinction between military and police. Two years after the Police Bill was enacted into law, he voiced his preference for "an army of police to a military army" in Ireland (Gash 185). Nevertheless, as police reform continued, Peel never counted out the regular army's role in police operations. Ireland seemed to merit a careful exception to the legal separation of standing armies and domestic policing. As Peel wrote to Hewett—who, for one, was tiring of army deployments to quell civil disturbances—"the army in this country is not stationed in it for those purposes for which an army is usually employed" (qtd. in Gash 187). Meanwhile, answering concerns of Anglo-Irish landowners who requested a stepping up in army numbers for protection of rural holdings, Peel spoke of the need to downsize domestic troop deployments, noting "so many instances wherein the military have been improperly called forth and their services employed in the mere promotion of the private ends of individuals" (qtd. in Gash 187). If such duplicity or double standards were in part politically driven, they no less established a pattern of unclear distinctions surrounding military and constabulary.

Peel's militarized vision of police became the reality that would dominate a century of British policing in Ireland. This was evident in the remarks of observers and the policies of administrators through the rest of the nineteenth century. Visiting Ireland in the 1870s, James Macaulay emphasized the paramilitary aspect of the country's police: "It is the merit of the force that its civil efficiency is as great as that of any body of police in the Empire, and in emergencies it has shown military efficiency equal to that of the best regular troops" (qtd. in Muenger 83). Police militarism remained a stated goal of executive authority as well. Boasting of the RIC in a January 1889 cabinet memo, Chief Secretary for Ireland Arthur Balfour called it "the finest body of drilled men in the world"; he claimed that the public acceptance of Irish constables was due in large measure to their local origins and shared religion, concluding "it would doubtless be possible (though not perhaps prudent) to preserve order in Ireland by aid of Constabulary alone, if, in consequences of foreign war, all the soldiers were withdrawn" (qtd. in Muenger 99–100). This view conveniently omitted the fact that the vast majority of the RIC leadership was drawn not from the Catholic working class but from the landed gentry and lesser Ascendancy. As Elizabeth Muenger argues, "Balfour glorified the morale of the Constabulary in his memorandum, but he was speaking only of a portion of the force, those on the level of a constable or below, when he described social or religious sympathies" (100).

As the constabulary assumed policing duties that for decades had been carried out by the army, it often looked and acted very much the same. This resemblance to the army was manifest in "centralised control, paramilitary character, and separation of police from people—all factors that reinforced each other" (Malcolm 39). As Muenger notes, "Training followed military lines; barracks resembled those of the army, and general procedural conduct was structured similarly" (83). In his history of British colonial police, Sir Charles Jeffries defined the RIC as a "para-military organization or gendarmerie, armed, and trained to operate as an agent of the central government in a country where the population was predominantly rural, communications were poor, social conditions were largely primitive, and the recourse to violence by members of the public who were 'agin the government' was not infrequent" (Jeffries 31).

The police effectively emerged as an additional standing army on Irish soil. The appearance of the force instilled this impression in officers and civilians alike. RIC rank and file donned various styles of uniform, initially soldiers' castoffs, later of intentional design. From the mid-nineteenth century, these included "scarlet cloaks with plumed brass helmets bearing the inscription 'Waterloo,' some in hussar uniform with short cloaks, others attired as riflemen riding pillion, and commanded by officers equally splendid and equally heterogeneous" (Gash 185). Such a presence showed Peel's police had every interest in projecting a grandiose military mien.

The aggressive attitude and paramilitary appearance were retained into the twentieth century as police continued to function as an auxiliary to the army. Officers were equipped very much like combat-ready soldiers who brandished arms as well as attitude from provincial boreens to city squares. Public perceptions of the police took note of their powerful presence and martial bearing. A fictional dramatic monologue in a January 1900 issue of the Gaelic League weekly *An Claideamh Soluis* reflects satirically on such military affectation by police when a rural townsman remarks of an arrogant constable, "He is only a policeman, but he has an accent on his speech that you would think he is a captain in the army" ("Two Men"). In his memoir of the War of Independence, Ernie O'Malley directs a slightly more subtle mix of derision and awe toward the peelers he knew in real life:

> They were fine-looking well-built men. Their movements, even their lack of movement, conformed to an outward induced sense of authority as if they wore an extra skin. They had a ceremonious dignity about them that made ritual out of what would seem to us unimportant details. . . . Their uniforms were blue black with a touch of green, the colour of the cheap ink we used at school. The colour darkened their appearance. They carried batons in heavy leathern cases, carbines and bayonets. They wore padded cupola helmets. (68)

Minus the firearms carried by the RIC, the Dublin Metropolitan Police were also equipped in military fashion for their community policing of the capital. Instead of guns or rifles, DMP constables were armed with truncheons and outfitted at first in capes and top hats, then later helmets and tunics. They originally wore rattles, and later whistles, to sound a warning and call for assistance. As Bloom's response in "Lestrygonians" shows, the imposing street presence of police in Ireland was designed to inspire strong reactions from the civilian population.

DMP training emphasized community patrol and surveillance techniques. The force exerted a close domestic vigilance over both its own men and the civilian population under its jurisdiction. The duty manual stresses an officer's attitude of skeptical surveillance down to the level of individual household: "Q. 15. What are you particularly required to make yourself acquainted with on your Beat? A. With the Streets, Thorough-fares, Courts, and Houses. I should also have a knowledge of the Inhabitants of each house, so as to be enabled to recognize their persons" (Penny n.p.).

The DMP became notorious for a culture of surveillance in central Dublin and the outlying areas. One early chief clerk of the force was known to boast that "the Dublin Police are, in one respect, very like to Howth Harbour, as no one could get into either without passing 'Ireland's Eye'" (Herlihy 30). It is therefore appropriate that "Cyclops," an episode replete with ocular references, begins with the narrator's encounter with a retired policeman, "old Troy of the D.M.P." (*U* 12.1).

It is worth considering the social commerce of "Two Gallants" amid the strong paternalistic and panoptical functions of Dublin police culture. The police presence enters "Two Gallants" indirectly through Corley, who happens to be the son of a police inspector. Above constable and sergeant, district inspector represented the highest attainable rank for an officer of the metropolitan police. Though not himself a member of the force, Corley has the same paramilitary swagger and strut, having "inherited his father's frame and gait" (*D* 45). He is his father's son in a political sense as well, being the archetype of the colonial subject who mimics the actions of the occupying forces. A policeman's attitude suffuses his entire demeanor, a fact that seems even more insidious than if he were an actual officer or official subaltern: "He walked with his hands by his sides, holding himself erect and swaying his head from side to side" (*D* 45). In addition, Corley's watchful attitude resembles the sort of vigilant patrol that would have been encouraged by his police-inspector father: "He always stared straight before him as if he were on parade and, when he wished to gaze after someone in the street, it was necessary for him to move his body from the hips" (*D* 45). Cognizant of seeing and being seen, Corley moves at an "easy pace and the solid sound of his boots had something of the conqueror in them" (*D* 49). Meanwhile, the target of his surveillance is herself depicted in militarized fashion as wearing "a white sailor hat" and "execut[ing] half turns on her heels" (*D* 48, 49).

Corley's blatant links to undercover operatives—"He was often to be seen walking with policemen in plain clothes, talking earnestly" (*D* 45)—put him not just in robotic imitation but in direct communication with the most ruthless branch of Dublin law enforcement: the G Division of the Dublin Metropolitan Police. *Ulysses* will confirm that he is "the eldest son of inspector Corley of the G Division" (*U* 16.131–32). This group of undercover detectives based in Dublin Castle was notorious for its secret informants and rough interrogation tactics. Bloom considers the ruthlessness of the G-men moments after he sees the uniformed DMP constables: "If a fellow gave them trouble being lagged they let him have it hot and heavy in the bridewell" (*U* 8.420–21). Some in Bloom's circle are police operatives as well: "Never know who you're talking to. Corny Kelleher he has Harvey Duff in his eye" (*U* 8.441–42). Harvey Duff was a police informant in Dion Boucicault's popular play *The Shaughraun*. We already know Kelleher for his "Policeman's shoulders" (*U* 6.685), a description that seems appropriately confirmed in this rumor of his covert association with the Castle.

Police mystique and intrigue enter into romantic interactions, too, as Bloom remarks how "those plainclothes men are always courting slaveys" (*U* 8.445–46). Courting his own slavey, or at least exploiting her generosity, the would-be G-man Corley embodies surveillance and deception. He is a walking example of how overzealous policing can breed distrust and degrade social relations, and ultimately the worst manifestation of Peel's congruent vision of police and the public. Bloom himself even assumes a kind of police cover by adopting the name of a notorious Dublin policeman as pseudonym for his clandestine correspondence.

To be sure, street surveillance was a longstanding tactic in Dublin policing. The DMP duty manual, published as early as 1840, asserts an aggressive form of surveillance that extends to action against troublesome persons: "Q. 78. Is it lawful for you to apprehend *suspicious* characters?" The stated answer to the rhetorical question offers several elaborations that amount to a rough typing of detainable suspects: "A. It is lawful for me when on duty to apprehend all loose and disorderly persons, whom I have just cause to *suspect* of any evil design, or whom I may find disturbing the public peace, or loitering in any bye place after night-fall, and not giving a satisfactory account of themselves" (Penny n.p., italics added).

Everything depends on the officer's discretion, itself derived from policing theory that trains him to recognize such categorical descriptions. While subjectivity is necessarily a common denominator of police work, in this context it erodes fundamental distinctions between observable criminal actions and distrustful expectations on the part of the patrolling officer. The public is not the police, and the police is not the public; rather, as embodiment of the *patria potestas* of the state, the policeman assumes practically limitless oversight and discretion. Emulating the patterns of a dysfunctional household, Dublin police culture revolves around a base of suspicion and surveillance backed by the option of unilateral force and control.

Like a policeman on the beat, a critical reader of *Dubliners* must detect and apprehend suspicious characters. As Mr. Doyle and Corley suggest, some of the more untrustworthy characters turn out to be those with links to the police. This notion of questionable police connections is overtly mentioned later in *Dubliners*. Like the constables Bloom spies in *Ulysses*, police and their civilian contacts can themselves arouse suspicion.

In "Grace," the "immense constable" who arrives on the scene of Mr. Kernan's barroom fall suggests certain social and geographic realities in contemporary police recruitment. His "suspicious provincial accent" (*D* 150) shows he is up from the country, as were many of his colleagues, or else suggests an eagerness to arrest. Either way, the phrase speaks volumes concerning police recruitment practices and community relations. Much as the British Army made a policy of posting soldiers from Wales or Yorkshire to the Irish garrison, DMP recruitment purposefully targeted rural counties in a strategic effort to police Dublin with outsiders who could avoid treasonous fraternization or other conflicts of interest. From a Dubliner's perspective, this made "suspicious" and "provincial" practically interchangeable terms for those rural strangers patrolling their city streets. For his part, Mr. Cunningham, "a Castle official only during office hours," shows his contempt for such well-fed culchies as constables when he describes the cabbage-catching game "supposed . . . to take place in the depot where they get these thundering big country fellows, *omadhauns*, you know, to drill" (*D* 160). Mr. Kernan, not so moved by the humor, only complains, "These yahoos coming up here . . . think they can boss the people. I needn't tell you, Martin, what kind of men they are" (*D* 160). In short, the country constable is wary and suspicious of the fallen drunk; his training makes him so. Another reading, however, given rural-urban tensions, suggests that suspicion might just as readily flow in the opposite direction from the inebriated Mr. Kernan, whose alcoholic stupor and Dublin background might both shape his dubious attitude toward the immense policeman. Indeed, "suspicious" and "provincial" are somewhat redundant terms for Dubliners who tended to see rural strangers patrolling city beats as constituting a form of domestic surveillance and control that reinforced the military occupation.

Arguably the most suspicious character apprehended by Dublin police at the turn of the century was a provincial policeman himself. In the late summer of 1900, Henry Flower was a constable at the Irishtown barracks in the E Division of the DMP. He was also the suspect in a possible murder. Flower became the target of public and police suspicion when he was identified as the last person seen with Bridget Gannon, a Baggot Street servant whose body was found in the River Dodder on 23 August. Flower was one of the constables involved in retrieving and transporting her body, and according to a colleague he "made a swift, anxious scrutiny of the young woman's appearance and muttered something under his breath" (Herlihy 55). The testimony of Gannon's friend Margaret Clowry named Flower as a possible suspect. Amid growing suspicion of foul play, Gannon's body was twice exhumed by the city coroner to check for causes of death besides drowning. Flower was arrested and held for trial. Further tragedy ensued when the Irishtown station sergeant, presumably due to the stress of the investigation, committed suicide by slitting his own throat. A month later the judge, Mr. Justice Gibson, suggested to a grand jury that, given the broken wall along the river, Gannon's death was probably an accidental drowning; if Flower had fled the scene, it was out of fear rather than guilt, a choice that was "disgraceful but not criminal" (Hardiman 83). The jury agreed, and Flower walked free. His police career was over, however, and DMP records show he left the force at that time ("Numerical Register").

The "Dodder Mystery," as it was dubbed by the *Freeman's Journal*, did not produce a conviction, but it did generate enough suspicion to keep public attention fixed on the police courts and on Henry Flower in particular. Newspaper transcripts of testimony offered all Dubliners the chance to imagine themselves detectives and vicariously apprehend suspicious characters. Whether it was an accidental drowning or a horrific murder followed by the legal system covering for one of its own, suspicion lingered in the public imagination for decades after the case was closed and Flower had left the force. Without identifying his source, John Garvin writes of a deathbed confession by Clowry to Gannon's murder some four decades later, leading Garvin to regard Flower as "the misfortunate constable of the E division" (56). If Clowry did in fact confess to the crime, her admission of guilt might well have altered public perception of Henry Flower—for those who still remembered him—when she resurrected the incident around 1940. But in 1904 or 1922, Flower remained for Joyce and his early readers a figure cloaked in public suspicion. Public trust in law enforcement likely suffered a parallel blow.

Still living in Dublin, Joyce would have found it as difficult to ignore the Henry Flower investigation as an American in the mid-1990s would the O. J. Simpson trial. Through late August and September, the gruesome details of the Gannon case dominated the *Freeman's Journal* and the *Daily Express* and, presumably, daily conversation. Joyce would likely have learned about the case firsthand from his father's friend Timothy Harrington, MP, the barrister (and future Lord Mayor) who served as Flower's counsel at the inquest (Herlihy 57). Whatever the truth about Flower's guilt or innocence, the case afforded Joyce a clear point of reference for considering the potential brutality and abuse of police power. As with so many aspects of *Ulysses*, he seems to have relished the opportunity to weave such realistic features of Dublin into the novel. But the decision to link such an allegedly violent person to a central character known for his tolerance and pacifism is especially intriguing. The name of the controversial policeman provided Joyce at least a curious coincidence with the surname of his central character. The synonymous floral connotations of Bloom and Virag (Hungarian for flower) of course function in marvelous thematic conjunction with the name Henry Flower. Claire Culleton rightly suggests that "Joyce might have wanted to exploit the suggestiveness of the name, since the trial was such a popular one in the daily press" (130). I would argue further that allusion to such an infamous and (possibly) corrupted constable poses broader questions about policing, violence, and male identity.

The moment he first assumes the tarnished policeman's identity to retrieve his letter from Martha Clifford, Bloom is eyeing the ideals of uniformed masculinity illustrated by a military recruiting bill on the post office wall. His inspection of the army poster reveals something of his anxiety and envy concerning the power of men in uniform, including not least Molly's father, as he wonders, "Where's old Tweedy's regiment?" (*U* 5.66). Gazing at one particular regimental figure, Bloom, not unlike Peel a century before, maintains a clear distinction between the army and police: "The King's own. Never see him dressed up as a fireman or a bobby" (*U* 5.74–74). In the pseudonymic sense, Bloom is dressed up as a bobby, one whose alleged sexual violence amounts to a serious violation of the public peace he was sworn to protect. His own extramarital correspondence symbolizes a threat not just to the domestic security of Number 7 Eccles Street but to the civic peace of Dublin. Additionally, as Gifford notes, the phrase "King's own" signifies his honorary membership in the regiment to which it is attached and "it could also be applied to the 'household regiments'" (86). Bloom's attention has therefore come to rest on the very terms that emphasize patriarchal possession and control to the highest degree.

Adopting the name of Henry Flower for his clandestine correspondence lets Bloom assume a strong and well-known masculine identity. As Adrian Hardiman observes, "The pen name Henry Flower would have been a very striking one in the Dublin of 1904" (80). Such a high-profile moniker would seem an odd choice for a secret epistolary affair. Yet a police identity also allows him to engage in a fantasy of instant celebrity and patriarchal authority. (Bloom even adds the honorific "Esq" for a touch of minor-aristocratic respectability.) We might read the Henry Flower pseudonym as Bloom's creative response to this problem of masculine identity and gender anxiety, an attempted corrective that satirizes the attraction to uniformed male authority by following it to its most abusive and fatal extreme. Whoever spies the name Henry Flower on the envelope—be it Martha Clifford, the postmistress, Molly, or the informed reader of *Ulysses*—will be reminded of the constable-cum-suspected murderer.

Still, even as he assumes this dubious name, there is little risk Bloom will take on the brutalizing aspects of state paternalism it represents. After all, he is not just Henry Flower but the mystical "father of thousands, a languid floating flower" (*U* 5.571–72). In this sense, he represents the hope for a pacific, procreative realignment of the *patria potestas*. Bloom faces the challenge of reorienting his power as father and householder along humane and productive lines in a city where that power is often corrupted and abused. His progress in this regard will ultimately determine not just his own connection to his living, lost, and surrogate children (Milly, Rudy, and Stephen Dedalus); it will stand as a metaphoric counterpoint to the militarization of paternalistic identity in the form of the police and the garrison.

Bloom's adoption of a disgraced constable suggests his revitalized rhetorical response to oppressive British policing in Ireland. He acknowledges the futility of fighting the entrenched, paternal order of police, as any anticolonial or insurrectionary action comes up short against a status quo backed by official force: "Useless words. Things go on same, day after day: squads of police marching out, back" (*U* 8.477–78). The patriarchal and paramilitary reality of the militarized police state remains in place, seemingly immovable. Nevertheless, through a subversive act of literary masquerade, Joyce highlights the tragic consequences of a corrupt power of the father at the interpersonal and national levels. In this regard Joyce's fiction, starting with the dysfunctional fathers of *Dubliners* and extending to Bloom's ambivalent attitude to police, formulates Joyce's public interrogation of police power and critique of the paternal tyranny in the house of Ireland.

5

Barracks and Brothels

> I was in company with the soldiers and they left me to do, you know, and the young man run up behind me. But I'm faithful to the man that's treating me though I'm only a shilling whore.
>
> *Ulysses* 15.4381–83

One of the more striking transformations in *Ulysses* is that of Cissy Caffrey from suburban child-minder to Nighttown prostitute. When she appears in "Nausicaa," the good sister minding younger brothers Tommy and Jacky on Sandymount Strand, the protean possibilities of the location are already evident from Stephen's early morning walk there. Even so, the revealing remark about her professional identity shows a drastically different person from several hours before. One might be tempted to dismiss her change as one more in the long line of hallucinatory details in "Circe," yet the duality is more than just fanciful invention. It is an accurate reflection of women's limited economic opportunities and dual social identities in early-twentieth-century Dublin. Whether Cissy is actually streetwalking or working at Bella Cohen's brothel, or merely a recycled figment of Bloom's imagination, her role as prostitute is set in conjunction with the largest, and most controversial, client of the Dublin sex industry: the British garrison.

Earlier in the day, Cissy's military affiliation was prefigured in her brothers' sailor suits and Martello-tower sandcastle (*U* 13.14, 42–45). During the mock interrogation of "Circe," the connection is confirmed by her alibi that she was "in company with the soldiers" (*U* 15.4381). The pun conjoins a casual phrase with an official designation for a military unit smaller than a battalion. (One might say, for example, the Coldstream Guards regiment was divided into four battalions and fourteen companies, or the Number Seven Company of the Guards is preparing for deployment.) In offering such unabashed disclosure of her occupation, Cissy embeds herself with the British military in Dublin in every sense of the word.

Exchanging private intimacies for privates' pay, she assumes a place in the sex trade and, with it, the language and identity of her military customers. Doing so, she becomes representative of countless Dublin women who turned to prostitution in the late nineteenth and early twentieth century, and whose common patrons were soldiers and army officers. By referencing the interdependence of British garrison and Dublin red-light district, she acknowledges the economic context that surrounded such a choice. Cissy joins in the camaraderie and jargon of the barracks, and even her bargain rate as "only a shilling whore" (*U* 15.4383) echoes the infamous weekly wage paid to British Army recruits well into the twentieth century. As Nora Barnacle's mother wrote of her son Tom's enlistment in December 1915, "at present he is only getting a shilling a Weeke he sined me half his pay than I am getting seperation allowance" (qtd. in Maddox 139). Taking the "king's shilling" was a hard choice made by the thousands of Irishmen who opted to serve in the army out of financial necessity rather than patriotic loyalty. Cissy's identification with the same monetary value suggests a parallel involvement of prostitutes in the imperial military mission.

The overt link between private and prostitute also appears in *A Portrait of the Artist as a Young Man* via Stephen Dedalus's thoughts of his "gloomy secret night" in the "squalid quarter of the brothels"; his anticipatory memory includes, among other sensory minutiae, "a photograph of two soldiers standing to attention" (*P* 96–97). The mundane detail is one of Joyce's many realistic images that form part of the brothel's expected décor; however, it seems to say much more owing to its surroundings and the limited-omniscient perspective of the narrative. "Standing to attention" suggests not simply a notion of upright infantry but a double entendre of phallic readiness, a meaning perhaps only fully realized in its context on the brothel wall. If in other locales—say a post office billboard or recruiting station door—pictures of soldiers might just be soldiers, here they are sexualized objects and sexual clientele. Awaiting their turn, the privates see themselves in the pinup on the wall, and the photograph serves to regularize their status and their territorial control—over the brothel, the women's bodies, the city overall.

These suggest a possible reading of the content and context of the photograph, but questions linger as to its pretext: besides Joyce's fiction and Stephen's memory, who put the photo there in the first place and why? Was it the house madam or one of her employees, in a gesture of genuine admiration or clever advertisement? Or a soldier-customer in a statement of boastful conquest? Neither confirming nor denying such possible explanations, the narrative merely creates a space for speculation. The photograph serves as one dynamic focal point of interpretation, another of Joyce's resonant lacunae, or what Richard Pearce terms the meaningful "(w)holes" of the Joycean text.[1] What we do know in most certain terms of the narrative is that Joyce's writing (and Stephen's perspective) put the photo there for our interpretation. There emerges from the placement a uniform semiotics that couples the British occupying forces with the Dublin skin trade. Like Cissy's alibi, the soldiers' photograph reinforces the clear alliance in Nighttown of sexual and armed services.

Dublin sex workers were "in company" with British soldiers not only through plying their trade on the streets and in the houses but, in a larger sense, showing their parallel subjection with the soldiers to the prevalent culture of militarism. From opposite ends of the carnal transaction, privates and prostitutes had much in common, as both groups constantly risked their physical and moral well-being in the mere effort to survive. In a depressed economy with limited prospects, many unemployed or underemployed women chose prostitution. They likely chose the sex trade for many of the same reasons their male counterparts opted for army life. Unmarried women unable to secure positions in domestic service often turned to full- or part-time solicitation to make ends meet, just as men displaced from industrial or agricultural jobs often found no alternative to enlisting. The rapid recharacterization of Cissy Caffrey speaks to the situation of countless Dublin women who had little choice but to follow the same path. To a great extent, that choice was circumscribed by a cultural ethos that encouraged this role and reinforced an administrative structure that did little to prevent prostitution and much to support it in military contexts.

Joyce's fiction reveals this militarized nature of the Dublin sex economy. Soldiers and police appear in frequent conjunction with streetwalkers and brothel workers, a correlation that effectively elides their social identities and illustrates their parallel subject positions. As the physical manifestations of British power, soldiers and police play a crucial, but contradictory, role in the sex industry; they do so in a colonized city where men as sexual competitors and women as sexualized commodities are alike enmeshed in the controversial climate of armed occupation. They are at once its enforcers and its beneficiaries, as the line between patronizing and policing the Dublin sex trade becomes increasingly blurred. At the same time, Joyce shows how prostitutes come to resemble the soldiers and constables they serve in a city where life is dictated by concerns of state security and spatial control. In the process, he challenges contemporary voices as diverse—and divergent—as military and law enforcement authorities and advanced Irish nationalists.

Critical readings of prostitution in Joyce have explored its depiction as both abstract literary trope and realistic reflection of colonial Dublin.[2] Some have emphasized as well Joyce's political response to a moralistic reform movement that targeted the red-light district much as it targeted Joyce's writing.[3] To these views I would add that prostitution in Joyce's Dublin is most effectively understood, as Cissy Caffrey explains, "in company with the soldiers" (U 15.4381)—that is, as consciously and constantly inscribed within the military realities of British-occupied Ireland. The prostitute functions in an ambiguous and problematic role, as a potentially coercive and subversive presence in contested urban spaces. Her collaboration or opposition to the military presence remains, like her professional identity, covert and unclear. Recognizing the centrality of the prostitute in Joyce's portrayal of the modern city, Clair Wills notes the equivocal status he affords her: "for Joyce, the prostitute acted as a kind of double agent" given her equal capacity (as disease carrier) to infect the occupying forces or bring down the entire city (92). For moral as well as medical reasons, the prostitute bespeaks promise and risk to the culture of Irish nationalism, which itself constructed an ideological binary of purity and contagion in rendering her both a subject of propaganda and a target of reform. At the same time, the British military regarded the sex worker as both occupational hazard and recruitment incentive, an alluring feature of military life that nevertheless required careful surveillance and control. The inherent power of such ambivalent status informs Joyce's depictions of prostitution and the soldiery, offering insight into another deep-seated effect of militarism in the social and economic life of Dublin. Through the literary symbiosis of barracks and brothels, Joyce reveals them as uneasy partners and codependent forces in his occupied city.

His portrayal of their historical connection begins as early as *Dubliners*. At the heart of the collection, the stories "Two Gallants" and "The Boarding House" illustrate the entanglement of paramilitary attitudes with the pursuit of commercial-sexual transactions. The companion stories participate in contemporary debates about public and private space, national politics and female identity. In *Ulysses* these themes resound in the "Sirens" and "Eumaeus" episodes, through the depiction of the streetwalker, and in "Circe," where Bella Cohen's brothel becomes a dynamic, dramatic locale in which issues of gender and sexuality conflate with occupation politics and military force. *Finnegans Wake* extends the motif, showing the link as an abiding concern for Joyce into his final decade. Overall, in the transactions of soldiers and sex workers, Joyce's literary treks into Nighttown depict the force of two mutually exploitative and interdependent systems that both traffic in human bodies.

Reading Joyce's fiction with an eye to its sexual and martial economies, it is important to consider how their interrelation was shaped by current realities. The British Army in Ireland during the first years of the twentieth century faced tasks of maintaining public order, securing troop levels, supplying overseas engagements, and preparing for future action. As the Second Boer War wound down in 1902, returning troops were nevertheless part of a dominant, escalating militarism throughout the United Kingdom and Europe. Fears of German invasion prompted many civilian and military leaders to regard all realms of society as part of a common effort to galvanize the nation for war. As during the Cold War some five decades later, or the War on Terror a century on, the sheer anticipation and anxiety over global conflict did much to create its own enveloping ideology and social conditions, some intended, others incidental. Life in occupied Dublin generated a unique set of socioeconomic circumstances that Joyce recorded and scrutinized in his fiction. At the interface of militarism and sexual commerce were the soldiers, police, and prostitutes all brought to serve the interests of the war machine. In their comings and goings through Joyce's texts, they bear an odd and ironic resemblance to each other, one that effectively emphasizes their essential connection and subordinate status as corporeal assets of the state.

Soldiers and Sex Workers

While militaries have long been predominantly male institutions, many have recognized the advantages of enlisting local women and civilians to serve noncombat needs. Women have been incorporated in the development and mobilization of armies through integration of their domestic, social, economic, and professional roles. Cynthia Enloe asserts how policies for recruiting and maintaining armed forces have evolved to exploit the social, economic, and sexual lives of women:

> The processes of military manpower acquisition are gendered processes. Ignore gender—the social constructions of "femininity" and "masculinity" and the relations between them—and it becomes impossible adequately to explain how military forces have managed to capture and control so much of society's imagination and resources. (*Does Khaki Become You?* 212)

Across diverse historical and geographical milieus, Enloe considers the roles women assume for economic survival in military settings; the role of camp follower or prostitute is consistently among these.[4] In cultural contexts ranging from medieval Europe to present-day Asia, military authorities consciously foster the interdependency of soldier and sex worker through manipulating the ideology of occupation and the economy of desire.

Women who work in the marketplace of sexual services that typically surrounds a base of military operations play a central role in building and maintaining the ranks of volunteer armed forces. In many cases, army leadership has knowingly encouraged the presence of female camp followers, since unfettered access to prostitution offers a strong enticement to service in volunteer armies. The British occupation of Ireland was no exception, implementing policies for inspecting and monitoring prostitutes in order to provide troops with access to safe sexual recreation. At the same time, militant Irish republicans viewed prostitution in highly politicized and problematic ways, often feigning moral concern as a pretense for a similar exploitation of the issue and individuals involved.

With troop numbers in Ireland averaging around 26,000 during the late nineteenth century and upwards of 35,000 by 1914, the army brought a constant demand for sexual commerce. Most soldiers were single men from their early twenties to late thirties who welcomed any opportunity to step out of the barracks in search of female company. Since room and board were covered, soldiers' weekly pay was often diverted to the erotic amusements of the backstreets or bordellos, where it provided a stable influx of cash to an economy that, even a half century after the Famine, was still operating at much reduced levels.

Wherever troops were stationed, streetwalkers and brothels soon materialized. The briskest trade centered quite predictably around the major base areas, so, as Maria Luddy remarks, "It was in towns which housed garrisons that prostitution was most public.... Indeed, every garrison town had its red-light district" (25). Dublin, Cork, and the Curragh, County Kildare, were among the places where prostitution became most visible.

Apart from the steady supply of soldier-customers, certain economic push factors drove the sex trade in Ireland during the period. With few options at home, many rural women migrated to cities and major towns. They arrived with expectations of working in hotels, restaurants, or domestic service, but found intense competition from so many others in the same situation. The result was high joblessness, underemployment, or at best relatively low wages in what was decidedly an employer's market. The best option for survival, for many, was to enter another marketplace altogether. Prostitution offered "viable means of earning or supplementing an income in a country which offered few employment opportunities for women" (Luddy 41). Through the final decades of the nineteenth century, it became an option for an increasing number of women in Dublin and other substantial garrison towns.

Unlike Belfast to the north, Dublin had not developed a strong industrial base; therefore, most employment in some way served the British civil and military administration headquartered in the city. The vast majority of jobs for women were in the service sector, including hotels, restaurants, shops, and private residences. Joyce's extensive roster of female characters employed as house servants or "slaveys" accurately reflects this economic trend. The large number of female emigrants who poured into Dublin to escape the Famine in the countryside only added to an employer's market, forcing many young women to seek other ways to earn a living. Prostitution became a major source of income, and, as Bonnie Kime Scott notes, "Brothels flourished, as *Ulysses* testifies, furnishing outlets for men who could not satisfy themselves with angels and income for single, ineligible women, who needed an independent wage for survival" (14).

Often a slide into casual prostitution was the result of chronic underemployment, intense material ambitions, or both. In *Finnegans Wake*, for example, the account of Luperca Latouche alludes to some of these socioeconomic factors. To start, her surname suggests a triple pun of sexual contact, cash borrowing (touched her for a shilling), and mental instability (touched in the head). When the life of her "sister-in-love" Lupita ends tragically, the "other soiled dove" finds "one day while dodging chores that she stripped teasily for binocular man and that her jambs were jimpjoyed to see each other, the nautchy girly soon found her fruitful hat too small for her and rapidly taking time, look, she rapidly took to necking, partying and selling her spare favours in the haymow or in lumber closets or in the greenawn" (*FW* 67.35–68.5).

No location being off limits, Luperca will even entertain her customers "in the sweet churchyard close," and if cash is unavailable, as is often the case in developing economies, she trades in kind, receiving "coal or an array of thin trunks" as barter for her services (*FW* 68.7–9). As cause for this particular descent into prostitution, the story suggests the basic economic need for new domestic service or housework. With her habit of "dodging chores," Luperca is certainly no Eveline. Her first customer, "binocular man," suggests at once sexual voyeur and field general, outfitted with the standard equipment for each role. As discussed in the previous chapter, visibility and surveillance were key practices for the military and law enforcement in Ireland. They were also essential strategies of the streetwalker.

Army recruitment policies and barracks rules evolved in tandem with the limited economic prospects for women. From the military perspective, prostitutes were both the boon and the bane of the armed forces in Ireland. They offered an unofficial fringe benefit to enlistment, a constant outlet for sexual recreation in convenient proximity to the garrison. At the same time, as potential carriers of sexually transmitted diseases, they posed a mortal danger to the men and, by extension, to the mission as a whole. The very concentrated nature of the sex industry could guarantee the exponential spread of disease. In this sense, prostitutes like Cissy Caffrey who consorted with the troops could become a most literal internal threat to national security. Cognizant of this, military authorities supported the sex trade through policies that ranged from police surveillance to medical monitoring.

For their part, various nationalist groups produced vocal opposition to the interactions of British soldiers and Irish women. Still, they managed to make the issue more about sovereignty and power politics than physical or moral well-being. They identified British forces in Ireland with sexual debasement. Advanced nationalist propaganda emphasized the interconnectedness of the sexual and military economies. Such a view was predicated upon a reductive contrast of Irish purity with English depravity that many republicans exploited to rhetorical ends. Despite their ideological opposition, for both British Army officials and militant Irish nationalists the strategic and political significance of military prostitution took precedence over any moral concern for the women whose lives were at the center of the situation. On both sides, questions of morality were often mere pretense for strategic posturing or political rhetoric.

By the first years of the twentieth century, there were more than eighty barracks in Dublin. Most of these were imposing structures intentionally designed to be the architectural and psychological center of their neighborhood. They fanned out across the north and south sides of the Liffey, distributing soldiers in a circular pattern that placed most districts within marching distance of one or more regimental bases. This abundant dispersion of troops, when combined with high unemployment rates for young women, helped to assure the dominance of prostitution in the Dublin economy.

The fact that many women worked apart from recognized brothels, while others relied on sexual commerce only seasonally or in times of scarce employment, made taking a precise census of prostitution a difficult task. Still, a high-water mark appears to have come in the mid-to-late nineteenth century. In 1845 there were 419 brothels in the city, and while this figure declined in the post-Famine years, it still averaged more than a hundred by the final decade of the century (Luddy appendix 3). In 1871 William Logan, an antiprostitution advocate and author of *The Great Social Evil*, was appalled at the vast number of nightwalkers he encountered in the city. Not surprisingly, Logan saw the most solicitation occurring close to military installations, whose location by this time corresponded predictably to the redlight districts of Dublin: "In a back-street in a neighborhood of the barracks there were, it was said, some 200 of those wretched girls" (qtd. in Fagan 11). Though he does not specify it by name, there is good reason to believe Logan was describing the most notorious of these neighborhoods, Monto.

By the last quarter of the nineteenth century the focal point of the Dublin sex industry was the district bounded by Mecklenburgh Street Lower (renamed Tyrone Street and later Railroad Street), Lower Gardiner, and Montgomery (now Foley) Streets. Called Monto, after the abbreviation for Montgomery Street, it was also known as the Kips, the Digs, and the Village. Another variant, Nighttown, coined by journalists, came to be preferred by Joyce, whose characters in *Ulysses* access the area from Mabbot Street, near Amiens Street (now Connolly) Station. The Monto area became a congregation point for active soldiers, war veterans, and working prostitutes; as one local historian records, many crippled sailors, former militiamen, and camp followers settled in the neighborhood (Fagan 10).

The variety of Nighttown brothels catered to the different social strata of the neighborhood clientele. Readily accessible to all the Northside barracks, Monto thrived as a nighttime destination for elite officers and rank-and-file soldiers. Additional visitors included dockers, sailors, aristocrats, and businessman. Police were known to visit in occasional vice raids, but more often on illegal shakedowns that were often combined with sexual recreation. As one resident recalled, "I never remember the police getting involved in Monto. They could not give a damn what was going on. Sure, they never bothered the madams or the men that worked for them" (qtd. in Fagan 33). Another recalled seeing British soldiers and police regularly talking with the most famous madams of the district (Fagan 31). Indeed, the long-term existence of houses of prostitution, despite their illegal nature, strongly suggests a collusive military authority and a crooked constabulary. As Maria Luddy asserts, "The fact that brothels were allowed to operate almost unhindered is indicative of some level of [police] corruption" (29).

Streetwalkers carried on a brisk outdoor trade in back lanes, while basic brothels offered modest rooms and beds for those prepared to spend a little more time and cash. The best-maintained and priciest establishments, called flash houses, were run by madams of considerable influence. These attracted the highest class of customer for evening entertainment that rotated between musical lounges and private boudoirs. The clientele reportedly included King Edward VII during a 1904 royal visit. Among the top-tier flash houses of the area, the one known as Becky Cooper's became Bella Cohen's in the "Circe" episode. Joyce would even have found entries for Cooper and other notable madams in his frequent sourcebook for Dublin commercial and residential listings, *Thom's Directory*. He also had firsthand experience of the atmosphere and personalities of these Monto establishments during his own visits there between 1898 and 1904.

Lesser red-light districts grew up near the military installations in and around Phoenix Park. In *Finnegans Wake* Joyce lends the name Lili Coninghams to a streetwalker known for turning her tricks and "conning the hams" of the Conyngham Street neighborhood bordering the Park (*FW* 58.30). Lili probably chose her location for its close proximity to the Royal Barracks, the Magazine Fort, and Marlborough Barracks, which would have undoubtedly supplied an endless line of customers for her trade. South of the Liffey,

French Street and its environs were home to a number of the earliest and most successful flash houses, all within close range of the Portobello and Wellington barracks. (It was later renamed Mercer Street in an unsuccessful bid by the Dublin Corporation to confuse and discourage repeat customers.) Indeed, if not for their sizeable population of "garrickson's" (*FW* 55.35), the bordellos of Monto and these other districts could never have thrived in such volume or duration.[5]

If barracks were built as blatant and permanent reminders of the military presence, brothels, on the other hand, were by necessity covert and fluctuating establishments. They tended to spring up wherever conditions were optimal, and then minimize their trade or vanish entirely whenever local markets or Corporation policies grew less hospitable. In one particular expansion of the sexual economy, during the return of army regiments to Dublin following the Boer War, overcrowding in barracks led to the billeting of many officers and troops in residential houses. In those private boardinghouses they often occupied quarters adjacent to those of young women. Thus from economic necessity emerged a dual-purpose residential space cohabited by unrelated males and females, soldiers and civilians. This arrangement set the stage in many parts of the city, even those outside the traditional boundaries of Nighttown, for a sort of casual residential prostitution. Particularly in neighborhoods faced with declining employment opportunities, the transition from basic lodging house to de facto brothel was neither long nor complicated (Fagan 10). Such close residential quartering became a space wherein occupation politics were most directly embodied and intimately enacted.

Doublin Spaces

Joyce first elucidates the controversial link between British soldiering and Irish prostitution in *Dubliners*. "Two Gallants" and "The Boarding House" illustrate the diffusive influence of the military and sexual economies in street life and residential space. The tandem functions and formal dualities in both stories demonstrate the extent to which the pairing of prostitution and the military had permeated everyday Dublin life. They depict the broader influence of this partnership on daily lives and relationships, even for those lacking any official association with the army or direct connection to the red-light district. Joyce shows how men and women could be conditioned by the prescribing discourses of those social contexts. They dictated gender roles and determined sexual attitudes that were mimicked by many ordinary Dubliners. Joyce records such imitative roles as colonial symptomatics emphasizing the militarized nature of social and sexual life.

"Two Gallants" combines themes of nocturnal surveillance and sexual solicitation in urban space, and represents Joyce's earliest contribution to a heated contemporary debate concerning the presence of soldiers and women in Dublin's nighttime streets. Starting from its sardonic title, the story achieves its full rhetorical effect through urbane modern parody of the courtly notion of gallantry. Joyce most likely developed his contemporary angle on the chivalric theme from his reading of the Italian historian Guglielmo Ferrero.[6] "Two Gallants" addresses the controversial point that Dubliners themselves might also be panderers and coconspirators in their own city's conquest. The story Joyce characterized so innocuously "with the Sunday crowds and the harp in Kildare street and Lenehan" as simply "an Irish landscape" manages a striking exposé of how paramilitary attitudes could define social and sexual mores in middle-class Ireland (L 2:166).

"Two Gallants" commingles themes of policing and prostitution through the duality of its main character, Corley. As discussed in the previous chapter, Corley's links to police are established in his familial history, physical mien, and behavioral attributes, as well as his social network. At the same time, starting from his surname, he is directly associated with prostitution, as evidenced by the way he "aspirated the first letter of his name after the manner of the Florentines," a deliberate narrative detail suggests a breathy pronunciation of his name as something close to *Whore*-lee (D 45).[7] Whether Corley intends to promote this sonic coincidence or remains utterly oblivious to it is unclear, but by cashing in on the evening flirtation at the end of the story, he lives up to this affected enunciation of his name and becomes a streetwalker himself in more than one sense of the word.

Like Cissy Caffrey taking the king's shilling, Corley is a hybrid creature of the sexual-military economy that dominates Dublin street life. He remarks how the girl motoring past him on Earl Street has turned to prostitution—"She's on the turf now" (D 47)—with a hint that it is due to his own corrupting influence; however, through his police informing and sexual services, he is in fact following the same parallel courses of selling himself to the highest bidder, citizen or state. The political ramifications of the transaction are clear, since, as Terence Brown observes, the small gold coin Corley readily accepts from the slavey at the end of the story can only be a sovereign (*D* 266n70). The wordplay generates a submerged conceit that speaks doubly to Corley's acceptance of the English monarchy, while verifying his ambiguous status as gigolo, procurer, or opportunistic subaltern.[8] Symbolic of his, and Ireland's, ongoing devaluation and lack of political autonomy, Corley will accept even less when Stephen lends him a half crown at the cabman's shelter (*U* 16.194–96). The political-monetary metaphor will resonate further in *Ulysses* with Stephen's loan of "Four shining sovereigns . . . Four omnipotent sovereigns" to Buck Mulligan (*U* 1.296–97) and Bloom's recollection of his last visit to Sweny's chemist shop: "I changed a sovereign I remember" (*U* 5.470).

The ultimate transaction occurs in a hazy convergence of sexual and financial profit-taking. The precise nature of the exchange is not entirely clear, leaving the reader to partake of the same vague sense of deception or trickery visited by Corley upon the slavey. Whatever has happened, it is far from the ideal notions of gallantry. Effectively, Corley and Lenehan are anything but what the story's title suggests them to be; as Susan Humphreys asserts, the story "subjects all senses of the word 'gallant' to irony, including its connotations of military bravery, nobility of conduct, glamorous appearance, and chivalrous treatment of women" (244).

Following this ambiguous sexual commerce on the street, "The Boarding House" examines the elision of the sexual with the commercial that resulted from contemporary redefinitions of residential space. Through the surprisingly dubious environment of a Hardwicke Street lodging house, Joyce emphasizes the dual identities of residents and home space that were becoming a reality of many Dublin neighborhoods around the turn of the twentieth century. If in the streets of "Two Gallants" distinctions between civilian and paramilitary and between seduction and solicitation become difficult to ascertain, much the same can be said of marriage and prostitution within the walls of Mrs. Mooney's house. It is not mere coincidence that these duplications emanate from a house that, like many others in its neighborhood and city, had under social and economic pressures come to serve two purposes. Margot Norris has noted the structural dualisms at work in the narrative, from the "double set of confessions" (of Polly to her mother and Doran to the priest) to the "double meditation" and "double sacrificial rites" of

Catholic mass and Doran as symbolic social offering (*Suspicious Readings* 95). It is worth considering how this sequence of pairings occurs in a private residence that, like many others, had come to double as a commercial establishment.

As with many Dublin dwellings of the period, Mrs. Mooney's collapses distinctions between private and public, state and domestic. Indeed, its very status as boardinghouse at a time when military policy encouraged soldiers to move off base would tend to ensure this. Some critics point to the socioeconomic pressure of urban crowding as creating the conditions for Polly and Bob's casual form of prostitution (Parascandola and McGarrity 148–50). By the first years of the century, this fact of residential life in Dublin was greatly amplified by the vast numbers of troops returning from action in South Africa as well as the general buildup of the British garrison amid invasion fears and anticipation of a Continental war. With barracks filled to capacity, army authorities instituted overflow housing policies by which many soldiers took lodgings in private residences and boardinghouses throughout the city, where, in contrast to the barracks, they lived directly among host families and fellow boarders.

The notion of prostitution in "The Boarding House" plays out across the story through numerous characters, starting with the matriarch of the house. We learn in the opening how Mrs. Mooney has escaped from both an abusive marriage and the butchering business, but these nonetheless continue to shape her methods of managing business and family: "She dealt with moral problems as a cleaver deals with meat: and in this case she had made up her mind" (*D* 58). The parallel is a telling one and reinforces the overlapping identities of the house itself. Following her inclination to cash in on her daughter's sexuality and availability, Mrs. Mooney turns her boardinghouse into yet another sort of meat market.[9] Under her roof, commercial concerns outweigh familial ones, not least among these the need to ease the economic burden on the household by having Polly married. For Mrs. Mooney, the affair with Bob Doran becomes not just about social honor but about financial opportunity. The mother's demand for her daughter's marriage to Doran seems less for the social propriety the match will offer the daughter than for the economic advantage it will bring the mother, as Mrs. Mooney is determined she will not become "like some mothers she knew who could not get their daughters off their hands" (*D* 60). Like many parents of the time, her hopes for marrying off her daughter elide the pragmatic with the sentimental, in what amounts to a form of "tacit prostitution" (Norris, *Suspicious Readings* 98). That the male residents refer to Mrs. Mooney as "The Madam" only confirms Doran's suspicion that her "boarding house was beginning to get a certain fame" (*D* 57, 61).

Indeed, Mrs. Mooney's pursuit of monetary gain through Doran shows her nickname to ring somewhat true and contradicts her efforts to see Polly enter without pressure into a sanctioned marriage of her choosing. As in the exchange of the gold coin at the end of "Two Gallants," the differences are blurred between courtship and commerce, sovereignty and individuality. This is evident in the term "reparation," which occurs three times across the story, relating the prospect of legal restitution to its origins in wartime compensation. In this way, the theme of prostitution runs parallel to a martial motif. After his lengthy confession to the parish priest concerning his relations with Polly, Doran is "almost thankful at being afforded a loophole of reparation" (*D* 60) as he prepares for his confrontation with Mrs. Mooney. The qualifying language reasserts the nebulous nature of the household, while the diplomatic metaphor, now reconfigured with its etymological link to military architecture, introduces the notions of combat and siege. Before it was a means of escape from social consequences or legal damages, a loophole was a feature of late-medieval castles and fortifications.[10] While the Mooney home is Georgian town house rather than medieval fortress, ideologically its hybrid status has a direct bearing on the lives within it.

There are no actual soldiers billeted at Mrs. Mooney's house, but a bellicose attitude no less governs the premises, implicitly suggesting the effects of such quartering policies on Dublin civilian life. The principal male characters emulate the military ethos and contribute to a subtle allegory of the garrison. Despite being at odds with each other over Polly, Jack Mooney and Bob Doran each symbolize aspects of the British military presence, suggesting the deep divisions of the Irish national household. References to the occupation resonate, for example, in Jack's name and physique—"a thick bulldog face and a pair of thick short arms" (*D* 63)—which suggest the archetypal English symbols Union Jack and John Bull. He brings this imposing presence to bear in the row with the music-hall *artiste* who makes a suggestive remark about Polly. Jack's threat "that if any fellow tried that sort of a game on with *his* sister he'd bloody well put his teeth down his throat, so he would" (*D* 63) strikes a cadence and vocabulary that would sound more at home in Cockney London than Northside Dublin. Jack is further described as being a good boxer and "fond of using soldiers' obscenities" (*D* 57), both suggestive of the dominant martial culture beyond the door.

Although at odds with Jack, Bob Doran embodies his own martial qualities. His surname is the Gaelic word for stranger, echoing the Irish nationalist euphemism "strangers in the house" that was code for the unwelcome Anglo-Saxon presence. His first name underscores the monetary transaction of the story. As the slang term for shilling, "Bob" potentially renders Polly Mooney, like Cissy Caffrey, a shilling whore. The name also carries combative and pugilistic connotations, as the *OED* variously defines "bob" as a verb meaning to strike or tap and as a noun suggesting a light blow, a counterpart to Jack Mooney's stated penchant for boxing. In all of these details, Mooney and Doran typify colonized subjects who imitate colonizing behaviors. Like Irish boys learning cricket or Shakespeare, they have become avid consumers and reproducers of the occupying culture. They become stand-ins for soldiers in much the same way Corley copies police, or just as many boardinghouses became substitutes for barracks. As such, these characters and spaces alike embody the notion of "mimicry" that Homi Bhabha, in *The Location of Culture*, terms "the sign of a double articulation; a complex strategy of reform, regulation, and discipline which 'appropriates' the Other as it visualizes power" (123). In their mimicry of colonial behaviors, Bob and Jack comprise a "double articulation" of militarized colonial subjects, proxies for the Anglo-Irish conflict.

This role is reinforced toward the end of the story when Doran, on his way to the fateful interview with Mrs. Mooney, passes Jack on the stairs "nursing two bottles of Bass" (*D* 63). The English identity of the product, the maternal-infant connotations of the verb, and the number two all reinforce the duality of colonial subject and mother country. During their momentary encounter, Bob and Jack "saluted coldly" (*D* 63), a gesture that echoes Corley's paramilitary posturing in "Two Gallants." If not actual soldiers, the men nonetheless emulate behavioral aspects of the English armed presence. Like Corley and Lenehan, they bring a sense of corrupted gallantry in from the street and across the threshold of Mrs. Mooney's house.

The one person who might finally be capable of escaping the ideological snares entangling those who reside in the boardinghouse appears to be Polly herself. When she waits in her bedroom during her mother's meeting with Doran, there is the possibility of growth through self-reflection, symbolized by Polly's gaze into the looking glass (*D* 63). What seems a potential for insight becomes merely another form of doubling emphasized in the optical imagery of the mirror. Like the quayside deliberations of Eveline, Polly's bedroom epiphany is grounded in inaction and forgetfulness rather than awareness and active choice. During her time upstairs, as she moves between the bed and the mirror, she entertains "hopes and visions" (*D* 64) for the future. Whatever these might be—marriage and family life with Bob Doran?—their precise identification goes unmentioned to the reader and undisclosed to the other characters. Instead, Polly's own agency is reduced to little more than a passive role of distracted expectancy: "Then she remembered what she had been waiting for" (*D* 64).

The only verifiable aspects of Polly's future "hopes and visions" are that they remain private and unexpressed. In effect, she waits while others determine her fate. Her ultimate passivity seems confirmation of marriage as an imposed role rather than a deliberate choice. In this way, the story collapses the distinctions between marriage and prostitution, echoing the social conundrum for women described in *Stephen Hero*: "A woman's body is a corporal asset of the State: if she traffics with it, she must sell it either as a harlot or as a married woman or as a working celibate or as a mistress" (*SH* 202). By the time her mother's voice interrupts Polly's reverie of escape, the trafficking of her own body is complete; arrangements have been made, though without Polly or the reader knowing the full nature or extent of their consequences.

If Polly's future remains vague at the end of "The Boarding House," Joyce's readers are afforded a glimpse of it during a brief sequel to the story in *Ulysses*. A narrative digression in the "Cyclops" episode confirms that Doran does go on to marry Polly. It also offers an unflinching verification that the marriage does not mark an end to the reputation of either one for sexual commerce. The "Cyclops" narrator describes Polly as a "little concubine of a wife . . . wagging her tail up the aisle of the chapel with her patent boots on" and Mrs. Mooney as "the old prostitute of a mother procuring rooms to street couples" (*U* 12.812–15). These insults come on the heels of an even more scandalous anecdote about a drunken Doran being caught in a compromising position with two prostitutes: "Night he was near being lagged only Paddy Leonard knew the bobby, 14A" (*U* 12.801–2). Doran's impunity suggests something of the lackadaisical attitude and social favoritism of Dublin Metropolitan Police concerning enforcement of laws against prostitution-related activities. The subsequent account of the incident constructs dualities on multiple levels:

> Blind to the world in a shebeen up in Bride street after closing time, fornicating with two shawls and a bully on guard, drinking porter out of teacups. And calling himself a Frenchy for the shawls, Joseph Manuo, and talking against the Catholic religion, and he serving mass in Adam and Eve's when he was young with his eyes shut, who wrote the new testament, and the old testament, and hugging and smugging. And the two shawls killed with the laughing, picking his pockets, the bloody fool and he spilling the porter all over the bed and the two shawls screeching laughing at one another. (*U* 12.802–10)

This juicy gossip is steeped in notions of doubleness: concrete and abstract, real and invented, sacred and profane. These include the pair of prostitutes and the two books of the Bible, as well as Doran's altar boy and adult personae, his real Irish identity and his faux French alter ego. The dualisms are etched into the stylistics of the prose, through repeated phrase pairings that include "Adam and Eve," "the new testament, and the old testament," "hugging and smugging," and "the two shawls screeching laughing at one another."

From these dualities and continuities emerge ironic disruptions or discontinuities as well. With a Dublin accent, Doran's false surname Manuo suggests a pun on the transactional nature of the scene: identifying himself as the Man-you-owe is especially ironic given his (additional) dual status as both client and robbery victim of the two prostitutes. When he "falls silently into an area" (*U* 15.695) before a house in Nighttown, Doran will assume still another identity, that of Elpenor, the drunken sailor whose fatal plunge from Circe's roof goes unnoticed by his comrades. Meanwhile, the act of "drinking porter out of teacups" illustrates the disorienting intoxication described earlier of Doran "on one of his periodical bends" (*U* 12.803–4, 5.107). At the same time, the fundamental mismatch symbolizes how bawdy public-house life has very much spilled over and onto any hopes or dreams for an abode of bliss. Amid the domestic and sexual turmoil, there remains a commercial underpinning. Even the setting of the incident on Bride Street produces an ironic distinction between marital and adulterous relations; or, seen another way, it reifies the implicit point of the original *Dubliners* story that marriage and prostitution in fact move very much along the same street.

Overall, "The Boarding House" constructs a theoretical context and realistic location for such mimicking behavior. Inherent to a rooming house is the sense of collapsed social distinctions and personal boundaries. The story effectively depicts a contemporary trend whereby Dublin residential spaces were transformed by the presence of the sexual and military economies. Mrs. Mooney's house undergoes a subtle but certain transformation from lodging to brothel, and its new status as doubled space becomes the definitive context, if not the ultimate cause, of the entire affair. It suggests the sort of ambivalent conditions that Bhabha regards as symptomatic of colonial occupation: the function of its space and the actions of its characters demonstrate how "the discourse of mimicry is constructed around an *ambivalence*; in order to be effective, mimicry must continually produce its slippage, its excess, its difference" (122). Such ambivalence is ultimately reflected in the nebulous definition of the house itself as it becomes the context and basis for the compromising actions and uncertain identities of its residents. As a story of transactions, negotiations, and their consequences, "The Boarding House" presents a revealing microcosm of occupied Dublin in which the sibling economies of militarism and prostitution redefine the fundamental natures of sexual identity and household space.

"Two Gallants" was completed in 1906 during the heat of a Roman summer. Joyce asked Grant Richards to insert it before "The Boarding House" in the manuscript he had submitted to him the previous fall, thus cementing the relation of the two as companion stories. Each needed the other as neighbor in order to deliver its full impact. Putting a price on artistic integrity was for Joyce a notion as troubling as selling one's body or ideology. Writing to Richards on 10 October 1906 to defend "Two Gallants" and other *Dubliners* stories against the censorial demands of their printer, Joyce most deliberately echoes the story's precise theme: "I cannot plead the excuse of starvation or houselessness for a deliberate prostitution of my talent or a deliberate and hypocritical mutilation of my work" (L 2:177). If the stories of *Dubliners* were properly going to record "a chapter in the moral history of my country" (L 2:177), then the theme of harlotry, in all its social, martial, and coital connotations, demanded inclusion. After much wrangling and nearly a decade of delay, Joyce would finally get his way. This significant and binding theme made it into *Dubliners*, showing the subtle interrelation of armed forces and prostitution. Their historical tandem formed a significant component in Joyce's reflections of social and spatial topography going forward.

Nightwalkers

As with all foreign occupations, the success of the British military mission in early-twentieth-century Dublin depended on the ability to move and to control movement in the city. Longstanding administrative links to police authority enabled the army to monitor the activity of the streets, particularly after nightfall. The Night Watch was the extent of Dublin law enforcement well into the nineteenth century. It was a church-based system overseen by wardens who assigned a set number of around fifteen watchmen to each of the twenty-one parishes. They rotated duties during evening hours, the biggest shift being 10 p.m. to 6 a.m. in the longer nights of the winter months. In 1836 the establishment of the Dublin Metropolitan Police led to a gradual phasing out of the watch and the inception of full day and night policing. The appearance of the First and Second Watch as patrollers and enforcers in "Circe" is something of an anachronism, more reminiscent of Victorian than Edwardian Dublin.

One element that remained constant, however, was the emphasis on nighttime tours of duty and foot patrol. The Metropolitan Police expanded methods of community policing and surveillance through most city neighborhoods. Their foot patrols were established along regular routes or beats that were intended to detect and deter criminal activity. They aimed at a combination of vision and visibility, of seeing and being seen, as it were. Like their London counterparts, Dublin bobbies did not carry firearms but nightsticks—the very name suggests suspicion of nocturnal hours as the time of crime. Headquartered at Dublin Castle, the DMP took many of its cues from the military authorities. In times of civil disorder such as the 1899 Boer War street protests or during all-out armed conflict like the Easter Rising, the police and the military acted in concert to quell unrest and control public space. Such policing strategies ensured a connection between politics and law enforcement that made anyone present on the street after dark a fundamental target of suspicion; with regard to legal codes, social assumptions, and political ideologies, the onus was on the individual to justify his reason for being there.

Prostitutes who solicited business in public spaces were arguably the most vulnerable to abuse or arrest on these grounds. Streetwalkers already stood at the lowest rung of the ladder of Dublin sexual commerce: detached from any madam or house, they were more visible and controversial than their counterparts who operated behind closed doors. While brothel workers frequently operated with little or no interference, the "nymphs of the pavement" lived under the constant scrutiny of police, military, and medical authorities. Women on the street at night were especially vulnerable because of the way legal codes were written to target suspected prostitutes rather than actual instances of prostitution. While the sale of sexual services was not illegal in itself, solicitation was, and women judged to be loitering without legitimate business could be charged with vagrancy or disturbing the peace.

Just what constituted legitimate business was ultimately left to the discretion of the guard on patrol. Under the Police Clauses Act of 1847, a woman could be arrested if a policeman thought her to be "a common prostitute or night walker loitering or importuning passengers for the purpose of prostitution" (qtd. in Luddy 28). The law did not outlaw prostitution or mandate a DMP constable to disrupt the actual transaction of money for sexual services; instead, it concentrated police efforts against the disruptive presence or attitude of women perceived to be prostitutes. Such efforts thus depended upon interpretive judgment of individual officers whose surveillance of their beat was intended to identify certain individuals as particularly common; depending on time and circumstance, virtually any unaccompanied young woman on the streets of Dublin attracted police suspicion.

In this regard, one of the more interesting sidelights of the 1900 police-court hearing of Henry Flower (discussed in chapter 4) came from the conflicting testimonies of his police colleague, Thomas Dockery, and a woman named Lizzie Kavanagh who lived with her brother and sister-in-law near the Irishtown barracks. Their depositional discrepancy speaks to the tension of police-civilian relations that defined the Bridget Gannon case, as well as to broader perceptions about female sexual identity and freedom of movement in urban space.

Constable Dockery had been on plainclothes duty the night of 22 August and claimed to have been walking with Kavanagh beyond the Lansdowne railway station at the time of Bridget Gannon's death. His alibi depended largely on corroborating testimony from Kavanagh, but she denied even knowing Dockery, much less being with him on the night in question ("Dodder Mystery: Inquest Resumed"). Kavanagh had good reason for claiming she had not been out walking the streets that night with Dockery or anyone else: two years earlier, she had twice been arrested and charged with the more disreputable variety of streetwalking. She paid a fine of ten shillings in each case and was immediately released. During her testimony in the Gannon inquest, authorities were quick to remind Lizzie Kavanagh of this conviction—a tactic that seemed calculated to divert suspicion away from the police in a case that already compromised police integrity. The *Freeman's Journal* published Kavanagh's responses from the witness stand to Dublin coroner Christopher Friery reading aloud from her arrest record:

> "Elizabeth Kavanagh, of Great Brunswick Street, no business, night-walker."
> "I am not a night-walker."
> "Read the charge sheet. Is that an accurate description of you?"
> "I do not consider myself common." (ibid.)

The terms of Kavanagh's arrest and her persistent defense of her character echo the language of a legal code rooted in contemporary assumptions about the dubious moral influence of nighttime urban space, particularly where single women were concerned. In this sense, the police-court discourse reflects the prevailing social attitude that the streets of the capital at night were necessarily the domain of law-enforcing men and unlawful women. For, much like the prostitutes themselves, the Dublin Metropolitan Police owed their power and success to their ability to make the rounds on foot, to recognize specific individuals, and to assess their intentions or "business," as the charge sheet for Lizzie Kavanagh states. In their surveillance of urban space, the police and soldiery engaged in nocturnal perambulation and reconnaissance that bore a striking resemblance to the activities of the women they intended to subvert. After all, the determination that one has "no business" for being on the street at night amounts to a moral judgment. For their part, the police and military patrols charged with making such judgments are equally dubious night walkers, who from an alternative political position might also be said to have "no business" being on the streets of Dublin, day or night.

Underlying such legal codes and law enforcement activities was a growing concern about the moral state of the city streets at night shared by groups as various and opposed as army and law enforcement authorities, suffragists, purity organizations, and militant Irish republicans. When police intervention appeared ineffective against the growing problem of streetside solicitation, some took it upon themselves to take back the nighttime urban space. Irish nationalist organizations and suffragist groups began to wage campaigns against prostitution with British troops in Dublin, but like the military authorities, they often approached the problem from angles of political autonomy and territorial sovereignty rather than concern for moral and physical welfare.

These politicized approaches included the circulation of leaflets and the formation of women's street patrols. If well intentioned, these efforts did little to address the root socioeconomic causes and consequences of prostitution. They generally ignored many of the broader causes of prostitution in Dublin, namely poverty, high unemployment, and limited social roles and economic opportunities for women. Dire poverty, chronic unemployment, increased rural outmigration, and squalid, overcrowded housing conditions left many women with few economic alternatives to street solicitation or brothel employment. But such realities were often ignored by a rhetoric that reductively identified Irishness with sexual restraint and purity while associating Englishness with moral debasement and debauchery. Some nationalist discourse even portrayed Dublin prostitutes and British soldiers as related sources of literal and metaphoric contagion of which Ireland needed to be cleansed before it might be returned to a pure state.

Despite their differing agendas, many voiced a similar unease at the women who crowded major thoroughfares each evening to solicit soldiers. Regardless of national orientation or religious persuasion, they seemed to share a late Victorian concern over social appearance and propriety:

> It was most often the visibility of prostitutes in Dublin which caused anxiety, an anxiety not only about the use of public space but the contamination of that space. The discussions which developed around prostitution focused on the idea of contagion, either in the spread of disease and/or immorality; prostitution was itself believed to be contagious. (Luddy 17)

The streets as well as the bodies of the streetwalkers became contested sites of political sovereignty and territorial control linked to national traits of sexual restraint and promiscuity. Within that context, many nationalists placed the issues of venereal disease and prostitution at the center of propaganda efforts against the British Army. They did so both to discredit the occupier and to discourage Irish enlistment. Even medical and scientific facts became rhetorical weapons in the battle over Irish national loyalty.[11]

Advanced-nationalist propaganda emphasized how prostitutes were, on the one hand, emblematic of a traditional feminine Ireland ravaged and victimized by an impure foreign invader. On the other hand, prostitutes were also depicted as being contagious occupiers of public space, to be shunned and avoided at all costs. In this regard they did not differ too much from their soldierly clientele. Joyce invited readers to consider this paradox when, as Clair Wills notes, he "placed the prostitute at the center of his complex refiguring of the metropolis in an Irish context" (79). Joyce's fiction renders the streetwalker or brothel worker with a kind of potent ambivalence and humane ambiguity. Consequently, Wills argues, she can be regarded as possessing a kind of "double-agent" status, such that "we must read the prostitute as a sign of both imperial domination (in her link with the barracks) and, through her association with venereal disease, the corruption of that political/military system" (90). In this case, the anxiety results from the unknown potential and unclear eventuality, whether intentional and politicized or unconsciously mediated.

Ulysses becomes a conduit for these competing discourses of surveillance and anxiety surrounding prostitution as it generates its own scrutiny of nighttime streetwalking. The novel explores the ironic overlap of police and paramilitary authority with sex industry, specifically through Bloom's multiple encounters with the "whore of the lane" (*U* 11.1250–51). This mysterious, anxiety-inducing streetwalker appears twice in the narrative and is referenced a third time in flashback. Joyce's multiple descriptions of her conflate the vocabulary of urban policing, military reconnaissance, rural commerce, and sexual solicitation. Integral to each chance meeting is the tactical advantage of seeing or disadvantage of being seen. Her recurring presence alludes to persistent, inevitable questions about streetwalking as sanctioned or illicit, male or female, military or civilian.

Early in "Eumaeus," having just enumerated for Stephen some of the "dangers of nighttown"—which notably include both "women of ill fame" and unscrupulous policemen (*U* 16.63, 76)—Leopold Bloom encounters one such danger firsthand on the margin of the red-light district. During the late-night respite at the cabman's shelter he glimpses "The face of a streetwalker glazed and haggard under a black straw hat... palpably reconnoitring on her own with the object of bringing more grist to her mill" (*U* 16.704–6). The concluding image offers a vivid sexual innuendo as well as an agricultural-mercantile metaphor hinting at the socioeconomic patterns of Dublin prostitution. In the reduced agrarian economy of the post-Famine decades, as we have seen, many rural women were forced to migrate to the city where, in the face of excessive competition for limited employment as chambermaids, waitresses, and domestics, a significant number resorted to prostitution to earn a living. The dynamic commercial analogy of rural Ireland is paired with a gesture of reconnaissance appropriate to garrison Dublin: the act of "palpably reconnoitring" suggests the streetwalker's adaptation to a new urban economy in which, ironically, and necessarily, she mirrors the men who at once police and patronize her illicit trade. The archaic French verb *reconnoître*—literally meaning "to recognize"—carries the longstanding military connotation of clandestine scouting either along or behind enemy lines. The Continental etymology also extends the conjoined notions of tactical spying and sexual intrigue that emerge in "Proteus" during the exiled republican dynamitard Kevin Egan's condemnation of Paris, which he deems a place of "Most licentious custom" (*U* 3.236).

Bloom's immediate reaction at seeing the streetwalker is to hide behind his copy of the *Evening Telegraph* in the hope she will not see him. Still, he cannot quite look away. As Katherine Mullin notes of the scene, "prostitute and slum become twin urban receptacles for a fascinated yet repulsed bourgeois gaze" (177). In an episode that incorporates the themes of concealment and disguise that mark its Homeric pre-text, Bloom looks to avoid recognition of his own identity, not unlike the prostitute herself looking to evade the attention of the authorities. He is fascinated by her presence, even while he tries to ignore it.

Nor is this the first time Bloom has tried desperately to avoid the power of the streetwalker's gaze. Her surveillant, policing aspect is established earlier with her initial appearance in "Sirens" when Bloom sees her coming along Ormond Quay. Her approach interrupts his meditation on the lyrics of "The Croppy Boy" and the identity of the man in the mackintosh—both also narratives of disguise and recognition—with a sudden, anxious exclamation: "O, the whore of the lane!" (*U* 11.1250–51). Just before Bloom ducks furtively into Lionel Marks's antique shop, the ensuing lines merge a description of the approaching woman with a recollection of his initial, compromising encounter with her on a nighttime street:

> A frowsy whore with black straw sailor hat askew came glazily in the day along the quay towards Mr Bloom. When first he saw that form endearing? Yes, it is. I feel so lonely. Wet night in the lane. Horn. Who had the? Heehaw shesaw. Off her beat here. What is she? Hope she. (*U* 11.1252–55)

The moment merges Bloom's awareness of the social danger of the woman recognizing him in the current moment with his recollection of its basis in the night he almost engaged her services. "Horn," as a category of musical instrument, fits within the dominant musical motif of "Sirens." Or it could mean one of the newest sounds of modernity: the automobile klaxon. Additionally, as sexual slang it suggests both arousal and cuckoldry, both of which are associated with Boylan's impending visit with Molly. That is, Bloom will be a horned husband because Boylan is a horny paramour, a fact that is all but verified in Lenehan's quip about Boylan's rush to leave the Ormond Hotel bar for Eccles Street: "Got the horn or what?" (*U* 11.432).

Not least of all, though, "horn" suggests a truncated version of "horney," a nineteenth-century slang term for watchman or policeman, or in Dublin terms Metropolitan Police constables (Gifford 168).[12] Even after encountering the intimidating police troop after their lunch, Bloom employs the term to strike a sympathetic note: "Can't blame them after all with the job they have especially the young hornies" (*U* 8.421–22). The same denotation appears in the mock-courtroom testimony of *Finnegans Wake*: "How do I know? Such my billet. Buy a barrack pass. Tell the horneys. Tell the robbers" (*FW* 507.24–25). In Bloom's memory of the wet night in the lane, the term conjoins his own state of sexual excitement and the accompanying concern that a patrolling policeman might stumble upon their backstreet solicitation. This notion is reinforced by Bloom's reference to the whore with the constabulary metaphor as being "Off her beat here" (*U* 11.1255). By way of such descriptions, the streetwalker mimics the power and presence of the very ones charged with enforcing rather than transgressing laws of public space and sexual commerce.

Each appearance of the woman in the straw hat is replete with parallels that equate the streetwalking of policing and of prostitution. The ambiguous and unanswered question "What is she?" shows Bloom wondering about either her occupational status, her proper location, or both: he ponders what she is as well as what she is doing there, in terms of normative social identities or economic categories. It is the very sort of question a constable, soldier, or night watchman would have asked a woman found unaccompanied on the street after dark.

The woman in the straw hat has her own ready-made answer to such interrogation: her disguise as laundress—"Psst! Any chance of your wash" (U 11.1255–56)—provides a perfect way past the legal and social obstacles to her profession. Thus the streetwalker suggests a practical cover as well as the countless women who served their harsh penance in the Magdalen laundries after being judged by legal and clerical authority to be outside the safe sexual categories (married woman or maiden). Adopting this legitimizing identity, she subverts the policing presence of male authorities and figures of a repressive state apparatus by assimilating some of its own operational techniques, and even anticipating one of its social punishments.

In tandem with her covert, policing patrol, the "whore of the lane" elicits appropriate connections with those related major forces of the occupation: the British Army and the Royal Navy. Her black straw sailor hat, one of many women's fashions that followed a Victorian trend of copying naval attire, is not only as stylish accessory and a useful disguise, but serves as a kind of walking advertisement. In "Circe," Kitty Ricketts is similarly described as "a bony pallid whore in navy costume" and wearing a "sailor hat" (U 15.2050, 2060). Like the soldiers' photograph Stephen notices on the brothel wall, the sailor hat makes an automatic connection and show of camaraderie with the main clientele of the Dublin sex trade. In his discussion with Lynch, Stephen cloaks the idea of prostitution in such metonymical terms when he compares it cynically to marriage: "Love gives and freedom takes. The woman in the black straw hat gave something before she sold her body to the State. Emma will sell herself to the State but give nothing" (SH 203).

Ulysses revises the woman in the black straw hat, adding the naval detail. Subsequent vocabulary follows suit, as for example when, upon learning the whore is acquainted with Molly, Bloom punningly concedes that she "Had me decked" (U 11.1256). Both remarks anticipate "Eumaeus" and the shelter keeper's sardonic reference to the whore by her nautical nickname: "The gunboat" (U 16.727). Presumably the moniker implies she patrols the Liffey quays with much the same frequency and presence as the

British warships that bring a fair number of her customers. It also connects her directly, if anachronistically, to the fighting between British forces and Irish rebels, since during the Easter Rising the gunboat HMS *Helga* used her three-pounders to shell the Volunteers in the GPO and central Dublin. Joyce's 1903–4 Paris notebook records, among a number of items under the heading "For Dubliners," the notation "The gunboat (whore)" (37). The military connection with sexual commerce had apparently come to Joyce's mind nearly two decades earlier during the initial conception of *Ulysses* as a story for *Dubliners*.

Bloom's desperate avoidance of the streetwalker's surveillance points to an additional connection between sexual commerce and militarism in Dublin. Fittingly, it can be traced back to the man with whom Joyce acquired firsthand experience of Nighttown, Oliver St. John Gogarty. After hearing Ben Dollard sing "The Croppy Boy" in the Ormond Hotel bar, Bloom has in mind one of the characters in that song, the army captain who disguises himself as a priest to entrap a young Irish insurgent in the United Irishmen Rising of 1798. In Bloom's reading of the song, the croppy boy "must have been a bit of a natural not to see it was a yeoman cap" (*U* 11.1248–49). The rank of yeoman originated in the eighteenth-century militia in Ireland and generally alluded to the predominance of Ascendancy-class Anglo-Irish in military service.

Now juxtaposed with the "frowsy whore," the term "yeoman" recalls another contemporary and somewhat scandalous usage by Joyce's erstwhile friend and Nighttown companion. In 1900, Oliver St. John Gogarty published in *Dublin Society* magazine his acrostic "Ode of Welcome" for Irish soldiers rotating back from action in South Africa.[13] The opening lines of the poetic parody collectively referred to the returning troops as "the gallant Irish yeoman." The tribute seems laudatory, patriotic, and sincere until, much like the yeoman who unmasks his true identity in "The Croppy Boy," the acrostic message in "Ode of Welcome" at last reveals itself in full:

> **T**he Gallant Irish yeoman
> **H**ome from the war has come
> **E**ach victory gained o'er foeman
> **W**hy should our bards be dumb.
>
> **H**ow shall we sing their praises
> **O**ur glory in their deeds

Renowned their worth amazes
Empire their prowess needs.

So to Old Ireland's hearts and homes
We welcome now our own brave boys
In cot and Hall; neath lordly domes
Love's heroes share once more our joys.

Love is the Lord of all just now
Be he the husband, lover, son,
Each dauntless soul recalls the vow
By which not fame, but love was won.

United now in fond embrace
Salute with joy each well-loved face
Yeoman: in women's hearts you hold the place.

Part of the effectiveness of Gogarty's poem resides in how it manages to speak to multiple readerships, as Enda Duffy argues, depending mainly on political allegiance (157). Anglo-Irish Unionists and Tories with respect for the traditional role of the yeomanry might take it at face value, even disregarding the emerging code of its first letters; ardent nationalists, especially those familiar with the treacherous yeoman in the story of "The Croppy Boy," would be more likely to buy into its subversive, mocking message. In this way, the poem achieves an unlikely fusion of British soldiers with Irish nationalists past and present. Even with the acrostic made visible, the pro-army attitude does not of necessity disappear. In fact, depending on how readers envision the moral agency of the whores, their sexual commerce might variously be read as dangerous, unfortunate, or even excusable, given what the troops have just been through. At the same time, any truly gallant quality of the yeoman seems in danger of being compromised entirely by this revelation of his seamier nighttime pursuits.

Ulysses brings both of these interpretations and their source texts into Bloom's divided consciousness concerning the woman in the black straw hat. His past solicitation and present avoidance recall the dual identities apparent in Gogarty's poem and the traditional rebel song. As he flees the whore's line of sight, he thinks of the "brighteyed and gallant" crowd back in the Ormond, then sees the "gallant pictured hero" Robert Emmet in the antique-shop window (*U* 11.1270, 1274). The confluence of covert prostitution with lauded military figure echoes the irony of Gogarty's controversial acrostic. For readers of *Dubliners*, the word recalls Corley and Lenehan, those other two contemporary gallants whose moral identity also becomes increasingly circumspect amid the militarized sexual transactions of Dublin street life.

Disgraced Capital, Soldiers' Paradise

On a typical summer evening at the start of the twentieth century, scores of young men in uniform walked the streets of Dublin ready to spend their weekly army wages. These bands of soldiers encountered groups of young women, some as young as fifteen, many of whom had come from the countryside in search of work. Most were unemployed, or at best underemployed, as household domestics, hotel chambermaids, waitresses, or flower girls. As social reformer Helena Molony observed at the time, "many thousands of innocent country girls, up in Dublin, at domestic service mostly, were dazzled by these handsome and brilliant uniforms with polite young men with English accents inside them and dazzled often with disastrous results to themselves" (qtd. in Luddy 170). Others were perhaps less naïve than Molony describes, but no less vulnerable to the pressures of surviving in a limited economy.

Both sides took advantage of a recent loosening of regulations that gave soldiers more freedom to move about the city. Free off-base movement for recruits was a boon to army enlistment and erotic commerce, two dynamic sectors in an otherwise slumping local economy. Troop numbers consequently increased, and regulars could be seen roaming the city center at night with money in their pockets and time on their hands. Many women capitalized on the financial windfall generated by the relaxed barrack rules. Nevertheless, there was public outcry against the overt solicitation taking place in the city center. Molony noted how downtown space became strictly divided, with the soldiers "confined to one side of O'Connell Street, i.e., the G.P.O. side. No respectable person—man or woman—would dream of walking on that side of the street after twilight" (qtd. in Luddy 170).

By the spring of 1904, the situation was regarded by many as a crisis with moral and political resonance. The *United Irishman* newspaper of 11 June lamented how "in the heart of the city at night-time conduct has been openly carried on by the British soldiery and the women who consort with them that could not be witnessed in the streets of any other city in the world" and one city official viewed "the 'immorality and indecency' along Westmoreland and O'Connell streets as worse than anything he had seen in Paris, Port Said, Cairo or Bombay" ("Dublin Corporation" 5). The Continental and colonial comparisons suggest a calculated appeal to both Irish nationalist and British imperialist pride: surely, the implication runs, the streets of Dublin will not be allowed to descend to the level of iniquity found in such distant outposts of empire, much less the wicked French capital.

This controversy of the streets was a longstanding issue that had been revived a few weeks earlier with a challenge to an army policy allowing soldiers unrestricted nighttime movement throughout the city. Formerly, troops were confined to barracks at night, but in an effort to boost recruitment during the Boer War, military authorities had begun to permit troops stationed in Dublin to spend free evening hours away from the barracks. A May 1904 resolution by the Dublin Corporation asking the army to amend or rescind the policy had garnered no response from the military authorities and scant support from Corporation members with conservative leanings and military sympathies. The *United Irishman* correspondent voiced doubts that any Tory member of the Dublin Corporation who had a daughter "would attempt to walk with her along the west side of O'Connell-street on a Sunday evening" ("Dublin Corporation" 5). Nevertheless, conservative politicians, as well as army and Castle authorities, refused to take action. The *United Irishman* reported on 15 June:

> The British Government has officially announced that it attaches no importance to the protest of the Dublin Corporation against the conduct carried on in the main streets of Dublin each night, and particularly on Sunday nights by the British soldiery, and that it intends to take no steps to prevent the continuance of scenes which have earned for Dublin abroad the reputation of being one of the most immoral cities in the world. . . . Dublin is nicknamed in the British army "The Soldiers' Paradise," because in no city in Great Britain or in any part of the British Empire is such latitude permitted to the soldiery as in Dublin. ("British Government" 5)

Without support from crucial quarters, the Corporation's request failed to gain traction for any significant policy changes. The situation spoke as much to matters of national sovereignty as it did to public morality: "Under the

British flag, in the twentieth century, the Corporation of Dublin has not power even to regulate the traffic in the streets" ("Dublin Corporation" 5).

From a nationalist perspective, sexual commerce and armed conquest became symptomatic metaphors as well as parallel, concrete reminders of Dublin's occupied status. Social reformers and nationalists alike saw the military authorities as pandering the very city itself to men in uniform. With little or no movement on the issue from the army or police, some groups took their own actions. Women's organizations distributed leaflets and established street patrols aimed at monitoring the sexual interaction of women and soldiers. These campaigns of influence and surveillance sought as much to establish their own political position as to solve the social problem or change the actual lives of women. Like military and police approaches to the issue, they concentrated their efforts on controlling nighttime urban space, rather than looking to remedy the social and economic circumstances that caused prostitution to become so prevalent in that space.

Joyce considers this problem of the streets in direct relation to the sexualized military identity that can be read in the visual rhetoric of recruiting. At the opening of "Lotus Eaters," as he departs the Westland Row Post Office, Leopold Bloom spies a "recruiting poster with soldiers of all arms on parade" (*U* 5.57). As Mark Wollaeger argues, the moment conveys Bloom's "insight into uniforms as a technique of recruitment and social control" (97). For beyond engaging with his sense of nationalism or patriotism, the poster leads Bloom along personal and psychological lines as he scans the ranks for the uniformed likeness of his father-in-law:

> He slipped card and letter into his sidepocket, reviewing again the soldiers on parade. Where's old Tweedy's regiment? Castoff soldier. There: bearskin cap and hackle plume. No, he's a grenadier. Pointed cuffs. There he is: royal Dublin fusiliers. Redcoats. Too showy. That must be why the women go after them. Uniform. Easier to enlist and drill. (*U* 5.65–70)

A lifelong civilian, Bloom shows an incredibly detailed interest in the finer points of regimental dress, a likely consequence of growing up in a city where social advantage could be determined even by shallow, sartorial connection to the colonial military hierarchy. This sociopolitical dynamic also acquires a personal significance for Bloom who, in looking for Tweedy's uniform among the many portrayed on the poster, effectively seeks out his lost connection with Molly.

"Penelope" will confirm Molly's longstanding infatuation with military men, which some readers attribute to her working out her father issues.[14] She does demonstrate some precise knowledge of uniformed servicemen when she recalls "the Queens own they were a nice lot its well the Surreys relieved them theyre always trying to show it to you every time" (*U* 18.548–49). Whatever her reasons, Molly is proof that "women go after them," a thought that might make Bloom's study of the recruiting poster also become a painful reminder of the decade lapse in intimate relations with Molly. His jocularity holds sway, however, in the sexually explicit and humorous double entendre that to attract feminine interest it might be "Easier to enlist and drill" (*U* 5.69–70).

Bloom's reading of the recruiting poster indicates how militarist ideology can become entwined with male sexual identity. It demonstrates how the garrison could be an intrusion not only on the Cartesian spaces of city and country but on the psychological territory of desire. As rival to native men and purchaser of native women, the occupier represents a doubly invasive threat, what Sheldon Brivic describes as "an extension of the general historical principle that the conqueror has a right to the women of the conquered, with men's competition deciding women's fates" (48). The parallel verities of military and sexual conquest are evident in Bloom's response to the poster.

After he has read this official rhetoric of recruiting, the dialogic nature of Bloom's thinking leads him to recall another side to the issue. It immediately takes the form of Irish nationalists' public outcry against the sexual menace of soldiers in Dublin:

> Maud Gonne's letter about taking them off O'Connell street at night: disgrace to our Irish capital. Griffith's paper is on the same tack now: an army rotten with venereal disease: overseas or halfseasover empire. Half baked they look: hypnotised like. Eyes front. Mark time. (*U* 5.70–73)

Bloom juxtaposes two contemporary voices on the issue, Maude Gonne and Arthur Griffith, ardent nationalists who tended to exploit the issue of street solicitation for political advantage while ignoring the social problems in need of solutions. Gonne—or at least Bloom's sound-bite version of her—makes the issue about territorial control; "Griffith's paper" focuses on contagious disease as medical evidence of the British contagion in Ireland. Both incorporate the sexual presence of soldiers into potent analogies of moral and national health.

During the Boer War, Gonne's *Inghinidhe na hÉireann* (Daughters of Ireland) organization published propaganda that targeted Irishwomen walking with men in British uniform. Married to Major John MacBride, Gonne was among the first modern Irish nationalists to openly support military methods, as evidenced by her involvement in the Howth gunrunning incident. Her approach to the issue of soldiers in the red-light districts also reflected this martial mindset. It took the course of anti-recruiting discourse, as her organization "got out leaflets on the shame of Irish girls consorting with the soldiers of the enemy of their country" (qtd. in Novick 267). Steeped in the rhetoric of total war and armed engagement, one leaflet loudly and directly proclaimed the political dangers of romantic liaisons with members of the British military:

> Irish Girls!
>
> Ireland has the need of the loving service of all her children. Irishwomen do not sufficiently realise the power they have to help or hinder the cause of Ireland's freedom. If they did, we should not see the sad sight of Irish girls walking through the streets with men wearing the uniform of Ireland's oppressor.... Irish girls, make a vow, not only that you will yourselves refuse to associate with any man who wears an English uniform, but that you will also try and induce your girl companions to do the same. (qtd. in Luddy 171)

In her attempt to clear the streets, the writer makes no direct reference to prostitution or sexual liaisons in general; rather, she keeps to the euphemistic high ground when addressing the general issue of women "walking through the streets" with British soldiers (ibid.). With her argument directed toward such cut-and-dried issues as individual choice and patriotic loyalty, the writer tends to avoid the more nuanced realities of economic survival that were a major reason why many Dublin women offered sexual services or otherwise consorted with British soldiers.

Bloom's summary of Arthur Griffith and Sinn Fein's commentary on the problem points to the urgent issue of sexually transmitted diseases that had become a public health crisis in Dublin and other garrison towns. The editorial criticism that echoes in Bloom's thoughts of "an army rotten with venereal disease: overseas or halfseasover empire" (*U* 5.72) characterizes the soldiers as devolving into a dazed and delirious state. In such conditions, army and empire run the distinct risk of being defeated by the invisible and invincible force. The trope is strategic and predictive, as the British military is already "halfseasover"—that is, logistically overextended across the empire and physically reeling from intoxication with rum. It is also half-seized-over with the debilitating effects of syphilis. Owing to her soldiers' unrestrained appetites and unclean dalliances, Britannia could well go from ruling the waves to losing still more of her overseas possessions, until the empire as well resembles a syphilitic shadow of its former self.

One likely source of Bloom's paraphrase comes from a three-article series Oliver St. John Gogarty wrote for Griffith's *United Irishman* newspaper in the fall of 1906. Titled "Ugly England," it decries the hypocrisy of a hypothetical Englishman called Sludge who "cries out again at the godlessness of the foreign Governments regarding their treatment of those women who associate with their soldiers" (3). Bloom's thoughts correspond with Gogarty's description of the British Army as "a body of men who, as their own statistics show, are already more than half leprous from venereal excess ... rottener and more immoral than any or all of the armies in Europe put together" (3). As evidence Gogarty alludes to the alleged sexual behavior of British troops stationed in India, where women are held captive in a state of sexual slavery worse than a harem and "debauched at the good pleasure of the Army" (3). Writing as a married medical man with an anti-British agenda, "O.G." assumes his own safe distance, even if his reinvention as Buck Mulligan—not to mention his own memoir, somewhat mischievously titled *Tumbling in the Hay*—would eventually ensure his eternal association with the flash houses of Monto.

Griffith's newspaper and media machine would remain very much on the same tack in the decade that followed. The same general arguments appear in Sinn Fein anti-recruiting propaganda linking the British soldiery to venereal disease and prostitution. In attempting to prove its assertion that "The British Army in which Irishmen are asked to enlist is the MOST IMMORAL

ARMY IN THE WORLD," a leaflet published by the organization in 1913 blamed such "loathsome diseases" as syphilis on the troops of the empire. As example, it claimed that more than 20 percent of British soldiers (212 out of every 1,000) were treated each year for venereal diseases; this was more than twice the rate of the next highest (Italy's) listed in a group of six major European armies (Novick 155). The pamphlet also cited supposedly official policies of subsidizing prostitution, albeit without listing any sources for its information, as in the following: THE ENGLISH GOVERNMENT PAYS annually £400 to Cork, £250 to Dublin, £100 to Naas, for accommodation FOR PROSTITUTES FOR their SOLDIERS. IRISHMEN—WHY DON'T YOU JOIN THE ARMY? (qtd. in Novick 155).

Joyce appears to have been well aware of the politicized nature of the syphilis issue.[15] He forwarded Gogarty's "Ugly England" piece to Stanislaus on 24 September 1906, followed by a letter saying, "I hope you will appreciate the full flavour. The part about the chummies is particularly rich" (*L* 2:164). He might have been recalling his own Monto forays with Gogarty. The topic remained on his mind when he wrote his brother ten days later:

> I wish some unkind person would publish a book about the venereal condition of the Irish; since they pride themselves so much on their immunity. It must be rather worse than England, I think. I know very little of the subject but it seems to me to be a disease like any other disease, caused by anti-hygienic conditions. I don't see where the judgement of God comes into it nor do I see what the word "excess" means in this connection. (*L* 2:170–71)

To some extent Joyce became the person to write that book. The theme of sexually transmitted disease recurs throughout *Ulysses*, from private thoughts to bawdy jokes. It represents a matter of personal dignity in the case of Mr. Breen receiving the cryptic four-letter postcard (*U* 8.320). Meanwhile, Bloom worries briefly that Boylan might pass syphilis to him through Molly. Beyond the personal, contagious diseases connect to concerns of national security as well; they pose an equal threat to British and Irish, soldier and whore, colonizer and colonized.

Finnegans Wake I.3 alludes to the epidemic threat looming over the military and red-light district in a brief recollection of military men engaging in the nightlife of Monto:

Tap and pat and tapatagain, (fire firstshot, Missiers the Refuseleers! Peingpeong! For saxonlootie!) three tommix, soldiers free, cockaleak and cappapee, of the Coldstream. Guards were walking, in (*pardonnez-leur, je vous en prie, eh?*) Montgomery Street" (*FW* 58.23–26).

Whether Coldstream Guards or Royal Dublin Fusiliers, this roving band will never refuse a leer to any woman as they move through the heart of the Monto. These "three tommix," or three Tommies (slang for British soldiers), are free to mix with women of the town, especially after the extended curfews and relaxed off-barracks restrictions that became standard operating procedure for the army in Ireland in the post–Boer War years. Presumably as a consequence of such freedoms, these guards exhibit sure and fluid signs ("cockaleak") of sexually transmitted diseases from head to toe, or *cap à pied* ("cappapee")—with a pun on the final French syllable that gives entirely new meaning to the old regimental name Coldstream.

The trio of syphilis, soldiers, and prostitution surfaces as well in *Ulysses*'s "Cyclops" episode. When the barroom discourse ranges from Arthur Griffith to Admiral Nelson to British "colonies and civilization" (*U* 12.1193–96), it is interrupted by the Citizen's cultural renouncement of all things English: "Their syphilisation, you mean . . . sons of whores' gets! No music and no art and no literature worthy of the name. Any civilisation they have they stole from us" (*U* 12.1197–1200). To ardent Irish nationalists like the Citizen, syphilis and other brothel maladies could prove more effective than armed force in ousting the occupier. The implication is that prostitution might play an unexpected role in the military liberation of the country: prostitutes in a sense become soldiers in a silent battle, armed with their own biological weaponry. Clair Wills expresses this paradoxical potential in her observation that "for Joyce the prostitute acted as a kind of double agent. Because of her putative function as disease carrier, she would corrupt the British troops, but the effects of venereal disease also contributed to the collapse of the city" (92–93).

This precise contradiction arises in "Eumaeus" as the "glazed and haggard" visage of the woman in the black straw hat plying her trade beside the cabman's shelter. For in all her potent, surveying aspect, she suggests syphilitic symptoms as well. Bloom, though not possessing the trained medical mind of Mulligan/Gogarty, nevertheless offers his prognosis to Stephen:

"It beats me, . . . medically I am speaking, how a wretched creature like that from the Lock hospital reeking with disease can be barefaced enough to solicit or how any man in his sober senses, if he values his health in the least. Unfortunate creature!" (*U* 16.728–31). He then speculates as to the physical cause and moral obligation concerning the woman's health—"Of course I suppose some man is ultimately responsible for her condition" (*U* 16.731–32)—before suggesting an administrative course of action requiring that "women of that stamp" be "licensed and medically inspected by the proper authorities" (*U* 16.741, 743). Doing so, Bloom paraphrases a set of legislative measures that had come under heavy scrutiny just prior to the turn of the century.

The Contagious Diseases Acts (CDA) of 1864 mandated military, police, and medical professionals to track the health of prostitutes in British and Irish garrison towns. It established a network of lock hospitals for medical inspection and incarceration of prostitutes as a means of protecting the military mission. Any woman arrested for prostitution could be required to have a physical examination; those who refused could face a month-long sentence in one of a network of lock hospitals. A prostitute discovered to have syphilis or another venereal disease could be held for up to three months. This period of maximum detention was extended with each renewal of the CDA, to six months in 1866 and to nine months by 1869 (Luddy 140). Such regulation was considered not just a way to sustain the sexual perquisites of those who enlisted in the armed forces; it was deemed a vital measure necessary to national security. By contrast, opponents of the Contagious Diseases Act argued how, in safeguarding the health of the troops, the act unlawfully compromised the rights of women and ultimately encouraged prostitution.

Westmoreland Lock Hospital became the center for CDA medical inspections and incarcerations in Dublin. It is most likely the location referenced by the prostitute Kitty Ricketts in "Circe" when she relates the recent tribulations of a colleague who has contracted syphilis from a soldier: "Mary Shortall that was in the lock with the pox that she got from Jimmy Pidgeon in the blue caps had a child off him that couldn't swallow and was smothered with the convulsions in the mattress and we all subscribed for the funeral" (*U* 15.2578–81). Allusion to the "blue caps" signifies the regimental field uniform of the Royal Dublin Fusiliers, clarifying the military's equal hand in the epidemic. Kitty's account of the child's debilitating physical condition and tragic end suggests the high costs of dealing with the epidemic under the CDAs and lock hospital system.

Moments later, the medical student Lynch brings that system under further scrutiny with a sardonic reference to contemporary syphilis research by Russian embryologist Ilya Metchnikoff: "And to such delights has Metchnikoff inoculated anthropoid apes" (*U* 15.2590). In 1904, Metchnikoff's pioneering work inoculating apes with the disease allowed him to compare the physiological reaction of humans with that of their primate cousins. It eventually helped prove the effectiveness of early chemotherapy for syphilis treatment.[16] The juxtaposition of such cutting-edge science with the preventable tragedy of Mary Shortall and her child calls into question the fundamental humaneness and medical wisdom of the CDAs. Another reading of Lynch's remark is that British authorities' treatment of Nighttown prostitutes is on a moral par with animal testing. The analogy is an apt one, given Ireland's long history as a laboratory of British colonialism in everything ranging from railroads and postal delivery to health care and social services. Even if Metchnikoff's work brings about scientifically valid and valuable results, the question remains whether the treatment of his subjects is justified by his scientific ends. The same can be said for the suffering of Dublin women and children despite or due to official policies for controlling sexually transmitted disease.

This direct regulation of prostitution ceased in 1886 after repeal of the CDA under mounting public pressure.[17] For Bloom to be endorsing lock hospitals and the medical inspection of prostitutes nearly twenty years later, as Katherine Mullin suggests, has him "recapitulating arguments which were implemented and vigorously contested during the first two decades of his life" (186). In another sense, though, his remarks are not a total anachronism. At the outbreak of the First World War there was renewed discussion about whether to reinstitute the Contagious Diseases Act, although the debate never led to any legislative action. Nevertheless, relaxed barracks regulations such as freedom of the streets and off-base lodging for many soldiers continued to exploit the advantages of the Dublin red-light districts in an effort to draw young, single men into the regimental ranks. The tenuous partnership of soldier and sex worker had remained a fixture of Dublin for decades. During *Ulysses*'s vibrant, dramatic representation of Nighttown in the "Circe" episode, Joyce's combative brothel scenes seek a resolution of the powerful tension of sexual and armed services underlying the subconscious life of the city.

Setting Things Rite

Prostitutes and prostitution in "Circe" have been variously read in relation to actions as disparate as theatrical performance and terrorist violence.[18] Their association with soldiers and the military presence in Dublin is explored in the episode via the shifting identities of Leopold Bloom and other characters. His reincarnation as various figures of the demimonde—including soldier, prostitute, panderer, prostitution client, and reformer—reveals numerous psychosexual conflicts and contradictions. At the same time, these psychological manifestations underscore the fluid economic realities of Monto. Within the general atmospherics of the episode, such exaggerated transformations form an appropriate portrait of Nighttown as a place of tenuous transactions. The uneasy alliance of the military and the sex trade reveals itself through a series of changing identities and interactions; ultimately, as the conflicting forces within Bloom and the red-light district approach critical mass, they anticipate the urban battlefield that central Dublin became in 1916.

The first glimpse of Nighttown through the Mabbot Street entrance features a pairing of prostitutes and soldiers that is an effective overture to the psychological and political tensions. While Cissy Caffrey sings in bawdy rhymes, the stage directions describe the redcoat privates Compton and Carr holding "swaggersticks tight in their oxters, as they march unsteadily rightaboutface and burst together from their mouths a volleyed fart. Laughter of men from the lane. A hoarse virago retorts" (U 15.48–50). The moment concentrates on the arrogance of the soldiers, in part showing Joyce's personal vendetta against British consul Percy Bennett and Henry Carr, a consulate staff member who in fact was an army veteran, concerning their legal dispute over the English Players in Zurich.[19]

In settling old personal scores, the scene shines a harsh, satirical light on the Dublin garrison in general, highlighting their brutish qualities and general intellectual shortcomings. The privates' deflating show of force meets only with derision and dissent, suggesting a pathway of resistance in the literary theater of the episode and the military theater of the city. Three serious functions of martial display—weaponry, drilling, and communications—are depicted as incompetent or incoherent. Ineffective weapons, imprecise marching, and nonsensical communications elicit only laughter from male onlookers.

The female audience is even less forgiving. The Virago's obscene rejoinder—"Signs on you, hairy arse. More power the Cavan girl" (*U* 15.53)—emphasizes Nightown as a partitioned, militarized zone with distinct markings of individual status and power. Her remark singles out and vaguely threatens the soldiers; it socially and geographically labels Cissy as one of the many country girls who sought opportunity in Dublin and resorted to prostitution to earn a living. In this regard the Virago voices allegiances in the conflict, along national and gender lines. Like a stadium cheer, her words are a simple expression of praise and support that exhibit the essence of political protest and cultural identity: the question of "more power," for nations as well as for individuals, is precisely what is at stake. In aligning herself with Cissy Caffrey, the Virago chooses sides in a division that runs along cultural as well as gender lines. The moment forms a preamble to the complementary yet conflicting forces that will contend across the episode, with escalating consequences.

The soldier-prostitute pairing develops further when the initial appearance of the Loiterers and Whores coincides with the ambiguous interactions between the drunken Navvy and Privates Compton and Carr. The Navvy's stage action—"gripping the two redcoats, staggers forward with them"—and exclamatory remark "Come on, you British army!" (*U* 15.613–14) might be read as either social invitation or political challenge. The ambiguity represents the unresolved questions in Irish relations. As the scene wavers between potential camaraderie and conflict, it features echoes of the Keogh-Bennett boxing match: "Say! What price the sergeantmajor?" and "Bennett? He's my pal. I love old Bennett" (*U* 15.624, 626)). These are framed by the Navvy's singing of the opening verse of the rebel song "The Boys of Wexford" commemorating the 1798 United Irishmen Rising, which begins to resolve any question as to where his political sympathies lie. The choice of song is appropriate to the opening of "Circe," since it, too, is a text that commingles themes of romantic companionship, monetary reward, and political loyalty. The very next verse introduces a suspicious offer by a yeoman captain's daughter who boldly proclaims her desire to elope with the speaker and enlist with him in the fight. She would be more than a typical camp follower, sacrificing her money, her sexual identity, and potentially her life for the cause: "A thousand pounds I'll bring / If you will fly from home with me, / And dress myself in man's attire / And fight for liberty." The narrator faces a test of his loyalty and desire in this decision of whether to form a dangerous alliance with a sworn enemy. Though he does not altogether refuse consorting with the enemy, he seems intent on disengaging the fiscal temptation from the romantic notions of love and patriotism when he vows her "shining eyes will be my prize." Like "Circe," the rebel song juxtaposes issues of sexual involvement, military loyalty, and financial gain. The gender-bending promise of the captain's daughter anticipates the sexual-identity transformations of the episode typified in the interaction of Bella/Bello and Bloom as, overall, this intertextual link to "The Boys of Wexford" speaks to the duplicitous fiscal and sexual transactions that characterize Joyce's Nighttown.

These prologue moments prepare the dramatic ground of "Circe" for the entry of the leading man Bloom, who takes on multiple roles relating to military and sexual services. These range from predatory solicitor of sexual favors to panderer to great social reformer, as a shifting series of identities and alleged offenses are brought to light. Among other crimes, Bloom is accused of making sexual advances toward a former domestic, of possessing a bomb, and of pimping women to British army officers. His soliciting of servant Mary Driscoll echoes many similar tales that girls in domestic service had to contend with: "He made a certain suggestion but I thought more of myself as poor as I am" (*U* 15.873). Bloom then shifts from being a john to a pimp, as the incident with Mary Driscoll enlarges to a broader charge of involving numerous women in the "white slave traffic," including the claim from Mrs. Bellingham that he "urged me . . . to misbehave, to sin with officers of the garrison" (*U* 15.1167, 15.1069–70). Sexual offenses parallel military ones, as soon afterward, in the guise of an Irish republican dynamitard like Kevin Egan, Bloom is discovered by the Dublin Watch to be in possession of an "Infernal machine with a time fuse" (*U* 15.1199).

In defending against these charges, he emerges as a great social reformer. He presents a fictitious regimental record, complete with heroic battle narrative, in an attempt to influence the jury in his favor and clear his name:

> On this day twenty years ago we overcame the hereditary enemy at Ladysmith. Our howitzers and camel swivel guns played on his lines with telling effect. Half a league onward! They charge! All is lost now!

Do we yield? No! We drive them headlong! Lo! We charge! Deploying to the left our light horse swept across the heights of Plevna and, uttering their warcry *Bonafide Sabaoth*, sabred the Saracen gunners to a man. (*U* 15.1525–30)

The war memorial speech conflates the Second Boer War siege of Ladysmith in 1899–1900 with the 1877 siege of Plevna. Molly recalls her father talking about Plevna, and Bloom owns Tweedy's copy of Sir Henry Montague Hozier's *History of the Russo-Turkish War* (U 18.690, 17.1385–87). Poetic echoes of Tennyson's "Charge of the Light Brigade," about the fateful British cavalry charge in the Crimea, add to a tone that seems intended to ensure a type of patriotic masculinity in these distorted wartime recollections.

Public trial and ceremonial speeches gradually give way to more sadomasochistic punishment, as the most radical transformations ensue inside Bella Cohen's brothel. When the madam as dominatrix assumes the masculinized form Bello, (s)he threatens to turn a feminized Bloom into a sexual commodity to be offered up to the military clientele: "My boys will be no end charmed to see you so ladylike, the colonel, above all, when they come here the night before the wedding to fondle my new attraction in gilded heels" or else "a maid of all work at a short knock" (*U* 15.3081–83, 3086–87). Both possibilities threaten to bring the newly androgynous Bloom into situations of human trafficking and degraded sexual subservience. The commercial potentialities, complete with a full and forceful gynecological inspection, depict him as something like a house slave or a workhorse on the auction block.

During the altercation with soldiers at Bella Cohen's, the intercourse of martial power and sexual commerce undergoes a fascinating final re-visioning. This occurs when the stage directions amplify Stephen's assault by Private Carr into a scene of epic battle. The stage directions show an attack on one individual becoming an attack on the entire city:

Brimstone fires spring up. Dense clouds roll past. Heavy Gatling guns boom. Pandemonium. Troops deploy. Gallop of hoofs. Artillery. Hoarse commands. Bells clang. Backers shout. Drunkards bawl. Whores screech. Foghorns hoot. Cries of valour. Shrieks of dying. Pikes clash on cuirasses. Thieves rob the slain. (*U* 15.4661–65)

For all its dramatic overtones, the scene realistically foretells the violent transformation of Dublin during the Easter Rising. John Boyle's *The Irish*

Rebellion of 1916, a copy of which Joyce owned in Trieste, describes the hellish nighttime sights and sounds of the city center during the week of fighting: "Searchlights and star shells, lighting up the darkness of the night, completed a picture that might not unnaturally be compared to that of Dante's Inferno. In many of the poorer streets the night was made more hideous by the shrieks of women and children terrified out of their senses by the loud and sustained bombardment" (92–93).

The "Brimstone fires" and "Dense clouds" (*U* 15.4661) of "Circe," then, suggest accurate premonitions of Easter Week, when much of the city center and adjacent neighborhoods would be accidentally or intentionally set ablaze during the fighting. One eyewitness, Maire Nic Shiubhlaigh, a cook in the Jacob's Biscuit Factory garrison, described the devastated Dublin cityscape from her vantage point in the midst of the combat:

> Over in the north the GPO was blazing fiercely; it seemed as though the flames had spread the length of O'Connell Street. There were huge columns of smoke. Around us, in the turret, the Volunteers were still keeping up a steady fire on British outposts nearby. In the distance the crackle of gunfire was accompanied by sudden little flashes. All around, through the darkness, bombed out buildings burned. From where we stood, the whole city seemed to be on fire. (qtd. in Foy and Barton 94)

Another major target of the conflagration was the Linenhall Barracks, which the narrator and Hynes pass on their way to the pub in "Cyclops." Thirty-two British military clerks were held there by Ned Daly and the Irish Volunteers First Battalion and pressed into service building barricades for several days before they were released. The Linenhall was then evacuated and fire-bombed to prevent its being retaken by British forces, detonations that resulted in an enormous fire that spread to nearby buildings, eventually consuming a number of surrounding tenements and a wholesale drug warehouse, lighting up the Dublin night. As one eyewitness recalled, it was "like a roaring furnace, really spectacular. Barrels of oil were projected high in the air and exploded with a loud report. A stifling smoke cloud shrouded the district. On Thursday night, it was as bright as day. A pin could be picked up by the glare overspreading the surrounding streets" (qtd. in Foy and Barton 116).

In "Circe" a gathering host of screaming war birds adds Irish mythic connotations to the battle scene, while the darkened midnight sun lends a biblical dimension (of the battle of Jericho). In the warriors sprouted from dragons' teeth, the symbolic roots of civil-military strife in ancient Thebes are notably present, as they "exchange in amity the pass of knights of the red cross and fight duels with cavalry sabres" (*U* 15.4681–82). These coincide with a continuous entourage of women with diverse backgrounds and identities, some rather menacing, others quite vulnerable. Some become participants in the armed struggle, others its innocent bystanders or potential victims: the screeching whores are followed by flying witches, half-undressed society ladies, and fancily dressed factory lasses who "toss redhot Yorkshire baraabombs" (*U* 15.4677), a corrupting, terroristic revision of the lyric performed earlier in "Wandering Rocks" by the highland troops of the viceregal cavalcade (*U* 10.1251–57).

While the initial cause of trouble is Cissy Caffrey's being jostled by Stephen, accidental contact that quickly escalates to serious internecine strife. Dueling Irish statesmen from several eras take part in a series of dialectic spars between various historical incarnations of armed and constitutional Irish nationalism: "Wolfe Tone against Henry Grattan, Smith O'Brien against Daniel O'Connell, Michael Davitt against Isaac Butt, Justin M'Carthy against Parnell, Arthur Griffith against John Redmond" (*U* 15.4682–85). Fundamental questions linger around many of these figures about the possibility for armed uprising to achieve national liberation without destroying the nation in the process. These conflicts are as soon displaced by anagrammatic revisions of individual names set ridiculously against themselves—"John O'Leary against Lear O'Johnny, Lord Edward Fitzgerald against Lord Gerald Fitzedward, The O'Donoghue of The Glens against The Glens of The O'Donoghue" (*U* 15.4685–88)—each suggestive of the eternal divisiveness of the individual as well as the internal divisions of the nation.

The psychic chaos and political disarray of the narrative can apparently only be righted—or rited—by the capable hands of Father Malachi O'Flynn and the Reverend Mr Hugh C Haines Love, the clerical reincarnations of Mulligan and Haines. In a reiteration of the mock mass from the novel's opening scene, the current ritual seeks a proper realignment of female and male. The poor old milkwoman is replaced by the fecund Mina Purefoy on the altar of the sacred feminine; the phallic military stronghold of the Martello tower morphs into an open umbrella, an image representing the ancient heraldic symbol of the masculine as well as a precise inversion of the feminine/chalice that rests on Mrs. Purefoy's pregnant belly. This heraldic semiotics is previously visible in the "gilt chevrons" of Major Tweedy's uniform, when he "gives the pilgrim warrior's sign of the knights templars" (*U* 15.4614–16), the first of two references to the legendary military protectors of the sacred feminine and Grail symbology.[20]

Taking their cue from Stuart Gilbert, critics tend to label the ritual a Black Mass.[21] Yet the stage directions refer in fact to a "camp mass" (*U* 15.4695), a phrase that more properly sustains the battlefield conceit. The inherent paradox of the repeated phrase "back to the front," when applied to the physical positioning of O'Flynn and Love, carries a connotation of gender reversal, as evidenced by the "lace petticoat and reversed chasuble" worn by Malachi O'Flynn (*U* 15.4692–93). Moreover, O'Flynn's "two left feet" point to the ancient, sinister notion of the left (L. *sinistra*) in association with the feminine. Perhaps most significantly, going "back to the front" suggests returning to the front lines in a military theater of operations, a term that had come into increasingly common usage during the entrenched combat of the First World War, when the moving trenches of the Western and Eastern Fronts determined the back-and-forth progression of the long engagement.[22] The potential of a return to futile and inconclusive warfare seems to suggest the utter precariousness of history, specifically of Ireland and Europe in their time of civil and international upheaval. The question of whether to turn back to the front or turn one's back to the front—and all the destructive masculinities and marginalized femininities engendered there—becomes integral to pacifying the world through love and a return to the sacred feminine. In this way, "Circe" extends the alignment of warrior and harlot in a camp mass that serves as climactic antidote to primarily masculine orthodoxies of calculated violence and sexual oppression. It foreshadows the battleground Dublin was to become in 1916. At the same time, it suggests that the city possesses the inherent creative energy and sexual power to deter the destructive impulses that threaten to overwhelm it.

Joyce's representation of militarism and prostitution in Dublin provides an accurate account of how the recruitment and maintenance of armed forces occurs in a broader context interweaving questions of political loyalty and social acceptability within an economy of desire. If streetwalkers and brothel workers seem to exist apart from the social, legal, and financial norms, Joyce shows us how, like the soldiers they served, they were never beyond the ken of imperial militarist policy. The similarity promotes an uneasy alliance. As Mark Osteen observes, "British soldiers in Nighttown claim to 'protect Ireland' but treat her as a whore" (337). By enmeshing questions of political loyalty and physical sacrifice within an economy of desire, Joyce's fiction repeatedly underscores how the British garrison remained an industry codependent with the sexual economy, though often duplicitous in its relation to it.

Overall, Joyce's fictional depiction of soldiers and sex workers describes women in the unsavory aspects of militaristic domination and economic competition. At the same time, it asks readers to consider how the presence of armed forces influences issues of political loyalty and social acceptability. As countless young women found employment in the sex industry of early-twentieth-century Dublin, their connection to men in military service was virtually inescapable. If brothels and brothel workers seemed to exist somewhere apart from the social, legal, or financial norms, Joyce shows how the women of Nighttown were, like the soldiers of the garrison, corporeal subjects of the state as well as its potent, autonomous agents capable of their own subtle surveillance and calculated control.

6

Reclamations

> I hope that in the very near future we will have no need for military establishments in this country. We have had enough of soldiering and of everything that appertains to soldiering, and I sincerely trust that in the near future all the military establishments in the country will be handed over to the citizens for a more useful purpose.
>
> Senator Thomas Farren, 28 July 1924

> Haines asked:
> —Do you pay rent for this tower?
> —Twelve quid, Buck Mulligan said.
> —To the secretary of state for war, Stephen added over his shoulder.
> They halted while Haines surveyed the tower and said at last:
> —Rather bleak in wintertime, I should say. Martello you call it?
>
> *Ulysses* 1.537–41

In the summer of 1924 the Irish Senate, Seanad Éireann, turned to the business of determining the future of many former British Army facilities now in possession of the Irish Free State. The second hearing of the State Lands Bill featured a divisive debate over what to do with the new nation's vast inheritance of barracks and other military buildings. It was just over two years since the Anglo-Irish Treaty had been signed, the Union Jack lowered, and the tricolor hoisted above scores of barracks and fortifications around Ireland. Centuries of British presence had given Dublin and the rest of the country some of its most valuable and formidable garrison structures. Barracks dominated city neighborhoods and county towns; naval lookout posts and gun batteries dotted the coastal zone from Howth Head to Galway Bay. In a resource-poor country with chronic housing shortages and severe overcrowding in working-class urban areas and rural districts, space was at a premium. Acres of new ground and well-maintained buildings offered a potential remedy. At the same time, a nation just out from under the colonial yoke felt a need to provide security measures for major cities and towns, coastlines, and a northern border whose existence, despite the treaty, remained highly contested, having recently been grounds for a painful civil war.

In the Seanad debate, political differences concerning the fate of these former army facilities lay along the military-civilian divide. Senator Colonel Maurice Moore asserted the need for military preparedness and for maintaining the barracks around Phoenix Park. Moore, a founding member of the Irish Volunteers and brother of the novelist George Moore, noted how the Collins and other nearby barracks were "the only place in Dublin where troops can be trained"; President William Cosgrave lightly countered with his own assessment that "we have pretty good [troop] accommodation for a non-militarist government" ("Public Debate" 962). In proof of his point, Cosgrave enumerated the many Dublin barracks, being careful to distinguish between those already renamed for Volunteers—including Kehoe (formerly Richmond), Collins (formerly Royal), Griffith (formerly Wellington) and McKee (formerly Marlborough)—and others, namely Portobello and Beggars Bush, yet to be "baptized" ("Public Debate" 963–64). The religious metaphor highlighted the deep import that such rechristening had for a collective national consciousness that was now busily engaged with reclaiming the functional and symbolic spaces of British occupation.

One needs only to peruse a few lines of the Seanad hearing transcript to detect the powerful reaction the British barracks evoked in the speakers. The army facilities comprised economic and strategic resources as well as potent historical reminders. For postwar, postindependence Ireland, the spatial remnants of British armed presence were a lingering, unresolved political issue. In *Military Geographies*, Rachel Woodward notes how "militarism and military activities in non-conflict situations exert control over space in ways and through means which frequently render this control invisible, in contrast to the more obvious controls exerted by military forces during and following armed conflicts" (3). In strolling—and testing—the boundaries of England's Lakenheath army base, she provides a case study in the social and psychological effects of contemporary British military geography. Woodward's observations demonstrate how the defense sector, even under the auspices of national security, has a strong impact on national landscapes, both physical and psychosocial.

The decolonization and nation-building under way in the first years of the Free State likewise depended on "material and discursive" control of landscape (Woodward 3). Over six centuries, the British fortress in Ireland had grown into an extensive network of strategic spaces and operational facilities. The question was just what proportion of them should be directly repurposed for the new Irish military. The Cosgrave government faced the choice of just how to deal practically and profitably with what were at once some of the most valuable properties in Ireland and some of the most painful reminders of Irish history. In effect, it was writing the first chapter in the history of the new state by revising some of the most controversial national spaces. In Cosgrave's relatively moderate view, even an avowedly "non-militarist government" would apparently maintain the status quo of militarized spaces. The soldier Maurice Moore went even further in emphasizing the primacy of army training even after the guns of the War of Independence and Civil War had gone silent.

Senator Thomas Farren voiced a somewhat different view on how the military infrastructure might serve the new nation. A Labour Party member, Farren had been a close associate of James Connolly in the Dublin Trades Council. He envisioned a demilitarized future for the spaces in question, a unique opportunity of "providing housing accommodation for the people" ("Public Debate" 963). In the immense barracks compounds Farren and others saw the potential to replace some of the Georgian tenements of Dublin that were in the worst state of disrepair. "As a civilian," Farren said in the Senate's State Lands Bill hearing, "I would be delighted if to-morrow every military establishment in Dublin, and indeed, in the whole of Ireland were given over for the purpose of providing housing accommodation for the very many people who are in need of it" (963). Farren's radical initiative for turning army bases into housing for the poor never quite took off, although some military facilities left undeveloped by Irish authorities did eventually turn into unofficial public housing that served the needs of one of the most overcrowded urban populations in Europe. For example, Beggars Bush, the first barracks surrendered by the British in 1922, was closed by Free State authorities soon after they took possession of it. Yet for several decades starting in the 1930s it became a magnet for squatters and homeless families with nowhere else to turn, proving that Farren's concerns about the Dublin housing crisis were legitimate.[1]

While the politicians of the new Free State deliberated over the meaning and future of Dublin's ubiquitous military geography, James Joyce had provided his own bold reconceptualization of such spaces. Two years prior to the Seanad Land Bill hearings, *Ulysses* initiated a demilitarization of Dublin geography. As the opening setting of the novel, the Martello tower achieves a primary and instantaneous focus on the fortified spaces of the city. It is a strong symbol of historical incongruity with which Joyce initiates his meditation on history. Joyce's description of the Sandycove tower emphasizes facts of political history alongside hints of current cultural transformation. As Buck Mulligan informs the English guest, it was one in a network of coastal fortifications built to defend against a Napoleonic naval invasion. Most of that network was constructed from 1804 to 1812, a few years after French aid had brought the United Irishmen limited military success in their 1798 Rising. A century later, Joyce has Buck Mulligan recall these historical facts of the Martellos' construction, while at the same time pointing out the intellectual cachet their tenancy has brought this particular tower: "But ours is the *omphalos*"(*U* 1.544).

Buck, Stephen, and Haines occupy the former military location as a private residence, though Stephen is quick to add that they still pay twelve pounds in rent to the war office (*U* 1.537–40).[2] Reclamation and demilitarization are under way, yet remain incomplete. Nevertheless, Mulligan imagines the Sandycove tower as a vital new focal point of artistic and cultural consciousness, setting it apart from the dozen or so others like it around Dublin. It is one of a number, though still unique. Such imaginative re-visioning of the locale also distinguishes it from its past use as gun battery, barracks, and lookout post. Thus the narrative statement "Haines surveyed the tower" (*U* 1.541) effectively reverses the Martello's function from agent to target of surveillance. This transformation from a site of military surveillance to one of cultural reconnaissance—from naval-gazing to navel-gazing, as it were—is envisioned, like the modern Irish state, as still a work in progress.

To a great extent, Joyce's fictional urban geography concerns itself with portraying the architectural and spatial realities of a Dublin dominated by military presence. Both *Dubliners* and *Ulysses* frequently orient themselves around key landmarks of British occupation or Irish insurrection, most notably those related to the period preceding and including the Easter Rising. At the same time, Joyce's Dublin is a city anxiously divided over questions of force. Unlike a republican rising or a Black and Tan reprisal, Joyce's writing does not seek to commandeer its urban locations; rather, it effects their imaginative transformation through the forces of language and narrative.

Joyce's Tour de Force

Critical interpretations of the Martello tower are often informed by a sense of political symbolism on the one hand and tangible, earthbound setting on the other.[3] A conflation of these views might be the best way to account for its rich range of potential meanings. Declan Kiberd suggests a blending of historical circumstance, narrative development, and literary structure when he argues the tower "poses the question of inappropriate form. Built by the British to forestall invasion by Napoleonic forces, it is now the edifice in which a homeless, disenchanted youth will improvise what freedom he can" (41).

At the same time, one must be careful of distorting or misreading the Martello tower's significance. Enda Duffy rightly cautions against overdetermining its meaning by projecting some misty archetype of Irish history when in fact the Sandycove tower was "in the first place, nothing more than a fashionably eccentric residence for a group of mildly bohemian young men" (40–41). Nevertheless, it is a complex, multivalent space at the beginning of a complex novel. It is meaningful within the episode and across the novel from a mythic standpoint as well. Towers and panoramic surveillance are prevalent in the Hebrew and Celtic mythologies that inform Joyce's fiction. Maria Tymoczko argues the tower is emblematic of Irish tradition and of Joyce's role as "master builder" of mythic, linguistic, and literary architectonics; she situates the Martello within a broader tower motif that binds Dublin to Gibraltar in the context of the novel, and *Ulysses* to early Irish myth: "In the mythic substructure there are the Tower of Babel that the Goidels help construct, as well as the pharos in Spain from which Ireland is sighted. The inhabitants of Dublin are preoccupied with towers" (53). Such preoccupation, it seems, is essential to de-occupation. For someone who spent his childhood and adult life moving among many addresses, a few weeks of one long-ago summer might not have seemed much. Yet, as strategic starting point for *Ulysses*, the Martello tower sets in motion some of the novel's changing spatial and ideological concerns.

These arrive in the form of overlapping social categories and authorities represented in the mimicry of Buck Mulligan. Readers of the opening scene of *Ulysses* rightly focus on Mulligan's ritual parody of the mass as initiating a motif of Irish Catholicism that runs through the novel:

> —Introobo ad altare Dei!
> ....
> Solemnly he came forward and mounted the round gunrest. He faced about and blessed gravely thrice the tower, the surrounding land and the awaking mountains. (*U* 1.5, 1.9–11)

They do so, however, often to the exclusion of another revealing impersonation. Shortly after his mock-mass invocation, Mulligan substitutes the voice of priest with that of another powerful authority figure in early-twentieth-century Ireland, the army drill sergeant:

> Buck Mulligan peeped an instant under the mirror and then covered the bowl smartly.
> —Back to barracks! he said sternly. (*U* 1.17–19)

Together the twin parodies complete the representation of both masters—the Catholic Church and the British imperial state—that Stephen Dedalus will shortly after speak of serving. His diary entries concluding *A Portait* previously anticipate this pairing in the symbolic image of four "soldiers of the ninetyseventh infantry regiment . . . at the foot of the cross . . . [who] tossed up dice for the overcoat of the crucified" (*P* 215). The anachronistic inclusion of contemporary British troops in the pivotal New Testament scene underscores the blood-sacrifice reading of Irish history and its most recent manifestation of Easter 1916.[4]

Back at the outset of *Ulysses*, Mulligan's mock-military demeanor peeps out from under his priestly performance just long enough to remind us where we are: a recently reclaimed military installation. From the very first lines, the demilitarized status of the location is conveyed in the versatile word "gunrest" (*U* 1.9). The curious compound suggests not just the swiveling platform that once supported a rooftop artillery piece but also the present ceasefire of this decommissioned gun battery. For the moment, at least, British guns are at rest. If the mock mass seems out of place in the morning air of Sandycove, through Mulligan's channeling of a sergeant's language the Martello tower effectively reverts to its original purpose by echoing the former voices and original intentions of a coastal fort turned seaside rental.[5] After all, only a few years have passed since the Martello at Sandycove was manned by the soldiers of the Fortieth Foot regiment.

With his parade-ground vocalization, Buck Mulligan invokes their recent presence and an additional sense of his nickname beyond its dandyish or venereal connotations: by the First World War, the term "buck" referred to enlisted American infantry, for instance in the phrase "buck private," which arrived in Europe with U.S. troops in 1917. The following year, Allan Thomson memorialized the phrase in his poem "John Doe Buck Private," whose first lines ask (and answer) the question

> Who was it, picked from civil life
> And plunged in deadly, frenzied strife
> Against a devil's dreadful might?
> Just plain "John Doe—Buck Private." (lines 1–4)

The simple phrase and supplementary voice of this Buck private effectively realign the rhetorical with the spatial. As opposed to the ironic effect of prayer, Mulligan's alter (and altar) egos demonstrate the disjuncture achieved by returning language to its proper place at improper moments. While it is probably safe to assume there has never been a regular mass celebrated atop the Martello tower, over the preceding century that same space was most certainly defined by military orders and commands. In this regard, Mulligan's characterization establishes right from the start of *Ulysses* a sense of reoccupied strategic space. Demilitarization is under way, but past occupiers and their signifying speech acts remain an active presence in a contested location, one that is being figuratively reclaimed and gradually dismantled by the new occupying force of the text. Mulligan's command might, in this sense, also amount to a statement or question about the future of this tower and other newly demilitarized spaces in Ireland—the same asked in the 1924 Lands Bill debates—namely, whether it too will go back to barracks.

Joyce's depiction of the Martello tower stresses its multiple functions as surveillance point, signal station and gun battery. Like other coastal forts, the Martellos were located and designed with great attention to panoptical power. "Telemachus" appropriately features a language of gazing and surveillance that relives this primary function. The opening pages of the novel atop the parapet feature an abundance of words to describe the acts of seeing in which Stephen and Buck engage. In the first third of the episode alone, there are more than two dozen words and phrases having to do with seeing or sight. These include peered (*U* 1.6, 1.24, 1.135), faced about (*U* 1.9–10), catching sight (*U* 1.11), looked coldly (*U* 1.14), peeped (*U* 1.17), shut your eyes (*U* 1.22), looked gravely (*U* 1.30), watching (*U* 1.37, 1.174), hold up on show (*U* 1.70), gazing over the handkerchief (*U* 1.72), gazed out over Dublin bay (*U* 1.75), Come and look (*U* 1.80–81), looked down (*U* 1.83), searching eyes (*U* 1.86), gazed at the fraying edge (*U* 1.101), saw the sea (*U* 1.106), You'll look spiffing (*U* 1.118), You look damn well (*U* 1.118–19), turned his gaze (*U* 1.125), smokeblue mobile eyes (*U* 1.126), Stephen's peering eyes (*U* 1.141–42), not seeing his face in a mirror (*U* 1.143), cracked lookingglass (*U* 1.146, 1.154), looked in Stephen's face (*U* 1.185), looking towards the blunt cape of Bray Head (*U* 1.181), gazing over the calm sea (*U* 1.224), veiling their sight (*U* 1.225), Look at the sea (*U* 1.231), seaward where he gazed (*U* 1.243).

Later in the episode, when the narrator recounts how "Haines surveyed the tower" (*U* 1.541), the traditional subject-object order is inverted, and the structure built for watching becomes the target of surveillance. Moreover, the Englishman's gesture of surveying recalls the infamous cartographic project of the Ordnance Survey, when British soldiers prepared the first comprehensive maps of Ireland in the early 1830s. Doing so, they quantified distances, redrew boundaries, and renamed Irish places with English translations. The Ordnance Survey in essence completed the geographic, economic and linguistic conquest of the Irish landscape.

Perhaps for this reason the precise questions of seeing and surveillance become important for the two Irish residents of the tower, specifically when Mulligan and Stephen are shown "looking towards the blunt cape of Bray Head that lay on the water like the snout of a sleeping whale" (*U* 1.181–82). When Robert Boyle considers the question "Can Bray Head Be Seen From the Martello Tower?" he tests more than Joyce's renowned knack for detailed recollection of geographic minutiae. In this rare instance, Joyce's spatial memory seems to fail him; however, the error might be intentional, Boyle notes, meant to underscore more what Stephen sees "in the mind's eye" and not in reality, since Bray Head cannot be seen from Sandycove even though the narrative of his thoughts paints such a vivid picture of it (131). Joyce/Stephen likely draws this image from childhood years spent at the house in 1 Martello Terrace, Bray, which "afford[ed] a fine, uninterrupted view of the esplanade and Bray Head" (Igoe 21). Intentional or not, this erroneous suggestion Bray Head could be seen from Sandycove lends the tower a sense of reconstructed history that, regardless of accuracy, replaces its original functions of defensive surveillance and destructive bombardment with imaginative vision and artistic license.[6]

The visual perspective from the tower in "Telemachus" might also be contrasted with Gogarty's actual experience. In the summer of 1904 he wrote to his friend George Bell of the panoramic pleasure of the Martello. Looking north, across Dublin Bay to Howth Head, he notes, "The view is splendid. . . . The mountainous arm of the Bay, changing with every cloud and affording wonderful successions of colour in pink on a hot and sunny day. Purple or cerulean on clouded days. And, on days when there is an intermittent sunshine the hill gleams yellow as if clothed with fields of corn" (qtd. in O'Connor 83). The poetic intoxication wears off when Gogarty looks in the opposite direction and finds the pastoral scene disrupted by a memorial obelisk crowning Killiney Hill. This intrusion of what he calls "conformity petrified" turns his serene hymn to natural beauty into a plan for what might be considered the first act of eco-terrorism, as he vows "Some night I may blow it up"; he casts himself in the role of republican dynamitard, secretly and gradually collecting a pound of explosives to carry out his plot (qtd. in O'Connor 83). The tone is facetious, to be sure, but also quite fitting for one standing on the parapet of the Martello, itself a former powder magazine and munitions depot, as Gogarty was well aware. Moreover, one would be hard pressed to imagine a more innocuous target for his fantasy demolition, since the obelisk that ruins the view for him was constructed as relief effort and monument for famine sufferers in 1740–41.[7]

The visual and panoramic aspects of the Martello tower anticipate more recent concepts of seeing and surveillance in the total-war theory of Paul Virilio. Virilio first perceived the connection in his examination of the remnants of Nazi bunkers and blockhouses on the Atlantic coast of France, so that as Steve Redhead notes, "the German bunkers, and the systematic photographs he took of them, were the start of a career for Virilio concentrating on military space" (18). Among the most formidable attributes Virilio observed in the German coastal defense system was its deliberate positioning for sightlines and their power of surveillance. As he writes in *Bunker Archeology*, "You could walk day after day along the seaside and never once lose sight of these concrete altars built to face the void of the oceanic horizon. The immensity of this project is what defies common sense; total war was revealed here in its mythic dimension" (*Bunker Archeology* 12). Reimagining the bunkers as "concrete altars," Virilio overlays the bare functionality of their architecture with a ritual, religious aspect. As Joyce does through the impersonating actions of Buck Mulligan, Virilio highlights both military and religious qualities of the former coastal installations.

In a later essay, *Speed and Politics*, Virilio returns to the surveillant potency of such fortifications:

> the military lookout-post offers the invader a constant view of the social environment, primary information. Social privilege is based on the choice of viewpoint (before attaching itself to accidents of fortune or birth), on the relative position that one manages to occupy, then organize in a space dominating the trajectories of movement, keys to communication, river, sea, road or bridge. (73)

In this regard, by managing to occupy a notorious military lookout post, *Ulysses* alerts readers from the start to the strategic and political, as well as social and cultural, powers of the visual inherent in the militarization of Dublin space.

The architectural history of the Martello tower resonates in Joyce's fictionalized reclamation of it. Constructed in 1804, Martello tower number 11 was one in a series of fortifications meant to defend the Irish coast from what many saw as inevitable invasion by Napoleonic forces. As Buck Mulligan says, "Billy Pitt had them built . . . when the French were on the sea" (*U* 1.543–44). In the Dublin region alone, more than two dozen Martello towers formed a continuous network extending north and south from the Pigeon House Fort. Twelve Martellos guarded the northern half of Dublin Bay, past Howth and out to Balbriggan, while fourteen towers guarded the southern reaches at regular intervals all the way to the village of Bray. Their purpose was to guard potential landing places in the bay through a combination of advance warning and direct combat. Like all Martello towers, the one at Sandycove functioned simultaneously as barracks, gun battery, lookout point, and signal station. Guns were always at the ready, but the preliminary defensive purpose was to alert military headquarters in Dublin to approaching enemy vessels. This was achieved through semaphoric communication with the towers immediately to the north and south. Tower number 11 commanded the southern reaches of Dublin Bay and worked directly in conjunction with the Dalkey Hill signal tower, about a half mile uphill to the southwest. In the event that an enemy sighting turned into combat, the number 11 gun battery had the potential to fire up to a mile offshore. Besides this range, it possessed a shot furnace that could heat leaden cannonballs to ignite the wooden sailing vessels of the era. In a fundamental way, the Martello stood literally for the most efficient kind of communication as well as the most deadly kind of force.

By 1867, with wooden ships and French invasion fears largely relics of the past, the armaments were removed from all of the Martellos with the exception of Sandycove, which was reequipped with an eighteen-pound rifle-barreled gun that remained in use until 1900 (Sutcliffe 123). Joyce's tower was therefore the very last in Ireland to be completely disarmed and demilitarized. Like a number of others, it was soon offered by the War Department for private use, whereupon Gogarty obtained his residential lease. This role as habitation was not entirely new. While a gun battery and signal station, the tower had also housed soldiers, specifically those of the 40th Regiment of Foot who came to man the twenty-pound guns. The popular bathing place at the base of the tower known as the Forty Foot takes its name from them, so Buck Mulligan's swim there in essence reenacts yet another regimental custom.

One of the first references to the Martellos in Ireland appears in John Carr's 1805 travelogue *The Stranger in Ireland*, which praises the towers on aesthetic rather than strategic grounds:

> Upon the sides of this coast is a long chain of equidistant Martello towers, which, if they have been constructed to embellish the exquisite scenery ... the object of building them has been successful. ... I believe it would require the inflamed imagination of the hero of Cervantes to discover one possible military advantage which they possess, placed as they are at such a distance, on account of the shallowness of the bay, from the possibility of annoying a hostile vessel. (qtd. in Kerrigan 176)

A little more than a decade later, in 1822, Sir Walter Scott's novel *Peveril of the Peak* describes them as being "built in such a fashion as if intended ... for the sole purpose of puzzling posterity" (qtd. in Sutcliffe 14). The comment reminds one of Joyce's own famous remark that his fiction would keep professors scratching their heads for centuries to come. Of course it was national defense, not intellectual pondering or scenic improvement, the builders had in mind.

The order to construct the Martello towers around Dublin came in 1804 from Lord Cathcart, commander of British forces in Ireland. The urgency for an Irish coastal defense network and advance warning system was spurred by French invasions at Bantry Bay, County Kerry, in 1796 and at Killala Bay, County Mayo, in 1798, both assisting Wolfe Tone and the United Irishmen. Robert Emmet's 1803 rebellion in Dublin also involved Irish nationalists operating in tandem with French allies. Therefore Mulligan's brief historical synopsis of the Martello towers for Haines—"Billy Pitt had them built... when the French were on the sea"—rings at least partially true. Yet while Prime Minister Pitt sought parliamentary approval for the project, it was very much a military undertaking from start to finish.

An initial list of recommended locations for the signal stations and Martello towers was devised by Admiral James Hawkins Whitshed in late 1803 and early 1804, following a full survey of the Irish coast. Cathcart's correspondence that spring demonstrates how rapidly the plan was put into action. On 6 April he wrote to Evan Nepean, secretary to the Lord Lieutenant, "I have no doubt his Excellency will find it adviseable to rely upon men of the best Genious and of the Greatest ability and Experience for the construction of Public Works, and also to select the best of Artificiers" (*Kilmainham Papers* vol. 18). Cathcart emphasized the need to employ workers on a large scale to complete the projected network of Irish Martellos in a timely manner: "many Contractors and Overseers, must be employed if they are to be soon ready, as the Coast is so extensive that it will otherwise be the Work of Years" (ibid.). It was only a few weeks before the project got under way, a clear reflection of how seriously was taken the threat of another Napoleonic invasion. By 25 April the army made an advance of £300 to a contractor named Ross. Apparently Ross believed men "of the best Genious and of the Greatest ability" were to be found not in Dublin but Scotland, whence he brought most of the workmen to begin building the first Martellos around Dublin Bay, including Sandycove. Aside from racial stereotypes concerning intelligence and craftsmanship, it is possible that involving Irish workmen in the project was deemed a security risk. In the spring and summer of 1804, exactly one hundred years before Bloomsday, the granite blocks of Joyce's tower were hoisted into place.

The fortress intended as a bulwark against one foreign invader of course did much to reassert the economic and military superiority of another. The British hold on crucial Irish ports and landing places, particularly around Dublin and Cork, was measurably strengthened by the presence of the rotund new forts. In another irony, this show of British strength against French invasion originated from a tower that stood not far from the birthplace of Napoleon himself. The British navy had first encountered the Martello design at Cap Mortella, Corsica, when fighting on the side of French royalist forces in February 1794. Two warships, the *Fortitude* and the *Juno*, lost six men and suffered dozens of casualties before the first Martello was finally taken. British naval officers were summarily and unanimously impressed with the fort's ability to withstand siege. Soon after, plans were made for construction of Martello towers in places such as Saint John, New Brunswick, to protect British holdings in North America, and within a decade on the coasts of England and Ireland.

Beside its historical and intercultural significance, the Martello tower is also an appropriate starting place for the novel due to its ambiguous etymology. "Martello" conflates aspects of its original location and function as filtered through a cultural and linguistic divide. It might stem from eighteenth-century British sailors' mispronunciation of Cap Mortella, which in turn takes its name from myrtle, a coastal shrub abundant in the region. Another theory suggests the name originates from earlier Mediterranean watchtowers of the Roman era, called in Italian *torri di martello,* in which a coastal alarm was sounded by ringing a bell with a *martello*, a hammer (Sutcliffe 21). Whether one, the other, or both explanations confer historical truth, the linguistic multiplicity in the name alone is an appropriate opening to a book that ultimately celebrates the power of multiculturalism over narrow-minded ideologies of language and national identity. Gogarty notes the etymological confusion surrounding the name, as well as the towers' appropriate resemblance to the artillery pieces they formerly contained: "Some say that these towers got their name from a sculptor's mallet, others from the name of the man who designed them. They all look like the muzzle of an old-fashioned cannon, ringed around the top" (*It Isn't* 85). The Martello tower, then, like the genre of the novel, is a Continental form imported to an Anglo-Irish context.

While Haines plays the role of occupying Englishman in "Telemachus," the true militarization of the empire is revealed in his total ignorance concerning the military geography of the setting. He has not heard of Martello towers, despite the fact that they were ubiquitous landmarks along the English and Irish coasts at the time. Of the 140 constructed, approximately 90 still stood at the turn of the twentieth century, the rest having been destroyed by naval artillery tests or coastal erosion. Still, Haines asks: "Martello you call it?" (*U* 1.542). The Mediterranean name itself suggests the mark Napoleonic France ultimately made on Anglo-Irish culture and geography. Ironically, while the Martellos were built to forestall a French military invasion, they enabled a a cultural incursion through the visual and architectural transformation of the coastal zone.

Ulysses acknowledges this by enacting Joyce's reclamation of Dublin along similar lines. The novel infiltrates intellectual barriers and penetrates cultural defenses, effecting a peaceful aesthetic invasion from the French capital. *Ulysses* represents, in this sense, the force of another kind of Irish revolutionary operating with French assistance to make a daring artistic incursion into the heart of a British military installation. Against the backdrop of nineteenth-century English invasion fears, from Napoleonic France to imperial Germany, the Martello tower setting announces *Ulysses* from the start as a mission to retake Ireland through artistic cunning. Joyce brings characters and readers immediately to the center of the coastal defense network that for exactly a century had existed to repel another French incursion. In this sense, *Ulysses* utilizes the Martello for purposes of renovation rather than destruction. Commencement of the book in medias res atop the Sandycove tower suggests Joyce's reinvasion and reimagining of Ireland—through the transnational form of the novel—is already under way. One of the most immovable structural remnants of the British military presence is thereby reappropriated and redefined for a newly independent Ireland.

Towers enter Bloom's consciousness in the opening lines of "Calypso," when he imagines seeing himself from his cat's perspective: "Wonder what I look like to her. Height of a tower? No, she can jump me" (*U* 4.29). While the reference is nonspecific, the tower readers already have in mind is the Martello from the opening episode. Besides Bloom's interest in scale and parallax, the moment demonstrates the overpowering aspect of the tower. His cat can jump him, but he cannot surmount the tower, is dwarfed by the military power and imperial privilege for which it both literally and figuratively stands. The tower motif will continue to occupy his thoughts in "Nausicaa," where the motif elides martial and marital themes. There Bloom associates one particular tower with notions of female sexual awakening (of both Milly and Molly), military force, and general brutality recounted in stories of Molly's time in Gibraltar: "Poor child! Strange moment for the mother too. Brings back her girlhood. Gibraltar. Looking from Buena Vista. O'Hara's tower. The seabirds screaming. Old Barbary ape that gobbled all his family. Sundown, gunfire for the men to cross the lines" (*U* 13.1203–6).

In this way the Gibraltar edifice offers a counterpoise to the Martello tower at the far end of the novel that effectively integrates Molly's personal history and sexuality with discourses of British militarism and Irish mythology. In "Penelope," as she ponders her afternoon tryst with Blazes Boylan, she thinks back to her first sexual experiences with Lieutenant Mulvey "under the rockgun near OHaras tower" (*U* 18.783). She has clearly told her husband about these earlier dalliances, causing O'Hara's tower to become his own important psychological landmark and symbol. The militarized spaces of Gibraltar will comprise a major element in Molly's concluding monologue, as Joyce makes great use of the historiographic contexts and geographic details of the British military colony. As Andrew Gibson notes, "In 'Penelope,' through Molly, Joyce lays siege to the great British, Protestant, imperial stronghold. . . . He repudiates the colonizer's definition of it and understanding of its meaning and value" (*Revenge* 260–61).[8] Indeed, British-occupied Gibraltar was among the best armed and most impenetrable fortresses in the world at the time, looming large in the public imagination as it does in Molly's memories of childhood and adolescence. To Gibson's insightful Gibraltar analysis we might add this former tower landmark that was the focal point for British control of the Rock.

In addition to these contemporary historical concerns, Gibraltar and the tower motif in *Ulysses* update the earliest founding myth of Ireland, also a story of strategic surveillance and spatial domination. The *Lebor Gabála Érenn* (*Book of Invasions*) relates how the Milesians came to Ireland after spying it from a high tower in Spain:

> Once when Ith, of a clear winter's evening was on top of Bregan's Tower, contemplating and looking over the four quarters of the world, it seemed to him that he saw a shadow and a likeness of a land and lofty island far away from him. He went back to his brethren, and told them what he had seen; and said that he was mindful and desirous of going to see the land that had appeared to him.

Like that of the Milesians, the journey of Joyce's characters commences from a tower-top vista of Ireland. Yet the towers in *Ulysses* are not just mystic vantage points but grounded structures built for purposes of panoptical surveillance, communication, and control. In contrast with the Milesians' outward gaze and distant longing, the towers in Ulysses point to more localized, introspective purposes of self-discovery and cultural liberation.

The tower image links other characters across the novel as well. Also in "Nausicaa," it is the focus of play and controversy for Tommy and Jacky Caffrey: "The apple of discord was a certain castle of sand which Master Jacky had built and Master Tommy would have it right go wrong that it was to be architecturally improved by a frontdoor like the Martello tower had" (*U* 13.42–45). In their location on Sandymount Strand, the boys are playing in the shadow of another century-old Martello, just a few miles north of that inhabited by Buck Mulligan and friends. The two young architects appear to be perfectly militarized subjects, a Royal Navy recruiter's dream, as they are "dressed in sailor suits with caps to match and the name *H.M.S. Belleisle* printed on both" (*U* 13.14–15). As in the tenancy dispute of Buck and Stephen, the miniature Martello replica represents conflict as opposed to the security and protection intended by its construction; the discrepancy is underscored by the reference to the Judgment of Paris, the prime mover of the siege of Troy and source of the original "apple of discord" (*U* 13.42). The analogy suggests the same competing alternatives of love and war for modern Dublin as for mythic Greece.[9] It prefaces the barroom debate in "Cyclops," where territorial dominion and national strength—or, as Bloom puts it, "Force, hatred, history, all that" (*U* 12.1481)—will remain questions of the moment for contemporary Ireland. In this manner the towers of *Ulysses* raise questions about how the characters of the novel might liberate themselves from the military spaces and structures that loom over them and over Ireland.

Like the Caffrey twins' sandcastle Martello, Joyce's adaptation of the novel, a literary form that entered Ireland through Continental and British channels, exhibits concern with artistic innovation of a familiar cultural form. The initial publication of *Ulysses* brings further irony to this imagined breach of a fortification originally intended to repel French invasion. Ireland of course had a history of French assistance in matters of political revolution and armed insurgency: the rebellions of 1794, 1798, and 1803 each involved the actual or anticipated arrival of French ships and firepower. So, too, Joyce's literary invasion of the island via *Ulysses*, in both its composition and publication, was an Irish action bolstered by French assistance. Joyce finished the novel in Paris during the last months of 1921, and French friends and locations assumed prominent roles both in and around the text. The novel reflects contemporary French literary influences as well, from the internal monologue technique of Édouard Dujardin to the prose stylistics of Marcel Proust, and others too numerous to enumerate here.[10] On a material level, the book would not have come into being without the efforts of Parisian typists and typesetters, not to mention the renowned Left Bank bookstore of Sylvia Beach.

Thus, Joyce's literary reconstructions of the Martello tower and other strategic places can be regarded as a well-conceived retaking of urban space and renouncing of militarist ideology. If we can believe Oliver St. John Gogarty, the Martello was originally claimed by Joyce with his writing. He recalls how in the spring of 1904 Joyce "was careful to leave some article of his as a symbol of possession before we moved in. The only movable thing he possessed was a roll of manuscripts which contained a score or so of poems written in his clear handwriting" (qtd. in O'Connor 86). The Martello tower's eventual rechristening as Joyce's Tower and the James Joyce Museum arguably speaks to the ultimate success of Joyce's invasion and reclamation of this garrison space. In *Ulysses*, coming back to Ireland begins boldly and definitely with coming "Back to barracks" (*U* 1.19). Without hesitation, the novel announces its radical purpose as a modernist guide to geographic and political reclamation: Ireland's newest book of invasion. The fact that the Martello tower remains a tentative residential space, under lease from the secretary of state for war, only further attests to its incomplete reappropriation. That Stephen, like Joyce, is its subtenant demonstrates the inconclusive nature of this reclamation process. In the transformative setting of the Martello tower, the novel fires its opening rhetorical shots both from within and against this contested space. Doing so, it declares its own project of confronting the entrenched ideology of militarism that was part of both the Irish past and the global present.

Theaters of Engagement

Part of the power of *Ulysses*'s literary geography rests in the fact that it memorializes the Irish capital in the decade prior to its destruction in the War of Independence. It is nearly impossible to read Joyce's depictions of Dublin before the Rising and ignore the significance of many of those same buildings and spaces leveled and vacant after 1916. In his account of Easter Week and its aftermath, Joseph O'Brien emphasizes this traumatic effect on the urban landscape:

"There remained one final victim of the Rising—the city itself. Damage to the buildings was extensive in the wake of fire and artillery, but it was almost entirely confined to Lower O'Connell Street, from O'Connell Bridge northwards" (268). A number of the most important architectural landmarks in *Ulysses* were among the blocks of the city center reduced to rubble. O'Brien's block-by-block enumeration of ruined properties includes many that feature in the social and economic lives of Joyce's characters, such as the "ruined hulks and tottering walls ... on the site of Clery's" (269), the department store whose popular summer sale enters the thoughts of both Bloom and Gerty MacDowell (U 5.194, 13.234). The newspaper world of "Aeolus," featured in Bloom's work as an advertising canvasser and Stephen's delivery of Mr. Deasy's op-ed piece about foot-and-mouth-disease, was also extremely hard hit. "Eason's, Freeman's Journal Company, and other printing and publishing houses" were all destroyed, along with Mooney's spirit merchant on Eden Quay and Wynn's Hotel on Abbey Street (O'Brien 269). The latter had become particularly significant for hosting the decisive November 1913 meeting that founded the Provisional Committee of the Irish Volunteers, marking the decisive split from John Redmond's Irish Party and National Volunteers and the start to the "period of overt militancy" (Grob-Fitzgibbon 44).

There were also some remarkable exceptions to the destruction. In the heart of O'Connell Street, just before the shell of the General Post Office, Nelson's Pillar, a potent monument to British military strength, amazingly withstood the fighting and conflagrations. (It would fall to an IRA incendiary device a half century later). Already a prominent landmark and transportation hub, the pillar becomes the point of physical and rhetorical focus at the opening of "Aeolus": "Before Nelson's Pillar trams slowed, shunted, changed trolley, started for Blackrock, Kingstown and Dalkey, Clonskea, Rathgar and Terenure, Palmerston Park and Upper Rathmines, Sandymount Green, Rathmines, Ringsend and Sandymount Tower, Harold's Cross. The hoarse Dublin United Tramway Company's timekeeper bawled them off" (U 7.1–5).

By the end of the episode, it has been further reclaimed and transformed in Stephen's story of "two Dublin vestals," Anne Kearns and Florence MacCabe, who "want to see the views of Dublin from the top of Nelson's pillar" (*U* 7.923, 931). Armed with brawn, panloaf, and twenty-four ripe plums, they ascend gradually and somewhat nervously to the top and, once there, gaze out on the rooftops of Dublin, arguing about the locations of various churches until they become giddy from the height. So they lie down, snacking on the plums and "peering up at the statue of the onehandled adulterer" (*U* 7.1017–18). Their momentary fears that the pillar might fall are soon forgotten in the somewhat reckless act of spitting the plumstones out between the railings and down to the street below. *A Pisgah Sight of Palestine or The Parable of the Plums*, as Stephen titles it (*U* 7.1057–58), shows two Dubliners seeing their city from a new vantage point, then turning that perspective into an occasion for reconfiguring their relation to it. They might seem an unlikely pair of revolutionaries, yet their simple outing, like Stephen's narrative, predicts a vision of extraordinary change by ordinary Dubliners.

* * *

Late in the evening of 16 June 2004, Dublin city center filled with pulsing techno rhythms, a massive crowd, and oversized literary caricatures. This finale event to the Re-Joyce Celebration during the one-hundredth anniversary of Bloomsday was dubbed *The Parable of the Plums*, after Stephen's narrative in the "Aeolus" episode. Only, for this dramatized version, bits of text rather than pits of fruit rained down on the crowd: thousands of tickets bearing *Aeolus* newspaper headlines were thrown to the winds and fluttered down on the throngs of people lining the streets. In some cases the headlines were veritable geographic speech acts, asserting their place in the midst of the same spaces they proclaimed, as in DEAR DIRTY DUBLIN and IN THE HEART OF THE HIBERNIAN METROPOLIS. A century after the fictional Bloomsday, the messages touched down in the heart of a much dearer (and perhaps less dirty) Dublin than Joyce might have imagined.[11] Many present were able to clutch these fragments of meaning right from the air or from the O'Connell Street pavement.

Through the verbal confetti could be glimpsed the large-headed caricatures of Molly and Leopold Bloom, Stephen Dedalus, Blazes Boylan, and Buck Mulligan, among other Joycean characters. Their dancing likenesses shared the stage with members of Dublin's Chinese, Brazilian, and Nigerian communities, in a performance choreographed by Barabbas Theatre Company artistic director Raymond Keane. Thousands of spectators watched 170 performers in three separate waves peacefully advance upon the General Post Office and the former site of Nelson's Pillar. The North Parade consisted of actors dressed as Edwardian Dubliners; an East Parade followed, featuring an Asian troupe performing a Chinese lion dance as they entered from Talbot Street. A third group, the West Parade, consisted of West African dancers performing a Togolese rain dance. If these appearances caused some in the crowd to wonder about the connection to Joyce, Matthew Spangler's discussion of the performance brilliantly emphasizes how its divergences from the plot and characters of *Ulysses* in fact reinforce Joyce's themes of "border crossing and cross-cultural pollination" as these relate to a modern Ireland redefined by immigration and ethnic diversity (57).

Indeed, *The Parable of the Plums* reflected the cosmopolitan face of twenty-first-century Ireland alongside the multicultural concerns posited by Joyce's text. Helen Monaghan, director of the James Joyce Centre and Joyce's grandniece, saw the pageant exploring for contemporary Ireland the same definition of national identity posited by Bloom in his confrontation with the bigoted Citizen: "A nation? ... A nation is the same people living in the same place" (*U* 12.1422–23). Monaghan emphasized to one interviewer this implicit attitude of multicultural inclusiveness at work in both the performance and the novel: "The kids that we're working with on 'Parable of the Plums' and the outreach education programme also feel like outsiders in their own city, whatever about the fact that they might be living here all their lives and their family might be Irish" (Ó Conghaile 10).

In this regard, the street pageant offered a kind of updating of the moment that is simultaneously the most hurtful and the most heroic in *Ulysses*. As Spangler asserts, the innovative freedom and rhetorical power of street theater enabled *The Parable of the Plums* to relate a Dublin story of economic and demographic change at least as pressing on the hundred-first Bloomsday as it was on the first (47). The fact that such street theater took place in the once-contested, previously militarized streets of Dublin city center contributed further still to the meaning of the event. In effect, *The Parable of the Plums* brought the O'Connell Street area full circle from a theater of military operations in 1916 to a theater of literary and cultural reclamation at the start of a new century for Ireland and for Joyce's book.

In that respect, the dramatic climax occurred when a telescope-toting caricature of Lord Nelson was elevated above the crowd atop a rented cherry (plum?) picker. For a few moments, the figure loomed large over O'Connell Street. He stood alone, suspended, until through his nautical spyglass he saw another figure on the rise: a Daedalian-winged, fedora-wearing Joyce, portrayed by actor Ken Fanning, who (with help of mast, wire, and harness) soon ascended even higher than the "onehandled adulterer." This displacement of the notorious naval commander by the newly reclaimed writer was staged on the former site of Nelson's Pillar, the setting for Stephen's story of the plumstone-spitting Dublin vestals, and now the location of the Millennium Spire. The towering 120-meter spire had itself only recently claimed the empty space left by the pillar nearly forty years before.

Above and beyond the competing monumental histories normally invoked by the "pavement island" of O'Connell Street (*U* 7.1067), with its string of statues from Daniel O'Connell to Father Mathew, the pageant took up a meaningful occupation of a renowned space of Irish military history. Besides retaking the space from the Lord Admiral, the event was also just a plumstone's throw from the General Post Office, the Easter Week headquarters for the Irish Volunteers and Citizen Army. Taking in the festivities before the bullet-pocked façade of the GPO, where Pearse and Connolly had issued the Proclamation of the Irish Republic, it was hard not to think of how the fundamental text of Irish modernism was being publicly *re*-claimed precisely where the foundational text of modern Ireland was first *pro*-claimed.

In these ways, *The Parable of the Plums* amounted to much more than the mere "parade down O'Connell Street" reported the next day in the *Irish Times*. The pageant signified the recuperation of a once-detested writer in a formerly contested space. This occurred, appropriately enough, through a merger of Joyce's literary geography with some of its contemporary spatial counterparts. In essence, the Barabbas (much like the Dedalus) *Parable* managed to liberate the space of central Dublin from the longstanding military geographies of Anglo-Irish conflict. Never far from the kinetic energy of the performance was the shimmering implication that the city had drastically altered in the eight decades since Joyce's portrayal of the very same streets.

The Bloomsday 100 street parade joins a growing list of examples that show Ireland's recent rehabilitation of Joyce's literary contribution and public image. As documented by Joseph Brooker in *Joyce's Critics*, that image itself has been quite literally reappropriated, if not rehabilitated in Ireland in recent years, appearing everywhere from Grafton Street souvenir shops to Irish currency to public statues (183, 208–16). Most noteworthy in the latter category is Joyce's ashplant-wielding likeness at the junction of O'Connell and North Earl Streets, which, incidentally, had an ideal vantage point from which to view his theatrical apotheosis that centennial evening.[12]

Some critics lament such Bloomsday fanfare as the wrong sort of recognition, since it tends to replace the solitary intellectual rigor of reading Joyce with a massive, mindless party.[13] On the other hand, there is a compelling counterargument to be made that wider public awareness and participation can assure the necessary economic support for the Joycean enterprise in academic circles, something much needed in a time when the humanities and literary studies continue their struggle to survive in a tightening educational marketplace. Recent critical efforts to bring Joyce's fiction back not just to Ireland but to the everyday reader offer a way to bridge this gap.[14] If the idea of Joyce is celebrated as one of Ireland's top cultural icons and commercial exports, then it might just be the engine to sustain the ideas of Joyce in the scholarly arena.

Whatever way we choose to read this recent reclamation of Joyce and the space of his hometown, it is worth remembering that to a great extent Joyce himself initiated the process. Some ninety years before his massive likeness and public image were part of this ritual reappropriation in the heart of Dublin, his own fictional project was already actively recording and reclaiming many of the same urban spaces. His fiction exhibits a constant concern for accurate records of cultural, geographic, and spatial detail. It demonstrates an awareness of the inherent power of place in Dublin, by remembering, rewriting, and consequently remaking urban geography. Oftentimes this means remembering and engaging the most difficult or painful experiences of those spaces, in order to reinvent their future. In her look at historical memory in the "Wandering Rocks" episode, Anne Fogarty observes:

> The material realities of life on June 16, 1904, supply significant coordinates for our reading of *Ulysses* and yet seem also to be erased by the very processes of fictionalization and re-invention. Joyce's

memorializing textuality obliterates, rearranges, and deconstructs the history and geopolitical spaces that it also pretends to safeguard and salvage. (56)

His depictions of the city's militarized spaces, in particular, many of which appear in compact, allusive (and elusive) form, reveal Joyce as master builder and rearranger, a modern counterpart to those "men of best Genious" and "best of Artificiers" sought by the designers and contractors for the Martello tower. Through his fictional reconstruction of Dublin's dynamic and contested geography, Joyce initiates a dismantling of the traumatic cultural memories of occupation and conflict. Doing so, he begins, not so unlike a new Free State senator, to imagine the future for a modern, nonmilitarist Irish state.

Afterword

Among the most memorable comments attributed to Joyce is that recalled by Jacques Benoist-Méchin to Richard Ellmann in 1956 concerning the unending critical conversation—and literary celebrity—Joyce hoped for *Ulysses* to generate. Joyce said to the French translator, "I've put in so many enigmas and puzzles that it will keep the professors busy for centuries arguing over what I meant, and that's the only way of insuring one's immortality" (qtd. in Ellmann 535). My ambition for this book is that it too might keep the professors—and, with them, the students and all other readers—busy with Joyce, albeit in less enigmatic or puzzling ways. In the best of all possible worlds, I might reasonably expect for its topic to become irrelevant or unnecessary; in the world as it is, I will realistically wish for it to sustain further discussion in Joyce scholarship and literary studies.

To that end, while I might have the practical demand of arriving at a final word for this volume, I do so in the definite hope that it will not be the last word on the subject.

Reaching the end of the project, I can see many fissures and gaps that, like the provocative ellipses in a *Dubliners* story, suggest sites for debate and opportunities for research. In selecting just six facets of an expansive topic, I have inevitably neglected or underrepresented many others that could well constitute entire book-length discussions in their own right.

Two additional subtopics come to mind for future thinking about Joyce and militarism. One would be to consider the early-twentieth-century science and technology that derive from and drive militarization. A starting point for this approach can already be found in Tom Rice's view of Joyce's late fiction with regard to its cultural transfer of cinema, radio, and television. Rice shows how *Finnegans Wake* in particular, with its abundance of battlefield references, demonstrates Joyce's late concerns about the threat of these emerging media technologies to advance totalitarian political programs. Recent studies of media and technology in military public relations, recruiting, and battlefield operations might also be brought into the discussion. These include computers and artificial intelligence, in the form of unmanned drones and robotics, that have become regular components of the twenty-first-century military-industrial complex.[1]

Other scientific and technological breakthroughs of Joyce's time were also co-opted and mobilized for military purposes, namely those related to the atom. Joyce died at the dawn of the nuclear age, four years before the U.S. bombings of Hiroshima and Nagasaki, but his late work showed an awareness of what lay ahead. As Jean-Michel Rabaté has observed, *Finnegans Wake* "relentlessly insists on its futurity, as when it 'invents' television and the atomic bomb at a time when these were only projects, mere possibilities, and scientific blueprints" (216).[2] Additional work in this area might be framed by the total-war theories articulated in the later writings of Paul Virilio. While media, science, and technology have progressed in almost unimaginable ways in the seventy years since Joyce's death, many of the questions and controversies surrounding their role in focusing industrial (and postindustrial) societies on military purposes remain unchanged.

Another area for additional work is the private-sector economics and corporatization of militarism. While I have concerned myself mostly with militarization at the levels of individual social formation and cultural identity, I have left much unsaid about the market forces at work. The role of the military entrepreneur and profit-taker was already taking shape in Joyce's time, as seen, for instance, in the description of Boylan's father as a tax dodger who made his money through dishonest horse dealing with the army in wartime (*U* 12.999–1001, 18.403). In his case, questionable business ethics dovetail with questions of just war or national loyalty. A decade after the attacks of 11 September 2001, the twenty-first century is tending still further in that direction. The unprecedented use of private contractors in the U.S. occupations of Iraq and Afghanistan has exploded into a multibillion-dollar industry, while on the home front the emergence of a "security state" has spawned an immense partnership of private industry and government that has become too large to oversee and too powerful to question.[3] These had their modern precursors a century ago, and any attempt to understand their rapid expansion might begin there.

If *Joyce and Militarism* manages to sustain these or other critical approaches in the near future, then I will consider it to have achieved its goal, not of guaranteeing its author's immortality, but of making its own modest contribution to a vast and ongoing project.

Notes

Introduction

1. Tom Rice considers the abundance of military references in the Butt and Taff episode in relation to the rise of television in the 1930s, arguing how, alongside a "verbivocovisual" TV set (*FW* 341.19) in HCE's pub, these form a parallel between the physical destruction of modern weapons and the cultural devastation of televisual technology. See *Cannibal Joyce*, 139–60.

2. The word "subjugation," including its derivative forms, occurs twenty-one times in the essay, while "force" appears five times.

3. See Ellmann, *James Joyce*, 72.

4. Patrick J. Hogan's complete minutes of the 11 February 1899 meeting read:

> An able paper entitled "The War Machine a State Necessity" was read by Mr. H. B. Kennedy. A vote of thanks was proposed by Mr. Clancy and seconded by Mr. O'Higgins, and spoken to by Messers. Clandillon, Skeffington, Fitzgerald Kenny, Walsh, Callan and Clery. Mr. Dawson delivered a comprehensive summing up. In reply to a vote of thanks proposed by Mr. Clery, seconded by Skeffington, he returned thanks in appropriate words.

5. See Duffy, *The Subaltern Ulysses*; Tymoczko, *The Irish Ulysses*; Nolan, *James Joyce and Nationalism*; Cheng, *Joyce, Race and Empire*; Gibson, *Joyce's Revenge*.

6. This international modernist view of Joyce was largely advanced by the Anglo-American critical enterprise of the early to middle twentieth century. It originated in early assessments by T. S. Eliot in "*Ulysses*, Order and Myth" (1922) and Ezra Pound in "Paris Letter: *Ulysses*" (1922), and was sustained in subsequent decades by such works as Stuart Gilbert, *James Joyce's* Ulysses (1930); Frank Budgen, *James Joyce and the Making of* Ulysses (1934); and F. R. Leavis, "Joyce and the Revolution of the Word" (1933). By midcentury and after, it was framed by the dominant biographical and critical perspectives of Richard Ellmann, *James Joyce* (1959), and Hugh Kenner, *The Pound Era* (1975) and *Joyce's Voices* (1978).

7. See Spoo, *James Joyce and the Language of History*; Fairhall, *James Joyce and the Question of History*.

Chapter 1. Joyce and Ideas of Militarism

1. "But there was an antagonist with whom he had not thought to cope, the British Philistine, that last bulwark of mediocrity in a world that was rushing into the future. The British Printer raised his Moral Thumb, blew his Moral Nose and lifted his Moral Eyebrows" (Gorman 148).

2. Following Stanislaus's lead in a 1954 BBC interview, Richard Ellmann in *James Joyce*, 228, specifies an intertextual link from Ferrero's *Europa giovane* to Dumas's *Three Musketeers*. A. Walton Litz examines this connection in more detail in "Two Gallants," in the Scholes and Litz critical edition of *Dubliners*, 368–78. Dominic Manganiello in *Joyce's Politics*, 50, posits *L'Europa giovane* as the sole source for Ferrero's writings about the "moral code of the soldier" and its connection to sexuality. Finally, R. B. Kershner in *Joyce, Bakhtin, and Popular Literature*, 83–86, makes a case for *The Three Musketeers* as Joyce's source in popular literature for the ideology of gallantry.

3. Ellmann suggests *L'Europa giovane*, 163–70, wherein "Ferrero finds a secret alliance between Puritanism, sexual aberration, and military destructiveness, using Bismarck as his example" (*L* 2: 133n), a claim echoed by Dominic Manganiello in *Joyce's Politics*, 50.

4. For a summary of theoretical approaches to militarism during the period, see Berghahn, *Militarism*, 7–30.

5. Garibaldi's distinction applied very much to his own reputation as well. To supporters a fighting hero of the Risorgimento and unification of Italy, by his detractors Garibaldi was, along with Bismarck and Clausewitz, considered among the consummate militarists of the nineteenth century.

6. The fact that Alexandre Dumas also edited Garibaldi's memoirs 1861 suggests a remarkable, if accidental, consistency to the embattled ideologies Joyce uses to recontextualize his publishing disagreement.

7. For a full account of Voigt's misadventure, see Stargardt, *The German Idea of Militarism*, 1–6. The event became the subject of radical playwright Carl Zuckmeyer's *Der Hauptmann von Köpenick* (1931), which was made into several feature films. Zuckmeyer's play remains required reading in most German secondary schools.

8. In England, these writers included John Trenchard and Andrew Fletcher. In Germany, Immanuel Kant published *Perpetual Peace: A Philosophical Sketch* (1795).

9. Liebknecht anticipates in this regard the famous warning in the January 1961 farewell speech of outgoing U.S. president Dwight D. Eisenhower, in which he spoke of the unprecedented "conjunction of an immense military establishment and a large arms industry" and warned the American people to beware of the "military-industrial complex."

10. There were certain exceptions to this general geopolitical divide. See, for example, Bertrand Russell's *Why Men Fight,* which argues for a "great and fundamental reconstruction of social and economic life" in order to elevate humankind above its natural tendency to war.

11. See Streets, *Martial Races: The Military, Race, and Masculinity in British Imperial Culture, 1857–1914.*

12. First published as *Europe's Optical Illusion* in 1909.

13. The total warship tonnage went from 87,000 in 1900 to 372,000 in 1914 (Kennedy 203 table 20).

14. For more on Clancy, see Kemmy, "George Clancy: Murdered Mayor" and "Portrait of the Martyr as a Young Man."

15. For a biography, see Levenson, *With Wooden Sword: A Portrait of Francis Sheehy-Skeffington, Militant Pacifist.*

16. For more about her father-in-law's early interest in Stead and his peace crusade, see Andrée Sheehy Skeffington, "Historical Background," 118–19.

17. For a biography, see Lyons, *The Enigma of Tom Kettle.*

18. See Gillespie and Stocker, *James Joyce's Trieste Library.* The titles range from Irish to European contexts, and across categories of literature, philosophy, and historiography. Of particular relevance are Edmondo De Amicis, *La Vita Militare* (1880); Henri Bergson, *The Meaning of the War: Life and Matter in Conflict* (1915); John F. Boyle, *The Irish Rebellion of 1916* (1916); Francis Sheehy Skeffington, *In Dark and Evil Days* (1916); and S. Parnell Kerr, *What the Irish Regiments Have Done* (1916).

19. See for example "The Economics of Nationalism" and "Labour: War or Peace?" in *The Day's Burden*. These writings reflect Kettle's strong commitment to socialism in the prewar years.

20. See Pašeta, "Thomas Kettle."

21. I borrow the term from Deleuze and Guattari. Their chapter "Treatise on Nomadology—The War Machine" in *A Thousand Plateaus*, describes the preeminence of militarized power, 387–467.

Chapter 2. Violent Exercise

1. For the development of the school sports culture and athletic values, see Mangan's *Athleticism in the Victorian and Edwardian Public School*. For the spread of British athletic pastimes to colonial locations, see *The Games Ethic and Imperialism.*

2. For an account of the event and the poetic tribute, see Fussell, *The Great War and Modern Memory*, 27–28.

3. See Summers, "British Militarism Before the Great War," 111–12.

4. See Kershner, *Joyce, Bakhtin, and Popular Literature*, 168–75, for a discussion of several literary parallels and dialogical links between *Portrait*, *Tom Brown*, and the school-story genre.

5. Dante's gruesome nursery rhyme seems to blend a sort of Promethean classical punishment with the action of the Morrigan, an Irish war goddess who appears in bird form to feed on the remains of fallen soldiers in the field. As Maria Tymoczko writes, "A striking aspect of certain early Irish mythic females is their connection with war: they may be leaders of armies or frankly supernatural characters like the Morrigan, a war goddess who can metamorphose into a carrion crow" (97). Dante's connection to

conflict, in the form of the Christmas dinner political argument, also suggests her loose affiliation with this mythic role.

6. Gibson cites the Intermediate Education (Ireland) Act of 1878 as contributing to a rise in the overall competitiveness of Irish schools. For Gibson's reading of the labyrinth trope in *Portrait*, see his essays "That Stubborn Irish Thing" and "Time Drops in Decay."

7. The fact that Rowan was ultimately captured, imprisoned, then forced into a penniless exile in America seems to undercut further the hope of his gallant action. The Rowan story, along with other Clongowes narratives, will be discussed at greater length in the next chapter.

8. Stonyhurst (1793), Mount St. Mary's (1842), and Beaumont (1861) were three Jesuit public schools founded in Britain following the easing of the Penal Laws in the late eighteenth century. Nearly six decades before Protestant public schools such as Marlborough and Harrow began organized athletic programs, Stonyhurst had been playing its own versions of cricket and football in which masters often played alongside students (Mangan, *Athleticism* 65).

9. See Rose, *Ignatius Loyola and the Early Jesuits*, 19–26.

10. Joyce's writing, like Stephen's thinking, is an exercise in poetic connection rather than literary invention, since other than Nasty Roche, the names are identifiable as actual classmates of Joyce. According to Kevin Sullivan, "of the sixteen boys who appear or are mentioned in this chapter, the names of four are pure invention, and these are only the boys who are shown in a really unflattering light" (48). These four are Simon Moonan, Athy, Tusker Boyle, and Corrigan. Barnes and Flowers were the names of actual cricket professionals who came to coach at Clongowes.

11. Remarkably, a Clongowes team defeated the Trinity College club in the first interscholastic match held in 1861.

12. For interpretive links between British sports and the 1857 Sepoy War in Joyce, see Cheng, "The General and the Sepoy: Imperialism and Power in the Museyroom," and Spencer-Jones, "Making Sport of Violence: The Presence of the Sepoy Mutiny in James Joyce's *Ulysses* and J. G. Farrell's *The Siege of Krishnapur*."

13. The word "rattle" also recurs several times in "The Dead," where it is associated with illness and mortality.

14. See E. L. Epstein's chapter on "Nestor" in Hart and Hayman, *James Joyce's Ulysses*, 17–28.

15. The newspaper began in early 1887 and lasted until mid-January 1888, most of it written and edited by Cusack, with substantial funding and business direction from Scots businessman and Celtic enthusiast A. Morrison Millar.

16. Gaelic football likely emerged as a sixteenth-century colonial offshoot of the British game. Well into the nineteenth century, it was still referred to as the Irish style of football, suggesting its derivative quality. Croke's acceptance letter to Michael Cusack terms it "football kicking, according to Irish rules."

17. See Cheng, "Nation Without Borders: Joyce, Cosmopolitanism, and the Inauthentic Ireland."

18. Joyce's University College classmate George Clancy, the inspiration for Davin, was also a hurling enthusiast. It was Clancy who in fact introduced Joyce to Michael Cusack, whom Joyce "liked little enough to make him model the narrow-minded and rhetorical Cyclops in *Ulysses*" (Ellmann 63).

19. Karen Steele describes the paper and its role in the nationalist movement in *Women, Press, and Politics during the Irish Revival*, 27–65.

20. For an overview of sovereignty structures in Irish mythology and *Ulysses*, see Tymoczko, *The Irish Ulysses*, 96–137.

21. Gifford, *Ulysses Annotated*, 285, lists "C. S. M'Garvey, tobacconist on Frederick Street North (significance unknown)." By the time *Portrait* was published in 1916, the reference to a tobacco shop opposite Findlater's Church for many Dublin readers would have immediately suggested Clarke and other masterminds of the Easter Rising.

22. In his *History of the Sinn Fein Movement and the Irish Rebellion of 1916*, Francis Jones offers this recollection: "The store was of a size that did not permit more than half a dozen men to stand in front of the counter at a time. There was just about enough space between the counter and the wall for two men to walk in together. Along the wall were arranged all of the important Dublin and Irish newspapers, weekly and monthly periodicals, and so forth. Behind the short and narrow counter was a large assortment of brands of tobacco, cigars, pipes, and cigarettes, with a side line of stationery. The window was occupied mainly by a cardboard representation of an Irish Round Tower, advertising the Banba brand of Irish tobacco. Both the window and the store itself were brilliantly lighted, and the whole place suggested care and attention and spotless cleanliness" (143).

23. The national anthem of Ireland, "The Soldier's Song" (1907), contains the lines "Tonight we man the gap of danger / In Erin's cause, come woe or weal / 'Mid cannons' roar and rifles' peal."

24. See Leeson, "Death in the Afternoon."

25. See Groden, "Joyce at Work on 'Cyclops.'"

26. The *Little Review* also printed the unrealistic weight of "56 pound shot." Both late corrections to the typescript suggest Joyce's concern with accuracy in the athletic and military details.

27. Later that year, the ban was "extended to cover athletics meetings held under GAA laws, and also to include men receiving pensions from British forces. Finally the 1906 congress declared any athlete ineligible for a GAA sports meeting if he had participated in any meeting sponsored by either the British military forces or the R.I.C." (de Búrca 71).

28. Patrick Ledden advances this point along with context on Croke and Cusack in "Bloom, Lawn Tennis, and the Gaelic Athletic Association."

29. See Cheng, "Nation Without Borders," 228–29.

30. Founded by brothers William and Robert Jacob in County Waterford in 1851, the bakery moved to Dublin a few years later and grew by the turn of the century into one of the city's largest employers. The Jacob brothers grew up in a Quaker home, yet

even the renowned pacifism of that denomination seems utterly lost or at least ironically betrayed when the iconic package for their product gets converted into deadly ordnance and the site of their enterprise is transformed into a fortress of urban warfare. For a history of the company and factory, including its role in the Easter Rising, see Ó Maitiú, *W&R Jacob*.

31. See de Búrca, *The GAA: A History*, and Puirséal, *The G.A.A. in Its Time*, for the major pro and con positions in this discussion.

32. The 1919 *Little Review* installment of the episode reads "weak heart." Thus the later emendation seems to add one more "shoneen game" to the list, this one with particularly upper-class Oxbridge connotations.

33. See Richard Brown's "Cyclopean Anglophobia and Transnational Community: Re-reading the Boxing Matches in *Ulysses*." Neil Davison in "Pugilism in *Ulysses*: Round Two," 726, discusses the significance of Jewish fighter Daniel Mendoza as a cultural model of Bloom's "new self-assurance" in "Ithaca." J. Lawrence Mitchell considers Joyce's dispute with Percy Bennett over the Zurich English Players a major ingredient of the Keogh-Bennett parody.

34. See Sugden, *Boxing and Society*, 10–21. Sugden traces the rise of British boxing to sports-minded eighteenth-century aristocrats who backed impoverished, newly urbanized members of the displaced agricultural classes.

35. A Fenian and a soldier in the 10th Hussars, Prince of Wales Regiment, O'Reilly was convicted for his part in an 1866 plot to infiltrate the British Army. After escaping from an Australian penal colony, he made his way to America, where he became a reporter for the Irish-American newspaper the *Boston Pilot*, covering such events as the attempted Fenian invasion of Canada in 1870. He is mentioned in *Stephen Hero* as a favorite of Father Healy, who cites O'Reilly during his literary debate with Stephen (157).

36. Bennett's rank of "sergeantmajor" recalls Stephen's athletics instructor and the militarized voice of physical culture at Belvedere.

37. See Foy and Barton, *The Easter Rising*, 18.

38. The phrase is often attributed to U.S. president Woodrow Wilson, who might have adapted it from H. G. Wells's 1914 book *The War That Will End War*.

Chapter 3. Gorescarred Books

1. See Fairhall, *James Joyce and the Question of History*. Fairhall regards Stephen's vision of destruction as "overdetermined" for its conflation of Irish nationalist dynamite campaigns, U.S. and European anarchist bombings, and the artillery attacks of the First World War, new phenomena that produced unprecedented numbers of casualties and, with them, an entirely new sense of man-made catastrophe (165).

2. For Viconian readings of Joyce, see Verene, "Coincidence, Historical Repetition, and Self-Knowledge," and Klein, "A Shout in the Street."

3. Even Armstrong's address, "Vico Road, Dalkey" (*U* 2.25), alludes not just to suburban respectability but to historical insight. In his *Scienza Nuova* (1725), Giambattista Vico posited a cyclical vision for human history that, alongside Blake's poetry and

Aristotelian theory, informs the meditation in "Nestor" on past struggle and future destruction.

4. For a reading of ethnicity and primitivism in the story, see my essay "Reluctant Indians" in *Irish Modernism and the Global Primitive*, edited by Maria McGarrity and Claire A. Culleton.

5. Herring also penned several detective stories in the popular Sexton Blake series for the Harmsworth papers, including "The Parachute King" (*Union Jack* 1.336, 29 September 1900), "The Clue of the Freckled Hand" (*Union Jack* 1.420, 5 October 1902), and "On Special Service (*Union Jack* 1.13, 11 August 1906). Herring later published the novels *Bold Bendigo: A Romance of the Open Road* (1927), *Sir Toby and the Regent* (1929), and *The Midnight Murder* (1932).

6. See Stanislaus Joyce, *My Brother's Keeper*, 79. Also see Ellmann, *James Joyce*, 47–48. Such precise simultaneity of fiction with fact anticipates the sort of historical and biographical parallelism prevalent throughout the remainder of *Dubliners*, *A Portrait of the Artist as a Young Man*, and *Ulysses*. It is akin to the oft-cited example of Joyce consulting Dublin postal and real estate records to ensure Leopold and Molly Bloom could inhabit 7 Eccles Street in June 1904.

7. Brandon Kershner sees Mahony and the narrator as each enacting a different literary plot: the Wild West tale for Mahony, the sea story for the narrator. But both fictional formulas ultimately fall short because they present a rigid, hierarchical structure rather than the "chronicles of disorder" the boys prefer (*Joyce, Bahktin* 36–37).

8. See "Land Leaguers Arrested," *New York Times*, 9 March 1881.

9. See Althusser, "Ideology and Ideological State Apparatuses."

10. Seamus Deane, "Dead Ends," 26.

11. The phrase "Hardly had the day dawned" comes from Caesar's *Commentarii de bello gallico* (Jackson and McGinley 12r). Joyce translated passages from the *Commentarii* in the Latin section of his June 1894 intermediate exams at Belvedere (Bradley 112).

12. Katherine Mullin in *James Joyce, Sexuality and Social Purity*, 41, positions the Harmsworth papers as "the first of several radically unstable intertexts in 'An Encounter' to blur the boundaries between texts condemned and texts recommended by adult guardians of youth."

13. See Kershner, *Joyce, Bakhtin, and Popular Literature*, 33.

14. For example, several numbers of the *Halfpenny Marvel* advertised the Mexican Repeater pistol from the Brandreth Manufacturing Company, Brighton: "A smart weapon for boys for in or out door sport. It holds the road against all comers . . . beautifully plated and perfectly harmless." The same could not be said for another item, the "Lord Robert's target pistol" produced by the Crown Gun Works of Birmingham, which could fire actual rounds. Its advertisement boasted that its noiseless ball cartridges could "kill birds and rabbits up to 50 yards [at a rate of] 9d. per 100. Shot, 1/6 per 100. 100 birds or rabbits may be killed at a cost of 9d. only."

15. Brian Ferguson and Neil Whitehead classify three types of militarization in the tribal zone: 1) wars of resistance and rebellion (against the state presence); 2) wars

by indigenous peoples under the controlling influence of the state (also called "ethnic soldiering"); 3) "wars between indigenous peoples responding to their own perceived interests in the changing circumstances of the tribal zone" (17–18).

16. See Livingstone, *The Geographical Tradition*.

17. See Meagher, *Meagher of the Sword*.

18. In the "Circe" episode of *Ulysses*, Lord Tennyson himself appears "in Union Jack blazer and cricket flannels" to recite part of the refrain from his famous poem (*U* 15.4396).

19. The Fenian movement began in New York City in 1859 and drew upon immigrant communities throughout the U.S. Northeast for much of the support leading up to the 1867 Rising.

20. See Gillespie, *Inverted Volumes Improperly Arranged*, appendix B.

21. The expression comes from the Roman legion's practice of confining conquered enemy soldiers with a yoke, from which is derived the verb "subjugate" (L. *sub jugum* = under the yoke).

22. See Benstock, *James Joyce: The Undiscover'd Country*, 122–23; Carlson, "James Joyce's Irish Nationalism," 290.

23. As Seamus Deane observes, "It is a sweet irony that the novel should have appeared in the year of the Easter Rising in Dublin" (Introduction, viii).

24. See Krell, *The Devil's Rope*; Razac, *Barbed Wire*; and Nigel Fountain's review of the two, "Bouquet of Thorns."

Chapter 4. Domestic Forces

1. Liebknecht lists the police among other subordinate elements in the militaristic state: "Militarism has in fact already become the central sun in one dominant field. . . . Around it revolves the solar system of class legislation, bureaucratism, police administration, class justice, and clericalism of all kinds" (42).

2. See Rice, *Cannibal Joyce*, chap. 8, "The Cultural Transfer of Film, Radio, and Television," 136–60.

3. Bloom's fantastical target would become all too real in another decade, as the first casualty of the Easter Rising was a DMP constable guarding the gates to Dublin Castle.

4. Dun Laoghaire (Dunleary) was named for a fifth-century High King: Laoghaire's *dun*, or fort, served as a base of operations for ancient naval raids against the British coast. The Anglicized name Kingstown, while effacing such ancient military connotations, confirmed the drastic reversal of national identity and territorial conquest. The south Dublin suburb is linked to another kind of brutal force in "A Painful Case" when Mrs. Sinico is "knocked down and killed by the engine of the ten o'clock slow train from Kingstown" (*D* 113).

5. The story, accompanied by a critical essay, is anthologized in Mark Spilka's *Eight Lessons in Love: A Domestic Violence Reader*.

6. The verb is repeated in the barroom greeting by the muscular English acrobat to

extend the paramilitary motif: "Weathers saluted them and told the company that they were out of the Tivoli" (*D* 91).

7. In 1920–21, Beggars Bush Barracks would become an even more telling focal point for the distortion of army and police functions when it served as a base of operations for the Black and Tan auxiliaries, a Royal Irish Constabulary unit consisting mostly of Great War veterans.

8. Another exotic luxury item for middle-class Dublin in the late nineteenth century, Smyrna figs were coveted across Europe and the Americas; by 1882, the year of Joyce's birth, they were being cultivated as far away as San Francisco, as growers sought ways to supply an expanding local market. See "Fig" in Bailey and Miller, *Cyclopedia of American Horticulture*, 587.

9. The ancient walls were no longer solid enough to repel the invasion of Tamerlane, who sacked the city in 1402, massacring most of its inhabitants.

10. As Richard Ellmann notes, as Joyce finished "The Dead" in 1907 he was "already preparing to write *Ulysses*" (367).

11. A correspondent wrote to *Notes and Queries: A Medium of Intercommunication for Literary Men, General Readers, Etc.*, 3rd ser., 7 (January–June 1865): 104, "London: 'I've a crow to pluck with you and a poke to put the feathers in,' is I think the usual North country proverb, the poke for the feathers being rather an important part of the threat, judging from the stress the speaker lays upon it."

12. The allegorical personification of Generals Janvier (January) and Fevrier (February) was a common descriptor for the effect of snow and winter temperatures on a military campaign. An 1855 *Punch* article states, "Russia has two generals in whom she can confide, Generals Janvier and Fevrier." And Rudyard Kipling, writing in 1908—the same year Joyce was finishing "The Dead"—notes, "Here, General January will stiffen him up." (Both examples are from the online *Oxford English Dictionary*, s.v. "general.") The journalistic idiom suggests snow as not simply present but a commanding presence.

13. See Dubber, *The Police Power: Patriarchy and the Foundations of American Government*, for a discussion of these philosophers in their relation to the evolution of the science of police from antiquity to modern Europe.

14. If not of his own formulation, their association with Peel reflects his major role in reforming police organization and function. See Lentz and Chaires, "The Invention of Peel's Principles."

Chapter 5. Barracks and Brothels

1. See Pearce, "Teaching for the (W)Holes."
2. See Wills, "Joyce, Prostitution, and the Colonial City"; McCarthy, "The Jewel-Eyed Harlots of His Imagination."
3. See Mullin, *James Joyce, Sexuality and Social Purity*, chap. 6, "Vice Crusading in Nighttown: 'Circe,' Brothel Policing and the Pornographies of Reform," 171–202.
4. See Enloe, *Globalization and Militarism: Feminists Make the Link* and *Maneu-*

vers: *The International Politics of Militarizing Women's Lives*. See also Harrison, *The First Casualty: Violence Against Women in Canadian Military Communities*.

5. The last of the Monto brothels was razed in 1925, the culmination of the antiprostitution campaign led by the lay Catholic social reform organization the Legion of Mary.

6. See Humphreys, "Ferrero Etc."

7. Terence Brown refers to this as an appropriate but "unconscious pun" on Corley's part (*D* 261n20), raising the perhaps inconclusive question of whether or not Corley recognizes the immorality of his actions.

8. See Hee-Whan Yun, "Male Prostitution as Irony."

9. Louis Parascandola and Maria McGarrity offer a materialist reading of the butcher shop–prostitution parallel: "The falling class status of Mrs. Mooney and her daughter result directly from the father's poor management of meat as a commodity. Mrs. Mooney, then, must replace that commodity for her daughter. She must cut a new piece of flesh to reclaim middle-class respectability for the house" (145). The subtext of the story is quite clear, the flesh of meat, the cutting of flesh, the preparation of it, all portend the sale of fresh meat in the marriage market.

10. The loophole or embrasure was originally a narrow slit or opening in a crenellated wall, through which archers fired at approaching enemies. The *OED* lists the first recorded occurrence from *Garrard's Art of Warre* (1591): "That not one of the towne do so much as appear at their defences or loop holes."

11. In his book *Conceiving Revolution*, Ben Novick examines how the propaganda of advanced nationalists relied on a definition of Irishness linked to moral and sexual purity.

12. Farmer and Henley, *A Dictionary of Slang and Colloquial English*, includes the following definitions: Hornie (or Horness). 1. A constable or watchman: also a sheriff. 2. The devil: generally Auld Hornie.

13. See O'Connor, *The Times I've Seen*, 22–23.

14. In her reading of "Penelope," Suzette Henke observes how Molly Bloom's long-standing attraction to soldiers—Lieutenant Harry Mulvey and the British officer Gardner—stems from her "having initially courted the attentions of a detached and distant patriarch" (132), her father, himself a career officer.

15. It may have already become a pressing private concern if, as some suggest, Joyce contracted syphilis during a 1903 or 1904 visit to Monto. There is a long-running controversy (which I will not try to resolve here) as to whether or not for Joyce venereal disease was more than just a fictional trope. Erik Schneider makes the case that Joyce suffered from syphilis while in Trieste. Martin Bock argues that simply living in fear of the disease was enough to influence Joyce. Bock convincingly locates the source of Joyce's syphilitic descriptions in contemporary medical dictionaries. Other critics read syphilis as literary theme or artistic influence: Burton Waisbren and Florence Walzl analyze the symbolic role of the disease in *Dubliners*; Vernon Hall and Waisbren regard syphilis as a dominant theme and preoccupation of *Ulysses*. In *James Joyce and the Burden of Disease*, Kathleen Ferris considers syphilis, in all its physical and emotional

consequences, as a dominant factor of Joyce's life and fiction. J. B. Lyons in "Thrust Syphilis Down to Hell" dismisses these views, arguing that Joyce never suffered from syphilis, whether congenital or contracted.

16. See Krause, "Metchnikoff and Syphilis Research."

17. Suffragist and activist Anna Maria Haslam was a leading force in the movement for repeal of the Contagious Diseases Acts. See Mary Cullen's chapter on Haslam in *Women, Power and Consciousness in Nineteenth-Century Ireland*.

18. In his chapter "Terrorism, Prostitution, and the Abject Woman," Enda Duffy reads the episode as a discourse on the "intimate revenge" of terrorism. Margot Norris in "Disenchanting Enchantment" considers theatricality and performance to be the driving force in "Circe."

19. For a summary of the English Players dispute, see Ellmann, *James Joyce*, 439–41.

20. The chevron (^), ancient representation of masculinity (phallus) and inverted counterpart to the chalice symbol of femininity, still holds a prominent place on the epaulettes and sleeves of European and American military uniforms. In *Finnegans Wake* the chevron also functions as the symbol of Shaun (the Post).

21. See Gilbert, *James Joyce's* Ulysses, 346; McCarthy, "Jewel-Eyed Harlots," 103.

22. According to the *OED*, the first recorded use of the term "front" to signify a place of military engagement dates to 1665 in Manley, *Grotius' Low Country Warres*. It becomes prevalent throughout the nineteenth and twentieth centuries, from the Napoleonic Wars to World War II.

Chapter 6. Reclamations

1. Today, Farren's vision has to some extent been finally realized, as the Beggars Bush compound now includes senior-citizen housing, along with the National Print Museum, the Labour Relations Commission, and the Irish Geological Survey.

2. The Sandycove Martello tower, which now houses the James Joyce Museum, represents one of the first sites in which Joyce was reclaimed by Ireland. Several other Martellos around Dublin have undergone further reclamation into multi-million-euro residences. For example, U2 front man Bono renovated the Martello tower in nearby Bray.

3. Vincent Cheng in *Joyce, Race*, 151–52, reads the Tower as "a synecdoche for the Irish condition without Home Rule: it is 'occupied' (in both domestic and imperial senses) by a British presence (Haines) and by a native collaborator." Enda Duffy emphasizes "its role as a prison (Joyce's Dublin version of, and mocking riposte to, the Tower of London), a definitively enclosed space, at once a defensive fort—a bunker—and a prison cell" (36–37).

4. For discussion of the blood-sacrifice theory of the Rising, see Townshend, *Easter 1916*.

5. The layout of the Martello tower at Sandycove was typical for the design across the British Empire, with the soldiers' barracks located on the first floor. By 1904 the barracks had been converted to the apartment where Joyce lived with Gogarty and Samuel

Chenevix Trench. The powder magazine occupied the ground level, connected to the barracks and the rooftop gun platform by a spiral staircase.

6. There is also a Martello tower two miles southeast on Dalkey Island, which is visible from the Sandycove Tower.

7. The inscription on the obelisk reads "Last year being hard with the poor, walks about these hills and this were erected by John Mapas, June 1742."

8. Gibson's chapter subtitle, "Guns guns guns," a phrase drawn from Joyce's notes for "Penelope," underscores the intended emphasis on military themes.

9. Paris gave the golden apple to Aphrodite in exchange for the love of Helen, instead of giving it to Athena, who promised him wisdom and skill in war, or to Hera, who promised him the kingdoms of Europe and Asia.

10. A partial list of critical works concerning Joyce's French literary influences includes, for Proust, Michael O'Sullivan's *The Incarnation of Language*, Richard Davenport-Hines's *A Night at the Majestic*, and Sarah Tribout-Joseph's *Proust and Joyce in Dialogue*, and for Dujardin, R. B. Kershner's "Joyce and Dujardin's *L'Initiation au péché et à l'amour*," and Liisa Dahl's "A Comment on Similarities Between Édouard Dujardin's *Monologue Intérieur* and James Joyce's Interior Monologue."

11. In June 2004, Dublin ranked as the fourteenth most expensive city in the world, according to a cost-of-living survey by Mercer Human Resource Consulting ("World's Most Expensive").

12. Lest any celebrity (even of the posthumous variety) become too widely sung or grandly praised, Dubliners have come to refer to the monument in typically deflating good humor as "The Prick with the Stick."

13. Brooker quotes Aengus Fanning from an *Irish Independent* article: "Some of it seems a bit hollow and hypocritical, because you know many taking part have not read the book and never will read it.... *Ulysses* has been turned into a jolly, beery, harmless romp. But it isn't.... There are some very dark places in it and on the whole its view of Ireland is not very flattering" (213).

14. See Kiberd, *Ulysses and Us*.

Afterword

1. See Singer, *Wired For War: The Robotics Revolution and Conflict in the Twenty-First Century*.

2. John Bishop notes how "Robert Anton Wilson, author of *The Illuminatus Trilogy*, in a reading that cleverly demonstrates the power of the postmodern reader, has discovered in *Finnegans Wake* . . . the formula for the hydrogen bomb" (xii).

3. See Singer, *Corporate Warriors: The Rise of the Privatized Military Industry*; Priest and Arkin, *Top Secret America*.

Works Cited

Althusser, Louis. "Ideology and Ideological State Apparatuses (Notes Towards an Investigation)." In *Lenin and Philosophy, and Other Essays*, translated by Ben Brewster, 127–86. New York: Monthly Review Press, 1971.
Amery, L. S. Comments on "The Geographical Pivot of History," by H. J. Mackinder. *Geographical Journal* 23.4 (1904): 439–441.
Angell, Norman. *The Great Illusion: A Study of the Relation of Military Power in Nations to Their Economic and Social Advantage.* New York: Putnam, 1910.
Attridge, Derek, and Marjorie Howes, eds. *Semicolonial Joyce.* Cambridge: Cambridge University Press, 2000.
Bailey, Liberty Hyde, and Wilhelm Miller. *Cyclopedia of American Horticulture.* New York: Macmillan, 1900.
Beja, Morris. *James Joyce: A Literary Life.* Columbus: Ohio State University Press, 1992.
Benstock, Bernard. *James Joyce: The Undiscover'd Country.* Dublin: Gill and Macmillan, 1977.
Berghahn, Volker R. *Militarism: The History of an International Debate, 1861–1979.* New York: St. Martin's Press, 1982.
Bergson, Henri. *The Meaning of the War: Life and Matter in Conflict.* London: T. Fisher Unwin, 1915.
Berlin, Peter. "Rugby: On Irish Turf, God Save the English." *New York Times*, 23 February 2007.
Bhabha, Homi K. *The Location of Culture.* London: Routledge, 1994.
Bishop, John. Introduction to *Finnegans Wake*, by James Joyce, vii–xxvii. New York: Penguin, 1999.
Blackstone, William. *Commentaries on the Laws of England.* Vol. 2. Chicago: Callaghan, 1899.
Bock, Martin. "Syphilisation and Its Discontents: Somatic Indications of Psychological Ills in Joyce and Lowry." In *Joyce/Lowry: Critical Perspectives*, edited by Patrick A. McCarthy and Paul Tiessen, 126–44. Lexington: University Press of Kentucky, 1997.
"Bomb Outrage in Rome." *New York Times*, 15 November 1906.
Boyle, John F. *The Irish Rebellion of 1916: A Brief History of the Revolt and Its Suppression.* London: Constable, 1916.

Boyle, Robert, S.J. "Can Bray Head Be Seen From the Martello Tower?" *James Joyce Quarterly* 20.1 (Fall 1982): 130–31.

Bradley, Bruce. *James Joyce's Schooldays*. New York: St. Martin's Press, 1982.

"British Government." *United Irishman*, 15 June 1904, 5.

Brivic, Sheldon. *Joyce's Waking Women*. Madison: University of Wisconsin Press, 1995.

Brooker, Joseph. *Joyce's Critics*. Madison: University of Wisconsin Press, 2004.

Brown, Richard. "Cyclopean Anglophobia and Transnational Community: Re-reading the Boxing Matches in Joyce's *Ulysses*." In Jones and Beja, *Twenty-First Joyce*, 82–96.

Budgen, Frank. *James Joyce and the Making of* Ulysses. London: Grayson and Grayson, 1934.

Bulwer-Lytton, Edward, 1st Baron Lytton. Despatch 62, 30 December 1858. In *British Columbia: Papers Relative to the Affairs of British Columbia . . . Copies of despatches from the Secretary of State for the Colonies to the Governor of British Columbia, and from the governor to the Secretary of State relative to the government of the colony*. London: Eyre and Spottiswoode, 1859–62.

Burke, F. P. "The Revival of the G.A.A.: An Appeal to the Young Men of Belfast." *Shan Van Vocht*, October 1898, 186.

Caesar, Julius. *Commentaries on the Gallic and Civil Wars with the Supplemental Books*. Translated by W. A. McDevitte and W. S. Bohn. New York: Harper and Brothers, 1897.

Calraide. "Learning Geography." *United Irishman*, 2 September 1899, 2.

Caraher, Brian. "Semicolonial Cities and Trieste Joyce: The Cultural Politics of Reading Joyce's Homeplaces." Review of *Occasional, Critical, and Political Writing*, by James Joyce. *James Joyce Quarterly* 38.3–4 (Spring–Summer 2001): 505–18.

Carey, Vincent. "John Derricke's 'Image of Irelande,' Sir Henry Sidney, and the Massacre at Mullaghmast, 1578." *Irish Historical Studies* 31.123 (May 1999): 305–27.

Carlson, Sandy. "James Joyce's Irish Nationalism, A Response to His Time: A Portrait of the Artist as a Young Man." *Arkansas Quarterly* 2.4 (October 1993): 282–98.

Carpenter, Kevin. *Penny Dreadfuls and Comics: English Periodicals for Children from Victorian Times to the Present Day*. London: Victoria and Albert Museum, 1983.

Chapman, David L. *Sandow the Magnificent: Eugen Sandow and the Beginnings of Bodybuilding*. Urbana: University of Illinois Press, 1994.

Cheng, Vincent. "The General and the Sepoy: Imperialism and Power in the Museyroom." In *Critical Essays on James Joyce's Finnegans Wake*, edited by Patrick A. McCarthy, 258–68. New York: G. K. Hall, 1992.

———. *Joyce, Race, and Empire*. Cambridge: Cambridge University Press, 1995.

———. "Nation Without Borders: Joyce, Cosmopolitanism, and the Inauthentic Ireland." In Gibson and Platt, *Joyce, Ireland, Britain*, 212–33.

———. "The Twining Stresses, Two by Two: The Prosody of Joyce's Prose." *Modernism/modernity* 16.2 (2009): 391–99.

Conrad, Joseph. *Heart of Darkness*. Edited by Paul O'Prey. New York: Penguin, 1983.

Corcoran, T., S.J., ed. *The Clongowes Record, 1814–1932*. Dublin: Browne and Nolan, 1932.

Costello, Peter. *James Joyce: The Years of Growth, 1882–1915*. West Cork, Ireland: Roberts Rinehart; London: Kyle Cathie, 1992.
Cronin, Mike. *Sport and Nationalism in Ireland: Gaelic Games, Soccer, and Irish Identity Since 1884*. Dublin: Four Courts, 1999.
Cullen, Mary. "Anna Maria Haslam." In *Women, Power and Consciousness in Nineteenth-Century Ireland*, edited by Mary Cullen and Maria Luddy, 161–96. Dublin: Attic Press, 1995.
Culleton, Claire A. *Names and Naming in Joyce*. Madison: University of Wisconsin Press, 1994.
Cunningham, Hugh. *The Volunteer Force: A Social and Political History, 1859–1908*. London: Croom Helm, 1975.
Cusack, Michael. *See* Miceal.
Dahl, Liisa. "A Comment on Similarities Between Édouard Dujardin's *Monologue Intérieur* and James Joyce's Interior Monologue." *Neuphiologische Mitteilungen* 73.1–2 (1972): 45–54.
Davenport-Hines, Richard. *A Night at the Majestic: Proust and the Great Modernist Dinner Party of 1922*. London: Faber and Faber, 2006.
Davison, Neil. "Pugilism in *Ulysses*: Round Two." *James Joyce Quarterly* 32.3–4 (Spring–Summer 1995): 722–28.
De Amicis, Edmondo. *La Vita Militare*. 1880. Napoli: Salvatore Romano, 1911.
Deane, Seamus. "Dead Ends: Joyce's Finest Moments." In Attridge and Howes, *Semicolonial Joyce*, 21–36.
———. Introduction to *A Portrait of the Artist as a Young Man*, by James Joyce. New York: Penguin Classics, 1993.
de Búrca, Marcus. *The GAA: A History*. 2nd ed. Dublin: Gill and Macmillan, 1999.
Deleuze, Gilles, and Félix Guattari. *A Thousand Plateaus: Capitalism and Schizophrenia*. Translated by Brian Massumi. 1987. London: Continuum, 2004.
Devitt, Michael, S.J. "Clongowes Wood." *Journal of the Archaeological Society of the County of Kildare and Surrounding Districts* 3 (1902): 203–15.
Devlin, Kimberly J. "Bloom and the Police: Regulatory Vision and Visions in *Ulysses*." *Novel: A Forum on Fiction* 29 (Fall 1995): 45–62.
Dibdin, Charles. "The Lass That Loves a Sailor." Music in the Works of James Joyce. www.james-joyce-music.com/extras/lasslovesailor.html.
"The Dodder Mystery: Fresh Inquest Opened; The Body Again Exhumed." *Freeman's Journal*, 10 September 1900, 2.
"The Dodder Mystery: Inquest Resumed." *Freeman's Journal*, 11 September 1900, 2.
"The Dodder Mystery: Servant Girl Drowned." *Freeman's Journal*, 28 August 1900, 3.
Doherty, Gerald. *Dubliners' Dozen: The Games Narrators Play*. Madison, N.J.: Fairleigh Dickinson University Press, 2004.
"Drowning in the Dodder: Inquest." *Freeman's Journal*, 22 August 1900, 3.
Dubber, Markus Dirk. *The Police Power: Patriarchy and the Foundations of American Government*. New York: Columbia University Press, 2005.

"Dublin Corporation." *United Irishman*, 11 June 1904, 1.
Duffy, Enda. *The Subaltern Ulysses*. Minneapolis: University of Minnesota Press, 1994.
Eisenhower, Dwight D. "Farewell Radio and Television Address to the American People." 17 January 1961. In *Public Papers of the Presidents: Dwight D. Eisenhower, 1960–61*, 1035–40. Washington, D.C.: Government Printing Office.
Eliot, T. S. "*Ulysses*, Order and Myth." 1923. In *Selected Prose*, edited by Frank Kermode, 175–78. London: Faber and Faber, 1975.
Ellmann, Richard. *James Joyce*. New York: Oxford University Press, 1959.
Enloe, Cynthia. *Does Khaki Become You? The Militarisation of Women's Lives*. London: Pluto, 1983.
———. *Globalization and Militarism: Feminists Make the Link*. Lanham, Md.: Rowman and Littlefield, 2007.
———. *Maneuvers: The International Politics of Militarizing Women's Lives*. Berkeley: University of California Press, 2000.
Fagan, Terry. *Monto: Madams, Murder, and Black Coddle*. Dublin: North Inner City Folklore Group, 2002.
Fairhall, James. *James Joyce and the Question of History*. Cambridge: Cambridge University Press, 1993.
Felski, Rita. "Remember the Reader." *Chronicle of Higher Education*, 19 December 2008, B8.
Ferguson, R. Brian, and Neil L. Whitehead, eds. *War in the Tribal Zone: Expanding States and Indigenous Warfare*. Santa Fe, N.M.: School of American Research Press, 1992.
Ferrall, Charles, and Anna Jackson. *Juvenile Literature and British Society, 1850–1950: The Age of Adolescence*. New York: Routledge, 2010.
Ferrero, Guglielmo. *L'Europa giovane*. Milan: Fratelli Treves, 1898.
———. *Militarism: A Contribution to the Peace Crusade*. Boston: L. C. Page, 1903.
Ferris, Kathleen. *James Joyce and the Burden of Disease*. Lexington: University Press of Kentucky, 1995.
Fitzpatrick, David. "Militarism in Ireland, 1900–1922." In *A Military History of Ireland*, edited by Thomas Bartlett and Keith Jeffery, 379–406. Cambridge: Cambridge University Press, 1996.
Fogarty, Anne. "States of Memory: Reading History in 'Wandering Rocks.'" In Jones and Beja, *Twenty-First Joyce*, 56–81.
Fountain, Nigel. "Bouquet of Thorns." Review of Krell, *The Devil's Rope*, and Razac, *Barbed Wire*. *Guardian*, 14 December 2002.
Foy, Michael, and Brian Barton. *The Easter Rising*. Stroud, Glos.: Sutton, 1999.
Fussell, Paul. *The Great War and Modern Memory*. New York: Oxford University Press, 1975.
"Gaelic Athletes and the National Movement." *Shan Van Vocht* 1 (May 1896): 88–89.
Garibaldi, Giuseppe. *Garibaldi: An Autobiography*. Edited by Alexandre Dumas. Translated by William Robson. London: Routledge, 1861.

———. "To the People of England." *Daily Telegraph*, 28 April 1864, 1.
Garvin, John. *James Joyce's Disunited Kingdom and the Irish Dimension*. Dublin: Gill and Macmillan, 1976.
Gash, Norman. *Mr. Secretary Peel: The Life of Sir Robert Peel to 1830*. Cambridge: Harvard University Press, 1961.
"Germany to Fight, Northcliffe Says." *New York Times*, 8 September 1909, 5.
Gibson, Andrew. *Joyce's Revenge*. New York: Oxford University Press, 2002.
———. "'That Stubborn Irish Thing': *A Portrait of the Artist* in History: Chapter 1." In Gibson and Platt, *Joyce, Ireland, Britain*, 85–103.
———. "'Time Drops in Decay': *A Portrait of the Artist* in History (ii), Chapter 2." *James Joyce Quarterly* 44.4 (Summer 2007): 697–717.
Gibson, Andrew, and Len Platt, eds. *Joyce, Ireland, Britain*. Gainesville: University Press of Florida, 2006.
Gifford, Don. *Ulysses Annotated: Notes for James Joyce's Ulysses*. With Robert J. Seidman. 2nd ed. Berkeley: University of California Press, 1988.
Gilbert, Stuart. *James Joyce's Ulysses*. 2nd ed. New York: Knopf, 1952.
Gillespie, Michael Patrick. *Inverted Volumes Improperly Arranged: James Joyce and His Trieste Library*. Ann Arbor, Mich.: UMI Research Press, 1983.
Gillespie, Michael Patrick, with Erik Bradford Stocker. *James Joyce's Trieste Library: A Catalogue of Materials at the Harry Ransom Humanities Research Center, The University of Texas at Austin*. Austin: The Center, 1986.
Gillis, John R., ed. *The Militarization of the Western World*. New Brunswick, N.J.: Rutgers University Press, 1989.
Gogarty, Oliver St. John. *It Isn't This Time of Year at All! An Unpremeditated Autobiography*. Garden City, N.Y.: Doubleday, 1954.
———. "Ode of Welcome." *Irish Society and Social Review*, June 1900.
———. *Tumbling in the Hay*. London: Constable, 1939.
———. "Ugly England." *United Irishman*, 15 September 1905, 3.
"Goldsmith (G.P.O.) v. Grattan (Sandyford)." *Celtic Times*, 2 April 1887, 2.
Goodrich, Samuel G. *Peter Parley's Tales About Ancient and Modern Greece*. 1832. Philadelphia: Charles DeSilver, 1864.
Gorman, Herbert. *James Joyce*. 1939. New York: Octagon, 1974.
Grob-Fitzgibbon, Benjamin. *Turning Points of the Irish Revolution: The British Government, Intelligence, and the Cost of Indifference, 1912–1921*. London: Palgrave Macmillan, 2007.
Groden, Michael. "Joyce at Work on 'Cyclops': Toward a Biography of *Ulysses*." *James Joyce Quarterly* 44.2 (Winter 2007): 217–45.
Hall, Vernon, and Burton A. Waisbren. "Syphilis as a Major Theme of James Joyce's *Ulysses*." *Archives of Internal Medicine* 140 (1980): 963–65.
Hardiman, Adrian. "Murder Most Joyce." *Dubliner*, June 2006, 79–80, 83.
Harrison, Deborah. *The First Casualty: Violence Against Women in Canadian Military Communities*. Toronto: J. Lorimer, 2002.

Hart, Clive, and David Hayman, eds. *James Joyce's* Ulysses: *Critical Essays*. Berkeley: University of California Press, 1974.

Hee-Whan Yun. "Male Prostitution as Irony: Corley and Lenehan." *James Joyce Journal* 12.1 (June 2006): 57–69.

Henke, Suzette A. *James Joyce and the Politics of Desire*. New York: Routledge, 1990.

Herlihy, Jim. *The Dublin Metropolitan Police: A Short History and Genealogical Guide, 1836–1925*. Dublin: Four Courts, 2001.

Herring, Paul. "Cochise the Apache Chief." *Halfpenny Marvel* 4.86 (25 June 1895): 1–16.

Hogan, Patrick J. "University College Dublin, Literary and Historical Society. Meeting Minutes of 11 February 1899." UCD Library Special Collections, Microfilm soc 2. 173.

Homer. *The Odyssey*. Translated by Robert Fitzgerald. 1961. New York: Farrar, Straus and Giroux, 1998.

Hosty, Patrick. "Old Clongowes Football." In Corcoran, *The Clongowes Record*, 129–130.

Howes, Marjorie. "'Goodbye Ireland I'm Going to Gort': Geography, Scale, and Narrating the Nation." In Attridge and Howes, *Semicolonial Joyce*, 58–77.

Howes, Marjorie, and Derek Attridge. Introduction to Attridge and Howes, *Semicolonial Joyce*, 1–20.

Hughes, Thomas. *Tom Brown's School-Days*. 1857. London: J. M. Dent, 1906.

Humphreys, Susan L. "Ferrero Etc.: James Joyce's Debt to Guglielmo Ferrero." *James Joyce Quarterly* 16.3 (Spring 1979): 239–51.

Igoe, Vivien. *James Joyce's Dublin Houses and Nora Barnacle's Galway*. Dublin: Lilliput, 2007.

Jackson, Alvin. *Ireland, 1798–1998: Politics and War*. Oxford: Blackwell, 1999.

Jackson, John Wyse, and Bernard McGinley, eds. *James Joyce's* Dubliners: *An Annotated Edition*. London: Sinclair-Stevenson, 1993.

Jeffries, Charles, Sir. *The Colonial Police*. London: Max Parrish, 1952.

Johnson, Chalmers. *The Sorrows of Empire: Militarism, Secrecy, and the End of the Republic*. New York: Metropolitan, 2004.

Jones, Ellen Carol, and Morris Beja, eds. *Twenty-First Joyce*. Gainesville: University Press of Florida, 2004.

Jones, Francis P. *History of the Sinn Fein Movement and the Irish Rebellion of 1916*. New York: P. J. Kenedy and Sons, 1917.

Joyce, Stanislaus. *My Brother's Keeper: James Joyce's Early Years*. London: Faber and Faber, 1958.

Kant, Immanuel. *Perpetual Peace: A Philosophical Sketch*. 1795. Translated by M. Campbell Smith. London: Allen and Unwin, 1917.

Kealey, Terence. *The Economic Laws of Scientific Research*. London: Palgrave Macmillan, 1997.

Kelly, Joseph. *Our Joyce: From Outcast to Icon*. Austin: University of Texas Press, 1994.

Kemmy, Jim. "George Clancy: Murdered Mayor" and "Portrait of the Martyr as a Young Man." In *Remembering Limerick*, edited by David Lee, 250–60. Limerick: Limerick Civic Trust, 1997.

Kennedy, Paul. *The Rise and Fall of the Great Powers: Economic Change and Military Conflict from 1500 to 2000*. New York: Random House, 1988.
Kenner, Hugh. *Joyce's Voices*. Berkeley: University of California Press, 1978.
———. *The Pound Era: The Age of Ezra Pound, T. S. Eliot, James Joyce and Wyndham Lewis*. London: Faber and Faber, 1975.
Kerr, S. Parnell. *What the Irish Regiments Have Done*. With *A Diary of a Visit to the Front*, by John E. Redmond. London: T. Fisher Unwin, 1916.
Kerrigan, Paul M. *Castles and Fortifications in Ireland, 1485–1945*. Cork: Collins Press, 1995.
Kershner, R. B. "Joyce and Dujardin's *L'Initiation au péché et à l'amour*: An Unacknowledged Debt." *James Joyce Quarterly* 26.2 (Winter 1989): 213–25.
———. *Joyce, Bakhtin, and Popular Literature: Chronicles of Disorder*. Chapel Hill: University of North Carolina Press, 1989.
———. "The World's Strongest Man: Joyce or Sandow?" *James Joyce Quarterly* 30.4 and 31.1 (Summer–Fall 1993): 667–93.
Kettle, Thomas M. *The Day's Burden: Studies Literary and Political and Miscellaneous Essays*. 1918. Freeport, N.Y.: Books for Libraries Press, 1968.
———. *The Ways of War*. 1917. New York: Scribner's, 1918.
Kiberd, Declan. *Ulysses and Us: The Art of Everyday Life in Joyce's Masterpiece*. New York: W. W. Norton, 2009.
"Killiney v. Feach." *Celtic Times*, 19 February 1887, 3.
Kilmainham Papers. Vol. 18. National Library of Ireland.
Klein, A. M. "A Shout in the Street: An Analysis of the Second Chapter of Joyce's *Ulysses*." In *Literary Essays and Reviews*, by A. M. Klein, edited by Usher Caplan and M. W. Steinberg, 342–66. Toronto: University of Toronto Press, 1987.
Knowles, Sebastian D. G. *The Dublin Helix: The Life of Language in Joyce's* Ulysses. Gainesville: University Press of Florida, 2001.
Krause, Richard M. "Metchnikoff and Syphilis Research During a Decade of Discovery, 1900–1910." *ASM News* 62.6 (1996): 307–10.
Krell, Alan. *The Devil's Rope: A Cultural History of Barbed Wire*. London: Reaktion, 2002.
"Land Leaguers Arrested: The Enforcement of the Coercion Law Begun." *New York Times*, 9 March 1881.
Landreth, Helen. *The Pursuit of Robert Emmet*. New York: Whittlesey, 1948.
Leavis, F. R. "Joyce and 'The Revolution of the Word.'" *Scrutiny* 2.2 (September 1933): 193–201.
Lebor Gabála Érenn (The Book of Invasions). In *Ancient Irish Tales*, translated by Tom Peete Cross and Clark Harris Slover, 3–27. 1947. New York: Barnes and Noble, 1969.
Ledden, Patrick. "Bloom, Lawn Tennis, and the Gaelic Athletic Association." *James Joyce Quarterly* 36.3 (Spring 1999): 630–34.
Lee, Richard B., and Richard H. Daly. "Man's Domination and Women's Oppression: The Question of Origins." In *Beyond Patriarchy: Essays by Men on Pleasure, Power,*

and Change, edited by Michael Kaufman, 30–44. Toronto: Oxford University Press, 1987.

Leeson, David. "Death in the Afternoon: The Croke Park Massacre, 21 November 1920." *Canadian Journal of History* 38.1 (April 2003): 43–67.

Lentz, Susan A., and Robert H. Chaires. "The Invention of Peel's Principles: A Study of Policing 'Textbook' History." *Journal of Criminal Justice* 35.1 (2007): 69–79.

Levenson, Leah. *With Wooden Sword: A Portrait of Francis Sheehy-Skeffington, Militant Pacifist*. Boston: Northeastern University Press, 1983.

Liebknecht, Karl. *Militarism and Anti-Militarism*. Translated by Grahame Lock. Cambridge: Rivers Press, 1973.

Livingstone, David N. *The Geographical Tradition: Episodes in the History of a Contested Enterprise*. Oxford: Blackwell, 1992.

Luddy, Maria. *Prostitution and Irish Society, 1800–1940*. Cambridge: Cambridge University Press, 2007.

Luxemburg, Rosa. "The Militia and Militarism." In *Rosa Luxemburg: Selected Political Writings*, edited by Robert Looker, translated by W. D. Graf, 76–92. New York: Random House, 1972.

Lyons, J. B. *The Enigma of Tom Kettle*. Dublin: Glendale Press, 1983.

———. "Thrust Syphilis Down to Hell." In *James Joyce: The Centennial Symposium*, edited by Morris Beja, Phillip Herring, Maurice Harmon, and David Norris, 173–83. Urbana: University of Illinois Press, 1986.

Lytton, Lord. *See* Bulwer-Lytton.

Mac Cana, Proinsias. *Celtic Mythology*. London: Hamlyn, 1970.

Maddox, Brenda. *Nora*. Boston: Houghton Mifflin, 1988.

Malcolm, Elizabeth. *The Irish Policeman, 1822–1922: A Life*. Dublin: Four Courts, 2006.

Mandle, W. F. *The Gaelic Athletic Association and Irish Nationalist Politics, 1884–1924*. Dublin: Gill and Macmillan, 1987.

Mangan, J. A. *Athleticism in the Victorian and Edwardian Public School: The Emergence and Consolidation of an Educational Ideology*. Cambridge: Cambridge Universtiy Press, 1981.

———. *The Games Ethic and Imperialism: Aspects of the Diffusion of an Ideal*. Harmondsworth: Viking Penguin, 1986.

Mangan, J. A., and Hamad S. Ndee. "Military Drill—Rather More Than 'Brief and Basic': English Elementary Schools and English Militarism." In *Militarism, Sport, Europe: War Without Weapons*, edited by J. A. Mangan, 67–99. London: Frank Cass, 2003.

Manganiello, Dominic. *Joyce's Politics*. London: Routledge and Kegan Paul, 1980.

Mangnall, Richmal. *Historical and Miscellaneous Questions*. New ed. London: Longman, Brown, 1857.

Marryat, Frederick. *Mr. Midshipman Easy*. 1836. New York: Century, 1906.

———. *The Naval Officer*. Paris: Baudry's, 1834.

McCarthy, Patrick. "The Jewel-Eyed Harlots of His Imagination." *Eire-Ireland* 17.4 (1982): 91–109.
McCourt, John. *The Years of Bloom: James Joyce in Trieste, 1904–1920*. Dublin: Lilliput Press, 2000.
Meagher, Thomas Francis. *Meagher of the Sword: Speeches of Thomas Francis Meagher in Ireland, 1846–48, His Narrative of Events in July 1848, Personal Reminiscences of Waterford, Galway, and His Schooldays*. Edited by Arthur Griffith. Dublin: Gill, 1916.
Meenan, James, ed. *Centenary History of the Literary and Historical Society of University College Dublin, 1855–1955*. 1956. Dublin: A. and A. Farmer, 2005.
Mengham, Rod. "Military Occupation in 'The Dead.'" In *Re: Joyce: Text, Culture, Politics*, edited by John Brannigan, Geoff Ward, and Julian Wolfreys, 77–86. New York: St. Martin's, 1998.
Miceal [Michael Cusack]. "Hurling: A Fine Art." *United Irishman*, 6 May 1899, 3.
———. "The Gaelic Athletic Association: Hurling." *United Irishman*, 24 March 1899, 3.
Mitchell, J. Lawrence. "Joyce and Boxing: Famous Fighters in *Ulysses*." *James Joyce Quarterly* 31.2 (Winter 1994): 21–30.
Morgan, David H. J. "Theater of War: Combat, the Military, and Masculinities." In *Theorizing Masculinities*, edited by Harry Brod and Michael Kaufman, 165–81. Thousand Oaks, Cal.: Sage, 1994.
Moss, Mark. *Manliness and Militarism: Educating Young Boys in Ontario for War*. Don Mills, Ont.: Oxford University Press, 2001.
"Mr. Chamberlain's Visit to Dublin." *Freeman's Journal*, 18 December 1899, 6.
Muenger, Elizabeth A. *The British Military Dilemma in Ireland: Occupation Politics, 1886–1914*. Lawrence: University Press of Kansas, 1991.
Mullin, Katherine. *James Joyce, Sexuality and Social Purity*. Cambridge: Cambridge University Press, 2003.
"Native Athletics in the Schools." *United Irishman*, 4 February 1904, 6.
Nelson, Claudia. *Boys Will Be Girls: The Feminine Ethic and British Children's Fiction, 1857–1917*. New Brunswick, N.J.: Rutgers University Press, 1991.
Nolan, Emer. *James Joyce and Nationalism*. New York: Routledge, 1995.
Norris, Margot. "Disenchanting Enchantment: The Theatrical Brothel of Circe" in *Ulysses En-Gendered Perspectives*, edited by Kimberly J. Devlin and Marilyn Reizbaum, 229–41. Columbia: University of South Carolina Press, 1999.
———. *Suspicious Readings of Joyce's Dubliners*. Philadelphia: University of Pennsylvania Press, 2003.
———. *Writing War in the Twentieth Century*. Charlottesville: University Press of Virginia, 2000.
Northcliffe, Alfred Harmsworth, Viscount. *Lord Northcliffe's War Book, with Chapters on America at War*. New York: G. H. Doran, 1917.
Novick, Ben. *Conceiving Revolution: Irish Nationalist Propaganda during the First World War*. Dublin: Four Courts, 2001.

"Numerical Register of the Dublin Metropolitan Police." National Archives of Ireland. MFA 6/3.

O'Brien, Joseph V. *Dear, Dirty Dublin: A City in Distress, 1899–1916*. Berkeley: University of California Press, 1982.

Ó Conghaile, Pol. "Bloom 100." *Irish Independent*, 17 June 2004, 7–12.

O'Connor, Ulick. *The Times I've Seen: Oliver St. John Gogarty: A Biography*. New York: I. Obolensky, 1963.

O'Hegarty, P. S. *A History of Ireland Under the Union*. London: Methuen, 1952.

Ó Maitiú, Seámus. *W&R Jacob: Celebrating 150 Years of Irish Biscuit Making*. Dublin: Woodfield Press, 2001.

O'Malley, Ernie. *On Another Man's Wound*. 1936. Dublin: Dufour, 1990.

O'Reilly, John Boyle. *The Ethics of Boxing and Manly Sport*. Boston: Ticknor, 1888.

Orwell, George. *The Road to Wigan Pier*. London: Gollancz, 1937.

Osteen, Mark. *The Economy of* Ulysses: *Making Both Ends Meet*. Syracuse, N.Y.: Syracuse University Press, 1995.

O'Sullivan, Michael. *The Incarnation of Language: Joyce, Proust and a Philosophy of the Flesh*. London: Continuum, 2008.

Parascandola, Louis, and Maria McGarrity. "'I'm a . . . Naughty Girl': Prostitution and Outsider Women in James Joyce's 'The Boarding House' and Eric Walrond's 'The Palm Porch.'" *CLA Journal* 50.2 (December 2006): 141–61.

Pašeta, Senia. "Thomas Kettle: 'An Irish Soldier in the Army of Europe'?" In *Ireland and the Great War: "A War to Unite Us All"?* edited by Adrian Gregory and Senia Pašeta, 8–27. Manchester: Manchester University Press, 2002.

Pearce, Richard. "Teaching for the (W)Holes." In *Approaches to Teaching Joyce's* Ulysses, edited by Kathleen McCormick and Erwin R. Steinberg, 97–104. New York: Modern Language Association, 1993.

Peel, Robert. *As Irish Secretary: From His Private Correspondence*. Vol. 2 of *Sir Robert Peel*. London: J. Murray, 1891–99.

Penny, Thomas. *Manual Relative to the Duty of the Dublin Metropolitan Police and the Carriage Regulations within the Police District of Dublin Metropolis*. Dublin: Alexander Thom, 1840.

Plock, Vike Martina. *Joyce, Medicine, and Modernity*. Gainesville: University Press of Florida, 2010.

Pounch, Seamus. "Statement by Seamus Pounch, 55, O'Curry Road, Fairbrothers Fields, Dublin." Bureau of Military History, 1913–21. WS 267. National Archives of Ireland.

Pound, Ezra. "Paris Letter: Ulysses." In *Pound/Joyce: The Letters of Ezra Pound to James Joyce, with Pound's Critical Essays and Articles about Joyce*, edited by Forrest Read, 194–200. New York: New Directions, 1967.

Priest, Dana, and William M. Arkin. *Top Secret America: The Rise of the New American Security State*. New York: Little, Brown, 2011.

"Public Rights in the Phoenix Park." *Freeman's Journal*, 16 June 1904, 3.

"Public Business: State Lands Bill Debate, 1924—Second Stage." Seanad Éireann, vol.

3, 28 July 1924. Díospóireachtaí Parlaiminte (Parliamentary Debates). http://historical-debates.oireachtas.ie/S/0003/S.0003.192407280006.html.

Puirséal, Pádraig. *The G.A.A. in Its Time*. Dublin: Purcell Family, 1982.

Rabaté, Jean-Michel. *James Joyce and the Politics of Egoism*. Cambridge: Cambridge University Press, 2001.

Rault, André. "George Alfred Henty: Romancier de la Jeunesse." In *Home, Sweet Home or Bleak House? Art et littérature à l'époque Victorienne*, 165–89. Paris: Belles Lettres, 1985.

Razac, Olivier. *Barbed Wire: A Political History*. Translated by Jonathan Kneight. London: Profile, 2002.

Redhead, Steve. *Paul Virilio: Theorist for an Accelerated Culture*. Edinburgh: Edinburgh University Press, 2004.

Rice, Thomas Jackson. *Cannibal Joyce*. Gainesville: University Press of Florida, 2008.

Richards, Jeffrey. *Imperialism and Juvenile Literature*. Manchester: Manchester University Press, 1989.

Riquelme, John Paul. "Joyce's The Dead: The Dissolution of the Self and the Police." In *Rejoycing: New Readings of Dubliners*, edited by Rosa M. Bollettieri Bosinelli and Harold F. Mosher Jr., 123–41. Lexington: University Press of Kentucky, 1998.

Robinson, Richard. "Buckley in a General Russia: *Finnegans Wake* and Political Space." In *Joyce in Trieste: An Album of Risky Readings*, edited by Sebastian D. G. Knowles, Geert Lernout, and John McCourt, 170–87. Gainesville: University Press of Florida, 2007.

Roos, Bonnie. "James Joyce's 'The Dead' and Bret Harte's *Gabriel Conroy*: The Nature of the Feast." *Yale Journal of Criticism* 15.1 (Spring 2002): 99–126.

Rose, Stewart. *Ignatius Loyola and the Early Jesuits*. London: Burns and Oates, 1871.

Russell, Bertrand. *Why Men Fight: A Method of Abolishing the International Duel*. New York: Century, 1917.

Said, Edward W. *Culture and Imperialism*. New York: Knopf, 1993.

Schneider, Erik. "'A Grievous Distemper': Joyce and the Rheumatic Fever Episode of 1907." *James Joyce Quarterly* 38.3–4 (Spring–Summer 2001): 453–75.

Scholes, Robert, and A. Walton Litz, eds. Dubliners: *Text, Criticism, and Notes*. New York: Viking, 1969.

Scott, Bonnie Kime. *Joyce and Feminism*. Bloomington: Indiana University Press, 1984.

Sheehy Skeffington, Andrée D. "Historical Background to the Testimonial to the Tsar of Russia Referred to in *Stephen Hero* and *A Portrait of the Artist*." *James Joyce Quarterly* 20 (Fall 1982): 117–20.

Sheehy Skeffington, Francis. *In Dark and Evil Days*. Dublin: J. Duffy, 1916.

———. Letter to *Critical Chronicle*, 14 September 1914. Sheehy Skeffington Papers. National Library of Ireland. MS 33.604(6).

———. "The Psychology of Peace and War." *Irish Citizen* 4.6 (26 June 1915): 42.

Sheehy Skeffington, Hanna. "British Militarism as I Have Known It." 1917. Tralee: Kerryman, 1946.

———. Introduction to F. Sheehy Skeffington, *In Dark and Evil Days*, i–xxviii.
Singer, P. W. *Corporate Warriors: The Rise of the Privatized Military Industry*. Updated ed. Ithaca, N.Y.: Cornell University Press, 2007.
———. *Wired For War: The Robotics Revolution and Conflict in the Twenty-First Century*. New York: Penguin, 2009.
Skeffington. *See* Sheehy Skeffington.
Smith, Rennie. *Militarism in Our Educational Institutions: The Menace of the Junior Cadet Corps and the O.T.C.* London: National Council for the Prevention of War, 1926.
Spangler, Matthew. "Winds of Change: Bloomsday, Immigration, and 'Aeolus' in Street Theater." *James Joyce Quarterly* 45.1 (Fall 2007): 47–67.
Spencer, Herbert. *The Principles of Sociology*. Vol. 2. 1899. New York: Appleton, 1906.
Spencer-Jones, Claire. "Making Sport of Violence: The Presence of the Sepoy Mutiny in James Joyce's *Ulysses* and J. G. Farrell's *The Siege of Krishnapur*." In *Picturing South Asian Culture in English: Textual and Visual Representations*, edited by Tasleem Shakur and Karen D'Souza, 32–45. Liverpool: Open House Press, 2003.
Spilka, Mark. "Power Games in Joyce's 'Counterparts.'" In *Eight Lessons in Love: A Domestic Violence Reader*, 187–200. Columbia: University of Missouri Press, 1997.
Spoo, Robert. *James Joyce and the Language of History: Dedalus's Nightmare*. New York: Oxford University Press, 1994.
———. "'Nestor' and the Nightmare: The Presence of the Great War in *Ulysses*." *Twentieth Century Literature* 32.2 (Summer 1986): 137–54.
Springhall, John. "'Healthy Papers for Manly Boys': Imperialism and Race in the Harmsworths' Halfpenny Papers of the 1890s and 1900s." In Richards, *Imperialism and Juvenile Literature*, 107–25.
Stargardt, Nicholas. *The German Idea of Militarism: Radical and Socialist Critics, 1866–1914*. Cambridge: Cambridge University Press, 1994.
Steele, Karen. *Women, Press, and Politics during the Irish Revival*. Syracuse, N.Y.: Syracuse University Press, 2007.
Streets, Heather. *Martial Races: The Military, Race, and Masculinity in British Imperial Culture, 1857–1914*. Manchester: Manchester University Press, 2004.
Sugden, John. *Boxing and Society: An International Analysis*. Manchester: Manchester University Press, 1996.
Sullivan, Kevin. *Joyce Among the Jesuits*. New York: Columbia University Press, 1958.
Summers, Anne. "Militarism in Britain before the Great War." *History Workshop Journal* 2 (1976): 104–23.
Sutcliffe, Sheila. *Martello Towers*. Newton Abbot, Devon: David and Charles, 1972.
Thomson, Allan P. "John Doe Buck Private." In *Great Poems of the World War*, edited by W. D. Eaton, 127. Chicago: T. S. Denison, 1922.
"Tipperary R.G.A. (Militia) Regimental Sports." *Cork Examiner*, 30 May 1904, 7.
Townshend, Charles. *Easter 1916: The Irish Rebellion*. London: Ivan R. Dee, 2006.
Tribout-Joseph, Sarah. *Proust and Joyce in Dialogue*. London: Legenda, 2008.

"Two Men From the Country: Hugh and Dermott." *An Claideamh Soluis*, 20 January 1900, 709.

Tymoczko, Maria. *The Irish Ulysses*. Berkeley: University of California Press, 1994.

Verene, Donald Philip. "Coincidence, Historical Repetition, and Self-Knowledge: Jung, Vico, and Joyce." *Journal of Analytical Psychology* 47.3 (2002): 459–78.

Virilio, Paul. *Bunker Archeology*. Translated by George Collins. Princeton: Princeton Architectural Press, 2008.

———. *Speed and Politics: An Essay on Dromology*. Translated by Mark Polizzotti. New York: Semiotext(e), 1986.

Waisbren, Burton A., and Florence L. Walzl. "Paresis and the Priest: James Joyce's Symbolic Use of Syphilis in 'The Sisters.'" *Annals of Internal Medicine* 80.6 (1974): 758–62.

Wells, H. G. *The War That Will End War*. London: Duffield, 1914.

White, Arnold. *Efficiency and Empire*. London: Methuen, 1901.

Wills, Clair. "Joyce, Prostitution, and the Colonial City." *South Atlantic Quarterly* 95.1 (Winter 1996): 79–95.

Winston, Greg. "Reluctant Indians: Irish Identity and Racial Masquerade." In *Irish Modernism and the Global Primitive*, edited by Maria McGarrity and Claire A. Culleton, 153–72. New York: Palgrave Macmillan, 2009.

Wollaeger, Mark. "Posters, Modernism, Cosmopolitanism: *Ulysses* and World War I Recruiting Posters in Ireland." *Yale Journal of Criticism* 6.2 (Fall 1993): 87–132.

Woodward, Rachel. *Military Geographies*. Malden, Mass.: Blackwell, 2004.

"World's Most Expensive Cities." CNNMoney.com, 14 June 2004. http://money.cnn.com/2004/06/11/pf/costofliving.

Yeats, W. B. *Purgatory*. In *Eleven Plays of William Butler Yeats*, edited by A. Norman Jeffares. New York: Collier, 1964.

Index

The Abbot (Scott), 133
Act of Union, 143, 145, 157, 159, 164
"Aeolus," 122, 253
Afghanistan, 121, 260
"After the Race" (Joyce), 158, 161–64
Alexander the Great, 169
Almond, Hely Hutchinson, 67
Amery, Leopold, 30
An Claideamh Soluis, 181
Angell, Norman, 34, 58
Anglo-Irish Treaty, 4, 236
"Araby" (Joyce), 133, 152
Aran Islands, 48, 173
Army, British, 1, 4; in "The Dead," 170; in Ireland, 43, 147, 169; Lock hospitals and, 226; policing in Ireland and, 159–60; prostitution and, 189–90, 192–94, 218–35; recruiting in Ireland, 57; recruiting poster in *Ulysses*, 220; sports and, 14, 65–83, 95 (*see also* Garrison games); venereal disease and, 223–25
Asculum, Battle of, 82
Athleticism: militarism and, 14, 63, 66–68, 70–71; school, 61, 66–67. *See also* Games ethic; Physical culture; Sports
Athleticism in the Victorian and Edwardian Public School (Mangan), 70
Atomic bomb, 260
Attridge, Derek, 124
Aughrim, Battle of, 175–76
Austria-Hungary, 9, 15

Baden-Powell, Robert, 46, 151
Balfour, Arthur, 180
Barabbas Theatre Company, 255
Barbed wire, 147–48
Barnacle, Nora, 17, 48
Barney, 177
Barracks, 167–68, 197; demilitarization of, 236–38
Barrett, J. J., 110
Barry, Kevin, 7, 48
Beach, Sylvia, 96, 252
Beckett, Samuel, 4
Beggars Bush barracks, 167–68, 238, 271n7
Beja, Morris, 5
Belfast, 195
Belgium, 56
Bell, George, 244
Belvedere College: in "An Encounter," 126, 129, 269n11; athletic facilities, 79–80, 89
Bennett, Percy, 106, 228
Benoist-Méchin, Jacques, 259
Berghahn, Volker, 24, 30–31, 264n4
Bhabha, Homi, 204, 207
Bismarck, Otto von, 25, 36, 58, 156, 264n3, 264n5
Black and Tan Auxiliary Forces, 51, 93, 159, 239. *See also* Royal Irish Constabulary
Blackstone, William, 178; *Commentaries*, 155–56, 161–62, 176
Blake, Sexton, 121
Bloody Sunday, 93, 110

Bloom, Leopold: as casualty of violence, 100; Easter Week destruction and, 253; as Henry Flower, 186–88; Giuseppe Garibaldi and, 26; Gibraltar and, 250; military recruiting and, 220; police and, 155, 177, 181–83; prostitution and, 212–13, 225–26, 228; Eugen Sandow and, 101–3; sports and, 98; tower motif and, 249–51; on trial in "Circe," 230–31; wartime loss and, 60
Bloom, Milly, 250
Bloom, Molly, 168, 214, 221, 250
Bloomsday, 254, 257
"The Boarding House" (Joyce), 20, 163; tacit prostitution in, 199, 201–5
Boer War, 46, 60, 65–66, 148, 151, 193, 199, 219, 222, 231; street protest in *Ulysses*, 160, 177
Bonaparte, Napoleon, 25, 36, 102, 146, 239, 248
Book of Invasions, 250. See also *Lebor Gabàla Érenn*
Boucicault, Dion, 183
Bowen-Colthurst, Captain John, 55
Boxing, 14, 103–8. See also Keogh-Bennett fight
Boylan, Blazes, 214, 250, 260
Boyle, John, 231
Boyle, Robert, 243
Boyne, Battle of the, 176
Boys' Brigade, 46, 151
Boy Scouts, 46, 151
Boys' Friend, 121
"The Boys of Wexford," 229
Boys' papers, 119–21, 123–24, 127, 130–31. See also Penny dreadfuls
Bray, 243
British Army. See Army, British
British Columbia, 133–35
British militarism, 37
"British Militarism as I Have Known It" (Sheehy Skeffington), 55
British Navy, 121, 215, 251. See also Navy, Royal
British Volunteer Force, 42, 44. See also Volunteering movement
Brivic, Sheldon, 221
Brooker, Joseph, 257, 274n14

Brothels, 197–98, 231; Bella Cohen's in "Circe," 198, 231; Becky Cooper's, 198; British soldiers and, 190–91, 194–95, 235; Dublin barracks and, 198–99
Brown, Richard, 105
Brown, Terence, 124, 164, 201, 272n7
Browne, Anthony, 137–38
Browning, Robert, 173
Bruni, Alessandro Francini, 17
Buck private, 242
Bulwer-Lytton, Edward, 133–35. See also Lytton, Lord
Bunker Archeology (Virilio), 244–45
Burke, F. P., 91
Butler, P. R., 139
Butt, Isaac, 233
Byron, Lord, 139, 147

Caesar, Julius, 128–29, 163–64
Caffrey, Cissy, 189–91, 228, 233
Caffrey twins, 251
"Calypso," 249
Canada, 121, 133
Cap Mortella, 248
Captain of Köpenick, 27, 33, 264n7. See also Voigt, Wilhelm
Caraher, Brian, 8
Carpenter, Kevin, 131
Carr, Henry, 228
Carr, John, 245
Carson, Edward, 44
Casement, Roger, 3
Cathcart, Lord, 247
Celtic Times, 83–84, 86
Chamberlain, Joseph, 177
"The Charge of the Light Brigade" (Tennyson), 139, 231
Charleys, 177
Chastenay, Madame de, 25
Cheng, Vincent, 18, 82, 86, 132, 266nn12,17, 273n3
Chevron, 234, 273n20
"The Christian Church an Imperial Power" (Newman), 6

"Circe," 44, 189–90, 193, 215, 226, 228–34
The Citizen, 7, 54, 225
Citizen Army, 4, 45, 53, 99, 106, 256. *See also* Irish Citizen Army
Civil War: American, 76, 139; Irish, 4, 238
Clancy, George, 51, 267n18
Clarke, Thomas, 89, 267n21
Clarke's tobacco shop, 89–90, 267nn21,22
Clery, Arthur, 10
Clongowes Record, 74
Clongowes Wood College, 51, 68, 71–72, 82, 136–40
Clonliffe Road incident, 81, 147
Clowry, Margaret, 185
"Cochise the Apache Chief" (Herring), 124–28; as intertext for "An Encounter," 126–28
Coldstream Guards, 189, 225
Collins Barracks, 237
Commentaries on the Laws of England (Blackstone), 155–56, 161–62, 176
Commentarii de bello gallico (Caesar), 128–29
Connolly, James, 4, 45, 238, 256
Conrad, Joseph, 129, 162
Conroy, Gabriel, 42, 158, 171–76
Contagious Diseases Acts, 226–27
Cooper-Donnelly prizefight, 104
Cork, 195
Cork Examiner, 95
Corley, 200–201, 218
Corsica, 248
Cosgrave, William, 237
Costello, Peter, 72
"Counterparts" (Joyce), 15, 17, 158, 165–68
The Count of Monte Cristo (Dumas), 19
Cricket, 37, 61, 68, 72, 266n8; in "An Encounter," 79; in *Finnegans Wake* Museyroom, 79; as imperial and martial indoctrination, 77–79
Crimean War, 2, 231
Croke, Archbishop Thomas, 96–99, 103, 267n28
Croke Park, 93–94, 109–10
Cromwell, Oliver, 137, 143

"The Croppy Boy," 213, 216
Cuchulain, 84
Culleton, Claire, 186
Culture and Imperialism (Said), 111, 153
Cumann na Bann (Irishwomen's Council), 46
Curragh, 104, 195
Cusack, Michael, 64, 83, 87, 90–91, 94, 96–97, 267n28; as "The Citizen" in "Cyclops," 94–98
"Cyclops," 61, 92–101, 107, 182, 225

Daily Express, 173, 186
Daily Mail, 131
Daily Telegraph, 24
Daly, Ned, 232
Daly, Richard, 172
Daughters of Ireland, 222. See also *Inghinidhe na hÉireann*
Davin, Mat: in *A Portrait of the Artist as a Young Man*, 86–89; George Clancy as inspiration for, 267n18
Davin, Maurice, 86
Davitt, Michael, 233
Dawson, William, 10
"The Dead" (Joyce), 15, 42–43, 158, 168–76
Dedalus, Stephen, 14, 19, 49, 225, 233, 239, 241; aversion to football in *A Portrait of the Artist as a Young Man*, 68–70, 76–77; as history teacher in "Nestor," 111–12
Deleuze, Gilles, 11, 13
Demilitarization: of public space, 15, 236–39, 251–58
Devitt, Michael, 138
Devlin, Kim, 157
Doherty, Gerald, 166
Doran, Bob, 204–6
Douglas, James (colonial governor of British Columbia), 133–35
Dublin, 195, 228, 274n11; barracks, 197, 236–38; dual military and residential space, 201–3; Easter Week destruction, 216, 231–32, 234, 253; literary and artistic reclamation, 238–40, 257
Dublin Castle, 183, 208

Dublin Corporation, 199, 219
Dubliners (Joyce), 4, 24, 152, 158, 161, 165, 176, 259; intended audience for, 20; intertexts in, 14; Joyce's descriptions of, 23, 26; publication dispute, 17–23; *Ulysses* as story for, 216
Dublin Metropolitan Police (DMP), 93, 155–56, 159–60, 177, 181–85, 206, 208–10, 270n3
Dublin Society, 216
Dublin Trades Council, 238
Dublin Watch, 177, 208, 230
Duffy, Enda, 217, 240, 273nn18,3
Dujardin, Édouard, 252
Dumas, Alexandre, 19, 21, 264n6
Dun Laoghaire, 116, 164, 270n4. *See also* Kingstown

Easter Rising, 4, 46–47, 55, 76, 89, 94, 99, 114, 216; blood-sacrifice symbolism, 107; depicted as Keogh-Bennett fight, 106–7; and police, 208; property damage, 231–32, 239, 253
Ecclesiasticus, 49
Eccles Street, 168, 187, 214
Edward VII, 198
Efficiency and Empire (White), 29, 65–66
Egan, Kevin, 213, 230
Egypt, 169
Ellmann, Richard, 2, 6, 7, 76, 139, 264n2, 264n3, 267n18, 273n19
Elpenor, 206
Emmet, Robert, 177, 217, 247
"An Encounter" (Joyce), 14, 20, 119–20; "Apache Chief" intertext in, 126–32, 135–36, 152
Engels, Friedrich, 31
English Players dispute, 228, 273n19
Enloe, Cynthia, 193–94
The Ethics of Boxing and Manly Sport (O'Reilly), 84–85, 104
Eton College, 72
"Eumaeus," 193, 212–16, 225–26
"Eveline" (Joyce), 166
Evening Telegraph, 213

The Extended German Military State in Its Social Significance (Tuch), 33

Fairhall, James, 11, 112
Famine, 170, 194, 213
Fanning, Ken, 256
Farrar, F. W., 78
Farren, Thomas, 236, 238
Farrington, 166–68
Felski, Rita, 16
Fenian Cycle, 84. *See also* Fenianism; Fianna
Fenianism, 46, 268n35, 270n19. *See also* Fenian Cycle; Fianna
Ferguson, Brian, 135
Ferrall, Charles, 117, 151
Ferrero, Guglielmo, 13, 14, 17, 20, 39, 200, 272n6; *L'Europa giovane*, 35, 264nn2,3; *Militarism*, 21, 35–38, 52
Fianna, 46; athletics and, 98. *See also* Fenian Cycle; Fenianism
Fianna Eireann scouting organization, 14, 46–47
FIFA, 109
Findlater's Church, 89, 267n21
Finnegans Wake (Joyce) 3, 4, 123, 156, 214, 259; and atomic bomb, 260; "Ballad of Persse O'Reilly," 75–76; dialogue of Butt and Taff, 2–4; "How Buckley Shot the Russian General," 2–3; Museyroom, 115; prostitution in, 193, 195–96, 224–25; and sports and war, 108–9
First World War, 4, 9, 11, 56, 112, 227, 234, 242. *See also* Great War
Fitzpatrick, David, 41
Flower, Henry: as Leopold Bloom's pen name in *Ulysses*, 187; as DMP constable, 185–86, 209
Fogarty, Anne, 257–58
Football: association, 14, 37, 61, 63, 66; Clongowes gravel in *A Portrait of the Artist as a Young Man*, 72–74; Gaelic, 85, 266n16; Rugby, 61–62, 110; Stonyhurst, 266n8
"Force" (Joyce), 5–9. *See also* "Subjugation"
Foreign games, 97. *See also* Garrison games; Shoneen games

"A Forgotten Small Nationality" (Sheehy Skeffington), 53
Fortieth Foot Regiment, 241, 246
Forty Foot, 246
Fountain, Nigel, 148
France, 57; Foreign Legion, 81, 86; military involvement in Ireland, 239, 245, 251–52
Franklin, Benjamin, 141
Frederick the Great, 138
Freeman's Journal, 185–86, 210
Free State, Irish. *See* Irish Free State
Friery, Christopher, 210
Front, 234, 273n22
Fussell, Paul, 112

Gaelic Athletic Association, 14, 64, 83–84, 86–87, 96; foreign games ban, 97, 109 (*see also* Rule Forty-Two); link to physical-force nationalism, 100–101, 267n27
Gaelic League, 51, 181
Gaelic sports, 61, 83–97; Irish republicanism and, 88–92; militarist aspects, 84–88; origins, 84–87. *See also* Football: Gaelic; Hurling
Galway Harbour Scheme, 48–50
Games ethic, 14, 63, 66–67, 70–71. *See also* Athleticism; Physical culture; Sports
Gannon, Bridget, 185, 209
Garibaldi, Giuseppe, 24–26, 40, 264n5
Garrison games, 61, 65–83. *See also* Foreign games; Shoneen games
Garvin, John, 185–86
G Division, 183. *See also* Dublin Metropolitan Police
General Post Office (GPO), 47, 106, 216, 218, 232, 253, 256
Germany: coastal blockhouses, 244; military buildup, 3–4, 193. *See also* Militarism: German; Prussianism
Gestapo, 156
Gibraltar, 168, 240, 250
Gibson, Andrew, 10, 68–70, 250
Gifford, Don, 26, 94, 98, 187
Gilbert, Stuart, 234, 273n21
Gillis, John R., 12

"God Save the Queen" (British national anthem), 110
Gogarty, Oliver St. John, 216, 223, 225; and Martello tower, 244–46, 248, 252
Gonne, Maud, 221–22
Good Friday Accord, 110
Goodrich, S. G., 140
Goosestepping, 156
Gorman, Herbert, 18, 139, 264n1
"Grace" (Joyce), 158, 166, 184–85
Grafton Street, 257
Grattan, Henry, 233
The Great Illusion (Angell), 34
Great Lockout, 45
The Great Social Evil (Logan), 197
Great War, 4, 9, 11, 56, 112, 227, 234, 242. *See also* First World War
Griffith, Arthur, 99, 145, 221, 223, 233
Griffith Barracks, 237
Groden, Michael, 93
Guattari, Félix, 11, 13

Hague Peace Conference, 52
Haines, 236, 239, 248–49
Halfpenny Marvel, 119–21, 123–24, 126, 130–31, 133
Hardiman, Adrian, 187
Harmsworth, Alfred, 119, 121–22; in "Aeolus," 123; in *Finnegans Wake*, 123. *See also* Northcliffe, Lord
Harmsworth, Harold, 119
Harrow School, 72
HCE, 2
Heart of Darkness (Conrad), 129, 162
Hemingway, Ernest, 60
Henty, G. A., 121
Herring, Paul, 124
Hiroshima, 260
Historical and Miscellaneous Questions for the Everyday Use of Young People (Mangnall), 114, 142
History of the Russo-Turkish War (Hozier), 231
HMS *Belleisle*, 251
HMS *Fortitude*, 248
HMS *Helga*, 216

Hobson, Bulmer, 46
Hockey, 81–82
Hogan, Michael, 93, 110
Homer, 213
Home Rule, 53, 57
Hooke, S. Clarke, 121
Horney, 214, 272n12
Hosty, Patrick, 74
Hove, W. P., 79
Howes, Marjorie, 124, 145
Howth gunrunning, 45, 222
Hozier, Montague, 231
Hudson's Bay Company, 134
Hughes, Thomas, 117; *Tom Brown's School-Days*, 61–63, 67
Humphreys, Susan, 20, 201
Hurling, 14, 64, 84–85, 89–92

Il Piccolo della Sera, 38, 39, 48
Imperialism: British, 14
Imperialism and Juvenile Literature (Richards), 117
In Dark and Evil Days (Sheehy Skeffington), 53–55
India, 155
Inghinidhe na hÉireann, 222. *See also* Daughters of Ireland
International Olympic Committee, 109
Invasion scare, 65, 121, 193
Iraq, 260
Ireland, 9, 15
"Ireland: Island of Saints and Sages" (Joyce), 7
Irish Citizen (newspaper), 53
Irish Citizen Army, 4, 45, 53, 99, 106, 256. *See also* Citizen Army
Irish Free State, 236, 257
Irish national anthem, 110, 267n23. *See also* "The Soldier's Song"
The Irish Rebellion of 1916 (Boyle), 231–32
Irish Republican Army (IRA), 253
Irish Republican Brotherhood (IRB), 44, 89, 101
Irish republicanism, 14, 83

The Irish Ulysses (Tymoczko), 267n20
Irish Volunteers, 14, 45–46, 51, 53, 99, 106, 216, 232, 253, 256. *See also* Volunteers
Italian Irredentism, 40
Italy, 9, 15
"Ivy Day in the Committee Room" (Joyce), 20, 166

Jackson, Alvin, 45–46
Jackson, Anna, 117, 151
Jackson, John Wyse, 124
Jacob's Biscuit Factory, 47, 99–100, 232, 267n30
James Joyce and the Language of History (Spoo), 14
James Joyce Centre, 255
James Joyce Museum, 252
Jeffries, Charles, 180
"John Doe Buck Private" (Thompson), 242
Johnson, Chalmers, 16
Joyce, Giorgio, 17
Joyce, James: dispute with Grant Richards, 17–20; on Irish currency, 257; at Martello Tower, 252; Paris notebook, 216; public image, 257; in Rome, 38–39, 207; statue, 257, 274n12; and syphilis, 224, 272n15; in Trieste, 17; university career, 5–10. *See also individual works*
Joyce, Race and Empire (Cheng), 18
Joyce, Stanislaus, 9, 10, 38, 40–41, 76, 79, 165, 224, 264n2
Joyce Among the Jesuits (Sullivan), 137
Joyce's Critics (Brooker), 257
Judgment of Paris, 251
Juvenile Literature and British Society, 1850–1950 (Ferrall and Jackson), 117

Kavanagh, Lizzie, 209–10
Keane, Raymond, 255
Kehoe Barracks, 237
Kelly, Joseph, 20
Kelly, P. C., 61

Kennedy, Hugh Boyle, 10
Kennedy, Paul, 29
Keogh-Bennett fight, 103–8, 229
Kershner, R. B., 19, 68, 102–3, 123, 131, 149, 264n2, 274n10
Kettle, Mary Sheehy, 55–56
Kettle, Thomas, 14, 51, 56–60, 82; death of, 56; references to in *Finnegans Wake*, 56; *The Ways of War* (essays), 57–59
Kiberd, Declan, 112, 240
Kingstown, 116, 164, 270n4. *See also* Dun Laoghaire
Kipling, Rudyard, 117, 271n12
Kitchener, Lord, 43, 57, 148
Knowles, Sebastian, 115

Lads' Drill Association, 151
Ladysmith, Battle of, 230
La Guerre et La Paix (Proudhon), 25
Lancers, 169, 173
Lands Bill Hearings, 236–38, 242
Lansdowne Road Stadium, 110
Larkin, Jim, 45
Larne gunrunning, 44
"The Lass of Aughrim," 174–75
The Last Days of Pompeii (Lytton), 133
The Leader, 92
Lebor Gabála Érenn, 250. *See also Book of Invasions*
Lee, Nelson, 121
Lee, Richard, 172
Leipziger Volkszeitung, 31
Lenehan, 200–201, 218
"Lestrygonians," 155, 159–61, 177
L'Europa giovane (Ferrero), 35, 264nn2,3
Lever, John, 50
Liberty Hall, 4
Liebknecht, Karl, 13, 27, 31–33, 156, 160, 264n9; *Militarism and Anti-Militarism*, 32
Liffey, River, 215
Linenhall Barracks, 232
Literary and Historical Society, UCD, 10
Littlehales, Edward, 179

Little Review, 93, 267n26
Livingstone, David, 136
Lloyd George, David, 122
The Location of Culture (Bhabha), 204
Locke, John, 159, 178
Lock Hospitals, 226–27
Logan, William, 197
Loophole, 203, 272n10
"Lotus Eaters," 220–23
Loyola, Ignatius, 71
Luddy, Maria, 195, 198
Luxemburg, Rosa, 31–32
Lytton, Lord, 133–35. *See also* Bulwer-Lytton, Edward

Macaulay, James, 180
MacBride, John, 222
Mac Cana, Proinsias, 88
Mac Cumhaill, Fionn, 46, 84, 98
MacDonagh, Thomas, 53, 99
Macmillan's, 27
Mafeking, Siege of, 46
Magazine Fort, 75–76
Magdalen laundries, 215
Maher, Michael, 71
Mangan, J. A., 63, 70
Mangnall, Richmal, 114, 142
Markeviecz, Countess Constance, 46
Marlborough Barracks, 237
Marryat, Captain, 118, 148–51
Martello Terrace, 243
Martello tower, 15, 189, 234, 236, 239–52
Marx, Karl, 31
Mason, Ellsworth, 7
Mathew, Father, 256
McDowell, Gerty, 253
McGinley, Bernard, 124
McKee Barracks, 237
Meagher, Thomas Francis, 139
"The Memory of the Dead" (Ingram), 54
Mengham, Rod, 170
Meredith, George, 76
Metchnikoff, Ilya, 227
Milesians, 250–51

Militarism, 12–13; American, 16, 260; British, 33–35, 37, 42, 55; in education, 152–53; etymology, 24–26; German, 14, 21, 27–29, 36, 48, 55, 59 (see also Prussianism); Irish, 41–48, 53 (see also Physical-force Irish nationalism); liberal capitalist definitions, 33–34; post-Marxist definitions, 31–33
Militarism (Ferrero), 21, 35–40
Militarism: An Appeal to the Man in the Street, 28
Militarism and Anti-Militarism (Liebknecht), 32
Militarist, 17, 18–19, 21, 27
Military Geographies (Woodward), 237–38
Military-industrial complex, 260, 264n9
Military Manoeuvres (Moynan), 1, 2
"The Militia and Militarism" (Luxemburg), 31–32
Milligan, Alice, 87
Ministry of Munitions, 122
"The Mirage of the Fishermen of Aran: England's Safety Valve in Case of War" (Joyce), 48–50
Modder River, Battle of, 60
Molony, Helena, 218
Monaghan, Helen, 255
Montaigne, Michel de, 7
Montgomery Street, 225
Monto, 15, 197–98, 206, 212, 223–25, 228. See also Nighttown; Red-light district
Mooney, Jack, 203–4
Mooney, Polly, 204–5
Moore, George, 237
Moore, Maurice, 237
Moore, Thomas, 133
Moran, D. P., 92
Morgan, David, 171
Morrigu, 173, 265n5
Moynan, Richard Thomas, *Military Manoeuvres*, 1
Mr. Midshipman Easy (Marryat), 150–51
Muenger, Elizabeth, 180
Mullaghmast, Massacre at, 90
Mulligan, Buck, 225, 233, 239, 240–41, 251
Mullin, Katherine, 133, 213, 227

Mulvey, Lieutenant, 250
Murphy, D. B., 50
Muscular Christianity, 61, 65, 82, 117

Nagasaki, 260
Nannetti, Joseph Patrick, MP, 92, 98
"Napoleon" (Meredith), 76
Napoleon. See Bonaparte, Napoleon
National efficiency, 29, 61
National Service League, 42
"A Nation Once Again," 99
"Nausicaa," 189, 249
The Naval Officer (Marryat), 148–50
Navy, Royal, 121, 215, 251. See also British Navy
Navy League, 42
Nelson, Lord Admiral, 225, 256
Nelson's Pillar, 253, 255
Nepean, Evan, 247
"Nestor," 14, 49, 153; athletics in, 81; education in, 111–16
Nevill, Wilfred Percy, 63
Newman, John Henry, 6, 147
Nic Shiubhlaigh, Maire, 232
Nighttown, 15, 197–98, 206, 212, 216, 223–25, 228. See also Monto; Red-light district
Norris, Margot, 16, 176, 201–2, 273n18
Northcliffe, Lord, 119, 121–22; in "Aeolus," 123; in *Finnegans Wake*, 123. See also Harmsworth, Alfred

O'Brien, Joseph, 253
Occasional, Critical, and Political Writing (Joyce), 7
O'Connell, Daniel, 233, 256
O'Connell Bridge, 253
O'Connell Street, 218–19, 232, 253, 255–57
"Ode of Welcome" (Gogarty), 216–17
O'Donovan Rossa, Jeremiah, 47
Odysseus, 99
Odyssey (Homer), 113
O'Hara's Tower, 250
O'Leary, John, 44
O'Malley, Ernie, 181
Ordnance Survey, 4, 243
O'Reilly, John Boyle, 84, 104

Ormond Quay, 213
Orwell, George, 22
Osteen, Mark, 235
"Oxen of the Sun," 10

Pamplona, Siege of, 71
Parable of the Plums: Bloomsday 2004 street pageant, 15, 254–57; in *Ulysses*, 254
Parnell, Charles Stewart, 170, 233
Pašeta, Senia, 59
Patria potestas (power of the father), 157–59, 163–64, 172, 184, 187–88
Peace Preservation Act, 179
Pearce, Richard, 191
Pearse, Padraig, 45, 256
Peel, Robert, 156, 161, 177–80
Peelers, 178
"Penelope," 168, 221, 250
Penny dreadfuls, 119–21, 123–24, 127, 130–31. *See also* Boys' papers
Peter Parley's Tales About Ancient and Modern Greece, 140–42
Peveril of the Peak (Scott), 246
Phoenix Park, 75, 92, 237
Physical culture, 14, 65–67, 81
Physical-force Irish nationalism, 98, 170
Pigeon House, 126, 245, 269n8
Pitt, William, 245, 247
Platt, Len, 10
Plevna, Siege of, 231
Plock, Vike, 102
Pluck, 119–21, 131, 133
Plunkett, Lieutenant Pasha, 93
Pola, 9, 39
Police: Blackstone's concept of, 15, 155–59; British Army and, 155–57, 159–60, 164, 178–81 (*see also* Dublin Metropolitan Police; Royal Irish Constabulary); history in Dublin and Ireland, 155, 157, 177–79; patriarchy and, 161–64; Robert Peel and, 177–80; prostitution and, 208–10
Police Acts of 1836, Constabulary and Dublin, 159
Police Bill of 1814, 178–79
Police Clauses Act, 209

Polyphemos, 99
Poor Richard's Almanac (Franklin), 141
Portobello Barracks, 55, 107, 199
A Portrait of the Artist as a Young Man, 4, 14, 53; juvenile reading and schoolbooks in, 136–39, 144–48, 152; prostitution and, 190–91; soldiers in, 190, 241; sports and, 61, 67–71, 76–78, 80–81
Posthomerica (Quintus), 170
Pounch, Seamus, 47, 99
Pound, Ezra, 94
Prague, Battle of, 138
Principles of Sociology (Spencer), 33
Prostitution: British soldiers and, 189–90, 193–208, 218–28; in *Dubliners*, 17, 199, 202–5; in *Finnegans Wake*, 193, 195–96; in *A Portrait of the Artist as a Young Man*, 190; in *Ulysses*, 189–90, 205–7, 212–16, 228–35
"Proteus," 213
Proudhon, Pierre, 25
Proust, Marcel, 252
Prussian guard, 156
Prussianism, 14, 21, 27–29, 36, 48, 55, 59, 156. *See also* Militarism: German
Purgatory (Yeats), 147
Pyrrhus, 82, 111, 116

Queensberry Rules, 104, 108
Quintus, 170

Rabaté, Jean-Michel, 260
Ranji, 79
Redhead, Steve, 244
Red-light district, 15, 197–98, 206, 212, 216, 223–25, 228. *See also* Monto; Nighttown
Redmond, John, 233, 253
Remarque, Erich Maria, 60
Review of Reviews, 52
Rice, Tom, 156, 259, 263n1
Richards, Grant, 17–22, 207
Richards, Jeffrey, 117
Richmond Barracks, 237
Ricketts, Kitty, 226–27
Riquelme, John Paul, 175–76
Roberts, Lord, 43, 269n14

Robinson, Richard, 2
Rome: bombings in, 40–41; Joyce's residency in, 9, 38, 165
Roos, Bonnie, 169
Rousseau, Jean-Jacques, 157, 178
Rowan, Hamilton, 69, 137
Royal Barracks, 237
Royal Dublin Fusiliers, 57, 220, 225–26
Royal Irish Constabulary (RIC), 93, 147, 159, 166, 178–81, 267n27
Royal Military Academy at Woolwich, 151
Rugby: football, 62, 66; played at Croke Park, 110 (*see also* Football); school, 67
Rule Forty-Two, 97, 109. *See also* Gaelic Athletic Association: foreign games ban
Ruskin, John, 151–52
Russo-Japanese War, 76

Said, Edward, 111, 145, 152–53
Sailor hat, 216
Sailor suit, 189
Sandow, Eugen, 62, 81, 101–3
Sandycove, 239, 241, 273n2
Sandymount Strand, 251
Sapper, 4
Schippel, Max, 31
Scott, Bonnie Kime, 6, 195
Scott, Sir Walter, 133, 135, 246
Seanad Éireann, 236–37
September 11th attacks, 260
Seven Years' War, 138
Sexually transmitted disease, 15, 212, 223–28. *See also* Contagious Diseases Acts; Syphilis; Venereal disease
Shan Van Vocht, 87–88
The Shaughraun (Boucicault), 183
Sheehy Skeffington, Francis, 3, 10, 14, 34, 44, 51–55, 107; *In Dark and Evil Days* (novel), 53–55; death of, 55; as McCann in *SH* (MacCann in *P*), 34–35, 52; on militarism in Ireland, 44, 53
Sheehy Skeffington, Hanna, 55
Shelbourne Road, 167
Shoneen games, 61, 98

Shot put, 94–96
Sinn Fein, 98, 145
"Sirens," 193, 214
Sirr, Henry Charles, 177
"The Sisters" (Joyce), 20, 118
Sluagh na h-Eireann, 92, 98
Smith, Rennie, 152
Smith, William Alexander, 46
Smyrna, 169–70
Soccer. *See* Football: Association
"The Soldier's Song," 110, 267n23. *See also* Irish national anthem
Somme, Battle of the, 56, 63, 82, 114
The Sorrows of Empire (Johnson), 16
South Africa, 43, 121
Sovereignty goddess, 88, 267n20
Spain, 240, 250
Spangler, Matthew, 255
Speed and Politics (Virilio), 245
Spencer, Herbert, 33–34, 36, 65
Spilka, Mark, 167
Spoo, Robert, 11, 13, 70, 81, 113, 263n7
Sports, 14, 63, 66–67, 70–71. *See also* Athleticism; Games ethic; Physical culture
Stargardt, Nicholas, 25, 264n7
State Lands Bill, 236
Stead, W. T., 52
St. Enda's School, 45
Stephen Hero, 52, 90, 91–92, 94, 160, 205
Stephens, James, 26
Stonyhurst College, 71–72, 266n8
The Stranger in Ireland (Carr), 246
Streetwalker, 212–16. *See also* Whore of the lane
"Subjugation" (Joyce), 5–9. *See also* "Force"
Sullivan, Kevin, 137, 140, 266n10
Summers, Anne, 42
Surveillance, 15; Martello tower and, 239, 242–45, 251; police, 182–88; streetwalkers and, 196, 208–15, 235
Synge, J. M., 49
Syphilis, 15, 212, 223–28. *See also* Contagious Diseases Acts; Sexually transmitted disease; Venereal disease

Tailtean games, 84, 95
"Telemachus," 242–44
Tennyson, Alfred, Lord, 139, 147, 231
Thompson, Allan, 242
Thom's Directory, 198
The Three Musketeers (Dumas), 19, 264n1
Times, 131
Tom Brown's School-Days (Hughes), 61–63, 67
Tone, Wolfe, 137, 233, 247
Tower of Babel, 240
Townshend, Charles, 14, 45, 100, 273n4
Transvaal Committee, 177
Trieste, 17, 24, 26, 38; military presence in, 39–40
Trinity College Dublin, 177
Troy, Siege of, 251
Tuatha Dé Danann, 85
Tuch, Gustav, 33
Tumbling in the Hay (Gogarty), 223
"Two Gallants" (Joyce), 17–18, 182–83, 199–201, 264n2
Tymoczko, Maria, 240

"Ugly England" (Gogarty), 223
Ulster Volunteer Force (UVF), 44–45, 53
Ulysses, 4, 14, 16, 152, 177, 201; demilitarization of Dublin in, 15, 239–52; idea of history in, 13; Russo-Japanese War in, 29; as story for *Dubliners*, 216
Union Jack, 119, 121, 133
United Irishman, 84, 85–86, 145, 218–19
United Irishmen Rising, 54, 137, 177, 216, 223, 229, 239
University College Dublin, 5–6, 10, 14, 51

Vane, Major Sir Francis, 55
Venereal disease, 15, 212, 223–28. *See also* Contagious Diseases Acts; Sexually transmitted disease; Syphilis
Victoria, Queen, 43
Virilio, Paul, 244–45, 260
Voigt, Wilhelm, 27, 33, 264n7. *See also* Captain of Köpenick

Volunteering movement, 42, 44. *See also* British Volunteer Force
Volunteers, 14, 45–46, 51, 53, 99, 106, 216, 232, 256. *See also* Irish Volunteers

"Wandering Rocks," 54
"The War Machine: A State Necessity" (Boyle Kennedy), 10
War machine theory of Deleuze and Guattari, 11, 13, 60, 265n21
War of Independence: American, 143; Irish, 51, 93, 181, 238, 252–53
Wellington, Duke of, 67
Wellington Barracks, 199, 237
Wellington Monument, 75, 176
Westmoreland Lock Hospital, 226
Westmoreland Street, 219
White, Arnold, 29, 65–66
Whitehead, Neil, 135
Whitshed, James Hawkins, 247
Whore of the lane, 212–16. *See also* Streetwalker
Wild Geese, 81, 87
Wild West: boys' stories and, 118–21; colonial trope in "An Encounter," 123–36
Wilhelm, Kaiser, 27–28, 57, 122
William III, King (William of Orange), 43, 174–75
Wills, Clair, 192, 212, 225
Wollaeger, Mark, 220
Woodward, Rachel, 237
Wright, Sergeant Major, 80
Writing War in the Twentieth Century (Norris), 16
Wyndham, George, 92

Yeats, W. B., 147
Yeoman, 216–17
Young Ireland, 99, 139

Zeppelins, 121
Zurich, 9

Greg Winston is professor of English at Husson University, where his research explores historical and postcolonial contexts of modern Irish and British literatures. His essays have previously appeared in, among other journals, *Études Irlandaises* and the *James Joyce Quarterly*, and in Blackwell's *Companion to the British and Irish Short Story*.

The University Press of Florida is the scholarly publishing agency for the State University System of Florida, comprising Florida A&M University, Florida Atlantic University, Florida Gulf Coast University, Florida International University, Florida State University, New College of Florida, University of Central Florida, University of Florida, University of North Florida, University of South Florida, and University of West Florida.

THE FLORIDA JAMES JOYCE SERIES

Edited by Sebastian D. G. Knowles

The Autobiographical Novel of Co-Consciousness: Goncharov, Woolf, and Joyce, by Galya Diment (1994)
Bloom's Old Sweet Song: Essays on Joyce and Music, by Zack Bowen (1995)
Joyce's Iritis and the Irritated Text: The Dis-lexic Ulysses, by Roy Gottfried (1995)
Joyce, Milton, and the Theory of Influence, by Patrick Colm Hogan (1995)
Reauthorizing Joyce, by Vicki Mahaffey (paperback edition, 1995)
Shaw and Joyce: "The Last Word in Stolentelling," by Martha Fodaski Black (1995)
Bely, Joyce, and Döblin: Peripatetics in the City Novel, by Peter I. Barta (1996)
Jocoserious Joyce: The Fate of Folly in Ulysses, by Robert H. Bell (paperback edition, 1996)
Joyce and Popular Culture, edited by R. B. Kershner (1996)
Joyce and the Jews: Culture and Texts, by Ira B. Nadel (paperback edition, 1996)
Narrative Design in Finnegans Wake: *The Wake Lock Picked*, by Harry Burrell (1996)
Gender in Joyce, edited by Jolanta W. Wawrzycka and Marlena G. Corcoran (1997)
Latin and Roman Culture in Joyce, by R. J. Schork (1997)
Reading Joyce Politically, by Trevor L. Williams (1997)
Advertising and Commodity Culture in Joyce, by Garry Leonard (1998)
Greek and Hellenic Culture in Joyce, by R. J. Schork (1998)
Joyce, Joyceans, and the Rhetoric of Citation, by Eloise Knowlton (1998)
Joyce's Music and Noise: Theme and Variation in His Writings, by Jack W. Weaver (1998)
Reading Derrida Reading Joyce, by Alan Roughley (1999)
Joyce through the Ages: A Nonlinear View, edited by Michael Patrick Gillespie (1999)
Chaos Theory and James Joyce's Everyman, by Peter Francis Mackey (1999)
Joyce's Comic Portrait, by Roy Gottfried (2000)
Joyce and Hagiography: Saints Above!, by R. J. Schork (2000)
Voices and Values in Joyce's Ulysses, by Weldon Thornton (2000)
The Dublin Helix: The Life of Language in Joyce's Ulysses, by Sebastian D. G. Knowles (2001)
Joyce Beyond Marx: History and Desire in Ulysses *and* Finnegans Wake, by Patrick McGee (2001)
Joyce's Metamorphosis, by Stanley Sultan (2001)
Joycean Temporalities: Debts, Promises, and Countersignatures, by Tony Thwaites (2001)
Joyce and the Victorians, by Tracey Teets Schwarze (2002)
Joyce's Ulysses *as National Epic: Epic Mimesis and the Political History of the Nation State*, by Andras Ungar (2002)
James Joyce's "Fraudstuff," by Kimberly J. Devlin (2002)
Rite of Passage in the Narratives of Dante and Joyce, by Jennifer Margaret Fraser (2002)
Joyce and the Scene of Modernity, by David Spurr (2002)
Joyce and the Early Freudians: A Synchronic Dialogue of Texts, by Jean Kimball (2003)
Twenty-first Joyce, edited by Ellen Carol Jones and Morris Beja (2004)
Joyce on the Threshold, edited by Anne Fogarty and Timothy Martin (2005)

Wake Rites: The Ancient Irish Rituals of Finnegans Wake, by George Cinclair Gibson (2005)
Ulysses *in Critical Perspective*, edited by Michael Patrick Gillespie and A. Nicholas Fargnoli (2006)
Joyce and the Narrative Structure of Incest, by Jen Shelton (2006)
Joyce, Ireland, Britain, edited by Andrew Gibson and Len Platt (2006)
Joyce in Trieste: An Album of Risky Readings, edited by Sebastian D. G. Knowles, Geert Lernout, and John McCourt (2007)
Joyce's Rare View: The Nature of Things in Finnegans Wake, by Richard Beckman (2007)
Joyce's Misbelief, by Roy Gottfried (2007)
James Joyce's Painful Case, by Cóilín Owens (2008)
Cannibal Joyce, by Thomas Jackson Rice (2008)
Manuscript Genetics, Joyce's Know-How, Beckett's Nohow, by Dirk Van Hulle (2008)
Catholic Nostalgia in Joyce and Company, by Mary Lowe-Evans (2008)
A Guide through Finnegans Wake, by Edmund Lloyd Epstein (2009)
Bloomsday 100: Essays on Ulysses, edited by Morris Beja and Anne Fogarty (2009)
Joyce, Medicine, and Modernity, by Vike Martina Plock (2010; first paperback edition, 2012)
Who's Afraid of James Joyce?, by Karen R. Lawrence (2010; first paperback edition, 2012)
Ulysses *in Focus: Genetic, Textual, and Personal Views*, by Michael Groden (2010; first paperback edition, 2012)
Foundational Essays in James Joyce Studies, edited by Michael Patrick Gillespie (2011)
Empire and Pilgrimage in Conrad and Joyce, by Agata Szczeszak-Brewer (2011)
The Poetry of James Joyce Reconsidered, edited by Marc C. Conner (2012; first paperback edition, 2015)
The German Joyce, by Robert K. Weninger (2012)
Joyce and Militarism, by Greg Winston (2012; first paperback edition, 2015)
Renascent Joyce, edited by Daniel Ferrer, Sam Slote, and André Topia (2013; first paperback edition, 2014)
Before Daybreak: "After the Race" and the Origins of Joyce's Art, by Cóilín Owens (2013; first paperback edition, 2014)
Modernists at Odds: Reconsidering Joyce and Lawrence, edited by Matthew J. Kochis and Heather L. Lusty (2015)
The Ecology of Finnegans Wake, by Alison Lacivita (2015)
James Joyce and the Exilic Imagination, by Michael Patrick Gillespie (2015)
Joyce's Allmaziful Plurabilities: Polyvocal Explorations of Finnegans Wake, edited by Kimberly J. Devlin and Christine Smedley (2015)
Exiles: A Critical Edition, by James Joyce, edited by A. Nicholas Fargnoli and Michael Patrick Gillespie (2016)

www.ingramcontent.com/pod-product-compliance
Lightning Source LLC
Chambersburg PA
CBHW021338230426
43666CB00006B/330